iege

Biology 1

Mary Jones

Richard Fosbery

Dennis Taylor

Series editor: Mary Jones

CAMBRIDGE
UNIVERSITY PRESS

PUBLISHED BY THE PRESS SYNDICATE OF THE UNIVERSITY OF CAMBRIDGE
The Pitt Building, Trumpington Street, Cambridge, United Kingdom

CAMBRIDGE UNIVERSITY PRESS
The Edinburgh Building, Cambridge CB2 2RU, UK
40 West 20th Street, New York, NY 10011-4211, USA
477 Williamstown Road, Port Melbourne, VIC 3207, Australia
Ruiz de Alarcón 13, 28014 Madrid, Spain
Dock House, The Waterfront, Cape Town 8001, South Africa

http://www.cambridge.org

First published 2000
Ninth printing 2004

Printed in the United Kingdom at the University Press, Cambridge

Typeface Swift   *System* QuarkXPress®

A catalogue record for this book is available from the British Library

ISBN 0 521 78719 X paperback

Produced by Gecko Ltd, Bicester, Oxon

Front cover photographs: *Syrphus ribesii* (hoverfly) and *Helianthus* (sunflower), © Ida Cook

Contents

Introduction   v

Acknowledgements   vi

Part 1: Foundation

1 Cell structure   2
Why cells?   3
Cell biology and microscopy   3
Animal and plant cells have features
    in common   4
Differences between animal and plant cells   4
Units of measurement in cell studies   5
Electron microscopes   7
Ultrastructure of an animal cell   11
Structure and functions of organelles   11
Ultrastructure of a plant cell   14
Two fundamentally different types of cell   16
Tissues and organs   17

2 Biological molecules   21
The building blocks of life   22
Polymers and macromolecules   22
Carbohydrates   23
Lipids   28
Proteins   30
Water   37
Inorganic ions   39

3 Enzymes   42
Enzymes reduce activation energy   43
The course of a reaction   44
Measuring reaction rate   46
Enzyme inhibitors   48

4 Cell membranes and transport   51
Phospholipids   51
Structure of membranes   52
Transport across the plasma membrane   54
Exchange surfaces   61

5 Genetic control of protein structure and function   65
The structure of DNA and RNA   65
DNA replication   67
DNA, RNA and protein synthesis   70
Gene technology   75

6 Nuclear division   79
The nucleus contains chromosomes   79
The structure of chromosomes   81
Two types of nuclear division   83
Mitosis in an animal cell   83
Cancer   88

7 Energy and ecosystems   92
Energy flow through organisms
    and ecosystems   93
Matter recycling in ecosystems   96

Part 2: Transport

8 The mammalian transport system   102
The cardiovascular system   103
Blood plasma and tissue fluid   108
Lymph   109
Blood   111
Haemoglobin   112
Fetal haemoglobin   115
Myoglobin   116
Problems with oxygen transport   117

9 The mammalian heart   120
The cardiac cycle   122
Control of the heart beat   124

10 Transport in multicellular plants   128
The transport of water   129
Translocation   138
Differences between sieve elements
    and xylem vessels   144

Part 3: Human Health and Disease

11 Introduction to health and disease   148
What is health?   148
What is disease?   148
The Human Genome Project   151
Health statistics   153

12 Diet   158
Calculating dietary requirements   159
When dietary requirements go unmet   165

13 Gaseous exchange and exercise   172
The gaseous exchange system   172
Breathing rate and heart rate   175
Energy and exercise   179

14 Smoking and disease   187
Tobacco smoke   187
Lung disease   188
Proving the links between smoking
   and lung disease   191
Cardiovascular diseases   193

15 Infectious diseases   203
Worldwide importance of infectious diseases   203
Cholera   203
Malaria   205
Aquired Immune Deficiency Syndrome (AIDS)   209
Tuberculosis (TB)   212
Antibiotics   215

16 Immunity   219
Defence against disease   219
Cells of the immune system   220
Active and passive immunity   227
Measles   231
Allergies   232

Appendix 1   236

Appendix 2   237

Answers to self-assessment questions   239

Glossary   253

Index   259

Introduction

Cambridge Advanced Sciences

The *Cambridge Advanced Sciences* series has been developed to meet the demands of all the new AS and A level science examinations. In particular, it has been endorsed by OCR as providing complete coverage of their specifications. The AS material is presented as a single text for each of biology, chemistry and physics. Material for the A2 year comprises six books in each subject: one of core material and one for each option. Some material has been drawn from the existing *Cambridge Modular Sciences* books; however, the majority is entirely new.

During the development of this series, the opportunity has been taken to improve the design, and a complete and thorough new writing and editing process has been applied. Much more material is now presented in colour. Although the existing *Cambridge Modular Sciences* texts do cover some of the new specifications, the *Cambridge Advanced Sciences* books cover every OCR learning objective in detail. They are the key to success in the new AS and A level examinations.

OCR is one of the three unitary awarding bodies offering the full range of academic and vocational qualifications in the UK. For full details of the new specifications, please contact OCR:

OCR
1 Hills Rd.
Cambridge CB1 2EU
Tel: 01223 553311

Biology 1 – the AS biology text

Biology 1 is all that is needed to cover the whole of the AS biology material. It is divided into three parts which correspond to the modules Biology Foundation, Transport, and Human Health and Disease. It is designed to be accessible to students with a double-award science GCSE background. This book combines entirely new text and illustrations with revised and updated material from *Foundation Biology, Central Concepts in Biology, Transport, Regulation and Control* and *Human Health and Disease*, formerly available in the *Cambridge Modular Sciences* series.

Part 1, Foundation, combines new text and figures with existing material. Chapters 1, 2, 3, 4 and 6 are based on *Foundation Biology* chapters 1, 3, 4, 5 and 2 respectively whilst chapters 5 and 7 are based on *Central Concepts in Biology* chapters 4 and 6 respectively. For the first time, key information is provided on some practical aspects of the specification, such as testing for the presence of various biological chemicals.

In Part 2, Transport, chapters 8 to 10 are largely based on chapters 1 to 3 of *Transport, Regulation and Control*. Chapter 10 includes an entirely new section on xerophytes.

Part 3, Human Health and Disease, is drawn from chapters 1 to 6 of the *Cambridge Modular Sciences* book of the same name. It benefits hugely from being converted from the original black and white into full colour. Throughout chapters 11 to 16 there is a great deal of new or revised text and illustrations to adapt this former second year option to AS level. The extensive epidemiological and other data that are provided have all been brought up to date and mention is made of the latest research and thinking on subjects such as the Human Genome Project and HIV/AIDS.

Acknowledgements

Photographs

1.1, 2.7, 4.13, 7.5a, Dr Jeremy Burgess/Science Photo Library; 1.3, Alfred Pasieka/Science Photo Library; 1.6, 1.11, 1.21a, 7.5b, A M Page, Royal Holloway College, University of London; 1.7a, 1.7b, 2.26, Claude Nuridsany & Marie Perennou/Science Photo Library; 1.10, 6.14a, 15.1, 16.17, Eye of Science/Science Photo Library; 1.13, Don Fawcett/Science Photo Library; 1.14, 1.19, 1.20, 1.24, 6.1, 6.2, 8.5, 9.1, 9.4a, 10.6c, 10.13, 16.1, 16.2, ©Biophoto Associates; 1.15, 13.3, Secchi-Leacaque-Roussel-Uclaf/CNRI/Science Photo Library; 1.16, 1.22, Dr Kari Lounatmaa/Science Photo Library; 1.17, 16.6, Dr Gopal Murti/Science Photo Library; 1.18, 2.23b, Bill Longcore/Science Photo Library; 1.26a, Professors P M Motta & S Makabe/Science Photo Library; 2.9, 4.11c, 10.14e, Geoff Jones; 1.26c, 13.1a, 13.1b, John Adds; 2.12, Peter Gould; 2.13, Tom McHugh/Science Photo Library; 2.20, Dr Arthur Lesk/Science Photo Library; 2.23a, 15.4, Omikron/Science Photo Library; 2.24d, J Gross, Biozentrum/Science Photo Library; 2.24e, Quest/Science Photo Library; 3.8, 11.1, Simon Fraser/RVI, Newcastle-upon-Tyne/Science Photo Library; 4.9, 16.8, J C Revy/Science Photo Library; 5.10, Professor Oscar Miller/Science Photo Library; 6.11, 6.13, Eric Grave/Science Photo Library; 6.12, Manfred Kage/Science Photo Library; 6.14b, 6.15a, 13.2, 14.8, 14.9, 16.19, Science Photo Library; 6.15b, James Stevenson/Science Photo Library; 7.5b, 8.12, 10.6b, 10.14c, 10.14d, ©Andrew Syred; 7.7, Vaughan fleming/Science Photo Library; 8.4, 8.10b, 12.8, 13.1c, Biophoto Associates/Science Photo Library; 8.18, Chris Bonnington Picture Library (©Doug Scott); 9.10, Simon Fraser/Coronary Care Unit, Freeman Hospital, Newcastle-upon-Tyne/Science Photo Library; 10.11, Martyn F Chillmaid/Science Photo Library; 10.14a, Andrew Syred/Science Photo Library; 10.14b, Sinclair Stammers/Science Photo Library; 10.17, Ann Langham, Bethany, Toronto, Canada; 12.2, Caritas Japan via Kyodo/Popperfoto/Reuters; 12.3, 15.2, Ahmed Jadallah/Popperfoto/Reuters; 12.4, Hulton Getty Picture Collection; 12.5, Panos Pictures (©Lana Wong); 12.6, Syndication International; 12.7, Dr Clare Gilbert, ICEH, University College London; 12.9, Cristina Pedrazzini/Science Photo Library; 13.7, Phil Wilson, Loughborough University; 14.2, GCa-CNRI/Science Photo Library; 14.3, Dr Tony Brain/Science Photo Library; 14.5, Mirror Syndication International; 15.6, NIBSC/Science Photo Library; 15.7, Kwangshin Kim/Science Photo Library; 15.8, T Falise/WHO; 16.14, Hutchison Picture Library; 16.15, Kamal Kishore/Popperfoto/Reuters

Diagrams

1.26b, 1.26d, Geoff Jones; 6.16, adapted from *Understanding Cancer and its Treatment*, ABPI; 11.2, data from *The World Health Report*, 1999, *Annex Table 4* The World Health Organisation; 11.3, from *Human Physical Health* D J Taylor, Cambridge University Press; 12.1, from *Dietary Reference Values, A Guide* Department of Health, 1991, HMSO; 13.4, adapted from *Advanced Biology Principles and Applications, Study Guide* C J Clegg et al, 1996, John Murray; 13.6, 13.10, adapted from *Essentials of Exercise Physiology* McArdle et al, 1994, Lea and Febiger; 13.9, adapted from *Textbook of Physiology and Biochemistry* Bell et al, 1976, 9th ed. Churchill Livingston; 13.11, adapted from *The Physiology of fitness* Brian J Sharkey, 3rd ed. Human Kinetics Books; 14.1, adapted from Tetley, *Biological Sciences Review*, May 1990; 14.4, adapted from *Smoking ASH*, 1994; 14.10, from *Coronary Heart Disease Statistics Book*, 1999, British Heart Foundation; 15.5, adapted from Brown, *Inside Science*, *New Scientist*, 18 April 1992; 15.10, 15.9, from the Global TB programme of the World Health Organisation; 16.10, adapted from *Biology of Microorganisms* Brook et al, 1994, Prentice-Hall; 16.3, 16.13, adapted from *Medical Immunology for Students* Playfair & Lydyard, 1995, Churchill Livingston; 16.16, from the World Health Organisation internet site

Tables

12.3, 12.4, 12.6, data from *Dietary Reference Values for Food Energy and Nutrients for the United Kingdom*, 1991, HMSO; 12.5, *Energy and Protein Requirements*, Report of a joint FAO/WHO/UNU meeting, 1995, World Health Organisation; 12.7, data from *The Food Labelling Regulations 1996*, Statutory Instruments 1996 No. 1499, HMSO; 12.9, adapted from *Diet and Nutrition Card, Student Activity Sheet*, 1994, World Vision UK; 13.1, 13.2, data from *Human Physiology, Foundations and Frontiers* Schauf et al, 1990, Times Mirror/Mosby College Publishing; 14.1, data from *Factsheet* No. 4, ASH; 14.4, data from *Factsheet* No. 1, ASH and *Coronary Heart Disease Statistics* Boaz & Rayner, 1995, British Heart Foundation; 14.3, World Health Organisation MONICA Project, 1989; 15.1, 15.2, 15.3, 15.4, data from World Health Organisation internet site; 15.5, data from *Biology of Microorganisms* Brook et al, 1994, Prentice-Hall

Picture Research: Maureen Cowdroy

Part 1
Foundation

CHAPTER 1

Cell structure

By the end of this chapter you should be able to:

1 describe and interpret drawings and photographs of typical animal and plant cells as seen using the light microscope;

2 explain the meanings of, and distinguish between, the terms *resolution* and *magnification* and calculate the linear magnification of drawings;

3 describe and interpret drawings and photographs of typical animal and plant cells as seen using the electron microscope, recognising rough and smooth endoplasmic reticulum (ER), Golgi apparatus, mitochondria, ribosomes, lysosomes, chloroplasts, plasma (cell surface) membrane, centrioles, cilia and the nucleus, including the nuclear envelope and nucleolus;

4 outline the functions of the structures listed in 3;

5 describe the structure of a prokaryotic cell, and compare and contrast the structure of prokaryotic cells with eukaryotic cells;

6 explain how cells are organised into tissues, with reference to squamous and ciliated epithelia, xylem and phloem;

7 explain the meaning of the terms *tissue* and *organ*, and state examples in animals and plants.

In the early days of microscopy an English scientist, Robert Hooke, decided to examine thin slices of plant material and chose cork as one of his examples. On looking down the microscope he was struck by the regular appearance of the structure and in 1665 he wrote a book containing the diagram shown in *figure 1.1*.

If you examine the diagram you will see the 'pore-like' regular structures that he called 'cells'. Each cell appeared to be an empty box surrounded by a wall. Hooke had discovered and described, without realising it, the fundamental unit of *all* living things.

Although we now know that the cells of cork are dead, further observations of cells in living materials were made by Hooke and other scientists. However, it was not until almost 200 years later that a general cell theory emerged from the work of two German scientists. In 1838 Schleiden, a botanist,

suggested that all plants are made of cells, and a year later Schwann, a zoologist, suggested the same for animals. The **cell theory** states that **the basic**

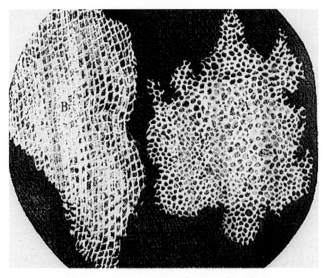

● **Figure 1.1** Drawing of cork cells published by Robert Hooke in 1665.

unit of structure and function of all **living organisms is the cell**. Now, over 150 years later, this idea is one of the most familiar and important theories in biology. To it has been added Virchow's theory of 1855 that **all cells arise from pre-existing cells by cell division**.

Why cells?

A cell can be thought of as a bag in which the chemistry of life is allowed to occur, partially separated from the environment outside the cell. The thin membrane which surrounds all cells is essential in controlling exchange between the cell and its environment. It is a very effective barrier, but also allows a controlled traffic of materials across it in both directions. The membrane is therefore described as **partially permeable**. If it were **freely permeable**, life could not exist because the chemicals of the cell would simply mix with the surrounding chemicals by diffusion.

Cell biology and microscopy

The study of cells has given rise to an important branch of biology known as **cell biology**. Cells can now be studied by many different methods, but scientists began simply by looking at them, using various types of microscope.

There are two fundamentally different types of microscope now in use: the light microscope and the electron microscope. Both use a form of radiation in order to create an image of the specimen being examined. The **light microscope** uses *light* as a source of radiation, while the **electron microscope** uses *electrons*, for reasons which are discussed later.

Light microscopy

The 'golden age' of light microscopy could be said to be the nineteenth century. Microscopes had been available since the beginning of the seventeenth century but, when dramatic improvements were made in the quality of glass lenses in the early nineteenth century, interest among scientists

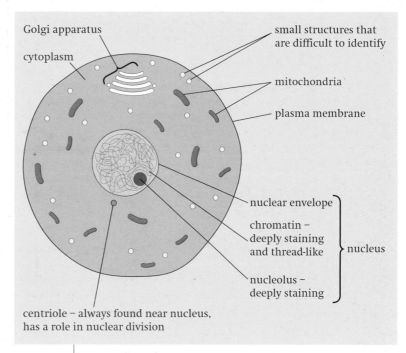

- **Figure 1.2** Structure of a generalised animal cell (diameter about 20 μm) as seen with a very high quality light microscope.

became widespread. The fascination of the microscopic world that opened up in biology inspired rapid progress both in microscope design and, equally importantly, in preparing material for examination with microscopes. This branch of biology is known as **cytology**. By 1900, all the structures shown in *figures 1.2, 1.3* and *1.4*, except lysosomes, had been discovered.

Figure 1.2 shows the structure of a generalised animal cell and *figure 1.4* the structure of a generalised plant cell as seen with a light microscope. (A generalised cell shows *all* the structures that

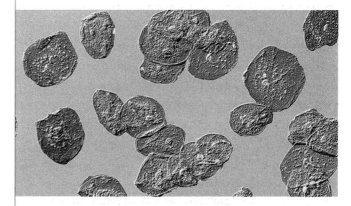

- **Figure 1.3** Cells from the lining of the human cheek (×300), showing typical animal cell characteristics: a centrally placed nucleus and many organelles such as mitochondria. The cells are part of a tissue known as squamous (flattened) epithelium (see page 19).

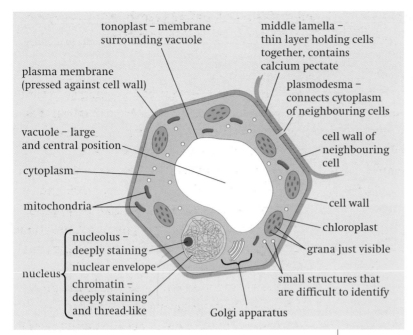

- **Figure 1.4** Structure of a generalised plant cell (diameter about 40 μm) as seen with a very high quality light microscope.

are typically found in a cell.) *Figure 1.3* shows some *actual* human cells.

SAQ 1.1

Using *figures 1.2* and *1.4*, name the structures that animal and plant cells have in common and those which are special only to animal or plant cells.

Animal and plant cells have features in common

In animals and plants each cell is surrounded by a very thin, **plasma (cell surface) membrane** which is too thin to be seen with a light microscope. Many of the cell contents are colourless and transparent so they need to be stained to be seen. Each cell has a **nucleus** which is a relatively large structure that stains intensely and is therefore very conspicuous. The deeply staining material in the nucleus is called **chromatin** and is a mass of loosely coiled threads. This material collects together to form visible separate chromosomes during nuclear division (see page 85). It contains **DNA (deoxyribonucleic acid)**, a molecule which contains the instructions that control the

activities of the cell (see chapter 5). Within the nucleus an even more deeply staining area is visible, the **nucleolus**, which is made of loops of DNA from several chromosomes.

The material between the nucleus and the plasma membrane is known as **cytoplasm**. Cytoplasm is an aqueous (watery) material, varying from a fluid to a jelly-like consistency. Many small structures can be seen within it. These have been likened to small organs and hence are known as **organelles**. An organelle can be defined as a **functionally and structurally distinct part of a cell**. Organelles themselves are often surrounded by membranes so that their activities can be separated from the surrounding cytoplasm. This is described as **compartmentalisation**. Having separate compartments is essential for a structure as complex as a cell to work efficiently. Since each type of organelle has its own function, the cell is said to show **division of labour**, a sharing of the work between different specialised organelles.

The most numerous organelles seen with the light microscope are usually **mitochondria** (singular **mitochondrion**). They are only just visible, but extraordinary films of living cells, taken with the aid of a light microscope, have shown that they can move about, change shape and divide. They are specialised to carry out aerobic respiration.

The use of special stains containing silver enabled the **Golgi apparatus** to be detected for the first time in 1898 by Camillo Golgi. The Golgi apparatus is part of a complex internal sorting and distribution system within the cell (see page 13).

Differences between animal and plant cells

The only structure commonly found in animal cells which is absent from plant cells is the **centriole**. Under the light microscope it appears as a small structure close to the nucleus (*figure 1.2*). It is involved in nuclear division (see page 85).

Individual plant cells are more easily seen with a light microscope than animal cells are because they are usually larger and surrounded by a relatively rigid **cell wall** outside the plasma membrane. The cell wall gives the cell a definite shape. It prevents the cell from bursting when water enters by osmosis, allowing large pressures to develop inside the cell (see page 57). Cell walls may also be reinforced for extra strength. Plant cells are linked to neighbouring cells by means of fine strands of cytoplasm called **plasmodesmata** (singular **plasmodesma**) which pass through pore-like structures in the walls of these neighbouring cells. Movement through the pores is thought to be controlled by their structure.

Apart from a cell wall, mature plant cells differ from animal cells in often possessing a **large central vacuole** and, if the cell carries out photosynthesis, in containing **chloroplasts**. The vacuole is surrounded by a membrane, the **tonoplast**, which controls exchange between the vacuole and the cytoplasm. The fluid in the vacuole is a solution of mineral salts, sugars, oxygen, carbon dioxide, pigments, enzymes and other organic compounds, including some waste products. Vacuoles help to regulate the osmotic properties of cells (the flow of water inwards and outwards) as well as having a wide range of other functions. For example, the pigments which colour the petals of certain flowers and parts of some vegetables, such as the red pigment of beetroots, are sometimes located in vacuoles.

Chloroplasts are relatively large organelles which are green in colour due to the presence of chlorophyll. At high magnifications small 'grains', or **grana**, can be seen in them. During the process of photosynthesis light is absorbed by these grana, which actually consist of stacks of membranes. Starch grains may also be visible within

chloroplasts. Chloroplasts are found in the green parts of the plant, mainly in the leaves.

Points to note

- You can think of a plant cell as being very similar to an animal cell but with extra structures.
- Plant cells are often larger than animal cells, although cell size varies enormously.
- Do not confuse the cell *wall* with the plasma *membrane*. Cell walls are relatively thick and physically strong, whereas plasma membranes are very thin. *All* cells have a plasma membrane.
- Vacuoles are not confined to plant cells; animal cells may have small vacuoles, such as phagocytic vacuoles (see page 60), although these are often not permanent structures.

We return to the differences between animal and plant cells as seen using the *electron* microscope on page 14.

Units of measurement in cell studies

In order to measure objects in the microscopic world, we need to use very small units of measurement which are unfamiliar to most people. According to international agreement, the International System of Units (SI units) should be used. In this system the basic unit of length is the **metre**, symbol **m**. Additional units can be created in multiples of a thousand times larger or smaller, using standard prefixes. For example, the prefix **kilo** means **1000** times. Thus 1 kilometre = 1000 metres. The units of length relevant to cell studies are shown in *table 1.1*.

It is difficult to imagine how small these units are, but, when looking down a microscope and seeing cells clearly, we should not forget how amazingly small the cells *actually* are. *Figure 1.5* shows the sizes of some structures. The smallest

Fraction of a metre	Unit	Symbol
one thousandth = 0.001 = 1/1000 = 10^{-3}	millimetre	mm
one millionth = 0.000 001 = 1/1 000 000 = 10^{-6}	micrometre	μm
one thousand millionth = 0.000 000 001 = 1/1 000 000 000 = 10^{-9}	nanometre	nm

μ is the Greek letter mu
1 micrometre is a thousandth of a millimetre
1 nanometre is a thousandth of a micrometre

● **Table 1.1** Units of measurement relevant to cell studies.

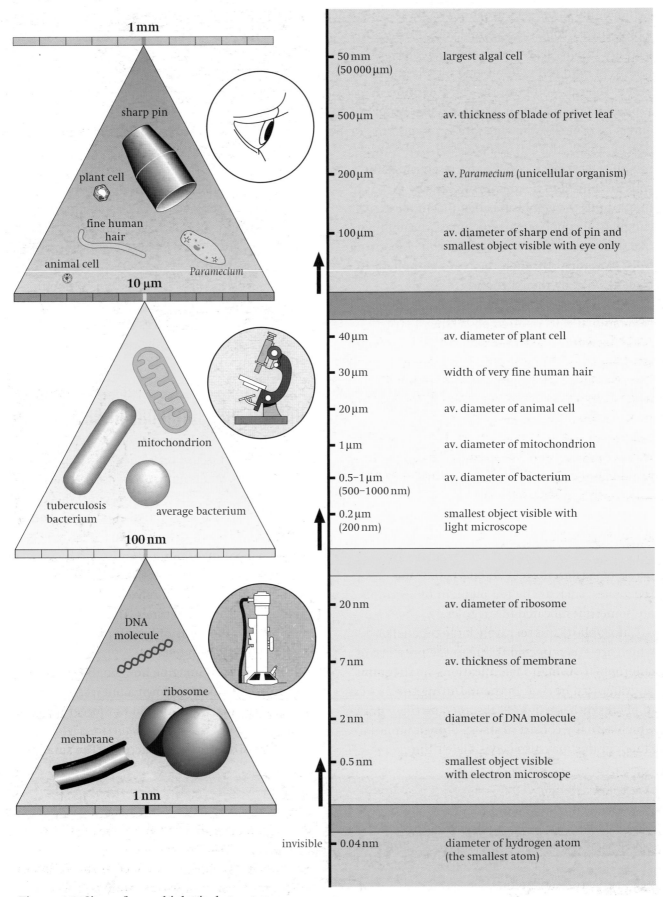

Figure 1.5 Sizes of some biological structures.

structure visible with only the human eye is about 50–100 μm in diameter. Your body contains about 60 million million cells, varying in size from about 5 μm to 20 μm. Try to imagine structures like mitochondria, which have an average diameter of 1 μm, or bacteria with an average diameter of 0.5 μm. The smallest cell organelles we deal with in this book, ribosomes, are only about 20 nm in diameter! When we consider processes such as diffusion (chapter 4), it is also helpful to have an appreciation of the distances involved.

Electron microscopes

Earlier in this chapter it was stated that by 1900 almost all the structures shown in *figures 1.2* and *1.4* had been discovered. There followed a time of frustration for microscopists because they realised that no matter how much the design of light microscopes improved, there was a limit to how much could ever be seen using light.

In order to understand the problem, it is necessary to know something about the nature of light itself and to understand the difference between **magnification** and **resolution**.

Magnification and resolution

Magnification is the **number of times larger an image is compared with the real size of the object.**

$$\text{magnification} = \frac{\text{size of image}}{\text{actual size of specimen}}$$

Figure 1.6 shows two photographs of sections through the same group of plant cells. The magnifications of the two photographs are the same. The real length of the central plant cell was about 150 μm. In the photographs, the length appears to be about 60 mm.

To calculate the magnification, it is easiest if we convert all the measurements to the same units, in this case micrometres. 60 mm is 60 000 μm, therefore

$$\text{magnification} = \frac{60\,000}{150}$$

$$= \times 400$$

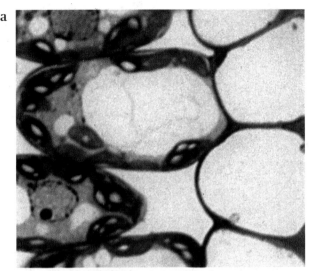

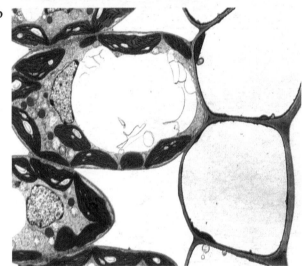

● **Figure 1.6** Photographs of the same plant cells seen **a** with a light microscope, **b** with an electron microscope, both shown at a magnification of about × 400.

SAQ 1.2

a Calculate the magnification of the drawing of the animal cell in *figure 1.2*.
b Calculate the actual length of the chloroplast in *figure 1.22*.

Although both photographs in *figure 1.6* are shown at the same magnification, you can see that **b**, the electron micrograph, is much clearer. (An electron micrograph is a picture taken with an electron microscope.) This is because it has greater resolution. **Resolution** is defined as **the ability to distinguish between two separate points**. If the two points cannot be **resolved**, they will be seen as one point. The maximum resolution of a light

● **Figure 1.7** The eye of a bee is sensitive to ultraviolet light and can see the guides which lead to the nectaries at the centre of the flower.   **a** In normal light, the nectar guides of the *Potentilla* flower cannot be seen by the human eye.   **b** In ultraviolet, they appear as dark patches.

microscope is 200 nm. This means that if two points or objects are closer together than 200 nm they cannot be distinguished as separate.

It is possible to take a photograph such as *figure 1.6a* and to magnify (enlarge) it, but we see no more *detail*; in other words, we do not improve resolution, even though we often enlarge photographs because they are easier to see when larger. Thus an increase in magnification is not necessarily accompanied by an increase in resolution. With a microscope, magnification up to the limit of resolution can reveal further detail, but any further magnification increases blurring as well as the size of the picture.

The electromagnetic spectrum

How is resolution linked with the nature of light? One of the properties of light is that it travels in waves. The length of the waves of visible light varies, ranging from about 400 nm (violet light) to about 700 nm (red light). The human eye can distinguish between these different wavelengths, and in the brain the differences are converted to colour differences. (Colour is an invention of the brain!) Some animals can see wavelengths that humans cannot. Bees, for example, can see ultraviolet light. Flowers that to us do not appear to have markings often have ultraviolet markings that guide bees to their nectaries (*figure 1.7*). If you happen to be sharing a dark room with a cobra, the cobra will be able to see *you*, even though you cannot see *it*, because warm bodies give off (radiate) infrared radiation which cobras can see.

The whole range of different wavelengths is called the electromagnetic spectrum. Visible light is only one part of this spectrum. *Figure 1.8* shows some of the parts of the electromagnetic spectrum. The longer the electromagnetic waves, the lower their frequency (all the waves travel at the same speed, so imagine them passing a post: shorter waves pass at higher frequency).

In theory, there is no limit to how short or how long the waves can be. Wavelength changes with energy: the greater the energy,

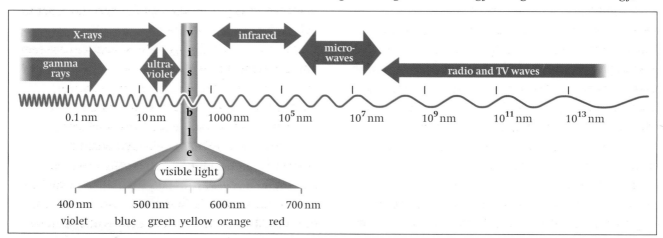

● **Figure 1.8** Diagram of the electromagnetic spectrum (the waves are not drawn to scale). The numbers indicate the wavelengths of the different types of electromagnetic radiation. Visible light is a form of electromagnetic radiation.

the shorter the wavelength (rather like squashing a spring!). Now look at *figure 1.9*, which shows a mitochondrion, some very small cell organelles called ribosomes (see page 12) and light of 400 nm wavelength, the shortest visible wavelength. The mitochondrion is large enough to interfere with the light waves. However, the ribosomes are far too small to have any effect on the light waves. The general rule is that **the limit of resolution is about one half the wavelength of the radiation used to view the specimen**. In other words, if an object is any smaller than half the wavelength of the radiation used to view it, it cannot be seen separately from nearby objects. This means that the best resolution that can be obtained using a microscope that uses visible light (a light microscope) is 200 nm, since the shortest wavelength of visible light is 400 nm (violet light). In practice, this corresponds to a maximum useful magnification of about 1500 times. Ribosomes are approximately 22 nm in diameter and can therefore never be seen using light.

If an object is transparent it will allow light waves to pass through it and therefore will still not be visible. This is why many biological structures have to be stained before they can be seen.

The electron microscope

Biologists, faced with the problem that they would never see anything smaller than 200 nm using a light microscope, realised that the only solution would be to use radiation of a shorter wavelength than light. If you study *figure 1.8*, you will see that ultraviolet light, or better still X-rays, look like possible candidates. Both ultraviolet and X-ray microscopes have been built, the latter with little success partly because of the difficulty of focussing X-rays. A much better solution is to use electrons. **Electrons** are negatively charged particles which orbit the nucleus of an atom. When a metal becomes very hot, some of its electrons gain so much energy that they escape from their orbits, like a rocket escaping from Earth's gravity. Free electrons behave like electromagnetic radiation. They have a very short wavelength: the greater the energy, the shorter the wavelength. Electrons are a very suitable form of radiation for microscopy for two major reasons. Firstly, their wavelength is

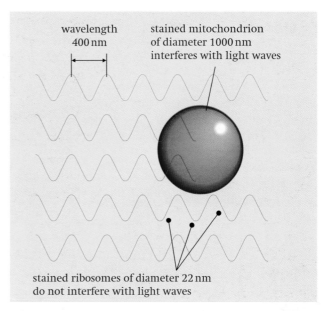

● **Figure 1.9** A mitochondrion and some ribosomes in the path of light waves of 400 nm length.

extremely short (at least as short as that of X-rays); secondly, because they are negatively charged, they can be focussed easily using electromagnets (the magnet can be made to alter the path of the beam, the equivalent of a glass lens bending light).

Electron microscopes were developed during the 1930s and 1940s but it was not until after the Second World War that techniques improved enough to allow cells to be studied with the electron microscope.

Transmission and scanning electron microscopes

Two types of electron microscope are now in common use. The **transmission electron microscope** was the type originally developed. Here the beam of electrons is passed *through* the specimen before being viewed. Only those electrons that are **transmitted** (pass through the specimen) are seen. This allows us to see thin sections of specimens, and thus to see inside cells. In the **scanning electron microscope**, on the other hand, the electron beam is used to scan the **surfaces** of structures, and only the **reflected** beam is observed. An example of a scanning electron micrograph is shown in *figure 1.10*. The advantage of this microscope is that surface structures can be seen. Also, great depth of field is obtained so that much of the specimen is in focus at the same time. Such a picture would be impossible to obtain with a light microscope, even using the

● **Figure 1.10** False-colour scanning electron micrograph (SEM) of the head of a cat flea (× 100).

same magnification and resolution, because you would have to keep focussing up and down with the objective lens to see different parts of the specimen. The disadvantage of the scanning electron microscope is that it cannot achieve the same resolution as a transmission electron microscope.

Viewing specimens with the electron microscope

It is not possible to see an electron beam, so to make the image visible the electron beam has to be projected onto a fluorescent screen. The areas hit by electrons shine brightly, giving overall a 'black and white' picture. The stains used to improve the contrast of biological specimens for electron microscopy contain heavy metal atoms which stop the passage of electrons. The resulting picture is therefore similar in principle to an X-ray photograph, with the more dense parts of the specimen appearing blacker. 'False-colour' images are created by processing the standard black and white image using a computer.

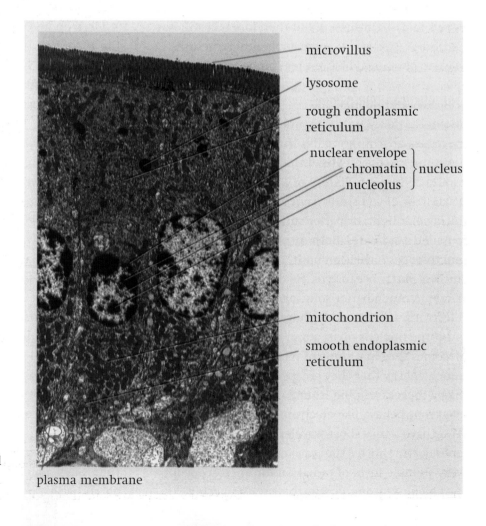

microvillus

lysosome

rough endoplasmic reticulum

nuclear envelope ⎫
chromatin ⎬ nucleus
nucleolus ⎭

mitochondrion

smooth endoplasmic reticulum

plasma membrane

● **Figure 1.11** A representative animal cell as seen with a transmission electron microscope. The cell is a small intestinal cell from a mouse (× 10 000).

To add to the difficulties of electron microscopy, the electron beam, and therefore the specimen and the fluorescent screen, must be in a vacuum. If electrons collided with air molecules, they would scatter, making it impossible to achieve a sharp picture. Also, water boils at room temperature in a vacuum, so all specimens must be dehydrated before being placed in the microscope. This means that only dead material can be examined. Great efforts are therefore made to try to preserve material in a life-like state when preparing it for the microscope.

SAQ 1.3

Explain why ribosomes are not visible using a light microscope.

Ultrastructure of an animal cell

The 'fine', or detailed, structure of a cell as revealed by the electron microscope is called its **ultrastructure**. *Figure 1.11* shows the appearance of a typical animal cell as seen with an electron microscope and *figure 1.12* is a diagram based on many other such micrographs.

SAQ 1.4

Compare *figure 1.12* with *figure 1.2*. Name the structures which can be seen with the electron microscope but not with the light microscope.

Structure and functions of organelles

Compartmentalisation and division of labour within the cell are even more obvious with an electron microscope than with a light microscope.

We now consider the structure and functions of some of the cell components in more detail.

Nucleus *(figure 1.13)*

The **nucleus** is the largest cell organelle. It is surrounded by two membranes known as the **nuclear envelope**. The outer membrane of the nuclear envelope is continuous with the endoplasmic reticulum *(figure 1.12)*. The nuclear envelope is conspicuously perforated by the **nuclear pores**. These allow exchange between the nucleus and the cytoplasm, e.g. mRNA and ribosomes leave the nucleus

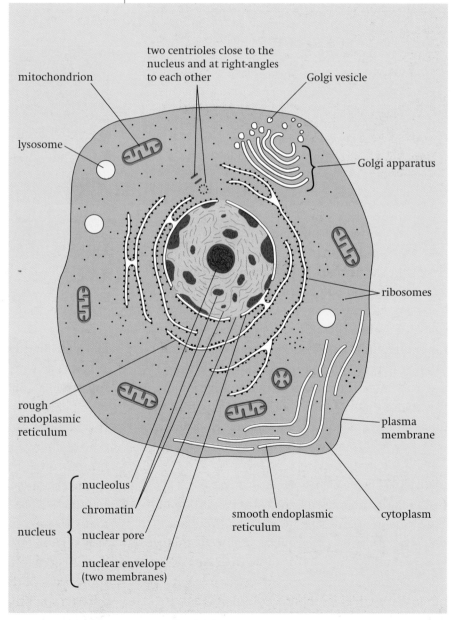

● **Figure 1.12** Ultrastructure of a typical animal cell as seen with an electron microscope. In reality, the endoplasmic reticulum is more extensive than shown and free ribosomes may be more extensive. Glycogen granules are sometimes present in the cytoplasm.

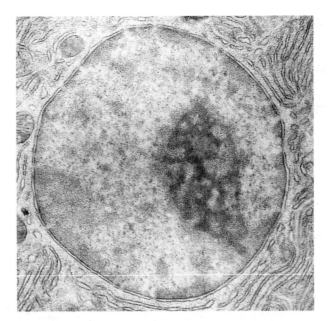

● **Figure 1.13** TEM of the nucleus of a cell from the pancreas of a bat (× 10 000). The circular nucleus displays its double-layered nuclear envelope interspersed with nuclear pores. The nucleolus is more darkly stained. Smooth endoplasmic reticulum is visible in the surrounding cytoplasm.

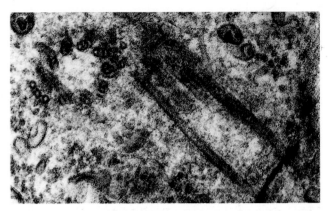

● **Figure 1.14** Centrioles in transverse and longitudinal section (TS and LS) (× 86 000). In TS the nine triplets of microtubules which make up the structure can be clearly seen.

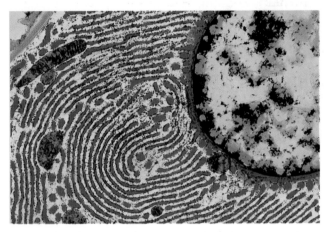

● **Figure 1.15** Coloured TEM of the rough ER (red stripes) covered with ribosomes (black dots) outside the nucleus (green) (× 7000).

and some hormones and nutrients enter the nucleus through the pores.

Within the nucleus, the chromosomes are in a loosely coiled state known as chromatin (except during nuclear division, see chapter 6). Chromosomes contain DNA which is organised into functional units called genes. Genes control the activities of the cell and inheritance; thus the nucleus controls the cell's activities. Division of the nucleus precedes cell division. Also within the nucleus, the **nucleolus** manufactures ribosomes, using the information in its own DNA.

Centrioles *(figure 1.14)*

Just outside the nucleus, the extra resolution of the electron microscope reveals that there are really *two* centrioles, not one as it appears under the light microscope (compare with *figure 1.2*). They lie close together at right-angles to each other. A centriole is a hollow cylinder about 0.4 µm long, formed from a ring of microtubules (a kind of cell scaffolding made of protein). These microtubules are used to grow the spindle fibres for nuclear division (see page 85).

Endoplasmic reticulum and ribosomes *(figure 1.15)*

When cells were first seen with the electron microscope, biologists were amazed to see so much detailed structure. The existence of much of this had not been suspected. This was particularly true of an extensive system of membranes running through the cytoplasm which became known as the **endoplasmic reticulum** (**ER**).

Attached to the surface of much of the ER are many tiny organelles, now known as **ribosomes**. At very high magnifications these can be seen to consist of two parts, a smaller and a larger subunit. In some areas of the cell, the ER lacks ribosomes and appears smooth. This is called **smooth ER** and is now known to have a different function from ribosome-covered ER, which is called **rough ER**. The membranes form a system of flattened sacs, like sheets, which are called **cisternae**. The space

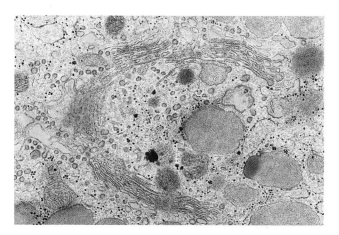

● **Figure 1.16** TEM of a Golgi apparatus (×30 000). A central stack of saucer-shaped sacs (cisternae) can be seen budding off small Golgi vesicles. These may form secretory vesicles whose contents can be released at the cell surface by exocytosis (for more details see page 60).

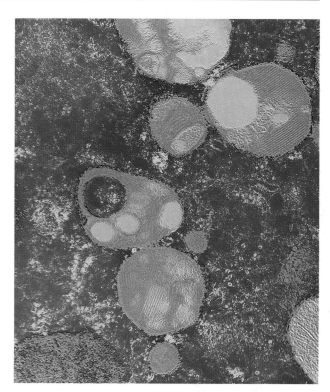

● **Figure 1.17** Lysosomes in a mouse kidney cell (×55 000). They contain membrane structures in the process of digestion (red) and vesicles (green). Cytoplasm is coloured blue here.

inside the sacs forms a compartment separate from the surrounding cytoplasm. The cisternae can go on to form the Golgi apparatus.

Ribosomes are the sites of protein synthesis (see pages 72–73). They are found free in the cytoplasm as well as on the rough ER. They are very small organelles, only about 22 nm in diameter and are made of **RNA** (ribonucleic acid) and protein.

The proteins that are manufactured on the ribosomes are transported throughout the cell by the rough ER. In contrast, the smooth ER makes lipids (page 28) and steroids (e.g. cholesterol and reproductive hormones).

Golgi apparatus (*figure 1.16*)

The Golgi apparatus is a stack of flattened sacs (**cisternae**). The stack is constantly being formed at one end from vesicles which bud off from the smooth ER, and broken down again at the other end to form **Golgi vesicles**.

The apparatus collects, processes and sorts molecules (particularly proteins from the rough ER), ready for transport in Golgi vesicles either to other parts of the cell or out of the cell (secretion). Golgi vesicles are also used to make lysosomes.

Lysosomes (*figure 1.17*)

Lysosomes are spherical sacs, surrounded by a single membrane and having no internal structure. They are commonly 0.1–0.5 μm in diameter. They

contain hydrolytic (digestive) enzymes which must be kept separate from the rest of the cell to prevent damage. Lysosomes are responsible for the breakdown (digestion) of unwanted structures, e.g. old organelles or even whole cells, as in mammary glands after lactation (breast feeding). In white blood cells they are used to digest bacteria (see endocytosis, page 60). Enzymes are sometimes released outside the cell, e.g. during replacement of cartilage with bone during development. The heads of sperm contain a special lysosome, the acrosome, for digesting a path to the ovum (egg).

Mitochondria (*figure 1.18*)

Mitochondria are slightly larger than lysosomes and are surrounded by two membranes (an envelope). The inner of these is folded to form finger-like **cristae** which project into the interior solution, or **matrix**.

The main function of mitochondria is to carry out the later stages of aerobic respiration. As a result of respiration, they make ATP, the universal energy carrier in cells (see chapter 7). They are also involved in synthesis of lipids (page 28).

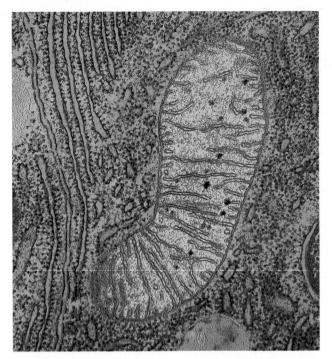

● **Figure 1.18** Mitochondrion (orange) with its double membrane (envelope); the inner membrane is folded to form cristae (×12 000). Mitochondria are the sites of aerobic cell respiration. Note also the rough ER (turquoise).

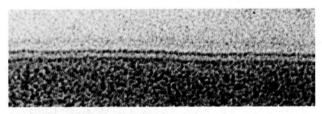

● **Figure 1.19** Plasma membrane (×250 000). At this magnification the membrane appears as two dark lines at the edge of the cell.

Plasma membrane *(figure 1.19)*

The plasma membrane is extremely thin (about 7 nm). However, at very high magnifications, at least ×100 000, it can be seen to have three layers (**trilaminar appearance**). This consists of two dark lines (heavily stained) either side of a narrow, pale interior. The membrane is partially permeable, controlling exchange between the cell and its environment. Membrane structure is discussed further in chapter 4.

Cilia *(figure 1.20)*

Some cells have long, thin extensions that can move in a wave-like manner. If there are just a few of these extensions, and they are relatively long,

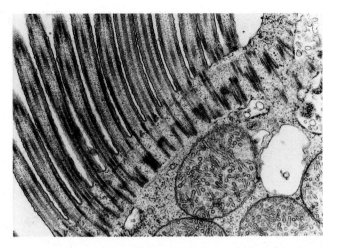

● **Figure 1.20** TEM of cilia in LS (×18 500).

then they are called **flagella** (singular **flagellum**). If there are many of them, and they are relatively short, then they are called **cilia** (singular **cilium**).

A cilium is usually about 3–4 μm long. It is covered with an extension of the plasma membrane, and it contains microtubules that extend throughout its length. These microtubules arise from a structure called a basal body, in the cytoplasm. The microtubules are arranged in an outer cylinder of 9 pairs, surrounding two central microtubules. Basal bodies are identical in structure to centrioles.

The movement of cilia and flagella is caused by the microtubules, which can slide against each other, causing the whole strucure to bend. Where there are many cilia on a cell, or a group of cells (as in ciliated epithelia, described on page 19), they all move in a coordinated manner, each slightly out of phase with its neighbour so that the overall effect looks rather like long grass rippling in the wind. As a result, substances around the cell are made to move or – if the cell is not fixed to anything – the cell itself is swept along as the cilia beat.

Ultrastructure of a plant cell

All the structures found in animal cells are also found in plant cells, except centrioles and – except very rarely – cilia. The appearance of a plant cell as seen with the electron microscope is shown in *figure 1.21a* and a diagram based on many such micrographs in *figure 1.21b*. The relatively thick cell wall and the large central

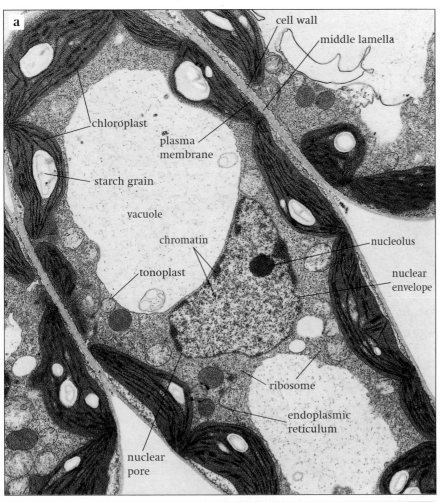

a
- cell wall
- middle lamella
- chloroplast
- plasma membrane
- starch grain
- vacuole
- chromatin
- nucleolus
- tonoplast
- nuclear envelope
- nuclear pore
- ribosome
- endoplasmic reticulum

Figure 1.21 Appearance of a representative plant cell as seen with an electron microscope. **a** An electron micrograph of a palisade cell from a soya bean leaf (×5600). **b** A diagram of the ultrastructure of a typical plant cell as seen with the electron microscope. In reality, the ER is more extensive than shown. Free ribosomes may also be more extensive.

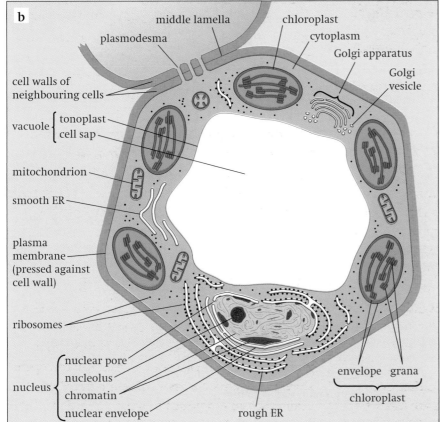

b
- middle lamella
- plasmodesma
- chloroplast
- cytoplasm
- Golgi apparatus
- Golgi vesicle
- cell walls of neighbouring cells
- vacuole { tonoplast, cell sap }
- mitochondrion
- smooth ER
- plasma membrane (pressed against cell wall)
- ribosomes
- nucleus { nuclear pore, nucleolus, chromatin, nuclear envelope }
- rough ER
- envelope grana
- chloroplast

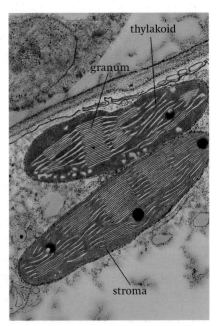

thylakoid, granum, stroma

Figure 1.22 Chloroplasts (×20 000). Parallel flattened sacs (thylakoids) run through the stroma and are stacked in places to form grana. Black circles among the thylakoids are lipid droplets.

vacuole are obvious, as are the chloroplasts (two of which are shown in detail in *figure 1.22*). These structures and their functions have been described on page 5.

SAQ 1.5

Compare *figure 1.21b* with *figure 1.4*. Name the structures which can be seen with the electron microscope but not with the light microscope.

Two fundamentally different types of cell

At one time it was common practice to try to classify *all* living organisms as either animals or plants. With advances in our knowledge of living things, it has become obvious that the living world is not that simple. Fungi and bacteria, for example, are very different from animals and plants, and from each other. Eventually it was realised that there are two fundamentally different types of cell. The most

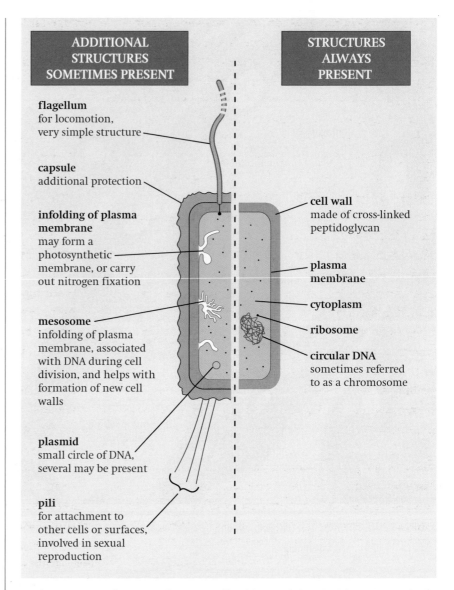

flagellum
for locomotion, very simple structure

capsule
additional protection

infolding of plasma membrane
may form a photosynthetic membrane, or carry out nitrogen fixation

mesosome
infolding of plasma membrane, associated with DNA during cell division, and helps with formation of new cell walls

plasmid
small circle of DNA, several may be present

pili
for attachment to other cells or surfaces, involved in sexual reproduction

ADDITIONAL STRUCTURES SOMETIMES PRESENT

STRUCTURES ALWAYS PRESENT

cell wall
made of cross-linked peptidoglycan

plasma membrane

cytoplasm

ribosome

circular DNA
sometimes referred to as a chromosome

● **Figure 1.23** Diagram of a generalised bacterium showing the typical features of a prokaryotic cell.

Prokaryotes	Eukaryotes
Average diameter of cell 0.5–5 µm	Cells commonly up to 40 µm diameter and commonly 1000–10 000 times the volume of prokaryotic cells
DNA is circular and lies free in the cytoplasm	DNA is not circular and is contained in a nucleus. The nucleus is surrounded by an envelope of two membranes
DNA is naked	DNA is associated with protein, forming structures called chromosomes
Slightly smaller ribosomes (about 18 nm diameter)	Slightly larger ribosomes (about 22 nm diameter)
No ER present	ER present, to which ribosomes may be attached
Very few cell organelles; none are surrounded by an envelope of two membranes	Many types of cell organelle present (extensive compartmentalisation and division of labour). Some organelles are bounded by a single membrane, e.g. lysosomes, Golgi apparatus, vacuoles; some are bounded by two membranes (an envelope), e.g. nucleus, mitochondrion; some have no membrane, e.g. ribosomes
Cell wall present	Cell wall sometimes present, e.g. in plants

● **Table 1.2** A comparison of prokaryotic and eukaryotic cells.

obvious difference between these types is that one *possesses a nucleus* and the other does not. Organisms that lack nuclei are called **prokaryotes** (*pro* means before; *karyon* means nucleus). All prokaryotes are now referred to as **bacteria**. They are, on average, about 1000 to 10 000 times smaller in *volume* than cells with nuclei and are much simpler in structure, for example their DNA lies free in the cytoplasm. Organisms whose cells possess nuclei are called **eukaryotes** (*eu* means true). Their DNA lies inside a nucleus. Eukaryotes include **animals**, **plants**, **fungi** and a group containing most of the unicellular eukaryotes known as **protoctists**. Most biologists believe that eukaryotes evolved from prokaryotes, one-and-a-half thousand million years after prokaryotes first appeared on Earth. We mainly study animals and plants in this book, but **all** eukaryotic cells have certain features in common. A generalised prokaryotic cell is shown in *figure 1.23*. A comparison of prokaryotic and eukaryotic cells is given in *table 1.2*.

SAQ 1.6

List the structural features that prokaryotic and eukaryotic cells have in common. Briefly explain why each of the structures you have listed is essential.

Tissues and organs

So far we have studied life at the cell level. Some organisms, such as bacteria, consist of one cell only. Many organisms are multicellular, consisting of collections of cells from several hundred to billions in total. One great advantage that multicellular organisms gain over unicellular organisms is greater independence from the environment, but a full discussion of this is outside the scope of this book. In these communities of cells, it is usual for the functions of the organism to be divided among groups of cells which become specialised, both structurally and functionally, for particular roles. We have already seen this distribution of function *within* cells, particularly eukaryotic cells, and have referred to it as 'division of labour'. Usually, specialised cells show division of labour by being grouped into **tissues**; the tissues may be further

grouped into **organs** and the organs into **systems**. Each tissue, organ or system has a particular function and a structure appropriate to that function. More precisely, we can define the terms as follows.

■ A **tissue** is a collection of cells, together with any intercellular secretion produced by them, that is specialised to perform one or more particular functions. The cells may be of the *same* type, such as parenchyma in plants and squamous epithelium in animals. They may be of *mixed* type, such as xylem and phloem in plants, and cartilage, bone and connective tissue in animals. The study of tissues is called **histology**.

■ An **organ** is a part of the body which forms a structural and functional unit and is composed of more than one tissue. Examples of plant organs are leaves, stems and roots; animal organs include the brain, heart, liver, kidney and eye.

■ A **system** is a collection of organs with a particular function, such as the excretory, reproductive, cardiovascular and digestive systems.

Figure 1.24 shows some examples of plant tissues within a leaf. *Figure 1.25* is based on *figure 1.24* and illustrates the relative positions of the tissues in a leaf. This is called a **plan diagram**. As its purpose is to show where the different *tissues* are, no individual cells are drawn.

Some examples of tissues

Several kinds of plant tissue are shown in *figure 1.24*. Whereas the palisade mesophyll is a tissue made up of many similar cells, all with the same function, the xylem tissue and phloem tissue are each made of several different types of cells. You can find out about the structure of xylem tissue and phloem tissue in chapter 10.

Two different animal tissues are squamous epithelium and ciliated epithelium. They are both **epithelial** tissues – that is, tissues which form sheets covering surfaces. Both of them are one cell thick, so they are said to be *simple* **epithelia**. The cells rest on a **basement membrane**, which, despite its name, is not a cell membrane; indeed, it is not part of the cells at all. The basement

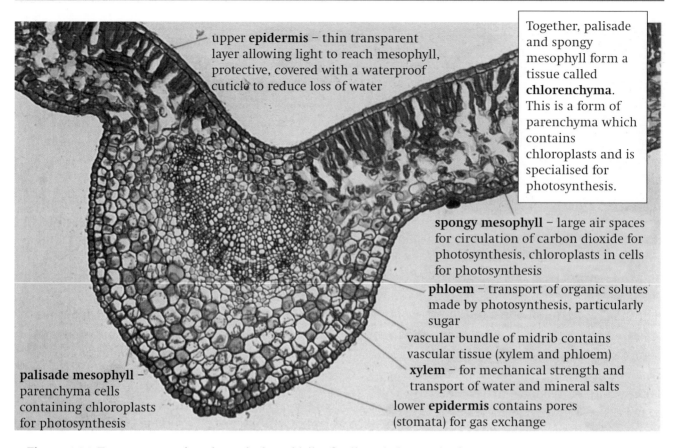

upper **epidermis** – thin transparent layer allowing light to reach mesophyll, protective, covered with a waterproof cuticle to reduce loss of water

Together, palisade and spongy mesophyll form a tissue called **chlorenchyma**. This is a form of parenchyma which contains chloroplasts and is specialised for photosynthesis.

spongy mesophyll – large air spaces for circulation of carbon dioxide for photosynthesis, chloroplasts in cells for photosynthesis

phloem – transport of organic solutes made by photosynthesis, particularly sugar

vascular bundle of midrib contains vascular tissue (xylem and phloem)

xylem – for mechanical strength and transport of water and mineral salts

lower **epidermis** contains pores (stomata) for gas exchange

palisade mesophyll – parenchyma cells containing chloroplasts for photosynthesis

● **Figure 1.24** Transverse section through the midrib of a dicotyledonous leaf, *Ligustrum* (privet) (×50). Tissues are indicated in bold type.

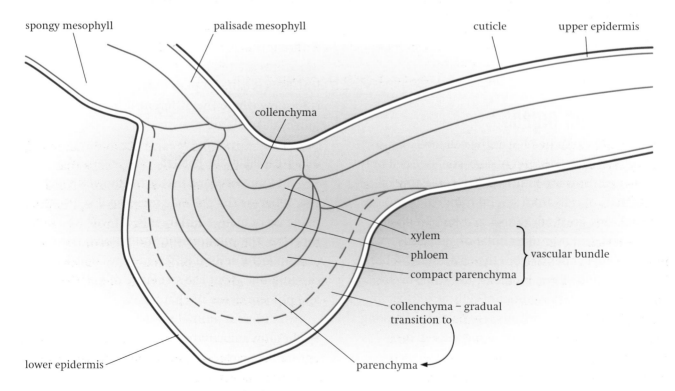

spongy mesophyll   palisade mesophyll   cuticle   upper epidermis

collenchyma

xylem
phloem
compact parenchyma
vascular bundle
collenchyma – gradual transition to

lower epidermis   parenchyma

● **Figure 1.25** A plan diagram of the transverse section through a privet leaf shown in *figure 1.24*. Parenchyma is a tissue made up of unspecialised cells. Collenchyma is made up of cells in which the walls are thickened with extra cellulose, especially at the corners, providing extra strength for support.

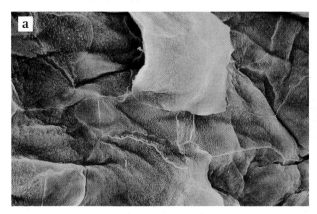

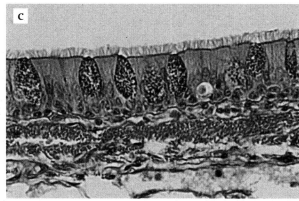

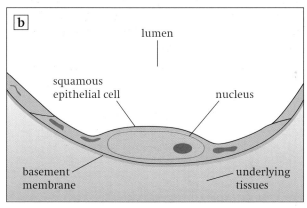

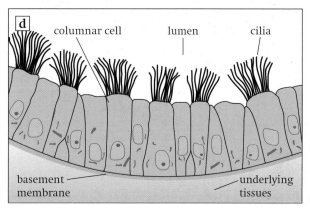

• **Figure 1.26**
a SEM of squamous epithelial cells on the surface of a healthy human cervix (× 1800). They have microvilli and tiny folds here. Borders between cells are coloured yellow. One cell is peeling away at the top. See also *figure 1.3*.
b Diagram of a section through squamous epithelium, as seen with a light microscope..
c Light micrograph of ciliated columnar epithelium (x 550) from the lining of a trachea. This epithelium also contains mucus-secreting goblet cells; the mucus is stained blue.
d Diagram of a section through ciliated columnar epithelium, as seen with a light microscope.

membrane is a network of collagen and glycoproteins (described on pages 36 and 53) that is secreted by the *underlying* cells, and that holds the epithelial cells in position.

Squamous epithelium (*figure 1.26a* and *b*) covers many surfaces in the human body, including the inner lining of the cheeks, the inner surfaces of blood vessels, and the inner surfaces of the atria and ventricles in the heart (chapter 9). It also forms the walls of the alveoli in the lungs. The individual cells are smooth, flat and very thin. They fit closely together, a little like tiles on a floor, thus providing a smooth, low-friction surface over which fluids can move easily. In the alveoli, the thinness of the cells allows rapid diffusion of gases between the alveoli and the blood (see chapters 4 and 13).

Ciliated epithelium (*figures 1.20* and *1.26c* and *d*), as its name suggests, is made up of cells that possess cilia. Sometimes these cells are shaped like cubes, making up *cuboidal* ciliated epithelium. This tissue is found, for example, lining the ends of the bronchioles in the lungs. Sometimes, the cells are tall and narrow, making up *columnar* ciliated epithelium. This tissue is found, for example, in the oviducts.

SAQ 1.7
Suggest the functions of the ciliated epithelium in
a the bronchioles and
b the oviducts.

SUMMARY

◆ All organisms are composed of units called cells.

◆ All cells are surrounded by a partially permeable membrane that controls exchange between the cell and its environment.

◆ The cells of animals and plants are compartmentalised and contain many similar structures: plasma membrane; cytoplasm containing mitochondria, endoplasmic reticulum (ER), lysosomes and ribosomes; and a nucleus with a nucleolus and chromatin.

◆ Animal cells also have centrioles and some-times cilia, whereas most plant cells have chloroplasts and a large central vacuole. Plant cells are also surrounded by rigid cell walls.

◆ Some of these structures are not visible with the light microscope because of the limit of resolution of light waves.

◆ Greater detail and smaller structures are seen with electron microscopes which use electron beams transmitted through (transmission electron microscope) or bounced off (scanning electron microscope) the specimen. However, only dead material can be viewed in electron microscopes.

◆ Prokaryote cells differ from eukaryote cells in being smaller, having free DNA in the cytoplasm, no endoplasmic reticulum or nucleus, few organelles and smaller ribosomes.

◆ In multicellular organisms, cells are organ-ised into groups called tissues. Groups of different tissues make up organs.

Questions

1 Briefly explain the differences between the following:
   a rough ER and smooth ER*,
   b cell wall and plasma membrane*,
   c chromatin and chromosome*,
   d nucleus and nucleolus*,
   e resolution and magnification,
   f scanning electron microscope and transmission electron microscope,
   g light microscope and electron microscope,
   h tissue and organ.
   (* With reference to both structure and function.)

2 What is meant by 'division of labour'? Show how it is important within eukaryotic cells.

3 Summarise the similarities and differences in structure between
   a prokaryote and eukaryote cells, and
   b animal and plant cells.

CHAPTER 2

Biological molecules

By the end of this chapter you should be able to:

1 understand the importance in biology of carbohydrates, lipids and proteins;

2 understand that although some important biological molecules are very large, they are made by the relatively simple process of joining together many small repeating subunits;

3 describe the basic structure of the main types of carbohydrates, namely monosaccharides, disaccharides and polysaccharides;

4 describe the structure of the ring forms of alpha- and beta-glucose;

5 describe the formation and breakage of a glycosidic bond, and its significance;

6 describe the structure of the polysaccharides starch, glycogen and cellulose and show how these structures are related to their functions in living organisms;

7 describe the basic structure and properties of triglycerides and phospholipids and relate these structures to their functions in living organisms;

8 distinguish between saturated and unsaturated fatty acids and lipids;

9 describe the structure of amino acids and the way in which peptide bonds are formed and broken;

10 describe the primary structure of polypeptides and proteins and how it affects their secondary and tertiary structure;

11 explain that the quaternary structure of a protein is formed by the combination of two or more polypeptide chains;

12 describe the importance of hydrogen bonds, disulphide bonds, ionic bonds and hydrophobic interactions in maintaining the three-dimensional structure of a protein;

13 discuss the ways in which the structures of haemoglobin and collagen are related to their functions;

14 describe the crucial role that water plays in maintaining life on Earth, both as a constituent of living organisms and as an environment;

15 outline the roles of inorganic ions in living organisms;

16 know how to test for reducing and non-reducing sugars, starch, lipids and proteins.

The study of the structure and functioning of biological molecules now forms an important branch of biology known as **molecular biology**. This is a relatively young science, but the importance of the subject is clear from the relatively large number of Nobel prizes that have been awarded in this field. It has attracted some of the best scientists, even from other disciplines like physics and mathematics.

Molecular biology is closely linked with biochemistry, which looks at the chemical reactions of biological molecules. The sum total of all the biochemical reactions in the body is known as **metabolism**. Metabolism is complex, but it has an underlying simplicity. For example, there are only 20 common amino acids used to make naturally occurring proteins, whereas theoretically there could be millions. Why is there this economy? One possibility is that all the manufacture and interactions of biological molecules must be controlled and regulated and, the more there are, the more complex the control becomes. (Control and regulation by enzymes will be examined in chapter 3.)

Another striking principle of molecular biology is how closely the structures of molecules are related to their functions. This will become clear in this chapter and in chapter 3. Our understanding of how structure is related to function may lead to the creation of a vast range of designer molecules to carry out such varied functions as large-scale industrial reactions and precise targetting of cells in medical treatment.

The building blocks of life

The four most common elements in living organisms are, in order of abundance, hydrogen, carbon, oxygen and nitrogen. They account for more than 99% of the atoms found in all living things. Carbon is particularly important because carbon atoms can join together to form long chains or ring structures. They can be thought of as the basic skeletons of organic molecules to which groups of other atoms are attached. Organic molecules always contain carbon.

It is believed that, before *life* evolved, there was a period of *chemical* evolution in which thousands of carbon-based molecules evolved from the more simple molecules that existed on the young planet Earth. Such an effect can be artificially created reasonably easily today given similar raw ingredients, such as methane (CH_4), carbon dioxide (CO_2), hydrogen (H_2), water (H_2O), nitrogen (N_2), ammonia (NH_3) and hydrogen sulphide (H_2S), and an energy source, for example an electrical discharge. These simple but key biological molecules, which are relatively limited in variety, then act as the building blocks for larger molecules. The main ones are shown in *figure 2.1*.

Polymers and macromolecules

The term **macromolecule** means 'giant molecule'. There are three types of macromolecule in living organisms, namely polysaccharides, proteins (polypeptides) and nucleic acids (polynucleotides). The prefix *poly* means 'many' and these molecules are **polymers**, that is macromolecules made up of many repeating subunits that are similar or identical to each other and are joined end to end like beads on a string. Making such molecules is relatively easy because the same reaction is repeated many times. This is **polymerisation**.

The subunits from which polysaccharides, proteins and nucleic acids are made are monosaccharides, amino acids and nucleotides respectively as shown in *figure 2.1*. This also shows two types of molecule which, although not polymers, are made up of simpler biochemicals. These are lipids and nucleotides. Natural examples of polymers are cellulose and rubber. There are many examples of industrially produced polymers, such as polyester, polythene, PVC (polyvinyl chloride) and nylon. All these are made up of carbon-based subunits and contain thousands of carbon atoms joined end to end.

We shall now take a closer look at some of the small biological molecules and the larger molecules made from them. (Organic bases and nucleic acids are dealt with in chapter 5).

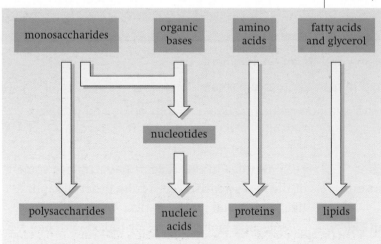

● **Figure 2.1** The building blocks of life.

Carbohydrates

All carbohydrates contain the elements carbon, hydrogen and oxygen. The second half of the name comes from the fact that hydrogen and oxygen atoms are present in the ratio of 2:1, as they are in water (*hydrate* refers to water). The **general formula** for a carbohydrate can therefore be written as $C_x(H_2O)_y$.

Carbohydrates are divided into three main groups, namely monosaccharides, disaccharides and polysaccharides.

Monosaccharides

Monosaccharides are **sugars**. They dissolve easily in water to form sweet solutions (*saccharide* refers to sweet or sugar). Monosaccharides have the general formula $(CH_2O)_n$ and consist of a **single** sugar molecule (*mono* means 'one'). The main types of monosaccharides, if they are classified according to the number of carbon atoms in each molecule, are **trioses** (3C), **pentoses** (5C) and **hexoses** (6C). The names of all sugars end with **-ose**.

SAQ 2.1 _____

The formula for a hexose is $C_6H_{12}O_6$ or $(CH_2O)_6$. What would be the formula of **a** a triose and **b** a pentose?

Molecular and structural formulae

The formula for a hexose has been written as $C_6H_{12}O_6$. This is known as the **molecular formula**. It is also useful to show the arrangements of the atoms which can be done by a diagram known as the **structural formula**. *Figure 2.2* shows the structural formula of glucose, a hexose which is the most common monosaccharide.

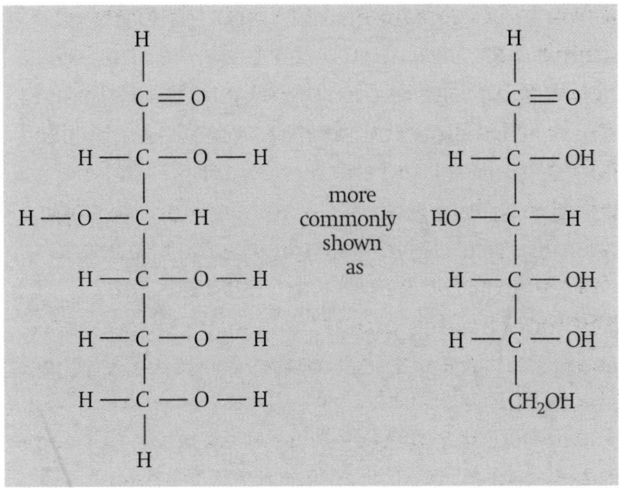

Ring structures

One important aspect of the structure of pentoses and hexoses is that the chain of

● **Figure 2.2** Structural formula of glucose. −OH is known as a hydroxyl group. There are five in glucose.

carbon atoms is long enough to close up on itself and form a more stable ring structure. This can be illustrated using glucose as an example. When glucose forms a ring, carbon atom number 1 joins to the oxygen on carbon atom number 5 (*figure 2.3*). The ring therefore contains oxygen, and carbon atom number 6 is not part of the ring.

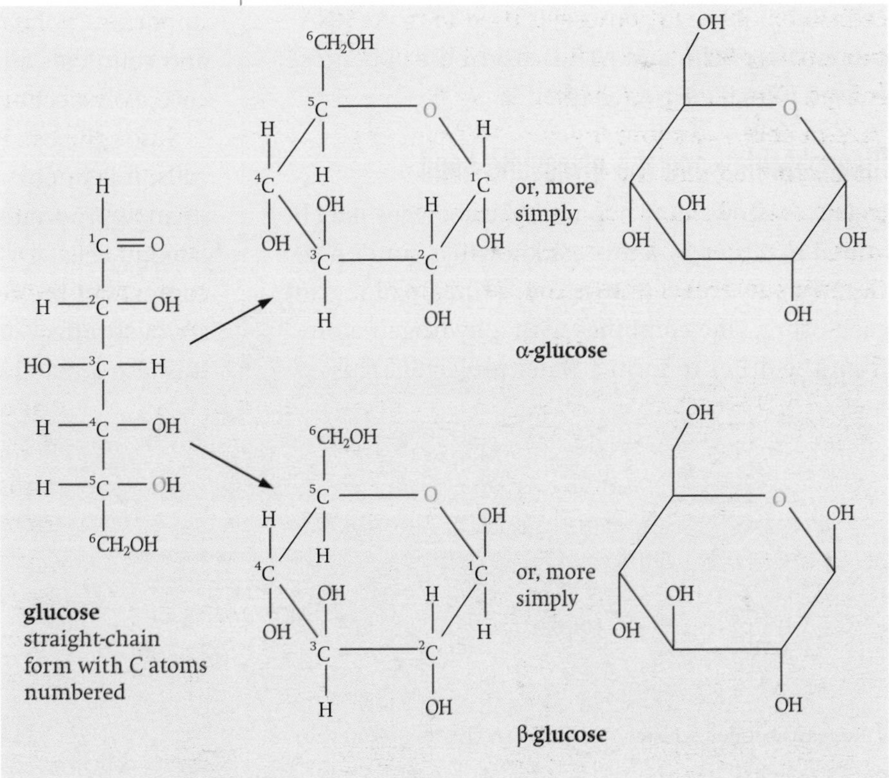

● **Figure 2.3** Structural formulae for the straight-chain and ring forms of glucose. Chemists often leave out the C and H atoms from the structural formula for simplicity.

You will see from *figure 2.3* that the hydroxyl group, −OH, on carbon atom 1 may be **above** or **below** the plane of the ring. The form of glucose where it is below the ring is known as α-**glucose** (**alpha-glucose**) and the form where it is above as β-**glucose** (**beta-glucose**). Two forms of the same chemical are known as **isomers**, and the extra variety provided by the existence of α- and β-isomers has important biological consequences, as we shall see in the structure of starch, glycogen and cellulose.

Roles of monosaccharides in living organisms

Monosaccharides have two major functions. Firstly, they are commonly used as a source of energy in respiration. This is due to the large number of carbon−hydrogen bonds. These bonds can be broken to release a lot of energy which is transferred to help make ATP (adenosine triphosphate) from ADP (adenosine diphosphate) and phosphate. The most important monosaccharide in energy metabolism is glucose.

Secondly, they are important as building blocks for larger molecules. For example, glucose is used to make the polysaccharides starch, glycogen and cellulose. Ribose (a pentose) is used to make RNA (ribonucleic acid) and ATP. Deoxyribose (a pentose) is used to make DNA (chapter 5).

Disaccharides and the glycosidic bond

Figure 2.4 shows how two monosaccharides may be joined together by a process known as **condensation**. Two hydroxyl (−OH) groups line up alongside each other. One combines with a hydrogen atom from the other to form a water molecule. This allows an oxygen 'bridge' to form between the two molecules, holding them together and forming a **disaccharide** (*di* means 'two'). The bridge is called a **glycosidic bond**. In theory any two −OH groups can line up and, since monosaccharides have many −OH groups, there are a large number of possible disaccharides. However, only a few of these are common in nature. Disaccharides, like monosaccharides, are sugars.

The reverse of this kind of condensation is the *addition* of water which is known as **hydrolysis** (*figure 2.4* again). This takes place during the digestion of disaccharides and polysaccharides when they are broken back down to monosaccharides. Like most chemical reactions in cells, hydrolysis and condensation reactions are controlled by enzymes.

Polysaccharides

Polysaccharides are polymers whose subunits are monosaccharides. They are made by joining many monosaccharide molecules by condensation. Each successive monosaccharide is added by means of a glycosidic bond, as in disaccharides. The final molecule may be several thousand monosaccharide units long, forming a macromolecule. The most important polysaccharides are starch, glycogen and cellulose, all of which are polymers of glucose. Polysaccharides are *not* sugars.

Since glucose is the main source of energy for cells, it is important for living organisms to store it in an appropriate form. If glucose itself accumulated in cells, it would dissolve and make the contents of the cell too concentrated, which would seriously affect its osmotic properties (see page 55). It is also a reactive molecule and would interfere

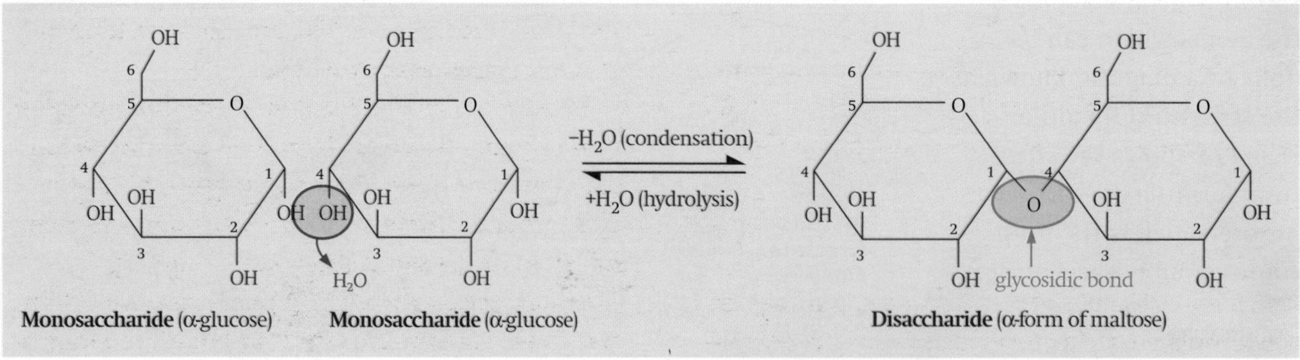

Monosaccharide (α-glucose)   Monosaccharide (α-glucose)   −H₂O (condensation)   +H₂O (hydrolysis)   Disaccharide (α-form of maltose)   glycosidic bond

Figure 2.4 Formation of a disaccharide from two monosaccharides by condensation. In this example, the glycosidic bond is formed between carbon atoms 1 and 4 of neighbouring monosaccharides. The process may be repeated many times to form a polysaccharide or reversed by hydrolysis.

Testing for the presence of sugars

If you have a solution that you suspect contains sugar, you can use **Benedict's reagent** to test it. Benedict's reagent is copper(II) sulphate in an alkaline solution and has a distinctive blue colour. If it is added to a **reducing agent** its Cu^{2+} ions will be **reduced** to Cu^+ resulting in a change of colour to the red of copper(I) sulphate. All monosaccharides and some disaccharides have this effect on Benedict's reagent. This is because they have a —C=O group somewhere in their molecules which can contribute an electron to the copper. They are therefore **reducing sugars**. In the process they themselves become **oxidised**.

reducing sugar + Cu^{2+} → oxidised sugar + Cu^+

Add Benedict's reagent to the solution you are testing and heat it in a water bath. If a reducing sugar is present, the solution will gradually turn through green, yellow and orange to brick red as the insoluble copper(I) sulphate forms a precipitate. As long as you use *excess* Benedict's reagent (more than enough to react with all of the sugar present) the intensity of the red colour is related to the concentration of the reducing sugar which you can then estimate. Alternatively you can use a colorimeter to measure subtle differences in colour precisely.

Some disaccharides are *not* reducing sugars, so you would get a negative result from the test as described so far. You must therefore go on to a second stage of the test to be certain whether such a **non-reducing** sugar is present. You need to break non-reducing disaccharides into their constituent monosaccharides, all of which are reducing sugars and *will* react with Benedict's reagent.

Heat the sugar solution with an acid to hydrolyse any glycosidic bonds present. This will release free monosaccharides. Benedict's reagent needs alkaline conditions to work so you need to neutralise the test solution now by adding an alkali such as sodium hydroxide. Add Benedict's reagent and heat as before and look for the colour change. If the solution goes red now but didn't in the first stage of the test, there is non-reducing sugar present. If there is *still* no colour change then there is no sugar of any kind present.

SAQ 2.2

a Why do you need to use *excess* Benedict's reagent if you want to get an idea of the concentration of a sugar solution?

b Outline how you could use the Benedict's test to estimate the concentration of a solution of a reducing sugar.

SAQ 2.3

You have a solution which you know contains sugar but you do not know whether it is reducing sugar, non-reducing sugar or a mixture of both. How can you find out?

with normal cell chemistry. These problems are avoided by converting it, by condensation reactions, to a storage polysaccharide, which is a convenient, compact, inert and insoluble molecule. This is in the form of starch in plants and glycogen in animals. Glucose can be made available again quickly by an enzyme-controlled reaction.

SAQ 2.4

What type of chemical reaction would be involved in the formation of glucose from starch or glycogen?

Starch and glycogen

Starch is a mixture of two substances, **amylose** and **amylopectin**. Amylose is made by many condensations between α-glucose molecules, as shown in figure 2.4. In this way a long, unbranching chain of several thousand 1,4 linked glucose molecules is built up. ('1,4 linked' means they are linked between carbon atoms 1 and 4 of successive glucose units.) The chains are curved (figure 2.5) and coil up into helical structures like springs, making the final molecule more compact. Amylopectin is also made of many 1,4 linked α-glucose molecules, but the chains are shorter than in amylose, and branch out to the sides. The branches are formed by 1,6 linkages, as shown in figure 2.6.

Mixtures of amylose and amylopectin molecules build up into relatively large starch grains which are commonly found in chloroplasts and in storage organs such as the potato tuber and the seeds of cereals and legumes (figure 2.7). Starch grains are easily seen with a light microscope, especially if stained; rubbing a freshly cut potato tuber on a glass slide and staining with iodine–potassium iodide solution (see box on page 26) is a quick method of preparing a specimen for viewing.

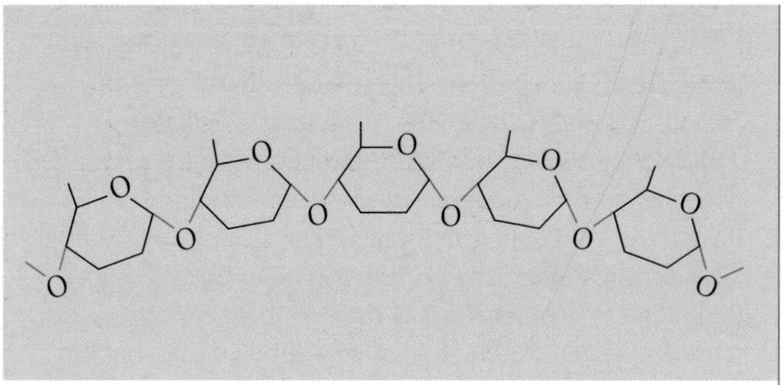

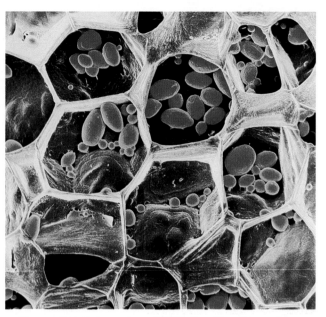

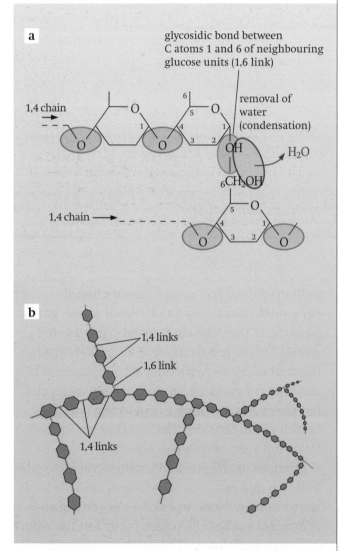

● **Figure 2.5** Arrangement of α-glucose units in amylose. The 1,4 linkages cause the chain to turn and coil. The glycosidic bonds are shown in red and the hydroxyl groups are omitted.

● **Figure 2.6** Branching structure of amylopectin and glycogen: **a** formation of a 1,6 link, a branchpoint; **b** overall structure of an amylopectin or glycogen molecule. Amylopectin and glycogen only differ in the amount of branching of their glucose chains.

● **Figure 2.7** False-colour SEM of a slice through a raw potato showing starch grains or starch-containing organelles (coloured red) within their cellular compartments (×200).

Testing for the presence of starch

Starch molecules tend to curl up into long spirals. The hole that runs down the middle of this spiral is just the right size for iodine molecules to fit into. The starch-iodine complex that forms has a strong blue–black colour.

So, to test for starch, you use something called 'iodine solution'. In fact, iodine won't dissolve in water, so the 'iodine solution' is actually iodine in potassium iodide solution. This solution is orange-brown. A blue–black colour is quickly produced if it comes into contact with starch.

Starch is never found in animal cells. Instead, a substance with molecules very like those of amylopectin is used as the storage carbohydrate. This is called **glycogen**. Glycogen, like amylopectin, is made of chains of 1,4 linked α-glucose with 1,6 linkages forming branches (*figure 2.6b*). Glycogen molecules tend to be even more branched than amylopectin molecules. Glycogen molecules clump together to form granules, which are visible in liver cells and muscle cells where they form an energy reserve.

SAQ 2.5

List five ways in which the molecular structures of glycogen and amylopectin are similar.

Cellulose

Cellulose is the most abundant organic molecule on the planet due to its presence in plant cell walls and its slow rate of breakdown in nature. It has a structural role, being a mechanically strong molecule, unlike starch and glycogen. However the only difference between cellulose and the latter is that cellulose is a polymer of β-glucose, not α-glucose. Remember that in the β isomer the −OH group on carbon atom 1 projects *above* the ring. In order to form a glycosidic bond with carbon atom 4, where the −OH group is *below* the ring, one glucose molecule must be upside down relative to the other, that is rotated 180°. Thus successive glucose units are linked at 180° to each other, as shown in *figure 2.8*.

This results in a strong molecule because the hydrogen atoms of −OH groups are weakly attracted to oxygen atoms in the same cellulose molecule (the oxygen of the glucose ring) and also to oxygen atoms of −OH groups in neighbouring molecules. These **hydrogen bonds** (see box on this page) are individually weak, but so many can form, due to the large number of −OH groups, that collectively they develop enormous strength. Between 60 and 70 cellulose molecules become tightly cross-linked to form bundles called **microfibrils**. Microfibrils are in turn held together in bundles called **fibres** by hydrogen bonding.

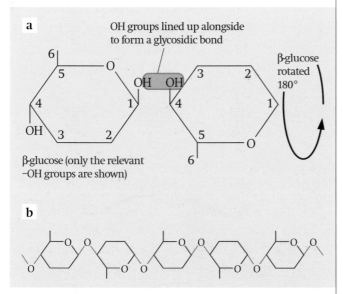

● **Figure 2.8 a** Two β-glucose molecules lined up to form a 1,4 link; **b** arrangement of β-glucose units in cellulose: glycosidic bonds are shown in red and hydroxyl groups are omitted.

Dipoles and hydrogen bonds

The atoms in molecules are held together because they share electrons with each other. Each shared pair of electrons forms a **covalent bond**. For example, in a water molecule, two hydrogen atoms each share a pair of electrons with an oxygen atom, forming a molecule with the formula H_2O.

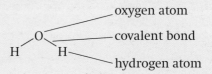

However, the electrons are not shared absolutely equally. The oxygen atom gets slightly more than its fair share, and so has a small negative charge, written δ^-. The hydrogen atoms get slightly less than their fair share, and so have a small positive charge, written δ^+.

This unequal distribution of charge is called a **dipole**. In water, the negatively charged oxygen of one molecule is attracted to the positively charged hydrogens of another, and this attraction is called a **hydrogen bond**. It is much weaker than a covalent bond, but still has a very significant effect. You will find out how hydrogen bonds affect the properties of water on pages 37–38.

Dipoles occur in many different molecules, particularly wherever there is an −OH, −C=O or N−H group. Hydrogen bonds can form *between* these groups, as the negatively charged part of one group is attracted to the positively charged part of another. These bonds are very important in the structure and properties of carbohydrates and proteins.

Molecules which have groups with dipoles are said to be **polar**. They are attracted to water molecules, because the water molecules also have dipoles. Such molecules are said to be **hydrophilic** (water-loving), and they tend to be soluble in water. Molecules which do not have dipoles are said to be **non-polar**. They are not attracted to water, and they are **hydrophobic** (water-hating). Such properties make possible the formation of plasma membranes, for example (chapter 4).

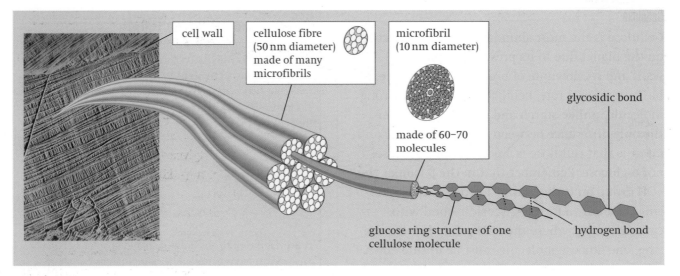

● **Figure 2.9** Structure of cellulose.

A cell wall typically has several layers of fibres, running in different directions to increase strength (*figure 2.9*). Cellulose comprises about 20–40% of the average cell wall; other molecules help to cross-link the cellulose fibres and some form a glue-like matrix around the fibres which further increases strength.

Cellulose fibres have a very high tensile strength, almost equal to that of steel. This means that if pulled at both ends they are very difficult to break, and makes it possible for a cell to withstand the large pressures that develop within it as a result of osmosis (page 57). Without the wall it would burst when in a dilute solution. These pressures help provide support for the plant by making tissues rigid, and are responsible for cell expansion during growth. The arrangement of fibres around the cell helps to determine the shape of the cell as it grows. Despite their strength, cellulose fibres are freely permeable, allowing water and solutes to reach the plasma membrane.

SAQ 2.6
Make a table to show three ways in which the molecular structures of amylose and cellulose differ.

Lipids
Lipids are a diverse group of chemicals. The most common type are the **triglycerides**, which are usually known as fats and oils. The main difference between them is that, at room temperature, fats are solid whereas oils are liquid.

Triglycerides
Triglycerides are made by the combination of three fatty acid molecules with one glycerol molecule. Fatty acids are organic molecules which all have a —COOH group attached to a hydrocarbon tail. Glycerol is a type of alcohol. The triglyceride molecule can be represented diagrammatically as shown in *figure 2.10*. The tails vary in length, depending on the fatty acids used.

Each of the three fatty acid molecules joins to glycerol by a condensation reaction as shown in *figure 2.11*. When a fatty acid combines with glycerol, it forms a glyceride, so when all three fatty acids have been added, the final molecule is called a **triglyceride**.

Triglycerides are insoluble in water but are soluble in certain organic solvents, including ether, chloroform and ethanol. This behaviour is due to the long hydrocarbon tails of the fatty acids. As the name suggests, these consist of a chain of carbon atoms (often 15 or 17 carbon atoms long) combined

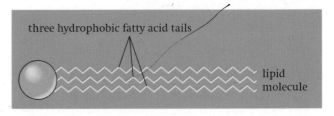

● **Figure 2.10** Diagrammatic representation of a triglyceride molecule.

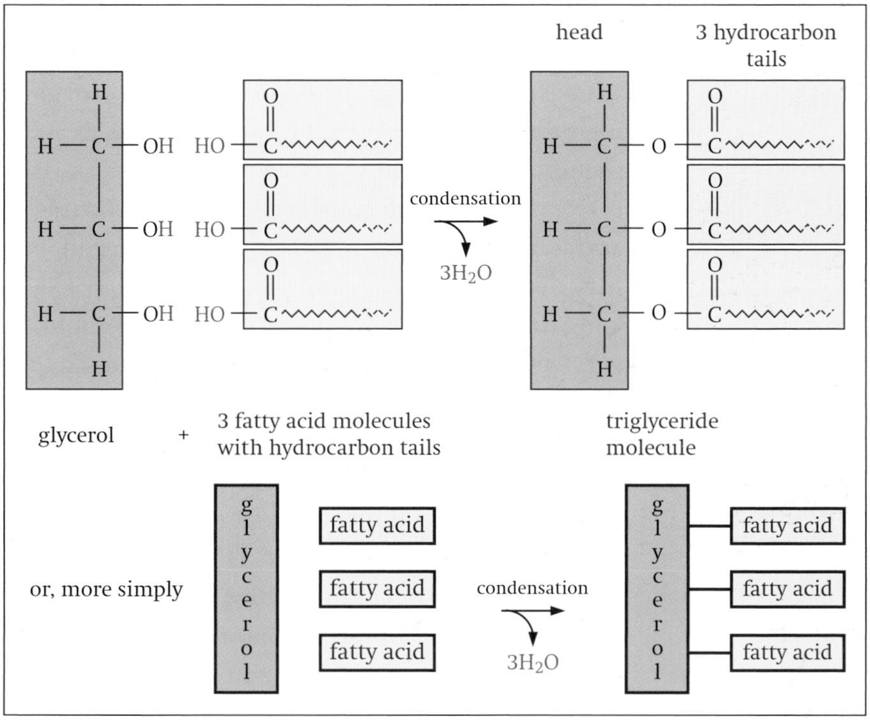

head   3 hydrocarbon
tails

glycerol   +   3 fatty acid molecules
with hydrocarbon tails

condensation
3H₂O

triglyceride
molecule

or, more simply

glycerol

fatty acid

fatty acid

fatty acid

condensation
3H₂O

glycerol

fatty acid

fatty acid

fatty acid

● **Figure 2.11** Formation of a triglyceride from glycerol and three fatty acid molecules.

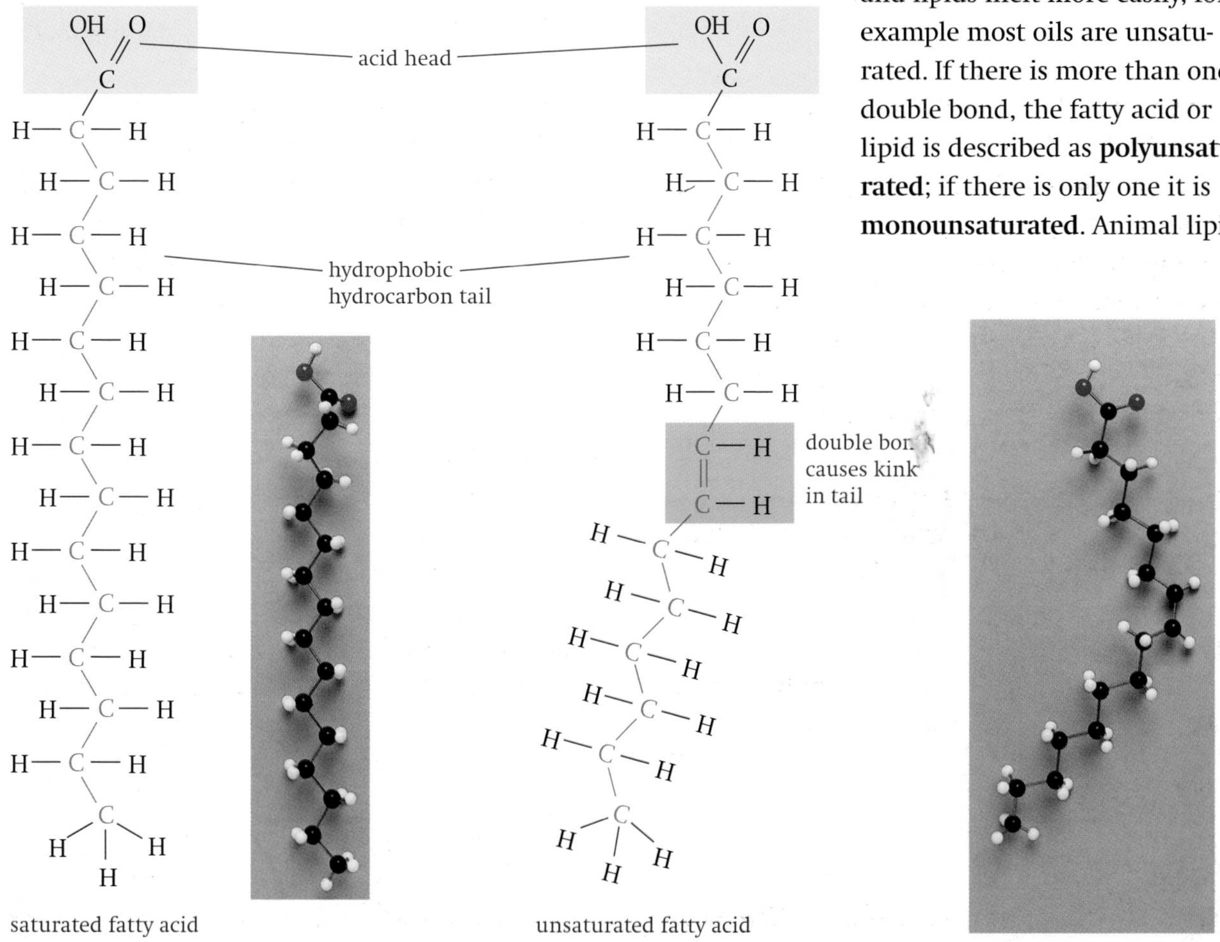

acid head

hydrophobic
hydrocarbon tail

double bond
causes kink
in tail

saturated fatty acid

unsaturated fatty acid

with hydrogen (*figure 2.12*). Unlike water molecules which are polar (see box on page 27) the fatty acid tails have no uneven distribution of electrical charge. Consequently, they will not mix freely with water molecules. Triglycerides are therefore **non-polar** and **hydrophobic**.

Saturated and unsaturated fatty acids and lipids

Some fatty acids have double bonds between neighbouring carbon atoms, like this: –C–C=C–C– (*figure 2.12* again). Such fatty acids are described as **unsaturated** (as they do not contain the maximum possible amount of hydrogen) and form unsaturated lipids. Double bonds make fatty acids and lipids melt more easily, for example most oils are unsaturated. If there is more than one double bond, the fatty acid or lipid is described as **polyunsaturated**; if there is only one it is **monounsaturated**. Animal lipids

● **Figure 2.12** Structure of a saturated and an unsaturated fatty acid. Photographs of models are shown to the right of each structure. In the models hydrogen is white, carbon is black and oxygen is red.

are often saturated and occur as fats, whereas plant lipids are often unsaturated and occur as oils, such as olive oil and sunflower oil.

Roles of triglycerides

Lipids make excellent **energy reserves** because they are even richer in carbon–hydrogen bonds than carbohydrates. A given mass of lipid will therefore yield more energy on oxidation than the same mass of carbohydrate (it has a higher calorific value), an important advantage for a storage product.

Fat is stored in a number of places in the human body, particularly just below the dermis of the skin and around the kidneys. Below the skin it

● **Figure 2.13** The desert kangaroo rat uses metabolism of food to provide the water it needs.

also acts as an **insulator** against loss of heat. Blubber, a lipid found in sea mammals like whales, has a similar function, as well as providing buoyancy. An unusual role for lipids is as a **metabolic source of water**. When oxidised in respiration they are converted to carbon dioxide and water. The water may be of importance in very dry habitats. For example, the desert kangaroo rat (*figure 2.13*) never drinks water and survives on metabolic water from its fat intake.

Phospholipids

Phospholipids are a special type of lipid. Each molecule has the unusual property of having one end which is soluble in water. This is because one of the three fatty acid molecules is replaced by a phosphate group which is polar (see box on page 27) and can therefore dissolve in water. The phosphate group is **hydrophilic** and makes the head of a phospholipid molecule hydrophilic, though the two remaining tails are still hydrophobic (*figure 2.14*). The biological significance of this will become apparent when we study membrane structure (see chapter 4).

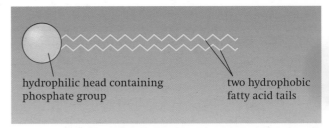

hydrophilic head containing phosphate group

two hydrophobic fatty acid tails

● **Figure 2.14** Diagrammatic representation of a phospholipid molecule.

Proteins

Proteins are an extremely important class of molecules in living organisms. More than 50% of the dry mass of most cells is protein. Proteins have many important functions. For example:

- they are essential components of cell membranes;
- the oxygen-carrying pigment haemoglobin is a protein;
- antibodies which attack and destroy invading microorganisms are proteins;
- all enzymes are proteins;

- hair and the surface layers of skin contain the protein keratin;
- collagen, another protein, adds strength to many tissues, such as bone and the walls of arteries.

Despite their tremendous range of functions, all proteins are made from the same basic components. These are **amino acids**.

Amino acids

Figure 2.15 shows the general structure of all amino acids and of glycine, the most simple amino acid. They all have a central carbon atom to which is bonded an **amine** group, $-NH_2$, and a **carboxylic acid** group, $-COOH$. It is these two groups which give amino acids their name. The third component bonded to the carbon atom is always a hydrogen atom.

The only way in which amino acids differ from each other is in the remaining, fourth, group of atoms bonded to the central carbon. This is called

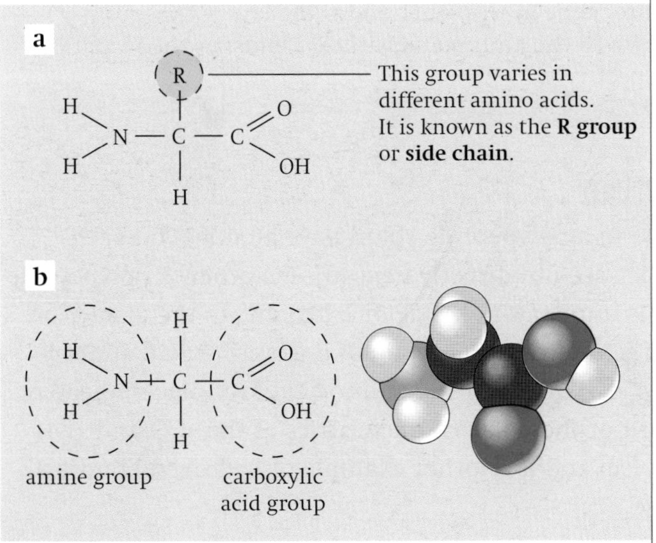

Figure 2.15 a The general structure of an amino acid. **b** Structure of the simplest amino acid, glycine, in which the R group is H, hydrogen. R groups for the 20 naturally occurring amino acids are shown in appendix 1.

the **R group** of which there are many different kinds. There are 20 different amino acids which occur naturally in the proteins of living organisms. (Many others have been synthesised in laboratories.) You can see their molecular formulae in appendix 1. You do not need to remember all of the different R groups! However, it is these R groups that are responsible for the three-dimensional shapes of protein molecules (page 33) and hence their functions.

The peptide bond

Figure 2.16 shows how two amino acids can join together. One loses a hydroxyl (–OH) group from its carboxylic acid group, while the other loses a hydrogen atom from its amine group. This leaves a carbon atom of the first amino acid free to bond with the nitrogen atom of the second. The bond is called a **peptide bond**. The oxygen and two hydrogen atoms removed from the amino acids form a water molecule. We have seen this type of reaction, a condensation reaction, in the formation of glycosidic bonds (*figure 2.4*) and in the synthesis of triglycerides (*figure 2.11*).

The new molecule which has been formed, made up of two linked amino acids, is called a **dipeptide**. Any number of extra amino acids could be added to the chain, in a series of condensation reactions. A molecule made up of many amino acids linked together by peptide bonds is called a **polypeptide**. A polypeptide is another example of a polymer and a macromolecule, like polysaccharides. A complete **protein** molecule may contain just one polypeptide chain, or it may have two or more chains which interact with each other.

In living cells, **ribosomes** are the sites where amino acids are linked together to form polypeptides. The reaction is controlled by enzymes. You can read more about this on pages 72–75.

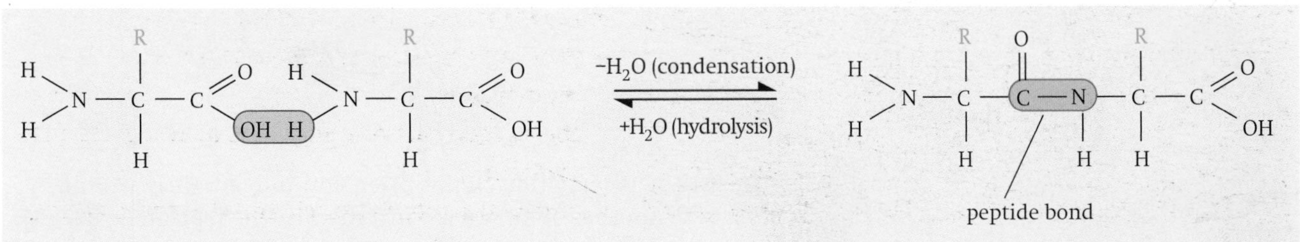

Figure 2.16 Amino acids link together by the loss of a molecule of water to form a peptide bond.

Polypeptides can be broken down to amino acids by breaking the peptide bonds. This is a hydrolysis reaction, involving the addition of water (*figure 2.16*), and naturally happens in the stomach and small intestine. Here, protein molecules in food are hydrolysed into amino acids prior to being absorbed into the blood.

Primary structure

A polypeptide or protein molecule may contain several hundred amino acids linked into a long chain. The types of amino acids contained in the chain, and the sequence in which they are joined, is called the **primary structure** of the protein. *Figure 2.17* shows the primary structure of ribonuclease.

There is an enormous number of different *possible* primary structures. Even a change in one amino acid in a chain made up of thousands may completely alter the properties of the polypeptide or protein.

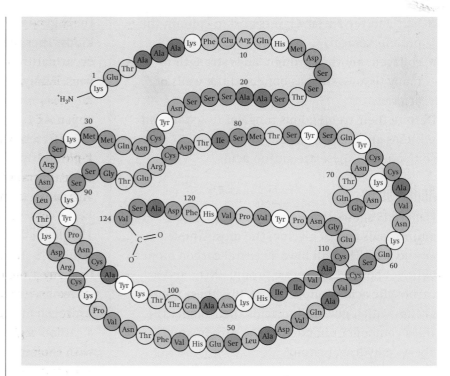

● **Figure 2.17** The primary structure of ribonuclease. Ribonuclease is an enzyme found in pancreatic juice which hydrolyses (digests) RNA (chapter 5). Notice that at one end of the amino acid chain there is an –NH$_3^+$ group, while at the other end there is a –COO$^-$ group. These are known as the amino and carboxyl ends, or the N and C terminals, respectively.

Secondary structure

The amino acids in a polypeptide chain have an effect on each other even if they are not directly next to each other. A polypeptide chain often coils into an α-**helix** (*figure 2.18a*) due to the attraction between the oxygen of the –CO group of one amino acid and the hydrogen of the –NH group of the amino acid four places ahead of it. This is a result of the polar characteristics of the –CO and –NH groups (*figure 2.19a*) and is another example of hydrogen bonding, (see box on page 27).

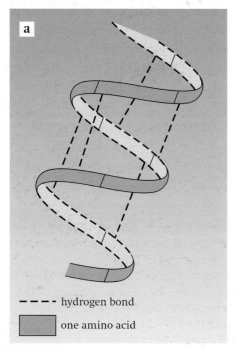

- - - - hydrogen bond

▨ one amino acid

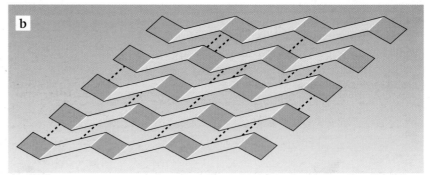

● **Figure 2.18 a** Polypeptide chains often coil into a tightly wound α-helix. **b** Another common arrangement is the β-pleated sheet. Both of these secondary structures are held in shape by hydrogen bonds between the amino acids.

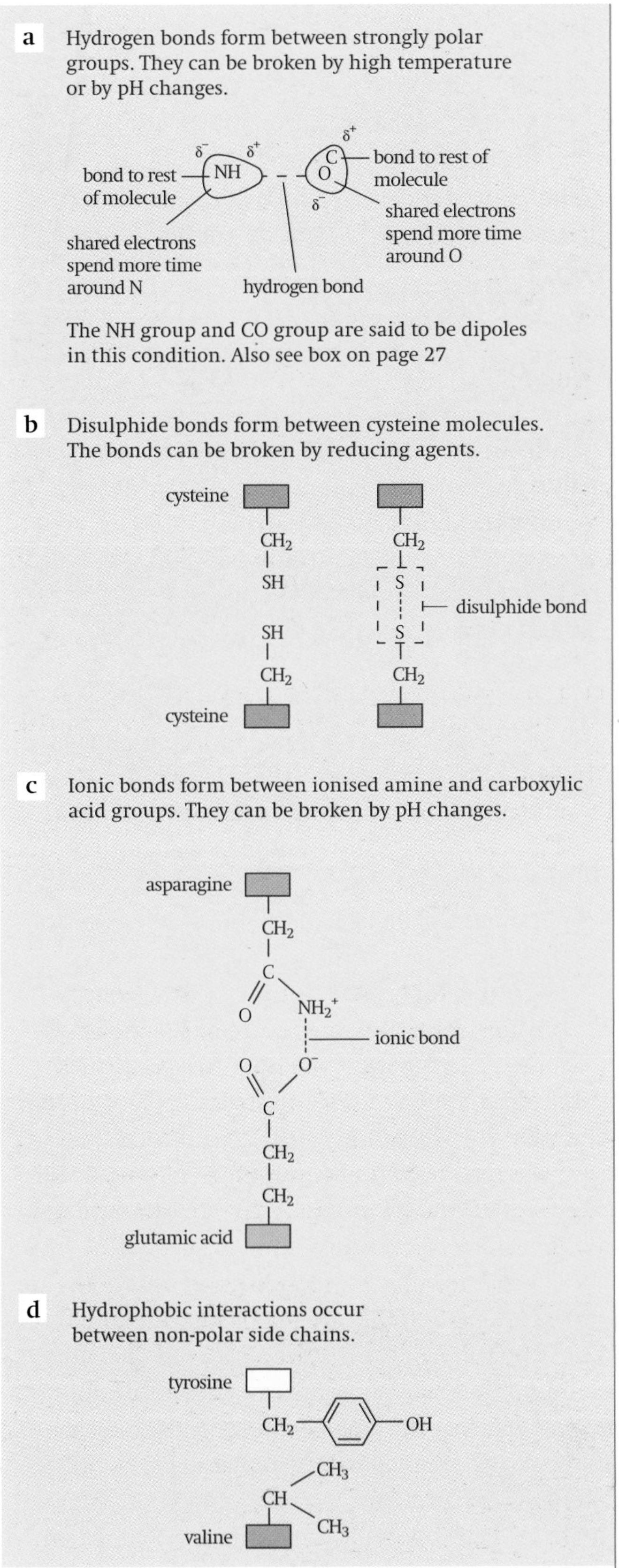

a Hydrogen bonds form between strongly polar groups. They can be broken by high temperature or by pH changes.

bond to rest of molecule — $\overset{\delta^-}{N}\overset{\delta^+}{H}$ — $\overset{\delta^+}{C}\overset{O}{}$ — bond to rest of molecule

shared electrons spend more time around N

hydrogen bond

shared electrons spend more time around O

The NH group and CO group are said to be dipoles in this condition. Also see box on page 27

b Disulphide bonds form between cysteine molecules. The bonds can be broken by reducing agents.

cysteine

CH_2

SH

SH

CH_2

cysteine

CH_2

S

S

CH_2

— disulphide bond

c Ionic bonds form between ionised amine and carboxylic acid groups. They can be broken by pH changes.

asparagine

CH_2

C

O NH_2^+

— ionic bond

O O^-

C

CH_2

CH_2

glutamic acid

d Hydrophobic interactions occur between non-polar side chains.

tyrosine

CH_2 — ⬡ — OH

CH_3

CH

CH_3

valine

● **Figure 2.19** The four types of bond which are important in protein secondary and tertiary structure: **a** hydrogen bonds, **b** disulphide bonds, **c** ionic bonds, **d** hydrophobic interactions.

Hydrogen bonds, although strong enough to hold the α-helix in shape, are easily broken by high temperatures and pH changes. As you will see, these effects on proteins have important consequences for living organisms.

Not all proteins coil into an α-helix. Sometimes a much looser, straighter shape is formed, called a β-**pleated sheet** (*figure 2.18b*). Other proteins show no regular arrangement at all. It all depends on which R groups are present and therefore what attractions occur between amino acids in the chain.

Tertiary structure

In many proteins, the secondary structure itself is coiled or folded. *Figure 2.20* shows the complex way in which a molecule of the protein myoglobin folds.

At first sight, the myoglobin molecule looks like a disorganised tangle, but this is not so. The shape of the molecule is very precise, and held in this exact shape by bonds between amino acids in different parts of the chain. The way in which a protein coils up to form a precise three-dimensional shape is known as its **tertiary structure**.

Figure 2.19 shows the four types of bonds which help to hold folded proteins in their precise shape.

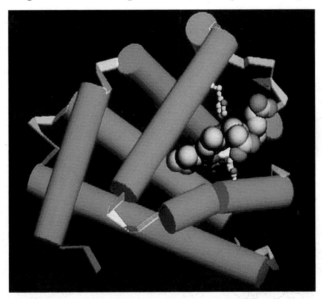

● **Figure 2.20** A computer graphic showing the secondary and tertiary structure of a myoglobin molecule. Myoglobin is the substance which makes meat look red. It is found in muscle, where it acts as an oxygen-storing molecule. The blue sections are α-helixes and are linked by sections of polypeptide chain which are more stretched out – these are shown in red. At the top right is an iron-containing haem group (see page 35).

Hydrogen bonds can form between a wide variety of R groups, including those of tryptophan, arginine and asparagine. **Disulphide bonds** form between two cysteine molecules. **Ionic bonds** form between R groups containing amine and carboxyl groups. (Which amino acids have these?) **Hydrophobic interactions** occur between R groups which are non-polar, or hydrophobic.

Quaternary structure

Many proteins are made up of two or more polypeptide chains. Haemoglobin is an example of this, having four polypeptide chains in each haemoglobin molecule. The association of different polypeptide chains is called the **quaternary structure** of the protein. The chains are held together by the same four types of bond as in the tertiary structure.

Globular and fibrous proteins

A protein whose molecules curl up into a 'ball' shape, such as myoglobin and haemoglobin, is known as a **globular protein**. In a living organism, proteins may be found in cells, in tissue fluid, or in fluids being transported, such as blood or in the phloem. All these environments contain water. Globular proteins usually curl up so that their non-polar, hydrophobic R groups point into

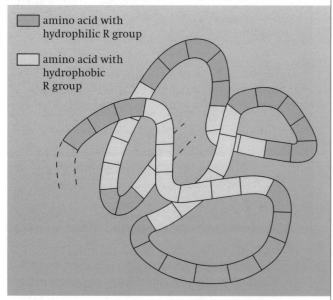

- **Figure 2.21** A schematic section through part of a globular protein molecule. The polypeptide chain coils up with hydrophilic R groups outside and hydrophobic ones inside, which makes the molecule soluble.

the centre of the molecule, away from their watery surroundings. Water molecules are excluded from the centre of the folded protein molecule. The polar, hydrophilic, R groups remain on the outside of the molecule. Globular proteins, therefore, are usually soluble, because water molecules cluster around their outward-pointing hydrophilic R groups (*figure 2.21*).

Many globular proteins have roles in metabolic reactions. Enzymes, for example, are globular proteins.

Many protein molecules do not curl up into a ball, but form long strands. These are known as **fibrous proteins**. Fibrous proteins are usually insoluble and many have structural roles. Examples include **keratin** in hair and the outer layers of skin, and **collagen** (see page 36).

Haemoglobin

Haemoglobin, the oxygen-carrying pigment found in red blood cells, is a globular protein. It is made up of four polypeptide chains. Two of these make an identical pair, and are called α chains. The other two make a different identical pair and are called β chains.

The haemoglobin molecule is nearly spherical (*figure 2.22*). The four polypeptide chains pack closely together, their hydrophobic R groups pointing in towards the centre of the molecule and their hydrophilic ones pointing outwards. Each β chain has a tertiary structure very similar to that of myoglobin (*figures 2.20* and *2.22*).

The interactions between the hydrophobic R groups inside the molecule are important in holding it in its correct three-dimensional shape. The outward-pointing hydrophilic R groups on the surface of the molecule are important in maintaining its solubility. In the disease sickle cell anaemia one amino acid, which occurs in a part of the amino acid chain of the β polypeptides on the surface of the curled-up molecule, is replaced with a different amino acid. The correct amino acid is glutamic acid which is polar. The substitute is valine which is non-polar. Having a non-polar R group on the outside of the molecule makes the haemoglobin much less soluble, and causes unpleasant and dangerous symptoms in anyone whose haemoglobin is all of this 'faulty' type (*figure 2.23*).

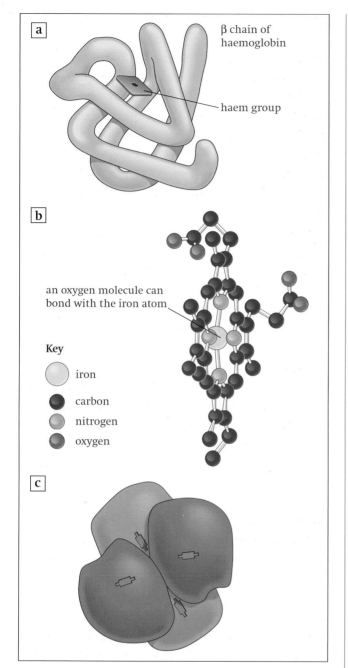

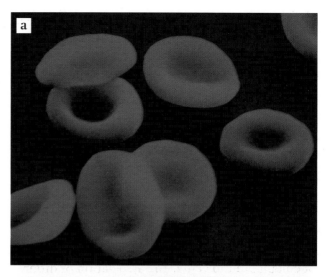

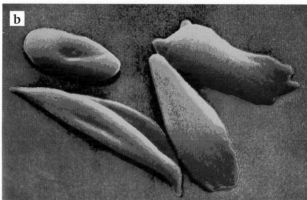

● **Figure 2.23 a** Human red blood cells. Each cell contains about 250 million haemoglobin molecules (×5500). **b** A scanning electron micrograph of red blood cells from a person with sickle cell anaemia. You can see both normal and sickled cells.

● **Figure 2.22** Haemoglobin. **a** Each haemoglobin molecule contains four polypeptide chains, one of which is shown here. Each polypeptide chain contains a haem group, shown in red. **b** The haem group contains an iron ion which can bond reversibly with an oxygen molecule. **c** The complete haemoglobin molecule is nearly spherical.

Each polypeptide chain contains a **haem group**, shown in *figure 2.22b*. A group like this, which is an important, permanent, part of a protein molecule but is not made of amino acids, is called a **prosthetic group**.

Each haem group contains an iron ion, Fe^{2+}. One oxygen molecule, O_2, can bind with each iron

ion. So a complete haemoglobin molecule, with four haem groups, can carry four oxygen molecules (eight oxygen atoms) at a time.

It is the haem group which is responsible for the colour of haemoglobin. This colour changes depending on whether or not the iron ions are combined with oxygen. If they are, the molecule is known as **oxyhaemoglobin**, and is bright red. If not, the colour is purplish.

Collagen

Collagen is a fibrous protein that is found in skin, tendons, cartilage, bones, teeth and the walls of blood vessels. It is an important **structural protein**, not only in humans but in almost all animals, and is found in structures ranging from the body wall of sea anemones to the egg cases of dogfish.

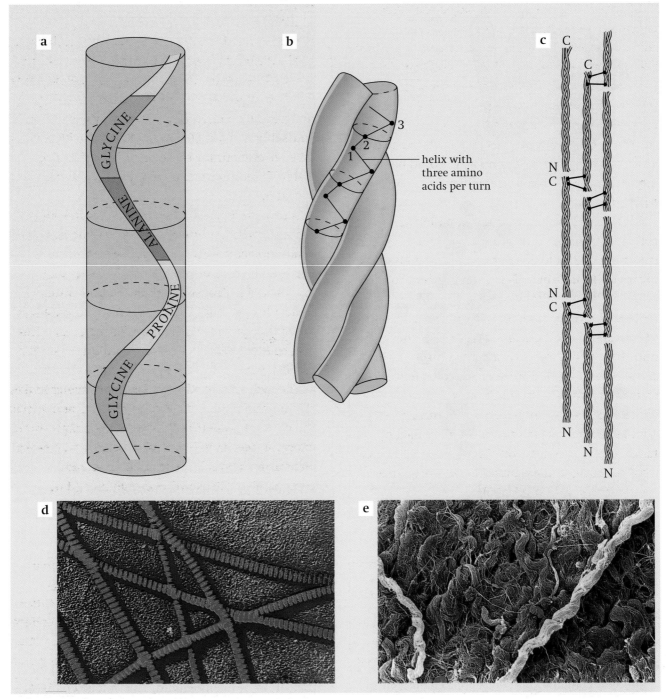

● **Figure 2.24** Collagen. The diagrams and photographs begin with the very small and work up to the not-so-small. Thus three of the polypeptide chains shown in **a** make up a collagen molecule shown in **b**; many of these molecules make up a fibril, shown in **c** and **d**; and many fibrils make up a fibre, shown in **e**.

a The polypeptides which make up a collagen molecule are in the shape of a stretched-out helix. Every third amino acid is glycine. **b** Three helixes wind together to form a collagen molecule. These strands are held together by hydrogen bonds.
c Many of these triple helixes lie side by side, linked to each other by covalent cross-links between the carboxyl end of one molecule and the amino end of another. Notice that these cross-links are out of step with each other; this gives collagen greater strength. **d** An SEM of collagen fibrils (×21 000). Each fibril is made up of many triple helixes lying parallel with one another. The banded appearance is caused by the regular way in which these helixes are arranged, with the staggered gaps between the molecules (shown in **c**) appearing darker.
e An SEM of human collagen fibres (×3 000). Each fibre is made up of many fibrils lying side by side. These fibres are large enough to be seen with an ordinary light microscope.

As shown in *figure 2.24*, a collagen molecule consists of three polypeptide chains, each in the shape of a helix. (This is not an α-helix as it is not tightly wound.) The three helical polypeptides then wind around each other to form a three-stranded 'rope'. Almost every third amino acid in each polypeptide is glycine. Its small size allows the three strands to lie close together and so form a tight coil. Any other amino acid would be too large. The three strands are held together by hydrogen bonds.

Each complete, three-stranded molecule of collagen interacts with other collagen molecules running parallel to it. Bonds form between the R groups of lysines in molecules lying next to each other. These cross-links hold many collagen molecules side by side, forming **fibres**. The ends of the parallel molecules are staggered; if they were not, there would be a weak spot running right across the collagen fibre. As it is, collagen has tremendous tensile strength, that is it can withstand large pulling forces. The human Achilles tendon, which is almost all collagen fibres, can withstand a pulling force of $300\,N$ per mm^2 of cross-sectional area, about one-quarter the tensile strength of mild steel.

Testing for the presence of proteins

All proteins have several amine, NH_2, groups within their molecules. These groups can react with copper ions to form a complex that has a strong purple colour.

The reagent used for this test is called **biuret reagent**. You can use it as two separate solutions – a dilute solution of copper(II) sulphate and a more dilute solution of potassium or sodium hydroxide – which you add in turn to the solution that you suspect might contain protein. A purple colour indicates that protein is present.

Alternatively, you can use a ready-made 'biuret solution' that contains both the copper(II) sulphate solution and the hydroxide ready-mixed. To stop the copper ions reacting with the hydroxide ions and forming a precipitate, this ready-mixed reagent also contains sodium potassium tartrate or sodium citrate.

SAQ 2.7
Where in a protein molecule are amino groups found?

Water

Water is arguably the most important biochemical of all. Without water, life would not exist on this planet. It is important for two reasons. Firstly, it is a major component of cells, typically forming between 70 and 95% of the mass of the cell. You yourself are about 60% water. Secondly, it provides an environment for those organisms that live in water. Three-quarters of the planet is covered in water.

Although it is a simple molecule, water has some surprising properties. For example, such a small molecule would exist as a gas at normal Earth temperatures were it not for its special property of hydrogen bonding to other water molecules (see box on page 27). Also, because it is a liquid, it provides a medium for molecules and ions to mix in and hence a medium in which life could evolve.

The hydrogen bonding of water molecules makes the molecules more difficult to separate and affects the physical properties of water. For example, more energy is needed to break these bonds and convert water from a liquid to a gas than in similar compounds, such as hydrogen sulphide (H_2S), which is a gas at normal air temperatures.

Water as a solvent

Water is an excellent solvent for ions and polar molecules (molecules with an uneven charge distribution such as sugars and glycerol) because the water molecules are attracted to them, collect around and *separate* them (*figure 2.25*). This is what happens when a chemical dissolves in water. Once

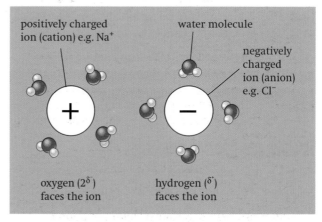

● **Figure 2.25** Distribution of water molecules around ions in a solution.

a chemical is in solution, it is free to move about and react with other chemicals. Most processes in living organisms take place in solution in this way.

By contrast, non-polar molecules such as lipids are insoluble in water and, if surrounded by water, tend to be *pushed together* by the water since the water molecules are attracted to *each other*. This is important, for example, in hydrophobic interactions in protein structure and in membrane structure (see chapter 4) and it increases the stability of these structures.

Water as a transport medium

Water is the transport medium in the blood, in the lymphatic, excretory and digestive systems of animals, and in the vascular tissues of plants. Here again its solvent properties are essential.

Thermal properties

As hydrogen bonding restricts the movement of water molecules, a relatively large amount of energy is needed to raise the temperature of water. This means that large bodies of water such as oceans and lakes are slow to change temperature as environmental temperature changes. As a result they are more stable habitats. Due to the high proportion of water in the body internal changes in temperature are also minimised, making it easier to achieve a stable body temperature.

Since a relatively large amount of energy is needed to convert water to a gas, the process of evaporation transfers a correspondingly large amount of energy and can be an effective means of cooling the body, as in sweating and panting. Conversely, a relatively large amount of energy must be transferred from water before it is converted from a liquid to a solid (ice). This makes it less likely that water will freeze, an advantage both for the bodies of living organisms and for organisms which live in water.

Density and freezing properties

Water is an unusual chemical because the solid form, ice, is less dense than its liquid form. Below 4°C the density of water starts to decrease. Ice therefore floats on liquid water and insulates the water under it. This reduces the tendency for large

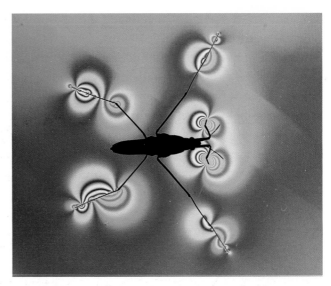

● **Figure 2.26** A pond skater standing on the surface of pond water. This was photographed through an interferometer which shows interference patterns made by the pond skater as it walks on the water's surface. The surface tension of the water means the pond skater never breaks through the surface.

bodies of water to freeze completely, and increases the chances of life surviving in cold conditions.

Changes in density of water with temperature cause currents which help to maintain the circulation of nutrients in the oceans.

High surface tension and cohesion

Water molecules have very high cohesion, in other words they tend to stick to each other. This is exploited in the way water moves in long, unbroken columns through the vascular tissue in plants (see chapter 10) and is an important property in cells. High cohesion also results in high surface tension at the surface of water. This allows certain small organisms, such as the pond skater, to exploit the surface of water as a habitat, allowing them to settle on or skate over its surface (*figure 2.26*).

SAQ 2.8

State the property of water that allows each of the following to take place and, in each case, explain its importance.

a The cooling of skin during sweating.

b The survival of fish in ice-covered lakes.

c The ability of insects, such as pond skaters, to walk on water.

d The transport of glucose and ions in a mammal.

Ion	Some roles in living organisms
Calcium, Ca^{2+}	Calcium phosphate is an important structural component of bones and teeth. Calcium ions are important in the transmission of electrical impulses across synapses, and in the contraction of muscles.
Sodium, Na^+	Sodium ions are involved in the transmission of nerve impulses along neurones. They contribute to the high concentration built up by the loop of Henle in the medulla of the kidney, thus enabling concentrated urine to be excreted so that water is conserved.
Potassium, K^+	With sodium, potassium ions are involved in the transmission of nerve impulses along neurones. They contribute to the control of turgidity of guard cells, and thus the opening and closing of stomata.
Magnesium, Mg^{2+}	Chlorophyll molecules contain magnesium. Some enzymes that catalyse the breakdown of ATP, called ATPases, have magnesium ions at their active sites.
Chloride, Cl^-	With sodium ions, chloride ions contribute to the high concentration built up by the loop of Henle in the medulla of the kidney, thus enabling concentrated urine to be excreted so that water is conserved. Chloride ions help to balance the positive charge of cations such as sodium and potassium, within and around cells.
Nitrate, NO_3^-	Plants use the nitrogen from nitrate ions to make amino acids and nucleotides.
Phosphate, PO_4^{3-}	Phosphate ions are used for making nucleotides, including ATP. With calcium, they form calcium phosphate, that gives bones their strength.
Iron, Fe^{2+}	Haemoglobin molecules contain iron in their prosthetic haem groups. Oxygen binds here for transport in the red blood cells.

● **Table 2.1** Some functions of eight of the most important ions required by living organisms. Note that many of the terms mentioned are explained in other chapters and books in this series.

Inorganic ions

All of the substances described in this chapter – carbohydrates, lipids, proteins and water – are made up of molecules. (A molecule is a group of atoms held together by covalent bonds.) But they are not the only type of substance that is important for the structure and metabolism of living organisms. All living things also need a wide variety of **ions**, as shown in *table 2.1*.

Ions are formed from individual atoms that have gained or lost one or more electrons and are therefore charged negatively or positively. Many are highly soluble in water (*figure 2.25*).

SUMMARY

◆ Molecular biology is the study of the structure and function of biological molecules.

◆ Many biological molecules are formed from smaller units that bond together. These include carbohydrates, lipids, proteins and nucleic acids. Molecules which are formed from repeating identical or similar sub-units are called polymers.

◆ Carbohydrates have the general formula $C_x(H_2O)_y$. Monosaccharides are the smallest carbohydrate units, of which glucose is the most common form. They are important energy sources in cells and also important building blocks for larger molecules. They may form straight-chain or ring structures and may exist in different isomeric forms. These are important because they bond together in different ways and so affect the structure of polysaccharides, such as starch, glycogen and cellulose. The glycosidic bond forms between monosaccharides by condensation and is broken by hydrolysis. Benedict's reagent can be used to test for reducing and non-reducing sugars.

◆ Starch is formed from some straight and some branched chains of α-glucose molecules and is an energy storage compound in plants. Glycogen is a branched α-glucose chain and is an energy storage compound in animals. Cellulose is a polymer of β-glucose molecules in which the chains are grouped together by hydrogen bonding to form strong fibres that are found in plant cell walls. 'Iodine solution' can be used to test for starch.

◆ Lipids are made from fatty acids and glycerol. They are hydrophobic and do not mix with water. They are energy storage compounds in animals, as well as having other functions such as insulation and buoyancy in marine mammals. Phospholipids have a hydrophilic phosphate head and hydrophobic fatty acid tails. This is important in the formation of membranes. The emulsion test can be used to test for lipids.

◆ Proteins are long chains of amino acids which fold into precise shapes. The sequence of amino acids in a protein, known as its primary structure, determines the way that it folds and hence determines its three-dimensional shape and function.

◆ Many proteins contain areas where the amino acid chain is twisted into an α-helix; this is an example of secondary structure. Further folding produces the tertiary structure. Often, more than one polypeptide associates to form a protein molecule. The association between different polypeptide chains is the quaternary structure of the protein. Tertiary and quaternary structures are held in place by hydrogen, covalent and ionic bonding and hydrophobic interactions.

◆ Proteins may be globular or fibrous. A molecule of a globular protein is roughly spherical. Most globular proteins are soluble and metabolically active. A molecule of a fibrous protein is less folded and forms long strands. Fibrous proteins are insoluble. They often have a structural role. Biuret reagent can be used to test for proteins.

◆ Water is important within bodies where it forms a large part of the mass of the cell. It is also an environment in which organisms can live. As a result of extensive hydrogen bonding, it has unusual properties that are important for life: it is liquid at most temperatures on the Earth's surface; its highest density occurs above its freezing point so that ice floats and insulates water below from freezing air temperatures; it acts as a solvent for ions and polar molecules and causes non-polar molecules to group together; it has a high surface tension which affects the way it moves through narrow tubes and forms a surface on which some organisms can live.

◆ Ions are charged particles, some of which are important in, for example, nerve impulse transmission, excretion from the kidneys and enzyme function. The protein haemoglobin relies on the presence of iron ions in its prosthetic haem groups for its ability to carry oxygen.

Questions

1. Discuss the biological importance of hydrogen bonding in
   a water and b proteins.

2. Show how the structure of
   a glycogen and
   b cellulose is related to its function in each case.

3. What is a monosaccharide? In what ways can the structure of monosaccharides vary?

4. With reference to one named protein, describe the meanings of the terms **primary structure, secondary structure, tertiary structure** and **quaternary structure**.

5. Discuss the ways in which the molecular structures of haemoglobin and collagen are related to their functions.

6. Copy and complete the table below to summarise the molecular structure and functions of the main groups of chemicals found in living organisms. Your table will need to be large so that you have plenty of space to include several examples in the last column, and several kinds of bonds in the penultimate column for proteins. (There is no example for water, of course!)

Chemical	Elements which it contains	Subunits from which it is made	Types of bonds which hold units together	Types of bonds which hold molecules in shape, or to other molecules	Examples and their functions
water	–	–			
carbohydrates					
proteins					
lipids					

CHAPTER 3

Enzymes

By the end of this chapter you should be able to:

1 explain that enzymes are globular proteins which act as catalysts;

2 explain the way in which enzymes act as catalysts by lowering activation energy;

3 describe examples of enzyme-catalysed reactions;

4 describe methods of following the time-course of an enzyme-controlled reaction;

5 discuss the ways in which temperature, pH, concentration of enzyme, concentration of substrate, and competitive and non-competitive inhibition affect the rate of enzyme-controlled reactions;

6 describe methods of investigating the effects of these factors experimentally.

Enzymes are protein molecules which can be defined as **biological catalysts**. A catalyst is a molecule which speeds up a chemical reaction, but remains unchanged at the end of the reaction. Virtually every metabolic reaction which takes place within a living organism is catalysed by an enzyme. Many enzyme names end in -ase, for example amylase, ATPase.

Enzymes are globular proteins. Like all globular proteins, enzyme molecules are coiled into a precise three-dimensional shape, with hydrophilic R groups (side-chains) on the outside of the molecule ensuring that they are soluble. Enzyme molecules also have a special feature in that they possess an **active site** (*figure 3.1*). The active site of an enzyme is a region, usually a cleft or

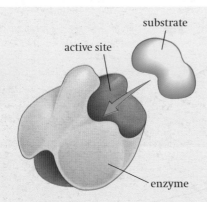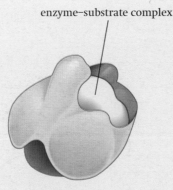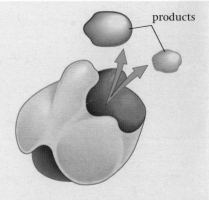

a An enzyme has a cleft in its surface called the active site. The substrate molecule has a complementary shape.

b Random movement of enzyme and substrate brings the substrate into the active site. An enzyme–substrate complex is temporarily formed. The R groups of the amino acids in the active site interact with the substrate.

c The interaction of the substrate with the active site breaks the substrate apart. The two product molecules leave the active site, leaving the enzyme molecule unchanged and ready to bind with another substrate molecule.

● **Figure 3.1** How an enzyme catalyses the breakdown of a substrate molecule to two product molecules.

depression, to which another molecule or molecules can bind. This molecule is the **substrate** of the enzyme. The shape of the active site allows the substrate to fit perfectly, and to be held in place by temporary bonds which form between the substrate and some of the R groups of the enzyme's amino acids. This combined structure is termed the **enzyme–substrate complex**. A simplified diagram is shown in *figure 3.2*.

Each type of enzyme will usually act on only one type of substrate molecule. This is because the shape of the active site will only allow one shape of molecule to fit. The enzyme is said to be **specific** for this substrate.

The enzyme may catalyse a reaction in which the substrate molecule is split into two or more molecules. Alternatively, it may catalyse the joining together of two molecules, as when making a dipeptide. Interaction between the R groups of the enzyme and the atoms of the substrate can break, or encourage formation of, bonds in the substrate molecule, forming one, two or more **products**.

When the reaction is complete, the product or products leave the active site. The enzyme is unchanged by this process, so it is now available to receive another substrate molecule. The rate at which substrate molecules can bind to the

enzyme's active site, be formed into products and leave can be very rapid. The enzyme catalase, for example, can bind with hydrogen peroxide molecules, split them into water and oxygen and release these products at a rate of 10^7 molecules per second.

Enzymes reduce activation energy

As catalysts, enzymes increase the rate at which chemical reactions occur. Most of the reactions which occur in living cells would occur so slowly without enzymes that they would virtually not happen at all.

In many reactions, the substrate will not be converted to a product unless it is temporarily given some extra energy. This energy is called **activation energy** (*figure 3.3a*).

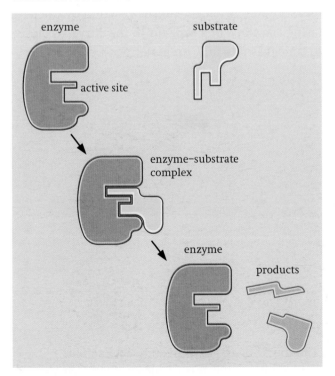

● **Figure 3.2** A simplified diagram of enzyme function.

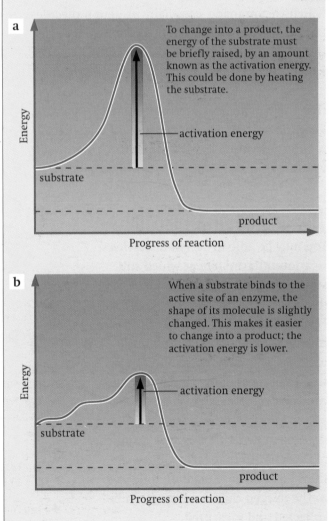

● **Figure 3.3** Activation energy **a** without enzyme, **b** with enzyme.

One way of increasing the rate of many chemical reactions is to increase the energy of the reactants by heating them. You have probably done this on many occasions by heating substances which you want to react together. In the Benedict's test for reducing sugar, for example, you need to heat the Benedict's reagent and sugar solution together before they will react (page 25).

Mammals, such as humans, also use this method of speeding up their metabolic reactions. Our body temperature is maintained at 37 °C, which is usually much warmer than the temperature of the air around us. But even raising the temperature of cells to 37 °C is not enough to give most substrates the activation energy which they need to change into products. We cannot raise body temperature much more than this, as temperatures above about 40 °C begin to cause irreversible damage to many of the molecules from which we are made, especially protein molecules. Enzymes are a solution to this problem because they *decrease* the activation energy of the reaction which they catalyse (*figure 3.3b*). They do this by holding the substrate or substrates in such a way that their molecules can react more easily. Reactions catalysed by enzymes will take place rapidly at a much lower temperature than they would without them.

The course of a reaction

You may be able to carry out an investigation into the rate at which substrate is converted into product during an enzyme-controlled reaction. *Figure 3.4* shows the results of such an investigation, using the enzyme catalase. This enzyme is found in the tissues of most living things and catalyses the breakdown of hydrogen peroxide into water and oxygen. (Hydrogen peroxide is a toxic product of several different metabolic reactions.) It is an easy reaction to follow as the oxygen that is released can be collected and measured.

The reaction begins very swiftly. As soon as the enzyme and substrate are mixed, bubbles of oxygen are released quickly. A large volume of oxygen is collected in the first minute of the reaction. As the reaction continues, however, the rate at which oxygen is released gradually slows down. The reaction gets slower and slower, until it eventually stops completely.

The explanation for this is quite straightforward. When the enzyme and substrate are first mixed, there is a large number of substrate molecules. At any moment, virtually every enzyme molecule has a substrate molecule in its active site. The rate at which the reaction occurs will depend only on how many enzyme molecules there are, and the speed at which the enzyme can convert the substrate into product, release it, and then bind with another substrate molecule. However, as more and more substrate is converted into product, there are fewer and fewer substrate molecules to bind with enzymes. Enzyme molecules may be 'waiting' for a substrate molecule to hit their active site. As fewer substrate molecules are left, the reaction gets slower and slower, until it eventually stops.

The curve is therefore steepest at the beginning of the reaction: the rate of an enzyme-controlled reaction is always fastest at the beginning. This rate is called the **initial rate of reaction**. You can measure the initial rate of the reaction by calculating the slope of a tangent to the curve, as close to time 0 as possible. An easier way of doing this

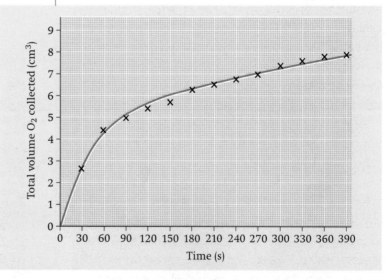

● **Figure 3.4** The course of an enzyme-catalysed reaction. Catalase was added to hydrogen peroxide at time 0. The gas released was collected in a gas syringe, the volume being read at 30 s intervals.

is simply to read off the graph the amount of oxygen given off in the first 30 seconds. In this case, the rate of oxygen production in the first 30 seconds is 2.7 cm^3 of oxygen per 30 seconds, or 5.4 cm^3 per minute.

SAQ 3.1

Why is it better to calculate the initial rate of reaction from a curve such as the one in *figure 3.4*, rather than simply measuring how much oxygen is given off in 30 seconds?

The effect of enzyme concentration

Figure 3.5a shows the results of an investigation in which different amounts of catalase were added to the same amount of hydrogen peroxide. You can see that the shape of all five curves is similar. In each case, the reaction begins very quickly (steep curve) and then gradually slows down (curve levels off). Because the amounts of hydrogen peroxide are the same in all five reactions, the total amount of oxygen eventually produced will be the same so, if the investigation goes on long enough, all the curves will meet.

To compare the rates of these five reactions, in order to look at the effect of enzyme concentration on reaction rate, it is fairest to look at the rate *right at the beginning* of the reaction. This is because, once the reaction is under way, the amount of substrate in each reaction begins to vary, as substrate is converted to product at different rates in each of the five reactions. It is only at the very beginning of the reaction that we can be sure that differences in reaction rate are caused only by differences in enzyme concentration.

To work out this initial rate for each enzyme concentration, we can calculate the slope of the curve 30 seconds after the beginning of the reaction, as explained earlier. Ideally, we should do this for an even earlier stage of the reaction, but in practice this is impossible. We can then plot a second graph, *figure 3.5b*, showing this initial rate of reaction against enzyme concentration.

This graph shows that the initial rate of reaction increases linearly. In these conditions, reaction rate is directly proportional to the enzyme concentration. This is just what common sense

says should happen. The more enzyme present, the more active sites will be available for the substrate to slot into. As long as there is plenty of substrate available, the initial rate of a reaction increases linearly with enzyme concentration.

SAQ 3.2

Sketch the shape of *figure 3.5b* if excess hydrogen peroxide was not available.

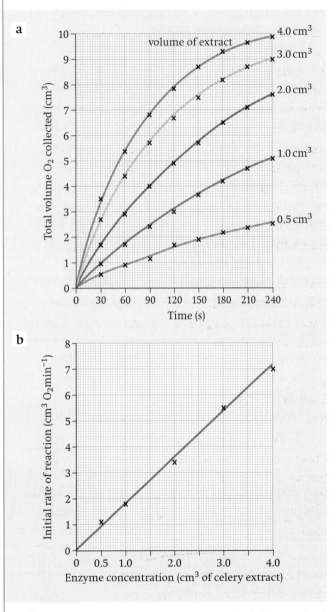

● **Figure 3.5** The effect of enzyme concentration on the rate of an enzyme-catalysed reaction.
a Different volumes of celery extract, which contains catalase, were added to the same volume of hydrogen peroxide. Water was added to make the total volume of the mixture the same in each case. **b** The rate of reaction in the first 30 s was calculated for each enzyme concentration.

Measuring reaction rate

It is easy to measure the rate of the catalase–hydrogen peroxide reaction, because one of the products is a gas, which is released and can be collected. Unfortunately, it is not always so easy to measure the rate of a reaction. If, for example, you wanted to investigate the rate at which amylase breaks down starch, it would be very difficult to observe the course of the reaction because the substrate (starch) and the product (maltose) remain as colourless substances in the reaction mixture.

The easiest way to measure the rate of this reaction is to measure the rate at which starch disappears from the reaction mixture. This can be done by taking samples from the mixture at known times, and adding each sample to some iodine in potassium iodide solution. Starch forms a blue-black colour with this solution. Using a colorimeter, you can measure the intensity of the blue-black colour obtained, and use this as a measure of the amount of starch still remaining. If you do this over a period of time, you can plot a curve of amount of starch remaining against time. You can then calculate the initial reaction rate in the same way as for the catalase–hydrogen peroxide reaction.

SAQ 3.3
a Sketch the curve you would expect to obtain if the amount of starch remaining was plotted against time.
b How could you use this curve to calculate the initial reaction rate?

It is even easier to observe the course of this reaction if you mix starch, iodine in potassium iodide solution and amylase in a tube, and take regular readings of the colour of the mixture in this one tube in a colorimeter. However, this is not ideal, because the iodine interferes with the rate of the reaction and slows it down.

The effect of substrate concentration

Figure 3.6 shows the results of an investigation in which the amount of catalase was kept constant, and the amount of hydrogen peroxide was varied. Once again, curves of oxygen released against time were plotted for each reaction, and the

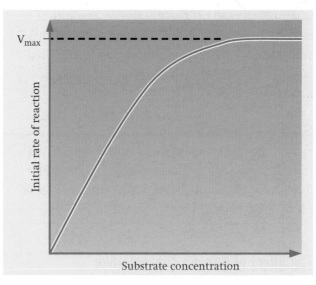

● **Figure 3.6** The effect of substrate concentration on the rate of an enzyme-catalysed reaction.

initial rate of reaction calculated for the first 30 seconds. These initial rates of reaction were then plotted against substrate concentration.

As substrate concentration increases, the initial rate of reaction also increases. Again, this is only what we would expect: the more substrate molecules there are around, the more often an enzyme's active site can bind with one. However, if we go on increasing substrate concentration, keeping the enzyme concentration constant, there comes a point where every enzyme active site is working continuously. If more substrate is added, the enzyme simply cannot work faster; substrate molecules are effectively 'queuing up' for an active site to become vacant. The enzyme is working at its maximum possible rate, known as V_{max}.

Temperature and enzyme activity

Figure 3.7 shows how the rate of a typical enzyme-catalysed reaction varies with temperature. At low temperatures, the reaction takes place only very slowly. This is because molecules are moving relatively slowly. Substrate molecules will not often collide with the active site, and so binding between substrate and enzyme is a rare event. As temperature rises, the enzyme and substrate molecules move faster. Collisions happen more frequently, so that substrate molecules enter the active site more often. Moreover, when they do collide, they do so with more energy. This makes it easier for bonds to be broken so that the reaction can occur.

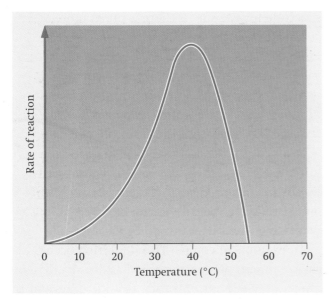

- **Figure 3.7** The effect of temperature on the rate of an enzyme-controlled reaction.

SAQ 3.4

How could you carry out an experiment to determine the effect of temperature on the rate of breakdown of hydrogen peroxide by catalase?

As temperature continues to increase, the speed of movement of the substrate and enzyme molecules also continues to increase. However, above a certain temperature the structure of the enzyme molecule vibrates so energetically that some of the bonds holding the enzyme molecule in its precise shape begin to break. This is especially true of hydrogen bonds. The enzyme molecule begins to lose its shape and activity and is said to be **denatured**. This is often irreversible.

At first, the substrate molecule fits less well into the active site of the enzyme, so the rate of the reaction begins to slow down. Eventually the substrate no longer fits at all, or can no longer be held in the correct position for the reaction to occur.

The temperature at which an enzyme catalyses a reaction at the maximum rate is called the **optimum temperature**. Most human enzymes have an optimum temperature of around 40 °C. By keeping our body temperatures at about 37 °C, we ensure that enzyme-catalysed reactions occur at close to their maximum rate. It would be dangerous to maintain a body temperature of 40 °C, as even a slight rise above this would begin to denature enzymes.

- **Figure 3.8** Not all enzymes have optimum temperatures of 40 °C. Bacteria and algae living in hot springs such as this one in Yellowstone National Park, USA, are able to tolerate very high temperatures. Enzymes from such organisms are proving useful in various industrial applications.

Enzymes from other organisms may have different optimum temperatures. Some enzymes, such as those found in bacteria which live in hot springs, have much higher optimum temperatures (*figure 3.8*). Some plant enzymes have lower optimum temperatures, depending on their habitat.

SAQ 3.5

Proteases are used in biological washing powders.
a How would a protease remove a blood stain on clothes?
b Most biological washing powders are recommended for use at low washing temperatures. Why is this?
c Washing powder manufacturers have produced proteases which can work at higher temperatures than 40°C. Why is this useful?

pH and enzyme activity

Figure 3.9 shows how the activity of an enzyme is affected by pH. Most enzymes work fastest at a pH of somewhere around 7, that is in fairly neutral conditions. Some, however, such as the protease pepsin which is found in the acidic conditions of the stomach, have a different optimum pH.

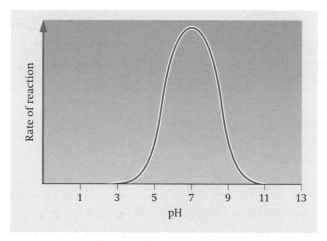

● **Figure 3.9** The effect of pH on the rate of an enzyme-controlled reaction.

pH is a measure of the concentration of hydrogen ions in a solution. The lower the pH, the higher the hydrogen ion concentration. Hydrogen ions can interact with the R groups of amino acids, affecting the way in which they bond with each other and therefore affect their 3D arrangement (see page 33). A pH which is very different from the optimum pH can cause denaturation of an enzyme.

SAQ 3.6

Trypsin is a protease secreted in pancreatic juice, which acts in the duodenum. If you make up a suspension of milk powder in water, and add trypsin, the enzyme digests the protein in the milk, so that the suspension becomes clear.

How could you carry out an investigation into the effect of pH on the rate of activity of trypsin? (A suspension of 4 g of milk powder in 100 cm^3 of water will become clear in a few minutes if an equal volume of a 0.5% trypsin solution is added to it.)

Enzyme inhibitors

As we have seen, the active site of an enzyme fits one particular substrate perfectly. It is possible, however, for some *other* molecule to bind to an enzyme's active site if it is very similar to the enzyme's substrate. This could **inhibit** the enzyme's function.

If an **inhibitor** molecule binds only briefly to the site there is competition between it and the substrate for the site. If there is much more of the substrate than the inhibitor present, substrate molecules can easily bind to the active site in the usual way and so the enzyme's function is unaffected. However, if the concentration of the inhibitor rises or the substrate falls, it becomes less and less likely that the substrate will collide with an empty site and the enzyme's function is inhibited. This is therefore known as **competitive inhibition** (*figure 3.10a*). It is said to be **reversible** (not permanent) because it can be reversed by increasing the concentration of the substrate.

An example of competitive inhibition occurs in the treatment of a person who has drunk ethylene glycol. Ethylene glycol is used as antifreeze, and is

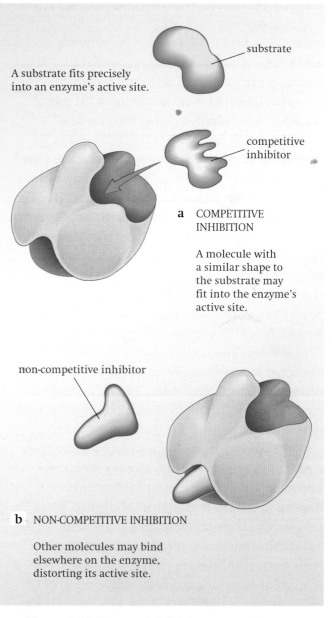

A substrate fits precisely into an enzyme's active site.

substrate

competitive inhibitor

a COMPETITIVE INHIBITION

A molecule with a similar shape to the substrate may fit into the enzyme's active site.

non-competitive inhibitor

b NON-COMPETITIVE INHIBITION

Other molecules may bind elsewhere on the enzyme, distorting its active site.

● **Figure 3.10** Enzyme inhibition.

sometimes drunk accidentally. It has also occasionally been added, illegally, to wine. Ethylene glycol is rapidly converted in the body to oxalic acid, which can cause irreversible kidney damage. However, the active site of the enzyme which converts ethylene glycol to oxalic acid will also accept ethanol. If the poisoned person is given a large dose of ethanol, the ethanol acts as a competitive inhibitor, slowing down the action of the enzyme on ethylene glycol for long enough to allow the ethylene glycol to be excreted.

Sometimes, the inhibitor can remain permanently bonded with the active site and therefore cause a permanent block to the substrate. No competition occurs as it does not matter how much substrate is present so this is **non-competitive irreversible inhibition**. The antibiotic penicillin works by permanently occupying the active site of an enzyme that is essential for the synthesis of bacterial cell walls.

A different kind of inhibition takes place if a molecule can bind to another part of the enzyme rather than the true active site. This can seriously disrupt the normal arrangement of hydrogen bonds and hydrophobic interactions holding the enzyme molecule in its 3D shape (see chapter 2).

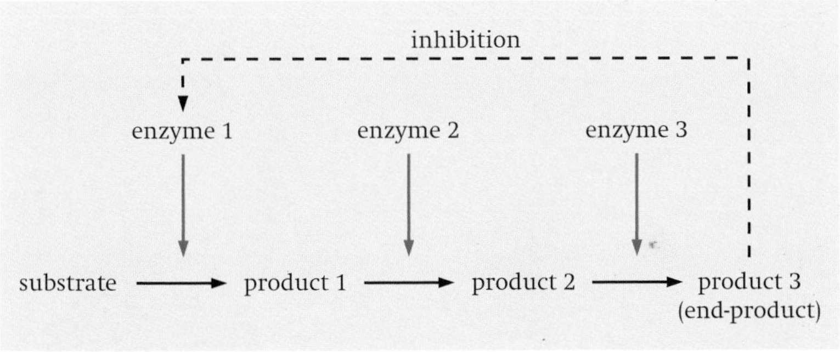

	Inhibitor binds to active site on enzyme	Inhibitor binds elsewhere on enzyme
Inhibitor binds briefly	Competitive reversible	Non-competitive reversible
Inhibitor binds permanently	Non-competitive irreversible	Non-competitive irreversible

● **Table 3.1** Types of enzyme inhibition

The resulting distortion ripples across the molecule to the active site making it unsuitable for the substrate. The enzyme's function is blocked no matter how much substrate is present so this is another type of **non-competitive inhibition** (*figure 3.10b*). It can be **reversible** or **irreversible**, depending on whether the inhibitor bonds briefly or permanently with the enzyme. Digitalis is an example of a non-competitive inhibitor. It binds with the enzyme ATPase, resulting in an increase in the contraction of heart muscle.

Inhibition of enzyme function can be lethal, but in many situations inhibition is essential. For example, metabolic reactions must be very finely controlled and balanced, so no single enzyme can be allowed to 'run wild', constantly churning out more and more product. One way of ensuring that this cannot happen is to use the **end-product** of a chain of reactions as an enzyme inhibitor (*figure 3.11*). As the enzyme converts substrate to product, it is slowed down because the end-product binds to another part of the enzyme and prevents more substrate binding. However, the end-product can lose its attachment to the enzyme and go on to be used elsewhere, allowing the enzyme to reform into its active state. As product levels fall, the enzyme is able to top them up again. This is **end-product inhibition** and is an example of **non-competitive reversible inhibition**.

A summary of the various types of inhibition can be found in *table 3.1*.

● **Figure 3.11** End-product inhibition. As levels of product 3 rise, there is increasing inhibition of enzyme 1. So, less product 1 is made and hence less product 2 and 3. Falling levels of product 3 allow increased function of enzyme 1 so products 1, 2 and 3 rise again and the cycle continues. This end-product inhibition finely controls levels of product 3 between narrow upper and lower limits and is an example of a feed-back mechanism.

SUMMARY

◆ Enzymes are globular proteins, which act as catalysts by lowering activation energy.

◆ Each enzyme acts on only one specific substrate, because there has to be a perfect match between the shape of the substrate and the shape of the enzyme's active site to form an enzyme–substrate complex.

◆ Anything which affects the shape of the active site, such as high temperature, a change of pH or the binding of a non-competitive inhibitor with the enzyme, will slow down the rate of the reaction.

◆ Competitive inhibitors also slow down the rate of reaction, by competing with the substrate for the active site of the enzyme.

Questions

1 What is an enzyme?

2 In mammals, such as humans, the temperature and pH of body fluids are kept constant. Discuss the reasons for this, in terms of the functioning of enzymes.

CHAPTER 4

Cell membranes and transport

By the end of this chapter you should be able to:

1 describe the fluid mosaic model of membrane structure and explain the underlying reasons for this structure;

2 outline the roles of phospholipids, cholesterol, glycolipids, proteins and glycoproteins in membranes;

3 outline the roles of the plasma membrane, and the roles of membranes within cells;

4 describe and explain how molecules can get in and out of cells (cross cell membranes) by the processes of diffusion, facilitated diffusion, osmosis, active transport, endocytosis and exocytosis;

5 describe the effects on animal and plant cells of immersion in solutions of different water potential;

6 describe the features of the gaseous exchange surface of the mammalian lung;

7 describe the features of root hairs that enable the uptake of ions by active transport.

In chapter 1 you saw that *all* living cells are surrounded by a membrane which controls the exchange of materials, such as nutrients and waste products, between the cell and its environment. Although extremely thin, the membrane must be capable of regulating this exchange very precisely. Within cells, particularly eukaryotic cells, regulation of transport across the membranes of organelles is vital. Membranes also have other important functions. For example, they enable cells to receive hormone messages. Therefore it is important to study the structure of membranes if we are to understand how these functions are achieved.

Phospholipids

An understanding of the structure of membranes depends on an understanding of the structure of phospholipids (see page 30). From phospholipids,

little bags can be formed in which chemicals can be isolated from the external environment. These bags are the membrane-bound compartments that we know as cells and organelles.

Figure 4.1a shows what happens if phospholipid molecules are spread over the surface of water. They form a single layer with their heads in the water, because these are polar (hydrophilic), and their tails projecting out of the water, because these are non-polar (hydrophobic). (The term 'polar' refers to the uneven distribution of charge which occurs in some molecules. The significance of this is also discussed on page 27.)

If the phospholipids are shaken up with water they can form stable structures in the water called **micelles** (*figure 4.1b*). Here all the hydrophilic heads face outwards into the water, shielding the hydrophobic tails, which point in towards each other. Alternatively, two-layered structures, called **bilayers**, can form in sheets (*figure 4.1c*). It is now

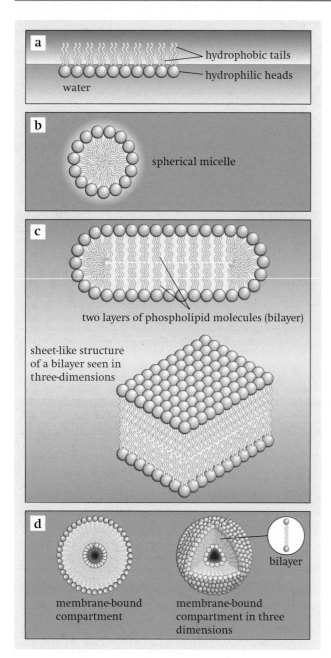

• **Figure 4.1** Phospholipids in water **a** spread as a single layer of molecules (a monolayer) on the surface of water, **b** forming micelles surrounded by water, **c** forming bilayers, **d** forming membrane-bound compartments.

known that this phospholipid bilayer is the basic structure of membranes (*figure 4.1d*).

Structure of membranes

The phospholipid bilayer is visible using the electron microscope at very high magnifications of at least × 100 000 (*figure 1.19*). The double black line visible using the electron microscope is thought

to show the two phospholipid layers. The bilayer (membrane) is about 7 nm wide.

Membranes also contain proteins. *Figures 4.2* and *4.3* show what we imagine a membrane might look like if we could see the individual molecules. This model for the structure of a membrane is known as the **fluid mosaic model**. The word 'fluid' refers to the fact that the individual phospholipid and protein molecules move around within their layer. The word 'mosaic' describes the pattern produced by the scattered protein molecules when the surface of the membrane is viewed from above.

Features of the fluid mosaic model

- The membrane is a double layer (**bilayer**) of phospholipid molecules. The individual phospholipid molecules move about by diffusion within their own monolayer.
- The phospholipid tails point inwards, facing each other and forming a non-polar hydrophobic interior. The phospholipid heads face the aqueous (water-containing) medium that surrounds the membrane.
- Some of the phospholipid tails are saturated and some are unsaturated. The more unsaturated they are, the more fluid the membrane. This is because the unsaturated fatty acid tails are bent (*figure 2.12*) and therefore fit together more loosely. As temperature decreases membranes become less fluid, but some organisms which cannot regulate their own temperature, such as bacteria and yeasts, respond by increasing the proportion of unsaturated fatty acids in their membranes.
- Most of the protein molecules float like mobile icebergs in the phospholipid layers, although some are fixed like islands to structures inside the cell and do not move about.
- Some proteins are embedded in the outer layer, some in the inner layer and some span the whole membrane. They stay in the membrane because they have hydrophobic portions (made from hydrophobic amino acids) which 'sit' among the hydrophobic phospholipid tails. Hydrophilic portions (made from hydrophilic amino acids) face outwards.
- The total thickness is about 7 nm on average.

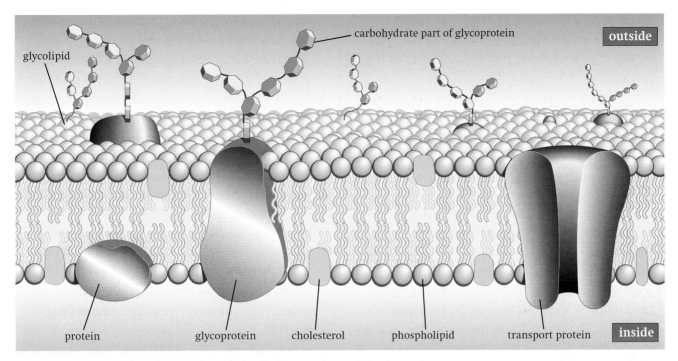

● **Figure 4.2** An artist's impression of the fluid mosaic model of membrane structure.

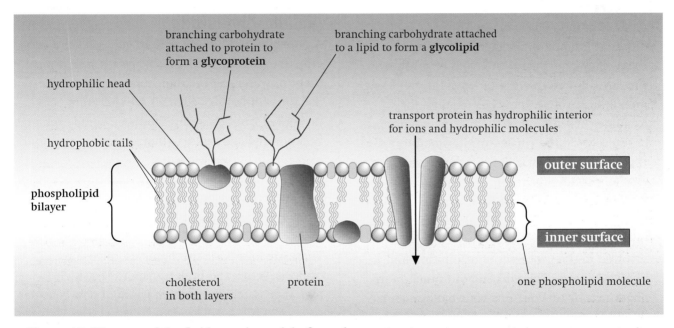

● **Figure 4.3** Diagram of the fluid mosaic model of membrane structure.

■ Many proteins and lipids have short, branching carbohydrate chains attached to the external surface of the membrane, thus forming **glycoproteins** and **glycolipids** respectively.

■ Molecules of cholesterol are also found in the membrane. Their function is described below.

Roles of the components of cell membranes

We have seen that cell membranes contain several different types of molecule – phospholipids,

cholesterol, proteins, glycolipids and glycoproteins. Each of these has a particular role to play in the overall structure and function of the membrane.

■ **Phospholipids**, as explained on page 51, form the bilayer which is the basic structure of the membrane. Because their tails are non-polar, it is difficult for polar molecules, or ions, to pass through them, so they act as a barrier to most water-soluble substances.

■ **Cholesterol** molecules, like phospholipids, have

hydrophilic heads and hydrophobic tails, so they fit neatly between the phospholipid molecules. They help to regulate the fluidity of the membrane, preventing it from becoming too fluid or too rigid. Cholesterol is also important for the mechanical stability of membranes, as without it membranes quickly break and cells burst open. The hydrophobic regions of cholesterol molecules help to prevent ions or polar molecules from passing through the membrane. This is particulary important in the myelin sheath (made up of many layers of membrane) around nerve cells, where leakage of ions would slow down nerve impulses.

- **Proteins** have a variety of functions within membranes. Many of them act as **transport proteins**. These provide hydrophilic channels or passageways for ions and polar molecules to pass through the membrane. This is described on pages 55 and 59. There are many different types of protein channel, each specific for a different kind of ion or molecule. Between them, they can control the types of substances that are allowed to enter or leave the cell. Other membrane proteins may be **enzymes**, for example those found in the plasma membranes of the cells on the surface of the small intestine that catalyse the hydrolysis of molecules such as disaccharides (page 24). Proteins also play important roles in the membranes of organelles. For example, in the membranes of mitochondria and chloroplasts, they are involved in the processes of respiration and photosynthesis. (You will find out much more about this if you continue your biology course to A2 level.)

- **Glycolipids** and **glycoproteins**. Many of the lipid molecules on the outer surfaces of plasma membranes, and most of the protein molecules, have short carbohydrate chains attached to them. These 'combination' molecules are known as **glycolipids** and **glycoproteins** respectively. The carbohydrate chains project out into the watery fluids surrounding the cell, where they form hydrogen bonds with the water molecules and so help to stabilise the membrane structure (see page 27). They also act as **receptor molecules**, binding with particular substances

such as hormones or neurotransmitters (the chemicals that enable nerve impulses to pass from one nerve cell to another). Different cells have different collections of receptor molecules in their membranes that will bind with particular substances. For example, only certain cells, such as those in the liver and muscles, have receptors for the hormone insulin. When insulin binds with these receptors, it triggers a particular series of chemical reactions in the cell. Other cells, as they do not have insulin receptors, are not affected by insulin.

One group of glycoproteins, known as antigens, are important in allowing cells to recognise each other. Each type of cell has its own type of antigen, rather like countries with different flags.

Transport across the plasma membrane

A phospholipid bilayer around cells makes a very effective barrier, particularly against the movement of water-soluble molecules and ions. The aqueous contents of the cell are therefore prevented from escaping. However, some exchange between the cell and its environment is essential.

SAQ 4.1
Suggest three reasons why exchange between the cell and its environment is essential.

There are four basic mechanisms, diffusion, osmosis, active and bulk transport, by which exchange is achieved, which we shall now consider.

Diffusion and facilitated diffusion

If you open a bottle of perfume in a room, it is not long before molecules of scent spread to all parts of the room (and are detected when they fit into membrane receptors in your nose). This will happen, even in still air, by the process of diffusion. **Diffusion** can be defined as the net movement of molecules (or ions) from a region of their higher concentration to a region of their lower concentration. The molecules move down a **concentration gradient**. It happens because of the natural kinetic energy (energy of movement) possessed by molecules or ions, which makes them move about at random. As a result of diffusion, molecules tend to reach an equilibrium situation where they are evenly spread within a given volume of space.

Some substances have molecules or ions that are able to pass through cell membranes by diffusion. The rate at which a substance diffuses across a membrane depends on a number of factors, including:

- the 'steepness' of the concentration gradient, that is the difference in the concentration of the substance on the two sides of the surface. If there are, for example, many more molecules on one side of a membrane than on the other, then at any one moment more molecules will be moving (entirely randomly) from this side than from the other. The greater the difference in concentration, then the greater the difference in the number of molecules passing in the two directions, and hence the faster the net rate of diffusion.
- temperature. At high temperatures, molecules and ions have much more kinetic energy than at low temperatures. They move around faster, and thus diffusion takes place faster.
- the surface area across which diffusion is taking place. The greater the surface area, then the more molecules or ions can cross it at any one moment, and therefore the faster diffusion can occur.
- the nature of the molecules or ions. Large molecules require more energy to get them moving than small ones do, so substances with large molecules tend to diffuse more slowly than ones with small molecules. Non-polar molecules diffuse more easily through cell membranes than polar ones, as they are soluble in the non-polar phospholipid tails.

The respiratory gases, oxygen and carbon dioxide, cross membranes by diffusion. Both can cross through the phospholipid bilayer directly between the phospholipid molecules. Oxygen is uncharged and non-polar, so crosses quickly. Carbon dioxide is a polar molecule but is small enough to pass through rapidly. Water molecules, despite being very polar, can diffuse rapidly across the phospholipid bilayer because they too are small enough. However, large polar molecules, such as glucose

and amino acids, cannot diffuse through the phospholipid bilayer. Nor can ions such as Na^+ or Cl^-. These can only cross the membrane by passing through hydrophilic channels created by protein molecules. Diffusion that takes place through these channels is called **facilitated diffusion**. *Facilitate* means 'make easy' or 'make possible', and this is what the protein channels do.

Plasma membranes contain many different types of protein channel, each type allowing only one kind of molecule or ion to pass through it. The movement of the molecules or ions is entirely passive, just as in ordinary diffusion, and net movement into or out of the cell will only take place down a concentration gradient from a high concentration to a low concentration. However, the rate at which this diffusion takes place depends on how many appropriate channels there are in the membrane, and on whether they are open or not. For example, the disease cystic fibrosis is caused by a defect in a protein which should be present in the plasma membranes of certain cells, including those lining the lungs, that normally allows chloride ions to move out of the cells. If this protein is not correctly positioned in the membrane, or if it does not open the chloride channel as and when it should, then the chloride ions cannot move out. The clinical effects are described in Part 3 of this book (page 150).

Osmosis

Osmosis is best regarded as a special type of diffusion involving water molecules only. In the explanations that follow remember that

solute + solvent = solution.

In a sugar **solution**, for example, the **solute** is sugar and the **solvent** is water.

In *figure 4.4* there are two solutions separated by a **partially permeable membrane**. This is a membrane which allows only certain molecules through, just like membranes in living cells. In the situation shown in *figure 4.4* solution B has a higher concentration of solute molecules than solution A has. Solution B is described as more concentrated than solution A, and solution A as more dilute than solution B.

First imagine the situation if the membrane were *not* present. Because B has the higher

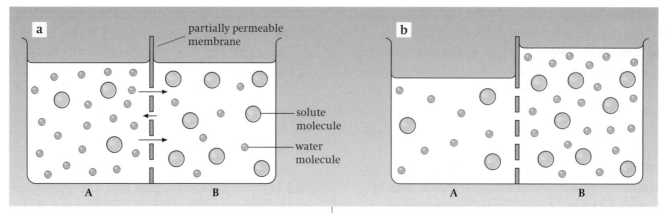

● **Figure 4.4 a** Before osmosis. Two solutions separated by a partially permeable membrane. The solute molecules are too large to pass through the pores in the membrane but the water molecules are small enough. **b** At equilibrium. As the arrows show, more molecules moved from A to B than from B to A so the net movement has been from A to B, raising the level of solution in B and lowering it in A.

concentration of solute molecules, there would be a **net** movement of solute molecules from B to A by diffusion (meaning more solute molecules would pass from B to A in a given time than from A to B). At the same time there would be a net movement of water molecules from A to B by diffusion because solution A has a higher concentration of water molecules than solution B has. Eventually, at equilibrium, the concentrations of water molecules and solute molecules in A would equal that in B.

Now consider the situation where a partially permeable membrane *is* present, as shown in *figure 4.4*. The solute molecules are too large to pass through the membrane, but water molecules can pass easily between solutions A and B, so the only molecules that can diffuse through the membrane are water molecules. There will therefore be a net movement of water molecules from A to B until an equilibrium is reached where solution A has the same concentration of water molecules (and therefore of solute molecules) as solution B. During the process the level of liquid in B will therefore rise and the level in A will fall. The fact that the movement of water molecules *alone*, and not of solute molecules, has brought about the equilibrium is characteristic of osmosis.

Water potential and solute potential

It is useful to be able to measure the tendency of water molecules to move from one place to another. This tendency is known as **water potential**. The symbol for water potential is the Greek letter psi, ψ. Water *always* moves from a region of higher water potential to a region of lower water potential. It therefore moves down a water potential gradient. Equilibrium is reached when the water potential in one region is the same as in the other. There will then be no net movement of water molecules. We can now define **osmosis** as **the movement of water molecules from a region of higher water potential to a region of lower water potential through a partially permeable membrane**.

In *figure 4.4a*, since water moves from A to B, solution A must have a higher water potential than solution B. Pure water has the highest possible water potential. The effect of solute molecules is therefore to *lower* the water potential.

By convention, the water potential of pure water is set at zero. Since solutes make water potential lower, they make the water potential of solutions *less* than zero, that is negative. The more solute, the more negative (lower) the water potential becomes. The amount that the solute molecules lower the water potential of a solution is called the **solute potential**. Solute potential is therefore always negative. The symbol for solute potential is ψ_s.

You should now be able to decide which solution in *figure 4.4a*, A or B, has the lower solute potential. The answer is that B has the lower (more negative) solute potential, and A has the higher solute potential (nearer zero and therefore less negative).

SAQ 4.2

In *figure 4.4b*, the solutions in A and B are in equilibrium, that is there is no net movement of water molecules now. What can you say about the water potentials of the two solutions?

Osmosis in animal cells

Figure 4.5 shows the effect of osmosis on an animal cell. Notice that if the water potential of the solution surrounding the cell is too high, the cell swells and bursts (*figure 4.5a*). If it is too low, the cell shrinks (*figure 4.5c*). This shows one reason why it is important to maintain a constant water potential inside the bodies of animals. In animal cells $\psi = \psi_s$, in other words water potential is equal to solute potential.

SAQ 4.3

In *figure 4.5*:

a which solution has the highest water potential?
b which solution has the lowest solute potential?
c in which solution is the water potential of the red cell the same as that of the solution?

Pressure potential

So far, the only factor we have examined which affects water potential is solute potential. It is possible for another factor to come into play, namely pressure. *Figure 4.6* shows a system like

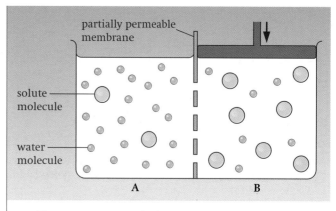

● **Figure 4.6** Two solutions separated by a partially permeable membrane. A piston is added, enabling pressure to be applied to solution **B**.

that in *figure 4.4*, except that a piston has been added, allowing pressure to be applied to solution B. We have seen that, without the piston, there is a net movement of water molecules from A to B. This can be prevented by applying pressure to solution B. The greater the pressure applied, the greater the tendency for water molecules to be forced back from solution B to solution A. Since the tendency of the water molecules to move from one place to another is measured as water potential, it is clear that increasing the pressure *increases* the water potential of solution B. The contribution made by pressure to water potential is known as **pressure potential**, and is given the symbol ψ_p. The pressure potential makes the water potential less negative and is therefore positive.

Osmosis in plant cells

Pressure potential is especially important in plant cells. Unlike animal cells, plant cells are surrounded by cell walls which are very strong and rigid (page 5). Imagine a plant cell being placed in pure water or a dilute solution (*figure 4.7a*). The water or solution has a higher water potential than the plant cell and water therefore enters the cell through its partially permeable plasma membrane by osmosis. Just like the animal cell, the volume of the cell increases but in the plant cell, the protoplast (the living part of the cell inside the cell wall) starts to push against the cell wall and

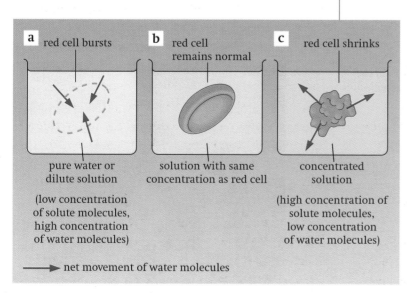

● **Figure 4.5** Movement of water into or out of red blood cells by osmosis in solutions of different concentration.

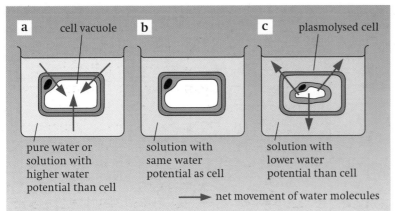

a   cell vacuole   b   c   plasmolysed cell

pure water or solution with higher water potential than cell

solution with same water potential as cell

solution with lower water potential than cell

→ net movement of water molecules

● **Figure 4.7** Osmotic changes in a plant cell in solutions of different water potential.

pressure starts to build up rapidly. This is the pressure potential and it increases the water potential of the cell until the water potential inside the cell equals the water potential outside the cell, and equilibrium is reached. The cell wall is so inelastic that it takes very little water to enter the cell to achieve this. The cell wall prevents the cell from bursting, unlike the situation when an animal cell is placed in pure water or a dilute solution. When a plant cell is fully inflated with water it is described

as **turgid**. For plant cells, then, water potential is a combination of solute potential and pressure potential. This can be expressed in the following equation:

$$\psi = \psi_s + \psi_p$$

Figure 4.7c shows the situation where a plant cell is placed in a solution of lower water potential. An example of the latter would be a concentrated sucrose solution. In such a solution water will *leave* the cell by osmosis. As it does so, the protoplast gradually shrinks until it is exerting no pressure at all on the cell wall. At this point the pressure potential is zero, so the water potential of the cell is equal to its solute potential (see the equation above). As the protoplast continues to shrink it begins to pull away from the cell wall (*figures 4.7c and 4.8*). This process is called **plasmolysis**, and a cell in which it has happened is said to be **plasmolysed**. Both the solute molecules and the water molecules of the external solution can pass through the freely permeable cell wall, and so the external solution remains in contact with the shrinking protoplast. Eventually, as with the animal cell, an equilibrium is reached when the water potential of the cell has decreased to that of the external solution. The point at which pressure potential has just reached zero and plasmolysis is *about* to occur is referred to as **incipient plasmolysis**.

The changes described can easily be observed with a light microscope using strips

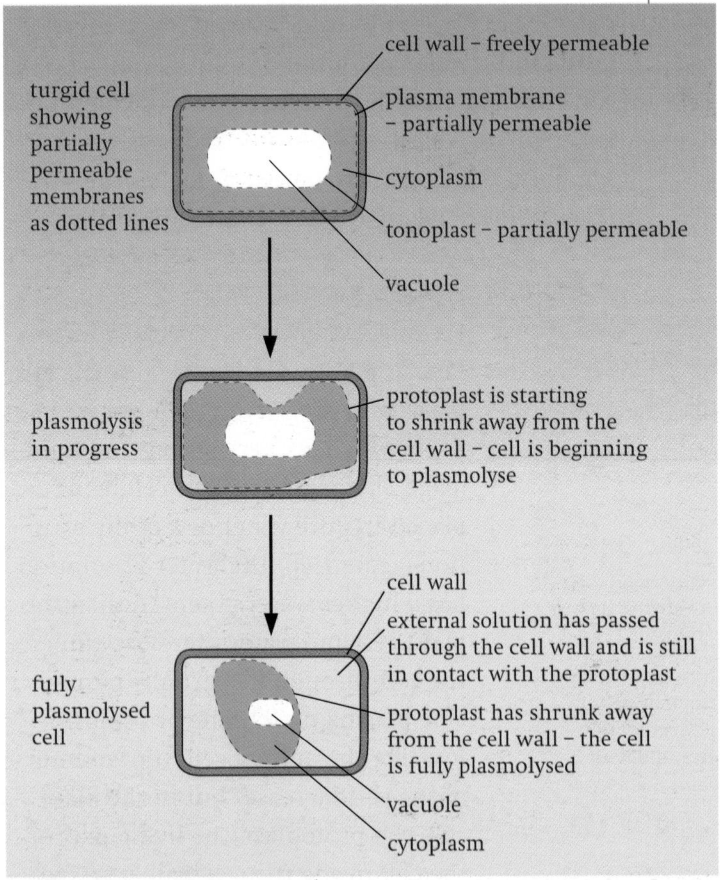

cell wall – freely permeable

turgid cell showing partially permeable membranes as dotted lines

plasma membrane – partially permeable

cytoplasm

tonoplast – partially permeable

vacuole

plasmolysis in progress

protoplast is starting to shrink away from the cell wall – cell is beginning to plasmolyse

cell wall

external solution has passed through the cell wall and is still in contact with the protoplast

fully plasmolysed cell

protoplast has shrunk away from the cell wall – the cell is fully plasmolysed

vacuole

cytoplasm

● **Figure 4.8** How plasmolysis occurs.

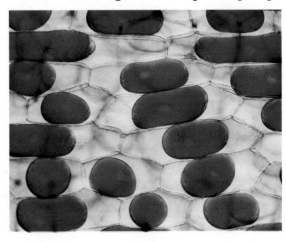

● **Figure 4.9** Light micrograph of red onion cells that have plasmolysed.

of epidermis peeled from rhubarb petioles or from the swollen storage leaves of onion bulbs and placed in a range of sucrose solutions of different concentration (*figure 4.9*).

SAQ 4.4

Two neighbouring plant cells are shown in the diagram.

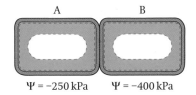

a In which direction would there be net movement of water molecules?

b Explain what is meant by *net movement*.

c Explain your answer to **a**.

d Explain what would happen if both cells were placed in (i) pure water, (ii) a $1\,mol\,dm^{-3}$ sucrose solution ($\psi = -3510\,kPa$).

SAQ 4.5

Figure 4.8 shows a phenomenon called plasmolysis. Why can plasmolysis not take place in an animal cell?

Active transport

If the concentration of particular ions, such as potassium and chloride, inside cells is measured it is often found that they are 10–20 times more concentrated inside than outside. In other words, a concentration gradient exists with a lower concentration outside and a higher concentration inside the cell. Since the ions inside the cell originally came from the external solution, diffusion cannot be responsible for this gradient because, as we have seen, ions diffuse from high concentration to low concentration. The ions must therefore accumulate *against* a concentration gradient.

The process responsible is called **active transport**. Like facilitated diffusion, it is achieved by special transport proteins, each of which is specific for a particular type of molecule or ion. However, unlike facilitated diffusion, active transport requires energy because movement occurs *up* a concentration gradient. The energy is supplied by the molecule ATP which is produced during respiration inside the cell. The energy is used to make the transport protein (sometimes called a **carrier protein**) change its 3D shape, transferring the molecules or ions across the membrane in the process (*figure 4.10*). The analogy of a 'kissing gate' can be used to imagine this: there is no direct route through the protein in one step; the 'gate' can only open to the far side once a molecule has entered the near side.

Active transport can therefore be defined as **the energy-consuming transport of molecules or ions across a membrane against a concentration gradient** (from a lower to a higher concentration) **made possible by transferring energy from respiration**. It can occur either into or out of the cell, depending on the particular molecules or ions and transport protein involved.

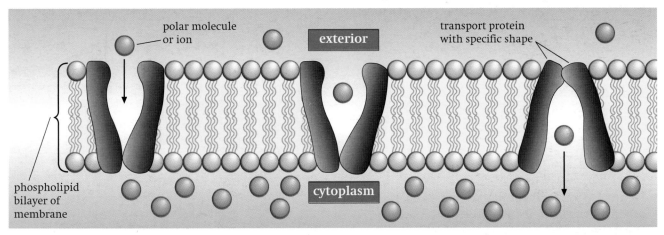

● **Figure 4.10** Changes in the shape of a transport protein during active transport. Here, molecules or ions are being pumped *into* the cell.

Active transport is important in reabsorption in the kidneys where certain useful molecules and ions have to be reabsorbed into the blood after filtration into the kidney tubules. It is also involved in the absorption of some products of digestion from the gut. In plants, active transport is used to load sugar from the photosynthesising cells of leaves into the phloem tissue for transport around the plant (chapter 10), and to load inorganic ions from the soil into root hairs (page 63).

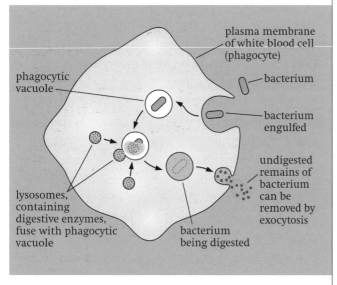

● **Figure 4.11a** Stages in phagocytosis of a bacterium by a white blood cell.

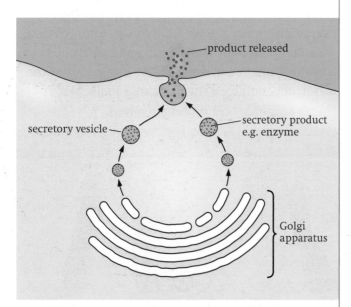

● **Figure 4.11b** Exocytosis in a secretory cell. If the product being secreted is a protein, the Golgi apparatus is often involved in chemically modifying the protein before it is secreted, as in the secretion of digestive enzymes by the pancreas.

Bulk transport

So far we have been looking at ways in which *individual* molecules or ions cross membranes. Mechanisms also exist for the bulk transport of large quantities of materials into cells (endocytosis) or out of cells (exocytosis).

Endocytosis involves the engulfing of the material by the plasma membrane to form a small sac, or 'endocytotic vacuole'. It takes two forms:

■ **phagocytosis** or 'cell eating' – this is the bulk uptake of solid material. Cells specialising in this are called **phagocytes**. The process is called **phagocytosis** and the vacuoles **phagocytic vacuoles**. An example is the engulfing of bacteria by certain white blood cells (*figure 4.11a*). Also see chapter 16.

■ **pinocytosis** or 'cell drinking' – this is the bulk uptake of liquid. The small vacuoles (vesicles) formed are often extremely small, in which case the process is called **micropinocytosis**. The human egg cell takes up nutrients from cells that surround it (the follicle) by pinocytosis.

Exocytosis is the reverse of endocytosis and is the process by which materials are removed from cells (*figure 4.11a* and *b*). It happens, for example, in the secretion of digestive enzymes from cells of the pancreas (*figure 4.11c*). Secretory vesicles carry the enzymes to the cell surface and release their contents. Plant cells use exocytosis to get their cell wall building materials to the outside of the plasma membrane.

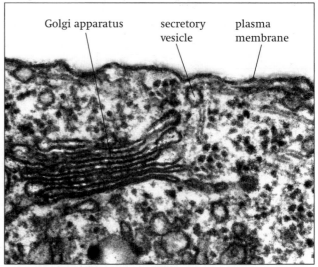

● **Figure 4.11c** EM of pancreatic acinar cell secreting protein.

Exchange surfaces

We have seen how substances may pass across membranes into and out of *cells* and *organelles* by a variety of passive and active processes. Substances such as gases, water and nutrients also pass into and out of whole *organisms*. We will look at two examples.

Gaseous exchange in mammalian lungs

Most organisms need a supply of oxygen for respiration. In single-celled organisms, the oxygen simply diffuses from the fluid outside the cell, through the plasma membrane and into the cytoplasm. In a multicellular organism such as a human, however, most of the cells are a considerable distance away from the external environment from which the oxygen is obtained. Multicellular organisms therefore usually have a specialised **gaseous exchange surface** where oxygen from the external environment can diffuse into the body, and carbon dioxide can diffuse out. In humans, the gaseous exchange surface is the **alveoli** in the lungs. *Figure 4.12* shows the distribution of alveoli in the lungs and their structure. Although each individual alveolus is tiny, they collectively have a

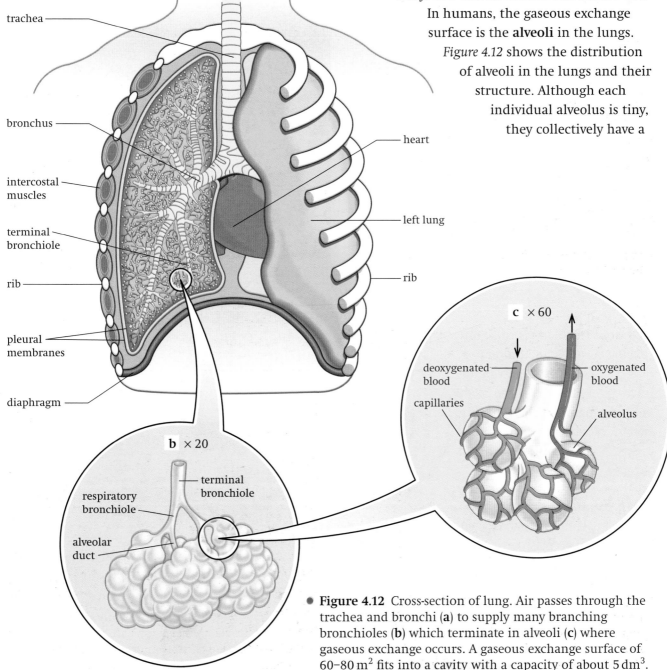

• **Figure 4.12** Cross-section of lung. Air passes through the trachea and bronchi (**a**) to supply many branching bronchioles (**b**) which terminate in alveoli (**c**) where gaseous exchange occurs. A gaseous exchange surface of 60–80 m² fits into a cavity with a capacity of about 5 dm³.

huge surface area, probably totalling around 70 m² in an adult. This increases the number of oxygen and carbon dioxide molecules that can diffuse through the surface at any one moment and so speeds up the rate of gaseous exchange.

The alveoli have extremely thin walls, each consisting of a single layer of squamous epithelial cells (*figure 1.26*) no more than 0.5 μm thick. Pressed closely against them are blood capillaries, also with very thin single-celled walls. The thinness of this barrier ensures that oxygen and carbon dioxide molecules can diffuse very quickly across it.

You will remember that diffusion is the net movement of molecules or ions down a concentration gradient. So, for gaseous exchange to take place rapidly, a steep concentration gradient must be maintained. This is done by breathing, and by the movement of the blood. Breathing brings supplies of fresh air into the lungs, with a relatively high oxygen concentration and a relatively low carbon dioxide concentration. Blood is brought to the lungs with a lower concentration of oxygen and a higher concentration of carbon dioxide than the air in the alveoli. Oxygen therefore diffuses down its concentration gradient from the air in the alveoli to the blood, and carbon dioxide diffuses down its concentration gradient in the opposite direction. The blood is constantly flowing through and out of the lungs so, as the oxygenated blood leaves, more deoxygenated blood enters to maintain the concentration gradients with each new breath. You can read more about this in chapters 8, 9 and 13.

SAQ 4.6 _____

How many times does an oxygen molecule cross a plasma membrane as it moves from the air into a red blood cell?

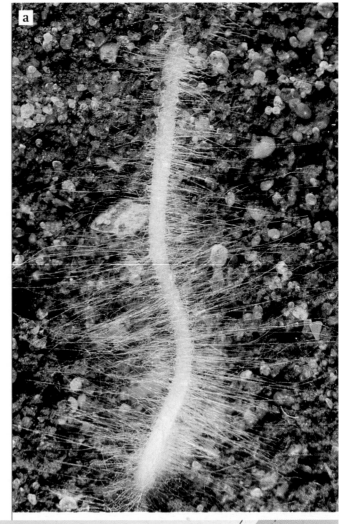

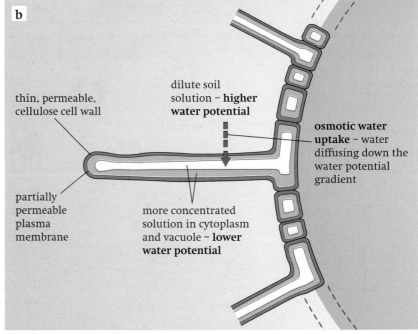

thin, permeable, cellulose cell wall

dilute soil solution – **higher water potential**

osmotic water uptake – water diffusing down the water potential gradient

partially permeable plasma membrane

more concentrated solution in cytoplasm and vacuole – **lower water potential**

● **Figure 4.13 a** A root of a young radish plant showing the root hairs. **b** Water uptake by a root hair cell. Mineral ions are also taken up but by active transport against the concentration gradient via carrier proteins.

Uptake of mineral ions in a plant root

A quite different specialised exchange surface is the **root hairs** of a flowering plant. Root hairs are very thin extensions of the cells that make up the outer layer, or **epidermis**, of a root. Each root hair is about 200–250 μm across. There may be thousands of them on each tiny branch of a root, so together they provide an enormous surface area that is in contact with the soil surrounding the root (*figure 4.13*).

Soil is made up of particles of minerals and humus. In between these particles are spaces that are usually filled with air. Unless the soil is extremely dry, there is a thin layer of water coating each soil particle. The root hairs make contact with water, and absorb it by osmosis. The water moves in because there is a lower concentration of solutes in the water in the soil than there is inside the root hair cell. The water potential outside the root hair is therefore higher than the water potential inside it, and water moves passively down the water potential gradient into the cells.

Mineral ions are also absorbed from the soil into root hair cells. If there is a higher concentration of a particular ion outside the root hair cell than inside it, then it can be taken up passively, by facilitated diffusion. More usually, however, the plant requires ions that are present in relatively low concentrations in the soil, while its cells already contain a higher concentration of that ion. In that case, the ions will be taken up by active transport, through carrier proteins, using energy to move them against their concentration gradient. Note that the cell wall provides absolutely no barrier to the diffusion of water molecules or mineral ions – they are all able to pass through it quite freely.

SAQ 4.7

Alveoli and root hairs are specialised exchange surfaces. What features do they share? How do these features help to increase the rate of exchange of substances across them?

SUMMARY

◆ The plasma membrane controls exchange between the cell and its environment. Special transport proteins are sometimes involved.

◆ Within cells, membranes allow compartmentalisation and division of labour to occur, within membrane-bound organelles such as the nucleus, ER and Golgi apparatus.

◆ Some chemical reactions take place on membranes as in photosynthesis and respiration. Membranes also contain receptor sites for hormones and neurotransmitters; possess cell recognition markers, such as antigens; and may contain enzymes, as with microvilli on epithelial cells in the gut.

◆ Diffusion is the net movement of molecules or ions from a region of their higher concentration to one of lower concentration. Oxygen and carbon dioxide cross membranes by diffusion through the phospholipid bilayer. Diffusion of ions and larger polar molecules through membranes is allowed by transport proteins.

◆ Water moves from regions of higher water potential to regions of lower water potential. When this takes place through a partially permeable membrane this diffusion is called osmosis. Pure water has a water potential of zero. Adding solute reduces the water potential by an amount known as the solute potential, which has a negative value. Adding pressure to a solution increases the water potential by an amount known as the pressure potential, which has a positive value.

◆ In dilute solutions, animal cells burst as water moves into the cytoplasm from the solution. In dilute solutions, a plant cell does not burst because the cell wall provides resistance to prevent it expanding. The pressure that builds up is the pressure potential. A plant cell in this state is turgid. In concentrated solutions, animal cells shrink whilst in plant cells the protoplast shrinks away from the cell wall in a process known as plasmolysis.

◆ Some ions and molecules move across membranes by active transport, against the concentration gradient. This needs a carrier protein and ATP to provide energy.

◆ Exocytosis and endocytosis involve the formation of vacuoles to move larger quantities of materials respectively out of, or into, cells by bulk transport. There are two types of endocytosis, namely phagocytosis and pinocytosis.

◆ Multicellular organisms often have surfaces that are specialised to allow exchange of substances to take place between their bodies and the environment. These include exchange surfaces such as alveoli in human lungs and root hairs of plants, which take up water and inorganic ions from the soil.

Questions

1   Explain how the properties of phospholipids are important in the formation of membranes.

2   Explain why plasma membranes are impermeable to most biological molecules.

3   Discuss the roles played by proteins in membranes.

4   Explain, with reference to suitable examples, what is meant by
    a facilitated diffusion and
    b active transport.

5   Certain cells of the pancreas make and secrete digestive enzymes. The following sequence of organelles is involved: ribosomes, ER, Golgi apparatus, Golgi vesicles. Summarise the role of these organelles and describe the process of exocytosis by which the enzymes are released.

CHAPTER 5

Genetic control of protein structure and function

By the end of this chapter you should be able to:

1 describe the structures of DNA and RNA, including the importance of base pairing and hydrogen bonding;

2 explain how DNA replicates semi-conservatively during interphase and interpret experimental evidence for this process;

3 know that a gene is part of a DNA molecule, made up of a sequence of nucleotides which codes for the construction of a polypeptide;

4 describe the way in which the nucleotide sequence codes for the amino acid sequence in the polypeptide;

5 describe how transcription and translation take place during protein synthesis, including the roles of messenger RNA, transfer RNA and ribosomes;

6 know that, as enzymes are proteins, their synthesis is controlled by DNA;

7 outline the principles of gene manipulation by biotechnology (genetic engineering);

8 describe how bacteria have been genetically modified to synthesise human insulin and outline the production of human factor VIII from genetically modified animal cells.

If you were asked to design a molecule which could act as the genetic material in living things, where would you start?

One of the features of the 'genetic molecule' would have to be the ability to **carry instructions** – a sort of blueprint – for the construction and behaviour of cells, and the way in which they grow together to form a complete living organism. Another would be the **ability to be copied** perfectly, over and over again, so that whenever the nucleus of a cell divides it can pass on an exact copy of each 'genetic molecule' to the nuclei of each of its 'daughter' cells.

Until the mid 1940s, biologists assumed that the 'genetic molecule' must be a protein. Only proteins were thought to be complex enough to be able to carry the huge number of instructions which would be necessary to make such a complicated

structure as a living organism. But during the 1940s and 1950s a variety of evidence came to light that proved beyond doubt that the 'genetic molecule' was not a protein at all, but DNA.

The structure of DNA and RNA

DNA stands for **deoxyribonucleic acid** and RNA for **ribonucleic acid**. As we saw in chapter 2, DNA and RNA, like proteins and polysaccharides, are **macromolecules** (page 22). They are also **polymers**, made up of many similar, smaller molecules joined into a long chain. The smaller molecules from which DNA and RNA molecules are made are **nucleotides**. DNA and RNA are therefore **polynucleotides**. They are often referred to simply as nucleic acids.

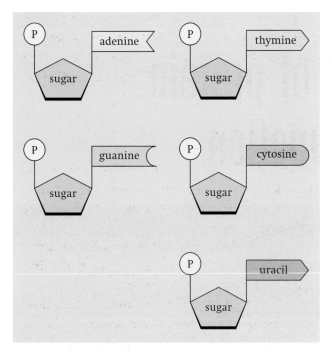

● **Figure 5.1** Nucleotides. A nucleotide is made of a nitrogen-containing base, a pentose sugar and a phosphate group ℗.

Nucleotides

Figure 5.1 shows the structure of nucleotides. Nucleotides are made up of three smaller components. These are:

■ a nitrogen-containing base;
■ a pentose sugar;
■ a phosphate group.

There are just five different nitrogen-containing bases found in DNA and RNA. In a DNA molecule there are four: **adenine**, **thymine**, **guanine** and **cytosine**. (Do not confuse adenine with adenosine which is part of the name of ATP – adenosine is adenine with a sugar joined to it; and don't confuse thymine with thiamine, which is a vitamin.) An RNA molecule also contains four bases, but the base thymine is never found. Instead, RNA molecules contain a base called **uracil**. These bases are often referred to by their first letters: **A**, **T**, **C**, **G** and **U**.

The pentose (5-carbon) sugar can be either **ribose** (in RNA) or **deoxyribose** (in DNA). As their

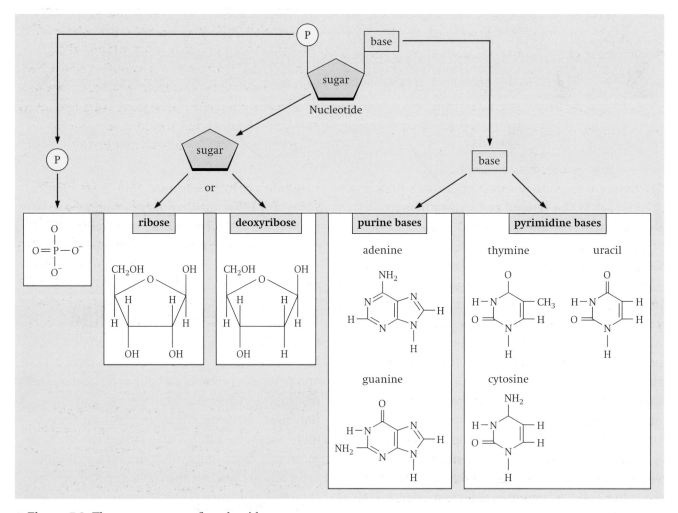

● **Figure 5.2** The components of nucleotides.

names suggest, deoxyribose is almost the same as ribose, except that it has one fewer oxygen atoms in its molecule.

Figure 5.1 shows the five different nucleotides from which DNA and RNA molecules can be built up. *Figure 5.2* shows the structure of their components in more detail; you do not need to remember these structures, but if you enjoy biochemistry you may find them interesting.

Polynucleotides

To form the polynucleotides DNA and RNA, many nucleotides are linked together into a long chain. This takes place inside the nucleus, during interphase of the cell cycle (page 83).

Figure 5.3a shows the structure of part of a polynucleotide strand. In both DNA and RNA it is formed of alternating sugars and phosphates linked together, with the bases projecting sideways.

DNA molecules are made of *two* polynucleotide strands lying side by side running in opposite directions. The two strands are held together by **hydrogen bonds** between the bases (*figure 5.3b* and *c*). The way the two strands line up is very precise.

The bases can be purines or pyrimidines. From *figure 5.2*, you will see that the two purine bases, adenine and guanine, are larger molecules than the two pyrimidines, cytosine and thymine. In a DNA molecule, there is just enough room between the two sugar–phosphate backbones for one purine and one pyrimidine molecule, so a purine in one strand must always be opposite a pyrimidine in the other. In fact, the pairing of the bases is even more precise than this. Adenine always pairs with thymine, while cytosine always pairs with guanine: **A** with **T**, **C** with **G**. This **complementary base pairing** is a very important feature of polynucleotides, as you will see later.

DNA is often referred to as the 'double helix'. This refers to the 3D shape that DNA molecules form (*figure 5.3d*). The hydrogen bonds linking the bases, and therefore holding the two strands together, can be broken relatively easily. This happens during DNA replication (copying) and also during protein synthesis (manufacture). As we shall see, this too is a very important feature of the DNA molecule, which enables it to perform its role in the cell.

RNA molecules, unlike DNA, remain as *single* strands of polynucleotide and can form a very different 3D structure. We will look at this later in the chapter when we consider protein synthesis.

DNA replication

We said at the beginning of this chapter that one of the features of the 'genetic molecule' would have to be the **ability to be copied** perfectly many times over.

It was not until 1953 that James Watson and Francis Crick used the results of work by Rosalind Franklin and others to work out the basic structure of the DNA molecule that we have just been looking at. To them, it was immediately obvious how this molecule could be copied perfectly, time and time again.

Watson and Crick suggested that the two strands of the DNA molecule could split apart. New nucleotides could then line up along each strand opposite their appropriate partners, and join up to form complementary strands along each half of the original molecule. The new DNA molecules would be just like the old ones, because each base would only pair with its complementary one. Each pair of strands could then wind up again into a double helix, exactly like the original one.

This idea proved to be correct. The process is shown in *figure 5.4*. This method of copying is called **semi-conservative replication**, because *half* of the original molecule is *kept* (conserved) in each of the new molecules. The experimental evidence for this process is described in the box on page 70.

DNA replication takes place when a cell is not dividing. This is in interphase in eukaryotic cells (chapter 6).

SAQ 5.1

a What other types of molecules, apart from nucleotides, are needed for DNA replication to take place? (Use *figure 5.4* to help you to answer this.) What does each of these molecules do?

b In what part of a eukaryotic cell does DNA replication take place?

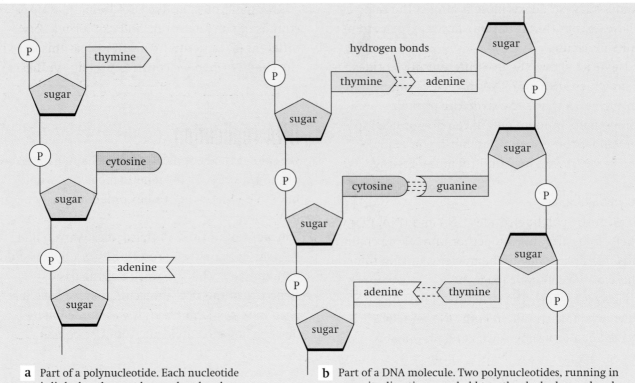

a Part of a polynucleotide. Each nucleotide is linked to the next by covalent bonds between their phosphates and sugars.

b Part of a DNA molecule. Two polynucleotides, running in opposite directions, are held together by hydrogen bonds between the bases. A links with T by two hydrogen bonds; C links with G by three hydrogen bonds. This is complementary base pairing.

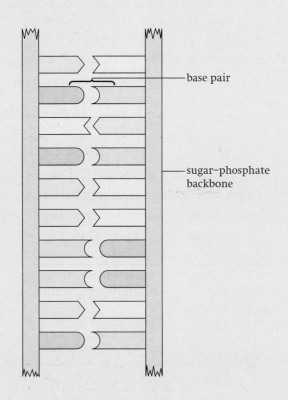

c A simplified diagram of a DNA molecule showing its backbone of alternating sugar–phosphate units, with the bases projecting into the centre creating base pairs.

d The DNA double helix.

● **Figure 5.3** The structure of DNA.

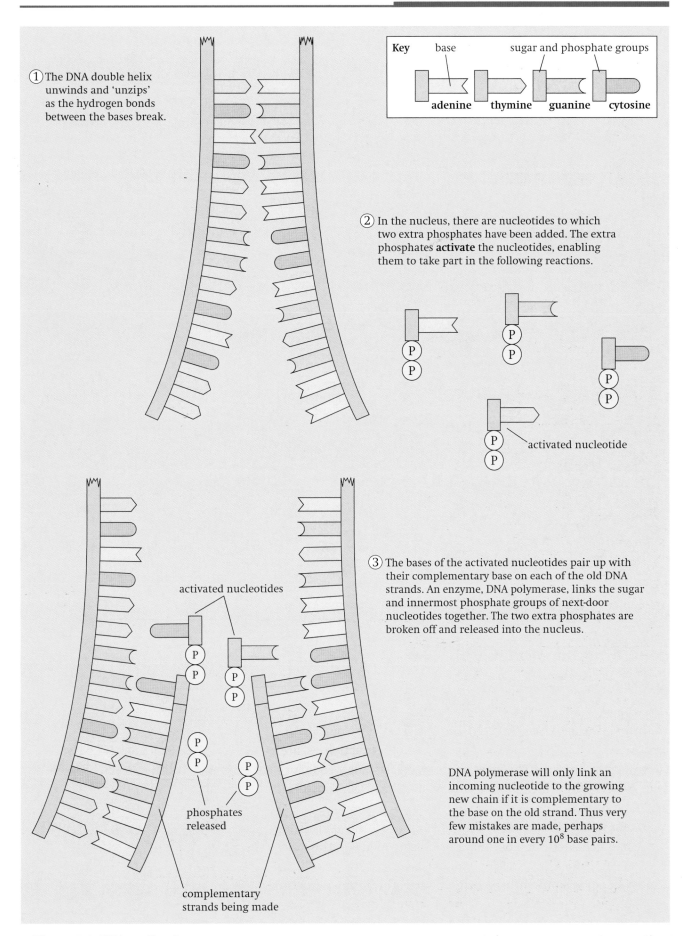

① The DNA double helix unwinds and 'unzips' as the hydrogen bonds between the bases break.

Key base   sugar and phosphate groups

adenine   thymine   guanine   cytosine

② In the nucleus, there are nucleotides to which two extra phosphates have been added. The extra phosphates **activate** the nucleotides, enabling them to take part in the following reactions.

activated nucleotide

activated nucleotides

phosphates released

complementary strands being made

③ The bases of the activated nucleotides pair up with their complementary base on each of the old DNA strands. An enzyme, DNA polymerase, links the sugar and innermost phosphate groups of next-door nucleotides together. The two extra phosphates are broken off and released into the nucleus.

DNA polymerase will only link an incoming nucleotide to the growing new chain if it is complementary to the base on the old strand. Thus very few mistakes are made, perhaps around one in every 10^8 base pairs.

● **Figure 5.4** DNA replication.

Experimental evidence for the semi-conservative replication of DNA

In the 1950s, no-one knew exactly how DNA replicated. Three possibilities were suggested:

- **conservative replication**, in which one completely new double helix would be made from the old one (*figure 5.5a*);
- **semi-conservative replication**, in which each new molecule would contain one old strand and one new one (*figure 5.5b*);
- **dispersive replication**, in which each new molecule would be made of old bits and new bits scattered randomly through the molecules (*figure 5.5c*).

Most people thought that semi-conservative replication was most likely, because they could see how it might work. However, to make sure, experiments were carried out in 1958 by Mathew Meselsohn and Franklin Stahl in America.

They used the bacterium *Escherichia coli* (*E. coli* for short), a common, usually harmless, bacterium which lives in the human alimentary canal. They grew populations of the bacterium in a food source that contained ammonium chloride as a source of nitrogen.

The experiment relied on the variation in structure of nitrogen atoms. All nitrogen atoms contain 7 protons, but the number of neutrons can vary. Most nitrogen atoms have 7 neutrons, so their relative atomic mass (the total mass of all the protons and neutrons in an atom) is 14.

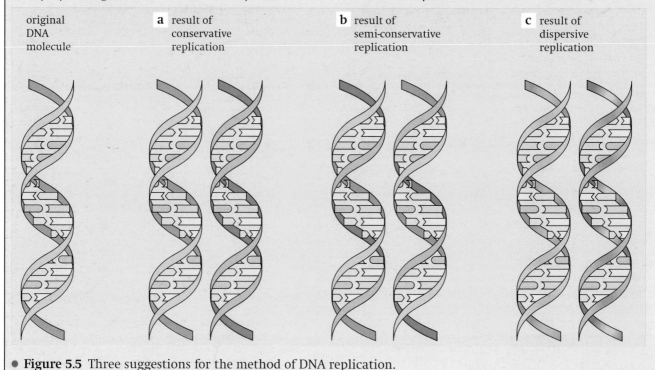

original DNA molecule

a result of conservative replication

b result of semi-conservative replication

c result of dispersive replication

● **Figure 5.5** Three suggestions for the method of DNA replication.

DNA, RNA and protein synthesis

DNA controls protein synthesis

How can a single type of molecule like DNA control all the activities of a cell? The answer is very logical. All chemical reactions in cells, and therefore all their activities, are controlled by enzymes. Enzymes are proteins. DNA is a code for proteins, controlling which proteins are made. Thus DNA controls the cell's activities.

Protein molecules are made up of strings of amino acids. The shape and behaviour of a protein molecule depends on the exact sequence of these amino acids, that is its primary structure (page 32). DNA controls protein structure by determining the exact order in which the amino acids join together when proteins are made in a cell.

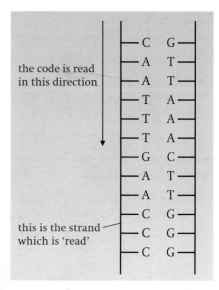

the code is read in this direction

C G
A T
A T
T A
T A
T A
G C
A T
A T
C G
C G
C G

this is the strand which is 'read'

● **Figure 5.7** A length of DNA coding for four amino acids.

Some nitrogen atoms have 8 neutrons, so their relative atomic mass is 15. These two forms are said to be **isotopes** of nitrogen.

The nitrogen atoms in the ammonium chloride that Meselsohn and Stahl supplied to the bacteria were the heavy isotope, nitrogen-15 (^{15}N). The bacteria used the ^{15}N to make their DNA. They were left in it long enough for them to divide many times, so that nearly all of their DNA contained only ^{15}N atoms, not nitrogen-14 (^{14}N). This DNA would be heavier than 'normal' DNA containing ^{14}N. Some of these bacteria were then transferred to a food source in which the nitrogen atoms were all ^{14}N. Some were left there for just long enough for their DNA to replicate once – about 50 minutes. Others were left long enough for their DNA to replicate two, three or more times.

DNA was then extracted from each group of bacteria. The samples were placed into a solution of caesium chloride and spun in a centrifuge. The heavier the DNA was, the closer to the bottom of the tube it came to rest.

Figure 5.6 shows the results of Meselsohn and Stahl's experiment.

SAQ 5.2

Looking at *figure 5.6*:

a Assuming that the DNA has reproduced semi-conservatively, explain why the band of DNA in tube 2 is higher than that in tube 1.

b What would you expect to see in tube 2 if the DNA had replicated conservatively?

c What would you expect to see in tube 2 if the DNA had replicated dispersively?

d Which is the first tube that provides evidence that the DNA has reproduced semi-conservatively and not dispersively? Explain your answer.

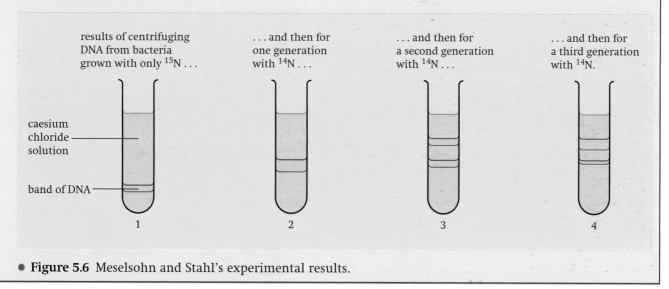

● **Figure 5.6** Meselsohn and Stahl's experimental results.

The triplet code

The sequence of bases or nucleotides in a DNA molecule is a code for the sequence of amino acids in a polypeptide. *Figure 5.7* shows a very short length of a DNA molecule, just enough to code for four amino acids.

The code is a three-letter, or **triplet**, code. Each sequence of three bases stands for one amino acid. The sequence is always read in one particular direction and on only one of the two strands of the DNA molecule. In this case, assume that this is the strand on the left of the diagram. Reading from the top of the left-hand strand, the code is:

C-A-A   which stands for the amino acid valine
T-T-T   which stands for the amino acid lysine
G-A-A   which stands for the amino acid leucine

C-C-C   which stands for the amino acid glycine

So this short piece of DNA carries the instruction to the cell: 'Make a chain of amino acids in the sequence valine, lysine, leucine and glycine'. The complete set of codes is shown in appendix 2.

SAQ 5.3

There are 20 different amino acids which cells use for making proteins.

a How many different amino acids could the triplet code code for? (Remember that there are four possible bases, and that the code is always read in just one direction on the DNA strand.)

b Suggest how the 'spare' triplets might be used.

c Explain why it could not be a two-letter code.

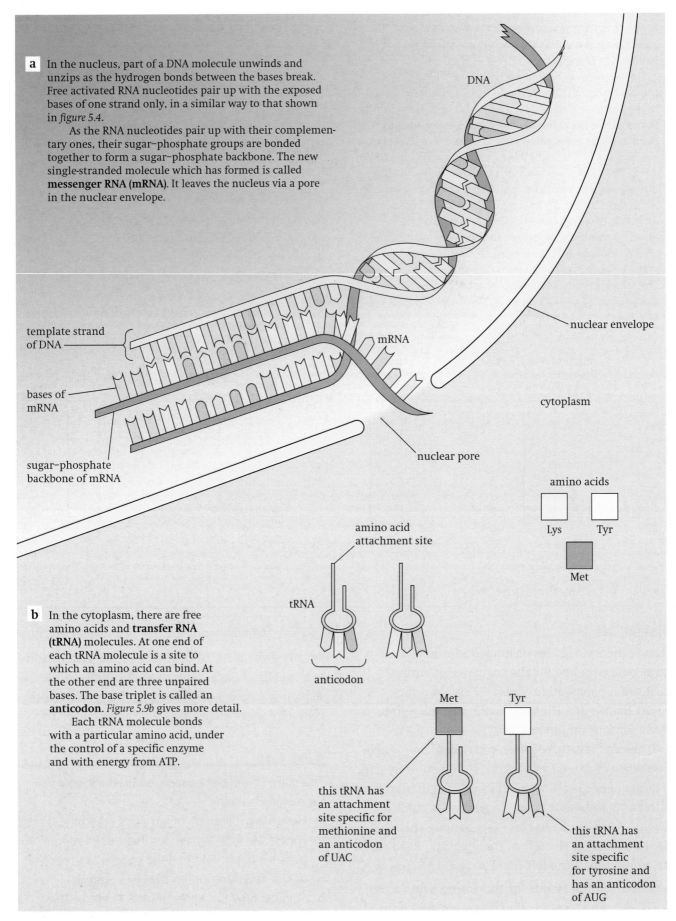

a In the nucleus, part of a DNA molecule unwinds and unzips as the hydrogen bonds between the bases break. Free activated RNA nucleotides pair up with the exposed bases of one strand only, in a similar way to that shown in *figure 5.4*.

As the RNA nucleotides pair up with their complementary ones, their sugar–phosphate groups are bonded together to form a sugar–phosphate backbone. The new single-stranded molecule which has formed is called **messenger RNA (mRNA)**. It leaves the nucleus via a pore in the nuclear envelope.

DNA

template strand of DNA

bases of mRNA

sugar–phosphate backbone of mRNA

mRNA

nuclear envelope

cytoplasm

nuclear pore

amino acids

Lys   Tyr

Met

amino acid attachment site

tRNA

anticodon

b In the cytoplasm, there are free amino acids and **transfer RNA (tRNA)** molecules. At one end of each tRNA molecule is a site to which an amino acid can bind. At the other end are three unpaired bases. The base triplet is called an **anticodon**. *Figure 5.9b* gives more detail.

Each tRNA molecule bonds with a particular amino acid, under the control of a specific enzyme and with energy from ATP.

Met   Tyr

this tRNA has an attachment site specific for methionine and an anticodon of UAC

this tRNA has an attachment site specific for tyrosine and has an anticodon of AUG

● **Figure 5.8** Protein synthesis – transcription.

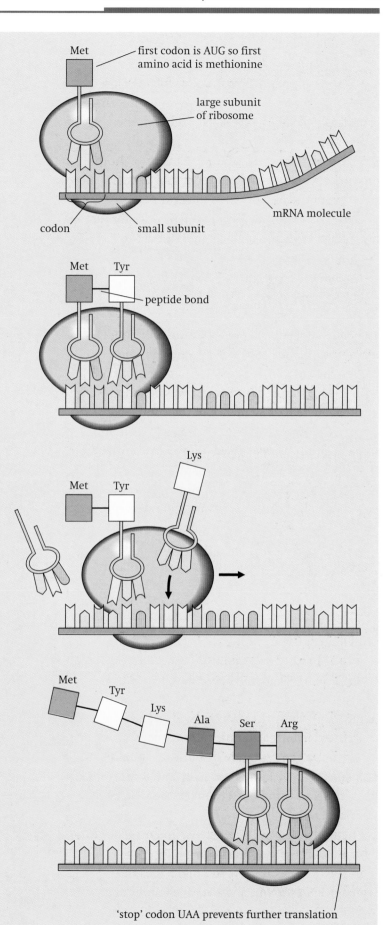

c Meanwhile, also in the cytoplasm, the mRNA molecule attaches to a ribosome. Ribosomes are made of ribosomal RNA (rRNA) and protein and contain a small and a large subunit. The mRNA binds to the small subunit. Six bases at a time are exposed to the large subunit.

The first three exposed bases, or **codon**, are *always* AUG. A tRNA molecule with the complementary anticodon, UAC, forms hydrogen bonds with this codon. This tRNA molecule has the amino acid methionine attached to it.

d A second tRNA molecule bonds with the next three exposed bases. This one brings a different amino acid. The two amino acids are held closely together, and a peptide bond is formed between them. This reaction is catalysed by the enzyme peptidyl transferase, which is found in the small subunit of the ribosome.

e The ribosome now moves along the mRNA, 'reading' the next three bases on the ribosome. A third tRNA molecule brings a third amino acid, which joins to the second one. The first tRNA leaves.

f The polypeptide chain continues to grow, until a 'stop' codon is exposed on the ribosome. This is UAA, UAC or UGA.

● **Figure 5.8 continued** Protein synthesis – translation.

Genes and genomes

DNA molecules can be enormous. The bacterium *E. coli* has just one DNA molecule which is four million base pairs long. There is enough information here to code for several thousand proteins. The total DNA of a human cell is estimated to be about 3×10^9 base pairs long. However, it is thought that only 3% of this DNA actually codes for protein. The function of the remainder is uncertain.

A part of a DNA molecule which codes for just one polypeptide is called a **gene**. One DNA molecule contains many genes. In humans, it is estimated that there are about 140 000 genes.

The total set of genes in a cell is called the **genome**. The genome is the total information in one cell. Since all cells in the same individual contain the same information, the genome represents the genetic code of that organism.

In 1990, an ambitious project was begun to work out the entire base sequence of the complete human genome. It is called the Human Genome Project, and is being carried out in laboratories all over the world. As there are about 3 billion bases in the human genome, you can see that this is a huge task. It is hoped that this information will help us to identify every human gene and then to find out how at least some of them affect human health. You can read more about this project in chapter 11.

Protein synthesis

The code on the DNA molecule is used to determine how the polypeptide molecule is constructed. *Figure 5.8* describes the process in detail, but briefly the process is as follows.

In the nucleus, a complementary copy of the code from a gene is made by building a molecule of a *different* type of nucleic acid, called **messenger RNA (mRNA)**, using one strand of the DNA as a template.

The mRNA leaves the nucleus, and attaches to a **ribosome** in the cytoplasm (page 12).

In the cytoplasm there are molecules of **transfer RNA (tRNA)**. These have a triplet of bases at one end and a region where an amino acid can attach at the other. There are at least 20 different sorts of tRNA molecules, each with a particular

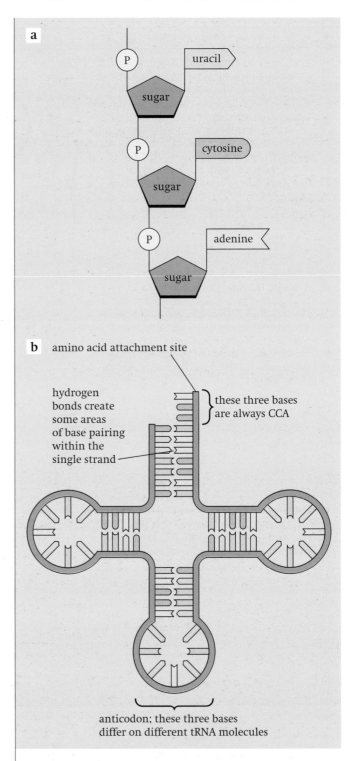

● **Figure 5.9** RNA.
a Part of a messenger RNA (mRNA) molecule.
b Transfer RNA (tRNA). The molecule is a single-stranded polynucleotide, folded into a clover-leaf shape. Transfer RNA molecules with different anticodons are recognised by different enzymes, which load them with their appropriate amino acid.

SAQ 5.4

Summarise the differences between the structures of DNA and RNA.

triplet of bases at one end and able to attach to a specific amino acid at the other (*figure 5.9*).

The tRNA molecules pick up their specific amino acids from the cytoplasm and bring them to the mRNA on the ribosome. The triplet of bases (an **anticodon**) of each tRNA links up with a complementary triplet (a **codon**) on the mRNA molecule. Two tRNA molecules fit onto the ribosome at any one time. This brings two amino acids side by side and a peptide bond is formed between them (page 31). Usually, several ribosomes work on the same mRNA strand at the same time. They are visible, using an electron microscope, as **polyribosomes** (*figure 5.10*).

So the base sequence on the DNA molecule determines the base sequence on the mRNA, which determines which tRNA molecules can link up with them. Since each type of tRNA molecule is specific for just one amino acid, this determines the sequence in which the amino acids are linked together as the polypeptide molecule is made.

The first stage in this process, that is the making of a mRNA molecule which carries a complementary copy of the code from part of the DNA molecule, is called **transcription**, because this is when the DNA code is **transcribed**, or copied, on to an mRNA molecule. The last stage is called **translation**, because this is when the DNA code is **translated** into an amino acid sequence.

SAQ 5.5

Draw a simple flow diagram to illustrate the important stages in protein synthesis.

Gene technology

The structure of DNA, and the way in which it codes for protein synthesis, was worked out during the 1950s and 1960s. Since then, this knowledge has developed to the level at which we can change the DNA in a cell, and so change the proteins which that cell synthesises. This is called genetic engineering or **gene technology**.

Insulin production

To explain the principles of gene technology, we will look at one example, that is the use of genetically modified bacteria to mass-produce human insulin.

One form of diabetes mellitus is caused by the inability of the pancreas to produce insulin. People with this disease need regular injections of insulin which, until recently, was extracted from the pancreases of pigs or cattle. This extraction was expensive, and many people did not like the idea of using insulin from an animal. Moreover, insulin from pigs or cattle is not identical to human insulin and so can have side-effects.

In the 1970s, biotechnology companies began to work on the idea of inserting the gene for human insulin into a bacterium, and then using this bacterium to make insulin. They tried several different approaches, finally succeeding in the early 1980s.

The procedure had several stages as described below and shown in *figure 5.11*.

Isolating the insulin gene

Insulin is a small protein. The first task was to isolate the gene coding for human insulin from all the rest of the DNA in a human cell. In this

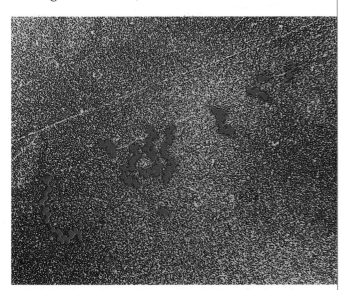

• **Figure 5.10** Protein synthesis in a bacterium. In bacteria, there is no nucleus, so protein synthesis can begin as soon as some mRNA has been made. Here, the long thread running from left to right is DNA. Nine mRNA molecules are being made, using this DNA as a template. Each mRNA molecule is immediately being read by ribosomes, which you can see as red blobs attached along the mRNAs. The mRNA strand at the left hand end is much longer than the one at the right, indicating that the mRNA is being synthesised working along the DNA molecule from right to left. (× 54 000)

Isolation of human gene

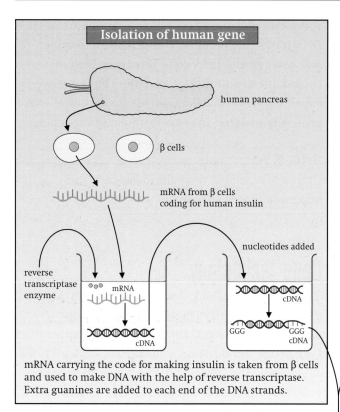

mRNA carrying the code for making insulin is taken from β cells and used to make DNA with the help of reverse transcriptase. Extra guanines are added to each end of the DNA strands.

Preparation of vector

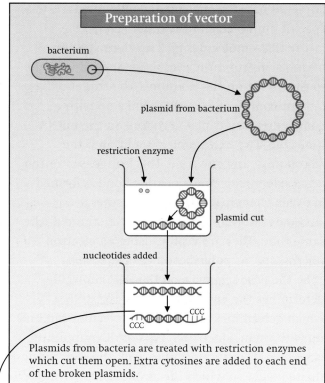

Plasmids from bacteria are treated with restriction enzymes which cut them open. Extra cytosines are added to each end of the broken plasmids.

Formation of recombinant DNA

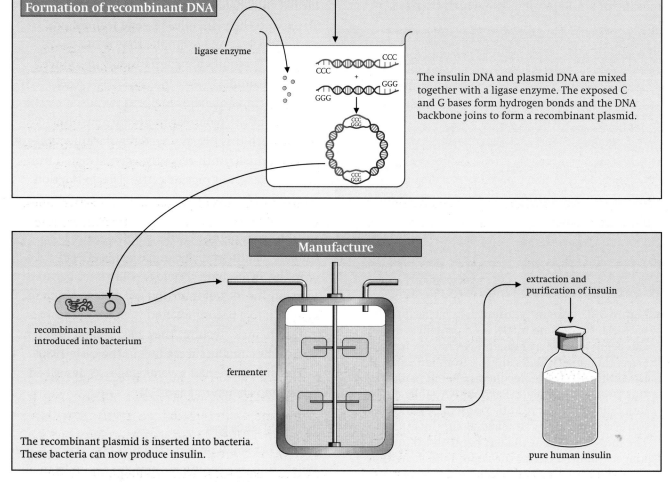

The insulin DNA and plasmid DNA are mixed together with a ligase enzyme. The exposed C and G bases form hydrogen bonds and the DNA backbone joins to form a recombinant plasmid.

Manufacture

The recombinant plasmid is inserted into bacteria. These bacteria can now produce insulin.

● **Figure 5.11** Producing insulin from genetically modified bacteria.

instance, there were problems in doing this directly. Instead, mRNA carrying the code for making insulin was extracted from the cells in a human pancreas that synthesise insulin, called β cells.

The mRNA was then incubated with an enzyme called **reverse transcriptase** which comes from a special group of viruses called **retroviruses**. As the name suggests, this enzyme does something which does not normally happen in human cells – it reverses transcription, causing DNA to be made from RNA. Complementary DNA (cDNA) molecules were formed from the mRNA from the pancreas cells. First, single-stranded molecules were formed, which were then converted to double-stranded DNA. These DNA molecules carried the code for making insulin; that is, they were insulin genes.

In order to enable these insulin genes to stick onto other DNA at a later stage in the procedure, they were given 'sticky ends'. This was done by adding lengths of single-stranded DNA made up of guanine nucleotides to each end, using enzymes.

Inserting the gene into a vector

In order to get the human insulin gene into a bacterium a go-between, called a **vector**, has to be used. In this instance the vector was a **plasmid**. A plasmid is a small, circular piece of DNA which can be found in many bacteria (page 16). Plasmids are able to insert themselves into bacteria so, if you can put your piece of human DNA into a plasmid, the plasmid can take it into a bacterium. (Viruses can act in a similar way to plasmids.)

To get the plasmids, the bacteria containing them were treated with enzymes to dissolve their cell walls. They were then centrifuged, so that the relatively large bacterial chromosomes were separated from the much smaller plasmids and the cell debris. The circular DNA molecule making up the plasmid was then cut open using a **restriction enzyme**. Once again, sticky ends were added, but this time the nucleotides used to make these single strands contained cytosine.

The cut plasmid and the cut human DNA were mixed together, and the C and G bases on their sticky ends paired up. The nucleotide backbones were linked using an enzyme called **DNA ligase**, so that the human insulin gene became part of the plasmid. This created **recombinant** DNA.

Inserting the gene into the bacteria

The plasmids were now mixed with bacteria. In the case of insulin, the bacterium was *E. coli*. A small proportion, perhaps 1%, of the bacteria took up the plasmids containing the insulin gene. These bacteria were separated from the others using antibiotic resistance provided by another gene which was introduced at the same time as the human insulin gene. When the bacteria were treated with antibiotic, only the ones containing the resistance gene (and therefore the insulin gene) survived.

The genetically modified bacteria are now cultured on a large scale. They secrete insulin, which is extracted, purified and sold for use by people with diabetes. It is called recombinant insulin because it is produced by organisms containing a combination of their own and human DNA.

Other uses of gene technology

Insulin production was one of the earliest success stories for gene technology. Since then, there have been many others. Other human protein hormones have been synthesised, for example human growth hormone. Enzymes are made for use in the food industry, for example, or in biological washing powders.

Gene technology can introduce genes into any organism, not just bacteria. Recent developments give hope for the success of **gene therapy** in humans, in which 'good' copies of genes are inserted into cells of people with 'defective' ones. This could be used to treat genetic diseases (see chapter 11). However, at the moment there are problems in getting the genes into enough cells for there to be any useful effect.

Genetically modified hamster cells are used by several companies to produce a protein called **human factor VIII**. This protein is essential for blood clotting, and people who cannot make it suffer from haemophilia. The human gene for making factor VIII has been inserted into hamster kidney and ovary cells that are then cultured in fermenters. The cells constantly produce factor VIII, which is extracted and purified before being used to treat people with haemophilia. These people need regular injections of factor VIII, which, before the availability of the recombinant factor VIII, came from donated blood. This carried risks of infection, such as with HIV (see chapter 15). Recombinant factor VIII avoids such problems.

Genes can be inserted into plants, too. Genes conferring resistance to pests can be extracted from a wild plant and inserted into a crop plant,

for example. However, people who are the possible future consumers of foods derived from such crops are not at all satisfied that this new technology is entirely safe (either for other organisms in the environment or for themselves) or desirable. There has therefore been considerable opposition to field trials of genetically modified crops.

SUMMARY

◆ DNA and RNA are polynucleotides, made up of long chains of nucleotides. A nucleotide contains a pentose sugar, a phosphate group and a nitrogen-containing base. A DNA molecule consists of two polynucleotide chains, linked by hydrogen bonds between bases. Adenine always pairs with thymine, and cytosine with guanine. RNA, which comes in several different forms, has only one polynucleotide chain, although this may be twisted back on itself, as in tRNA. In RNA, the base thymine is replaced by uracil.

◆ DNA molecules replicate during interphase. The hydrogen bonds between the bases break, allowing free nucleotides to fall into position opposite their complementary ones on each strand of the original DNA molecule. Adjacent nucleotides are then linked, through their phosphates and sugars, to form new strands. Two complete new molecules are thus formed from one old one, each new molecule containing one old strand and one new.

◆ The sequence of bases (or nucleotides) on a DNA molecule codes for the sequence of

amino acids in a protein (or polypeptide). Each amino acid is coded for by three bases. A length of DNA coding for one complete protein or polypeptide is a gene.

◆ During protein synthesis, a complementary copy of the base sequence on a gene is made, by building a molecule of mRNA against one DNA strand. The mRNA then moves to a ribosome in the cytoplasm. tRNA molecules with complementary triplets of bases temporarily pair with the base triplets on mRNA, bringing appropriate amino acids. As two amino acids are held side by side, a peptide bond forms between them. The ribosome moves along the mRNA molecule, so that appropriate amino acids are gradually linked together, following the sequence laid down by the base sequence on the mRNA.

◆ DNA may be transferred from one species to another by means of gene technology. This technology has been used to produce bacteria that synthesise insulin, and mammalian cells that synthesise human factor VIII.

Questions

1 Discuss the ways in which the structure of DNA allows it to carry out its functions.

2 Search recent newspapers and scientific magazines (for example *New Scientist*) for current examples of gene technology in the news. With reference to one or more such examples, discuss:

● your own feelings towards the potential usefulness and harm which may result from gene technology;

● the level of understanding of journalists and members of the public concerning the science behind these issues.

CHAPTER 6

Nuclear division

By the end of this chapter you should be able to:

1 explain the need for the production of genetically identical cells within an organism, and hence for precise control of nuclear and cell division;

2 distinguish between haploid and diploid;

3 explain what is meant by homologous pairs of chromosomes;

4 describe how nuclear division comes before cell division and know that replication of DNA takes place during interphase;

5 describe, with the aid of diagrams, the behaviour of chromosomes during the mitotic cell cycle and the associated behaviour of the nuclear envelope, plasma membrane and centrioles;

6 name the main stages of mitosis;

7 explain that as a result of mitosis, growth, repair and asexual reproduction of living organisms is possible;

8 explain why gametes must be haploid and that this is achieved by meiosis (reduction division);

9 explain how cancers are a result of uncontrolled cell division and list factors that can increase the chances of cancerous growth.

All living organisms grow and reproduce. Since living organisms are made of cells, this means that cells must be able to grow and reproduce. Cells reproduce by dividing and passing on their genes (hereditary information) to 'daughter' cells. The process must be very precisely controlled so that no vital information is lost. We have seen how this is achieved at the molecular level (chapter 5). We shall now examine the cellular level, particularly in eukaryotes.

In chapter 1 we saw that one of the most conspicuous structures in eukaryotic cells is the nucleus. Its importance has been obvious ever since it was realised that the nucleus always divides before a cell divides. Each daughter cell therefore contains its own nucleus. This is important because the nucleus controls the cell's activities. It does this through the genetic

material DNA. In chapter 5, we saw how DNA is able to act as a set of instructions, or code, for life.

So, nuclear division combined with cell division allows cells, and therefore whole organisms, to reproduce themselves. It also allows multicellular organisms to grow. The cells in your body, for example, are all genetically identical (apart from the gametes); they were all derived from one cell, the zygote, which was the cell formed when two gametes from your parents fused.

The nucleus contains chromosomes

Just before a eukaryotic cell divides, a number of characteristic thread-like structures gradually become visible in the nucleus. They are easily seen because they stain intensely with particular stains. They were originally termed **chromosomes**

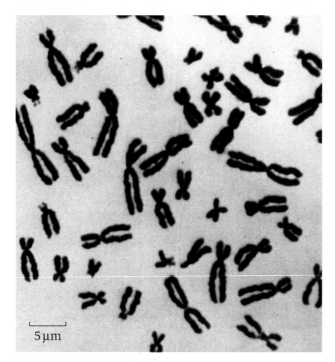

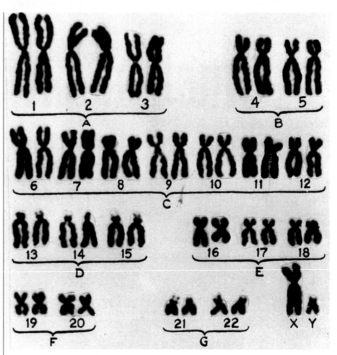

● **Figure 6.1** Photograph of a set of chromosomes in a human male, just before cell division. Each chromosome is composed of two chromatids held at the centromere. Note the different sizes of the chromosomes and positions of the centromeres.

● **Figure 6.2** Karyotype of a human male, prepared from *figure 6.1*. Non-sex chromosomes (autosomes) are placed in the groups A to G. The sex chromosomes (X, female; Y, male) are placed separately.

because *chromo* means 'coloured' and *somes* means 'bodies'. The number of chromosomes is characteristic of the species. For example, in human cells there are 46 chromosomes, and in fruit fly cells there are only 8. *Figure 6.1* shows the appearance of a set of chromosomes in the nucleus of a human cell. *Figure 6.2* shows the same chromosomes rearranged and *figure 6.3* is a diagram of the same chromosomes.

SAQ 6.1

Look at *figures 6.1, 6.2* and *6.3* and try to decide why the chromosomes are arranged in the particular order shown.

A photograph such as *figure 6.2* is called a **karyotype**. It is prepared by cutting out individual chromosomes from a picture like *figure 6.1* and rearranging them. Note the following.

■ There are matching pairs of chromosomes. These are called **homologous pairs**. Each pair is given a number. In the original zygote, one of each pair came from the mother and one from the father. *Figure 6.3* shows the complete set of 23 chromosomes that derived from just one of

the parents. Accurate and precise nuclear division during growth results in all cells of the body containing the two sets of chromosomes. There is more detail of this later in the chapter.

■ The pairs of chromosomes can be distinguished because each pair has a distinctive banding pattern when stained.

■ Two chromosomes are displayed to one side. These are the **sex chromosomes**, which determine the sex. All the other chromosomes are called **autosomes**. It is conventional to position the two sex chromosomes to one side in a karyotype so that the sex of the organism can be recognised quickly. In humans, females have two X chromosomes, and males have one X and one Y chromosome. The Y chromosome has a portion missing and is therefore smaller than the X chromosome.

Each chromosome has a characteristic set of genes which code for different features. The Human Genome Project (see chapters 5 and 11) is investigating which genes are located on which chromosomes. For example, we now know that the gene for the genetic disease cystic fibrosis is located on chromosome 7.

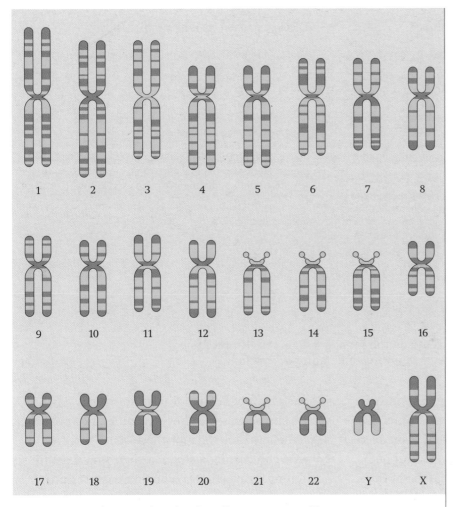

- **Figure 6.3** Diagram showing banding patterns of human chromosomes when stained. Green areas represent those regions that stain with ultraviolet fluorescence staining; orange areas are variable bands. Note that the number of genes is greater than the number of stained bands. Only one chromosome of each pair is shown except for the sex chromosomes which are both shown.

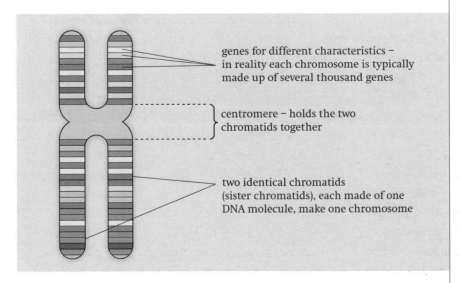

genes for different characteristics – in reality each chromosome is typically made up of several thousand genes

centromere – holds the two chromatids together

two identical chromatids (sister chromatids), each made of one DNA molecule, make one chromosome

- **Figure 6.4** Simplified diagram of the structure of a chromosome.

Haploid and diploid cells

When animals other than humans are examined, we again find that cells usually contain two sets of chromosomes. Such cells are described as **diploid**. This is represented as **2n**, where n = number of chromosomes in one set of chromosomes.

Not all cells are diploid. As we shall see, gametes have only one set of chromosomes. A cell which contains only one set of chromosomes is described as **haploid**. This is represented as **n**. In humans, therefore, a 2n body cell has 46 chromosomes, and a gamete has 23.

The structure of chromosomes

Before studying nuclear division, you need to understand a little about the structure of chromosomes. *Figure 6.4* is a simplified diagram of the structure of a chromosome. It can be seen that the chromosome is really a double structure. It is made of two identical structures called **chromatids**. This is because during the period between nuclear divisions, which is known as **interphase**, each DNA molecule in a nucleus makes an identical copy of itself (see chapter 5). Each copy is contained in a chromatid and the two chromatids are held together by a characteristic narrow region called the **centromere**, forming a chromosome. The centromere can be found anywhere along the length of the chromosome, but the position is characteristic for a particular chromosome, as

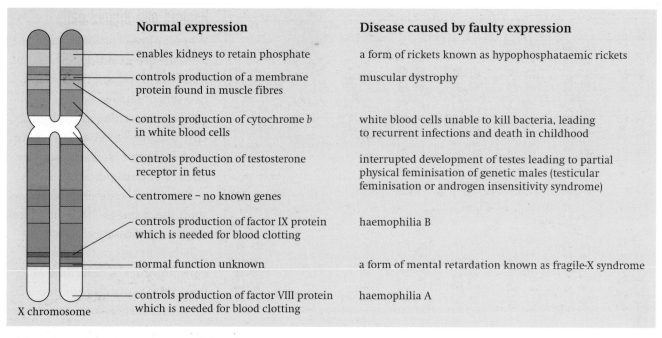

Normal expression	Disease caused by faulty expression
enables kidneys to retain phosphate	a form of rickets known as hypophosphataemic rickets
controls production of a membrane protein found in muscle fibres	muscular dystrophy
controls production of cytochrome *b* in white blood cells	white blood cells unable to kill bacteria, leading to recurrent infections and death in childhood
controls production of testosterone receptor in fetus	interrupted development of testes leading to partial physical feminisation of genetic males (testicular feminisation or androgen insensitivity syndrome)
centromere – no known genes	
controls production of factor IX protein which is needed for blood clotting	haemophilia B
normal function unknown	a form of mental retardation known as fragile-X syndrome
controls production of factor VIII protein which is needed for blood clotting	haemophilia A

X chromosome

● **Figure 6.5** Locations of some of the genes on the human female sex chromosome (the X chromosome) showing the effects of normal and faulty expression.

figures 6.2 and *6.3* show. **Each chromatid contains one DNA molecule.** As you know from chapter 5, DNA is the molecule of inheritance and is made up of a series of genes. Each gene is one unit of inheritance, controlling one characteristic of the organism. The fact that the two DNA molecules in sister chromatids, and hence their genes, are identical is the key to precise nuclear division.

The gene for a particular characteristic is always found at the same position, or **locus** (plural **loci**), on a chromosome. *Figure 6.5* shows a map of some of the genes on the human female sex chromosome which, if faulty, are involved in known genetic diseases.

Each chromosome typically has several hundred to several thousand gene loci, many more than shown in *figure 6.4*. The total number of different genes in humans is thought to be about 30 000.

Homologous pairs of chromosomes

The word *homologous* means 'similar in structure and composition'. Each member of a homologous pair of chromosomes comes from one of the parents. In humans 23 chromosomes come from the female parent (the **maternal chromosomes**), and 23 from the male parent (the **paternal chromosomes**). There are therefore 23 homologous pairs.

Each member of a pair possesses genes for the same characteristics. They may differ, however, in exactly how they code for those characteristics. A gene controlling a characteristic may exist in different forms (**alleles**) which are expressed

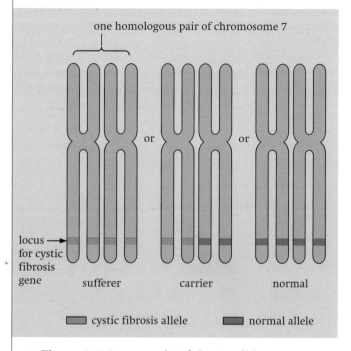

one homologous pair of chromosome 7

or   or

locus for cystic fibrosis gene

sufferer   carrier   normal

☐ cystic fibrosis allele   ▬ normal allele

● **Figure 6.6** An example of the possible combinations of one gene's alleles on a homologous pair of chromosomes. Note that sister chromatids within each chromosome have identical copies of the gene. The variation occurs between whole chromosomes.

differently. For example, the condition known as cystic fibrosis is caused by a faulty allele of a gene that codes for a chloride channel protein needed to produce normal mucus. The **mutant** or **mutated** (changed) allele causes production of very thick mucus which leads to cystic fibrosis. If both homologous chromosomes have a copy of the faulty allele, the person will suffer the disease; if only one copy of the faulty allele is present the person will not suffer the disease, but is termed a **carrier**. The possibilities are shown in *figure 6.6*.

Two types of nuclear division

Figure 6.7 shows a brief summary of the life cycle of an animal, such as a human. Two requirements must be satisfied.

1 **Growth** When a diploid zygote (one cell) grows into a multicellular diploid adult the daughter cells must keep the same number of chromosomes as the parent cell. The type of nuclear division that occurs here is called **mitosis**.

2 **Sexual reproduction** If the life cycle contains sexual reproduction, there must be a point in the life cycle when the number of chromosomes is halved (*figure 6.8*). This means that the gametes contain only one set of chromosomes rather than two sets. If there was no point in the life cycle when the number of chromosomes halved then it would double every generation. The type of nuclear division that halves the chromosome number is called **meiosis**. Gametes are always haploid as a result of meiosis.

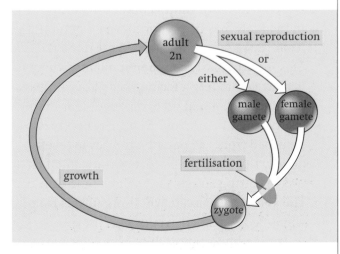

● **Figure 6.7** Outline of the life cycle of an animal.

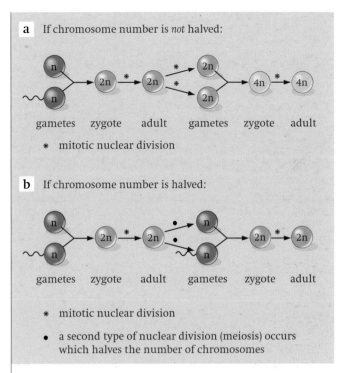

a If chromosome number is *not* halved:

gametes   zygote   adult   gametes   zygote   adult

*   mitotic nuclear division

b If chromosome number is halved:

gametes   zygote   adult   gametes   zygote   adult

*   mitotic nuclear division

●   a second type of nuclear division (meiosis) occurs which halves the number of chromosomes

● **Figure 6.8** A life cycle in which the chromosome number is **a** not halved, **b** halved.

Mitosis in an animal cell

Mitosis is nuclear division that produces two genetically identical daughter nuclei, each containing the same number of chromosomes as the parent nucleus. A diploid nucleus that divides by mitosis produces two diploid nuclei; a haploid nucleus produces two haploid nuclei. Mitosis, like meiosis, is a form of **nuclear division** and is part of a precisely controlled process called the **cell cycle**.

The cell cycle

The cell cycle is the period between one cell division and the next. It has three phases, namely **interphase**, **nuclear division** and **cell division**. These are shown in *figure 6.9*.

During interphase the cell grows to its normal size after cell division and carries out its normal functions, synthesising many substances, especially proteins, in the process. At some point during interphase, a signal may be received that the cell should divide again. The DNA in the nucleus replicates so that each chromosome consists of two identical chromatids, each containing one copy of that chromosome's DNA.

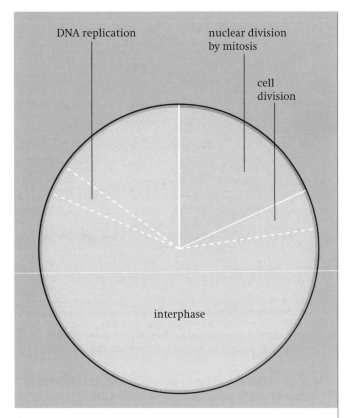

● **Figure 6.9** The mitotic cell cycle.

Nuclear division follows interphase. The whole cell then divides.

The length of the cell cycle is very variable, depending on environmental conditions and cell type. On average, root tip cells of onions divide once every 20 hours; epithelial cells in the human intestine every 10 hours.

In animal cells, cell division involves constriction of the cytoplasm between the two new nuclei, a process called **cytokinesis**. In plant cells it involves the formation of a new cell wall between the two new nuclei.

Mitosis

The process of mitosis is best described by annotated diagrams as shown in *figure 6.10*. Although in reality the process is continuous, it is shown here divided into four main stages for convenience, like four snapshots from a film. The four stages are called **prophase**, **metaphase**, **anaphase** and **telophase**.

Most nuclei contain many chromosomes, but the diagrams in *figure 6.10* show a cell containing only four chromosomes for convenience (2n = 4). Colours are used to show whether the chromosomes are from the female or male parent. An animal cell is used as an example. The behaviour of chromosomes in plant cells is identical. However, plant cells do not contain centrioles and, after nuclear division, a new cell wall must form between the daughter nuclei. It is chromosome behaviour, though, that is of particular interest. *Figure 6.10* summarises the process of mitosis diagrammatically. *Figures 6.11* (animal) and *6.12* (plant) show photographs of the process as seen with a light microscope.

Biological significance of mitosis

■ The nuclei of the two daughter cells formed have the same number of chromosomes as the parent nucleus and are genetically identical. This allows growth of multicellular organisms from unicellular zygotes. Growth may occur over the entire body, as in animals, or be confined to certain regions, as in the meristems (growing points) of plants.

■ Replacement of cells and repair of tissues is possible using mitosis followed by cell division. Cells are constantly dying and being replaced by identical cells. In the human body, for example, cell replacement is particularly rapid in the skin and in the lining of the gut. Some animals are able to regenerate whole parts of the body, as, for example, the arms of a starfish.

■ Mitosis is the basis of asexual reproduction, the production of new individuals of a species by one parent organism. This can take many forms. For a unicellular organism, such as *Amoeba*, cell division inevitably results in reproduction. For multicellular organisms, new individuals may be produced which bud off from the parent in various ways (*figure 6.13*). This is particularly common in plants, where it is most commonly a form of vegetative propagation in which a bud on part of the stem simply grows a new plant. This eventually becomes detached from the parent and lives independently. The bud may be part of the stem of an overwintering structure such as a bulb or tuber. The ability to generate whole organisms from single cells, or small groups of cells, is becoming important in biotechnology and genetic modification (engineering).

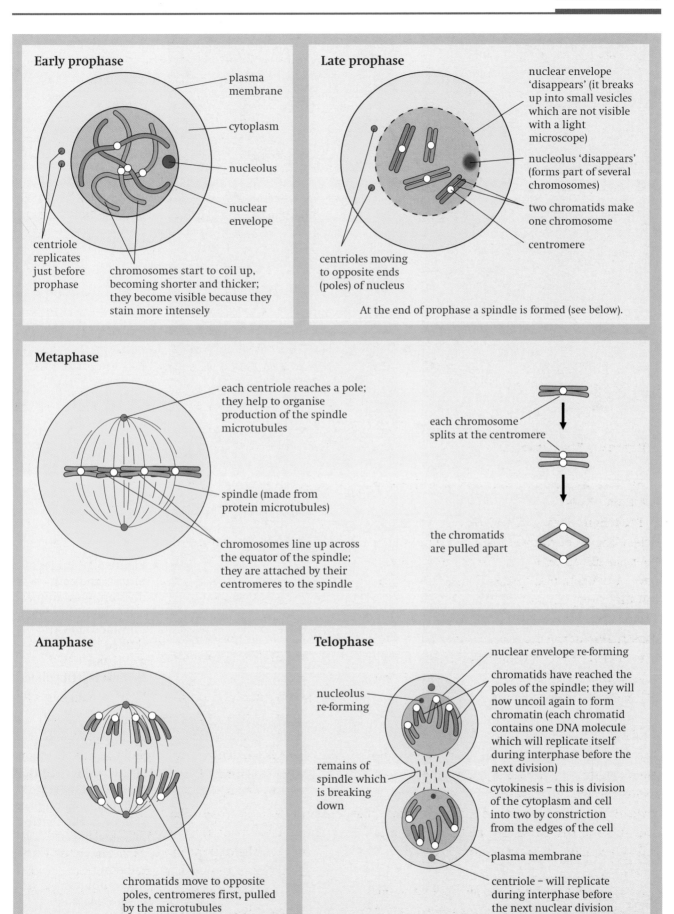

- **Figure 6.10** Mitosis and cytokinesis in an animal cell.

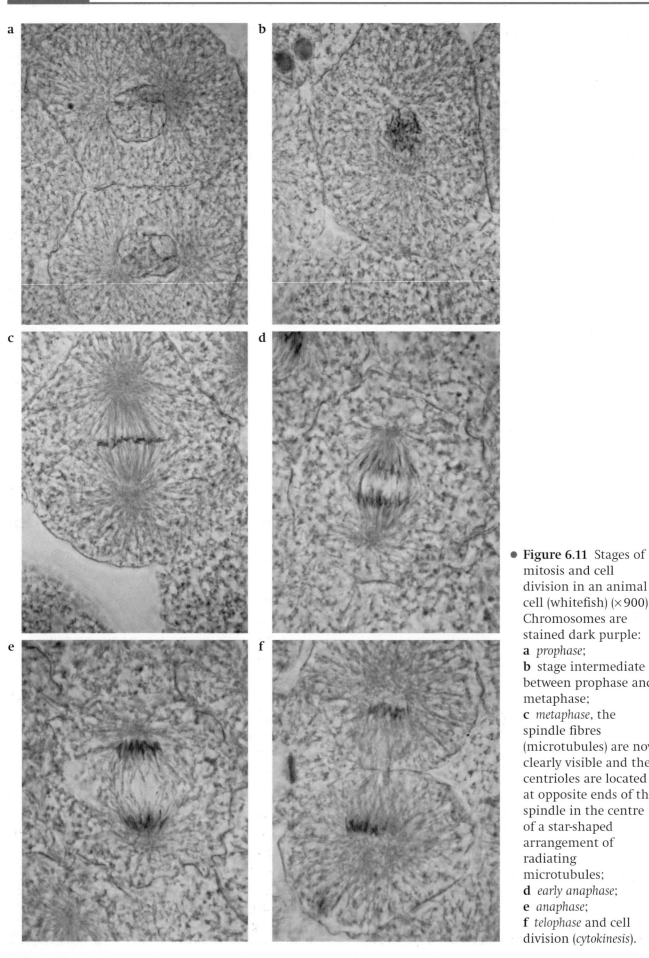

● **Figure 6.11** Stages of mitosis and cell division in an animal cell (whitefish) (×900). Chromosomes are stained dark purple:
a *prophase*;
b stage intermediate between prophase and metaphase;
c *metaphase*, the spindle fibres (microtubules) are now clearly visible and the centrioles are located at opposite ends of the spindle in the centre of a star-shaped arrangement of radiating microtubules;
d *early anaphase*;
e *anaphase*;
f *telophase* and cell division (*cytokinesis*).

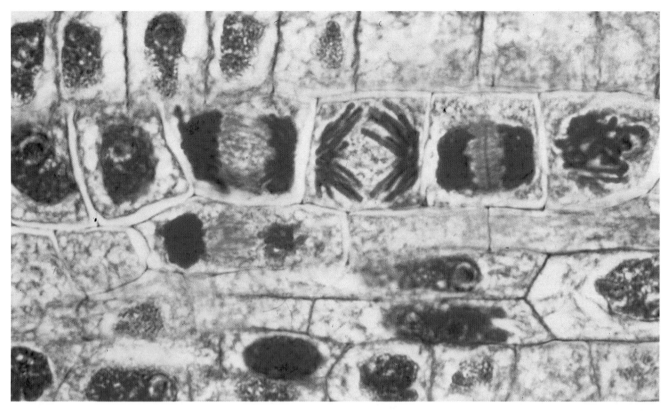

● **Figure 6.12** LS onion root tip showing stages of mitosis and cell division typical of plant cells (×400). Try to identify the stages based on information given in *figure 6.10*.

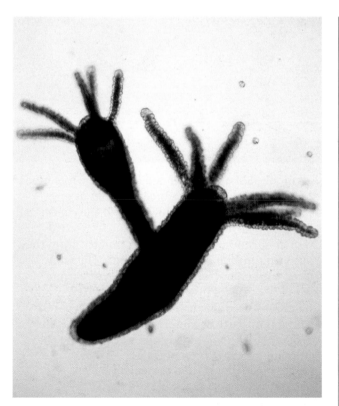

● **Figure 6.13** Asexual reproduction by budding (×60). *Hydra* lives in fresh water, catching its prey with the aid of its tentacles. The bud growing from its side is genetically identical to the parent and will eventually break free and live independently.

SAQ 6.2

a In the mitotic cell cycle of a human cell:
  (i) how many chromatids are present as the cell enters mitosis?
  (ii) how many DNA molecules are present?
  (iii) how many chromatids are present in the nucleus of each daughter cell after mitosis and cell division?
  (iv) how many chromatids are present in the nucleus of a cell after replication of DNA?

b Draw a simple diagram of a cell which contains only one pair of homologous chromosomes (i) at metaphase of mitosis, (ii) at anaphase of mitosis.

c What chemical subunits are used to synthesise new DNA molecules during replication of DNA?

d Of what elements are these subunits made?

e State two functions of centromeres during nuclear division.

f Thin sections of adult mouse liver were prepared and the cells stained to show up the chromosomes. In a sample of 75 000 cells examined, nine were found to be in the process of mitosis. Calculate the length of the cell cycle in days in liver cells, assuming that mitosis lasts 1 hour.

Cancer

Cancer is one of the most common diseases of developed countries, accounting for roughly one in four deaths. Lung cancer alone caused about one in 17 of all deaths in Britain in the 1990s, 1 in 13 deaths in men and 1 in 27 deaths in women. It is the most common form of cancer in men, while breast cancer is the leading form of cancer in women. There are, in fact, more than a hundred different forms of cancer and the medical profession does not think of it as a single disease. Cancers show us the importance of controlling cell division precisely, because cancers are a result of uncontrolled mitosis. Cancerous cells divide repeatedly, out of control, and a **tumour** develops which is an irregular mass of cells. The cells usually show abnormal changes in shape (*figure 6.14*).

Carcinogens

Cancers are thought to start when changes occur in the genes that control cell division. We have encountered **mutated** genes before when considering different alleles of genes in homologous pairs of chromosomes (page 83). The particular term for a mutated gene that causes cancer is an **oncogene** after the Greek word *onkos* meaning 'bulk' or 'mass'. A change in any gene is called a **mutation**. Mutations are not unusual events, and *most* mutated cells are either crippled in some way that results in their early death or are destroyed by the body's immune system. Since most cells

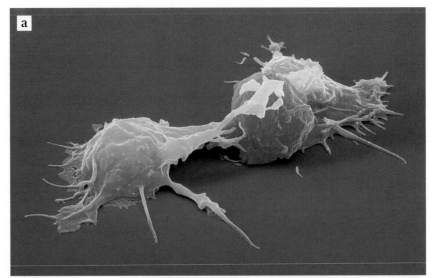

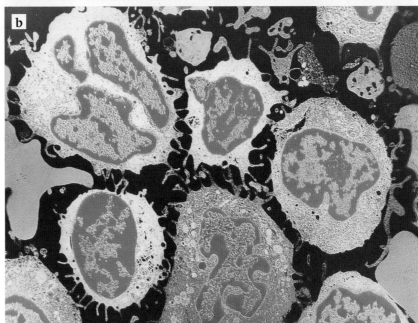

● **Figure 6.14 a** False-colour SEM of a cancer cell (red) and white blood cells (yellow). White blood cells gather at cancerous sites as an immune response. They are beginning to flow around the cancer cell which they will kill using toxic chemicals (×4500).
b False-colour TEM of abnormal white blood cells isolated from the blood of a person suffering from hairy-cell leukaemia. The white blood cells are covered with characteristic hair-like, cytoplasmic projections. Leukaemia is a disease in which the bone marrow and other blood-forming organs produce too many of certain types of white blood cells. These immature or abnormal cells suppress the normal production of white and red blood cells, and increase the sufferer's susceptibility to infection (×6400).

can be replaced, this usually has no detrimental effect on the body. Cancerous cells, however, manage to escape both possible fates, so, although the mutation may originally occur only in one cell, it is passed on to all that cell's descendents. By the time it is detected, a typical tumour usually contains about a thousand million cells.

It is thought that a single mutation cannot be responsible for cancer but that several independent rare 'accidents' must all occur in one cell. A factor which brings about any mutation is called a **mutagen** and is described as **mutagenic**. Any agent that causes cancer is called a **carcinogen** and is described as **carcinogenic**. So, some mutagens are carcinogenic.

Some of the factors which can increase mutation rates, and hence the likelihood of cancer, are as follows.

■ *Ionising radiation*

This includes X-rays, gamma rays and particles from the decay of radioactive elements. They cause the formation of damaging ions inside cells which can break DNA strands. Ultraviolet light, although it does not cause the formation of damaging ions, can also damage genes. Depletion of the ozone layer is causing concern because, as a result, more ultraviolet light will penetrate to the Earth's surface and could result in an increase in cases of skin cancer.

■ *Chemicals*

Many different chemicals have been shown to be carcinogenic. About 25% of all cancer deaths in developed countries are due to carcinogens in the tar of tobacco smoke (*figure 6.15*). Certain dyes, such as a group known as the aniline dyes, are also well-known carcinogens. All these chemicals damage DNA molecules.

■ *Virus infection*

Some cancers in animals, including humans, are known to be caused by viruses. Burkitt's lymphoma, the most common cancer in children in certain parts of Africa, is caused by a virus. Another causes a form of leukaemia (cancer of the white blood cells). Papilloma viruses are responsible for some cancers, and include two types that have been linked with cervical cancer, a disease that can be

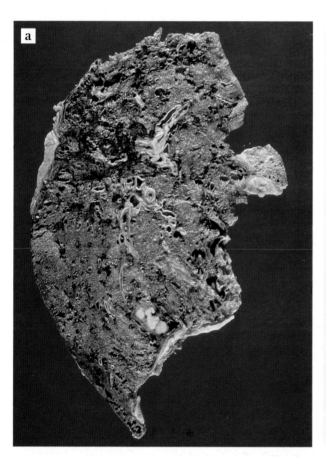

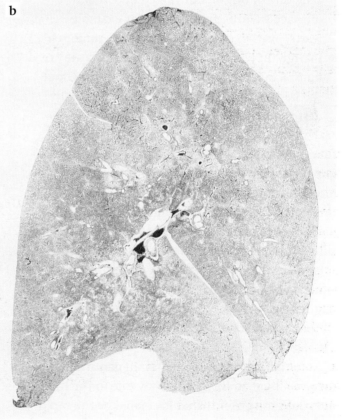

● **Figure 6.15 a** Lung of a patient who died of lung cancer, showing rounded deposits of tumour (bottom, white area). Black tarry deposits throughout the lung show the patient was a heavy smoker.

b Section of a healthy human lung. No black tar deposits are visible.

transmitted sexually. Viruses that cause cancer usually carry oncogenes, or regulatory genes that can become oncogenes.

■ *Hereditary predisposition*
Cancer tends to be more common in some families than others, indicating a genetic link. In most cases it is believed that the disease *itself* is not inherited, but susceptibility to the factors that cause the disease is inherited. However, some forms of cancer do appear to be caused by inheritance of a single faulty gene. For example, the inherited form of retinoblastoma, which starts in one or both eyes during childhood and spreads to the brain, causing blindness and then death if untreated, is caused by an error on chromosome 13.

Benign or malignant?

A small group of tumour cells is called a **primary growth**. There are two types:

■ **benign** tumours, which do not spread from their site of origin, but can compress and displace surrounding tissues, for example warts, ovarian cysts and some brain tumours;

■ **malignant** (cancerous) tumours, which are far more dangerous since they spread throughout the body, invade other tissues and eventually destroy them.

Malignant tumours interfere with the normal functioning of the area where they have started to grow. They may block the intestines, lungs or blood vessels. Cells can break off and spread through the blood and lymphatic system to other parts of the body to form **secondary growths**. The spread of cancers in this way is called **metastasis**. It is the most dangerous characteristic of cancer, since it can be very hard to find secondary cancers and remove them.

The steps involved in the development of cancer are shown in *figure 6.16*.

Note that both benign and malignant tumours involve a huge drain on the body due to the high demand for nutrients that is created by the rapid and continual cell division.

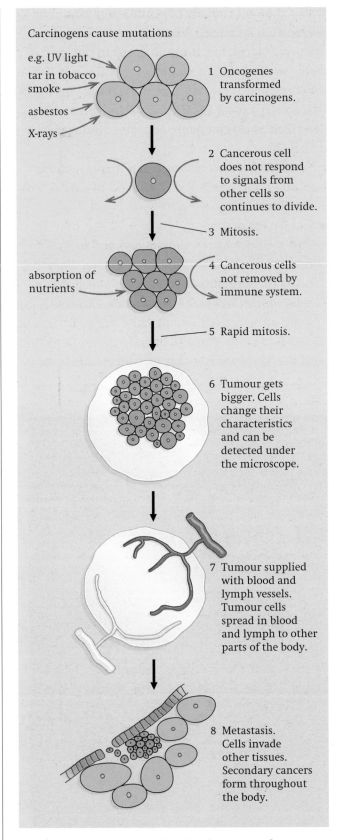

Carcinogens cause mutations

e.g. UV light
tar in tobacco smoke
asbestos
X-rays

1 Oncogenes transformed by carcinogens.

2 Cancerous cell does not respond to signals from other cells so continues to divide.

3 Mitosis.

absorption of nutrients

4 Cancerous cells not removed by immune system.

5 Rapid mitosis.

6 Tumour gets bigger. Cells change their characteristics and can be detected under the microscope.

7 Tumour supplied with blood and lymph vessels. Tumour cells spread in blood and lymph to other parts of the body.

8 Metastasis. Cells invade other tissues. Secondary cancers form throughout the body.

● **Figure 6.16** Stages in the development of cancer.

SUMMARY

◆ Cell division is needed so that organisms can grow and reproduce. It involves division of the nucleus followed by division of the cytoplasm.

◆ During nuclear division the chromosomes become visible. Each is seen to be formed of two chromatids. The chromosomes of a body cell can be photographed and arranged in order of size as a karyotype. This shows that each cell has either one set of chromosomes, known as haploid, or two sets of chromosomes, known as diploid. In the diploid condition, one set comes from the female parent and one from the male parent. Gametes are haploid cells.

◆ Body cells divide in the process of mitosis to produce two identical daughter cells whose nuclei contain the same number of chromosomes as the parent cell. This allows growth and repair of a multicellular organism and is the basis of asexual reproduction.

◆ Meiosis halves the number of chromosomes in the nucleus. This prevents chromosome number doubling in each generation of organisms which reproduce sexually.

◆ Cancers are caused by uncontrolled mitosis, possibly as the result of a mutation in a gene or genes which control cell division. Agents which cause cancer are known as carcinogens and include ionising radiation, many chemicals and viruses. Some cancers have a hereditary link.

Questions

1 Explain the link between cancer and mitosis. Describe how the chances of cancer developing in the human body may be increased.

2 Using photographs, such as shown in *figure 6.12*, how could you estimate the relative length of each stage of mitosis?

3 Explain clearly the meaning of the following terms: haploid, diploid, zygote, homologous pair of chromosomes, centromere, autosome, chromatid.

CHAPTER 7

Energy and ecosystems

By the end of this chapter you should be able to:

1 define the terms *habitat*, *niche*, *population*, *community* and *ecosystem*, and describe examples of each;

2 explain the terms *producer*, *consumer* and *trophic level*, and state examples of these in specific food chains and food webs;

3 describe how energy is transferred through food chains and food webs;

4 explain how energy losses occur along food chains, and understand what is meant by *efficiency* of transfer;

5 describe how nitrogen is cycled within an ecosystem.

So far in this book we have been looking at living things at a very small scale, considering what goes on in organisms in terms of the molecules from which they are built and the structure of their cells. In this chapter we change focus entirely, moving up in scale to think about how whole communities of living organisms interact with each other and with their environment. This branch of biology is called **ecology**.

We will consider two important themes in ecology: the flow of energy through ecological systems and the cycling of materials within those same ecological systems. In order to do this you need to become familiar with some of the specialist terms used in ecology. Ecology has its own set of terms, each with a precise meaning that may differ slightly from the meaning of the word when used in everyday life. Five of these are defined here and you will meet others later in this chapter.

■ A **habitat** is a **place where an organism lives**. The habitat of an oak tree might be the edge of an area of deciduous woodland. The habitat of a leaf-mining caterpillar might be inside a leaf on the oak tree.

■ A **population** is **a group of organisms of the same species, which live in the same place at the same time, and can interbreed with each**

other. All of the oak trees in the wood, for example, make up a population of oak trees. However, if the oak trees in a nearby wood can interbreed with those in the first wood, then they too belong to the same population.

■ A **community** is **all the organisms, of all the different species, living in a habitat**. The woodland community includes all the plants – oak trees, ash trees, grasses, hawthorn bushes, bluebells and so on – all the microorganisms and larger fungi, and all the animals which live in the wood.

■ An **ecosystem** is a **relatively self-contained, interacting community of organisms, and the environment in which they live and with which they interact**. Thus the woodland ecosystem includes not only the community of organisms, but also the soil, the water in the rain and streams, the air, the rocks and anything else which is in the wood. As you will see later in this chapter, energy flows into the ecosystem from outside it (as sunlight), flows through the organisms in the ecosystem (as food) and eventually leaves the ecosystem (as heat). Matter, on the other hand – that is, atoms and molecules of substances such as carbon and nitrogen – cycles round an ecosystem, where some atoms are reused over and over again by different organisms.

No ecosystem is entirely self-contained; organisms, energy and matter in one ecosystem do interact with those from other ecosystems. Nevertheless, the concept is a useful one, because it allows you to focus on something of a manageable size.

You can think of ecosystems on different scales. You could consider the surface of a rotting crab apple to be an ecosystem, with its own community of moulds and other organisms, or you could think of the whole hedgerow in which the crab apple tree is growing as an ecosystem.

■ The **niche** of an organism is **its role in the ecosystem**. The niche of an oak tree is as a producer of carbohydrates and other organic substances which provide food for other organisms in the ecosystem. It takes carbon dioxide from the air and returns oxygen to it. Its roots penetrate deeply into the soil, where they take up water and minerals. Water vapour diffuses from its leaves into the air. These leaves provide habitats for myriads of insects and other animals. It is almost impossible to provide a complete description of the niche of any organism, because there are so many ways in which it interacts with other components of the ecosystem of which it is a part.

Energy flow through organisms and ecosystems

Living organisms need a constant supply of energy to stay alive. At the most basic level, energy is required to drive many of the chemical reactions that take place within living cells. If these **metabolic reactions** stop, then all of the cell's activities stop and it dies. We have already seen that energy is needed for active transport across membranes (page 59) and to achieve cell growth and division. In mammals such as ourselves, large amounts of energy are required to maintain body temperature above that of our surroundings. There are many more such examples of the never-ending demand for energy.

Inside every cell, the immediate source of energy is **ATP** or **adenosine triphosphate**. ATP is the energy 'currency' of a cell. Each cell in every kind of living organism makes its own ATP as and when it needs it. Astonishing amounts of ATP are made every day. You, for example, probably make about 40 kg of ATP inside your cells every day, using it up almost immediately to supply energy for your cells' activities. When energy is required, the ATP is broken down by hydrolysis and its energy used for whatever the cell needs.

So, to keep your cells going you need energy from ATP, and to make ATP you need energy from somewhere else. The source of energy for making ATP is other organic molecules such as carbohydrates, lipids and proteins (see chapter 2). These molecules are high in energy which can be released and used to make ATP as they are broken down in the process of **respiration**. Respiration happens in every living cell, and its whole purpose is to make ATP.

How is energy stored in carbohydrates, lipids and proteins in the first place? It is achieved inside the mesophyll cells of plant leaves. Here, sunlight is captured by chlorophyll in the chloroplasts (page 5) and used to supply energy to drive the reactions of **photosynthesis**. Carbon dioxide from the air and water drawn up from the soil react together to produce carbohydrates and, in the process, energy is transferred from sunlight and converted into chemical energy in the carbohydrate molecules. The plant uses these carbohydrate molecules to make lipids and proteins which also contain some of this energy. When the plant requires energy for its metabolism, it breaks down some of these molecules in respiration and makes ATP.

This, then, is how all living organisms get their energy. Photosynthesis in plants converts sunlight energy to chemical energy in organic molecules. Animals eat plants, obtaining some of this chemical energy in the molecules they take in. Plants and animals then break down these organic molecules in the process of respiration, transferring energy to ATP molecules. The ATP can then itself be broken down to release its energy for use in metabolic reactions. This whole pattern of energy flow is summarised in *figure 7.1*. If you continue your biology studies into the second year, you will cover this subject in more detail (see *Biology 2* in this series).

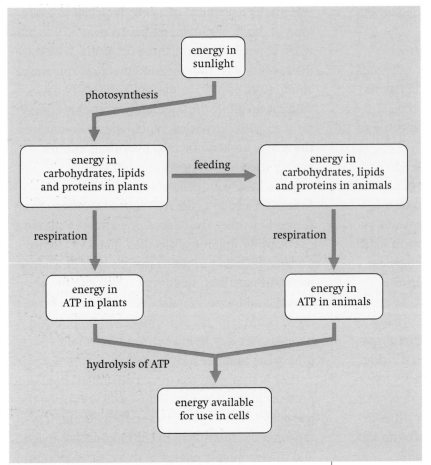

● **Figure 7.1** Energy flow through organisms and ecosystems.

Ultimately, therefore, green plants and other photosynthetic organisms have the essential role of providing the entire input of energy to an ecosystem. They are **producers**. The carbohydrates and other organic chemicals which they synthesise serve as supplies of chemical energy to all of the other organisms in the ecosystem. These other organisms, which include all the animals and fungi, and many of the microorganisms, consume the organic chemicals made by plants. They are **consumers**.

Food chains and food webs

The way in which energy flows from producer to consumers can be shown by drawing a **food chain**. Arrows in the food chain indicate the direction in which the energy flows. A simple food chain in a deciduous wood could be:

> oak tree → winter moth caterpillar →
> great tit → sparrowhawk

In this food chain, the oak tree is the producer, and the three animals are consumers. The caterpillar is a **primary consumer**, the great tit a **secondary consumer** and the sparrowhawk a **tertiary consumer**. These different positions in a food chain are called **trophic levels**. (*Trophic* means 'feeding'.)

Within this woodland ecosystem, there will be a large number of such food chains. The inter-relationships between many food chains can be drawn as a **food web**. *Figure 7.2* shows a partial food web for such an ecosystem. You can pick out many different food chains within this web.

You may notice that a particular animal does not always occupy the same position in a food chain. While herbivores such as caterpillars and rabbits tend *always* to be herbivores, and therefore always primary consumers, carnivores often feed at several different trophic levels in different food chains. Thus the fox is a primary consumer when it eats a fallen crab apple, a secondary consumer when it eats a rabbit, and a tertiary consumer when it eats a great tit. Animals which regularly feed as both primary and higher-level consumers, such as humans, are known as omnivores.

The food web also shows the importance of a group of organisms called **decomposers**. Most decomposers live in the soil, and their role in an ecosystem is to feed on **detritus** (dead organisms and waste material, such as dead leaves, faeces and urine). You can see that energy from *every* organism in the ecosystem flows into the decomposers. Decomposers include many bacteria, fungi, and also some larger animals such as earthworms. Sometimes, the term 'decomposer' is used only for bacteria and fungi, which feed saprotrophically, while the larger animals are called **detritivores**, meaning 'detritus feeders'. Decomposers are a largely unseen but vitally important group within every ecosystem. You will find out more about their roles in the nitrogen cycle on pages 97–100.

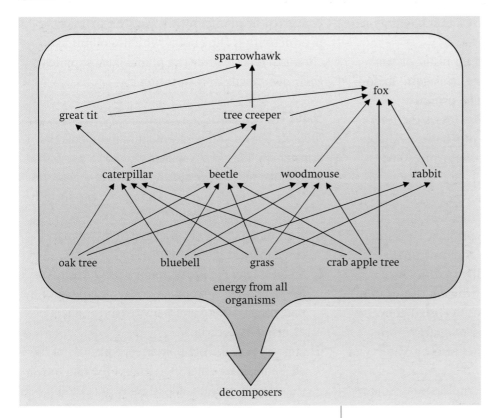

● **Figure 7.2** A food web in oak woodland.

Energy losses along food chains

Whenever energy is transferred from one form, or from one system, to another some is always lost as heat. As energy passes along a food chain, large losses from the food chain occur at each transfer, both within and between the organisms. *Figure 7.3* shows these losses for a simple food chain.

Of the sunlight falling onto the ecosystem, only a very small percentage is converted by the green plants into chemical energy. In most ecosystems, the plants convert less than 3% of this sunlight to chemical energy. The reasons for this inefficiency include:

■ some sunlight missing leaves entirely, and falling onto the ground or other nonphotosynthesising surfaces;

■ some sunlight being reflected from the surfaces of leaves;

■ some sunlight passing through leaves, without being trapped by chlorophyll molecules;

■ only certain wavelengths of light being absorbed by chlorophyll;

■ energy losses as energy absorbed by chlorophyll is transferred to carbohydrates during photosynthesis.

The chemical potential energy, now in the plants' tissues, is contained in various organic molecules, especially carbohydrates, lipids and proteins. It is from these molecules that the primary consumers in the ecosystem obtain their energy supply. However, in most plants, almost half of the chemical potential energy stored by plants is used by the plants themselves. They release the energy by respiration, using it for purposes such as active

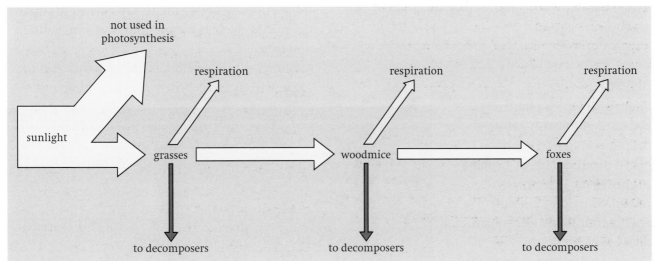

● **Figure 7.3** Energy losses in a food chain.

transport. During these processes, much energy is lost to the environment as heat.

What is left is then available for other organisms, which feed on the plants. Once again, losses occur between the plants and the primary consumers. The reasons for these losses include:

- not all of the parts of the plants being available to be eaten, such as woody tissues and some roots;
- not all of the parts of the plants eaten being digestible, so that not all of the molecules can be absorbed and used by the primary consumer;
- energy losses as heat within the consumer's digestive system, as food is digested.

As a result of the loss of energy during respiration in the plants, and the three reasons listed above, the overall efficiency of transfer of energy from producer to primary consumer is rarely greater than 10%.

Similar losses occur at each trophic level. So, as energy is passed along a food chain, less and less energy is available at each successive trophic level. Food chains rarely have more than four or five links in them because there simply would not be sufficient energy left to support animals so far removed from the original energy input to the producers. If you *can* pick out a five-organism food chain from a food web, you will probably find that the 'top' carnivore also feeds at a lower level in a different food chain.

SAQ 7.1

Energy losses from mammals and birds tend to be significantly greater than those from other organisms. Suggest why this is so.

Productivity

The rate at which plants convert light energy into chemical potential energy is called **productivity**, or **primary productivity**. It is usually measured in kilojoules of energy transferred per square metre per year ($kJ\,m^{-2}\,year^{-1}$).

Gross primary productivity is the total quantity of energy

converted by plants in this way. **Net primary productivity** is the energy which remains as chemical energy after the plants have supplied their own needs in respiration.

SAQ 7.2

Table 7.1 shows some information about energy transfers in three ecosystems.

a Calculate the figures for respiration by plants in the alfalfa field, and the net primary productivity of the young pine forest.

b How much energy is available to the primary consumers in the rain forest?

c Suggest why the gross primary productivity of the rain forest is so much greater than that of the pine forest. (There are many reasons – think of as many as you can.)

d Suggest why the net primary productivity of the alfalfa field is greater than that of the rain forest. (Again, you may be able to think of several reasons.)

Matter recycling in ecosystems

Living organisms require not only a supply of *energy*, but also a supply of *matter* from which to build their bodies. The elements from which this matter is made are mostly hydrogen, carbon and oxygen, which are contained in all the organic molecules within organisms. Proteins and nucleotides (chapters 2 and 5) also contain nitrogen, and some proteins contain sulphur. Phosphorus is an important component of nucleotides. Other elements are needed in smaller quantities, such as magnesium, calcium, iodine and iron.

Atoms of these elements are used over and over again within an ecosystem, or passed into other

	Mature rain forest in Puerto Rico	Alfalfa field in USA	Young pine forest in England
Gross primary productivity ($kJ\,m^{-2}\,year^{-1}$)	188 000	102 000	51 000
Respiration by plants ($kJ\,m^{-2}\,year^{-1}$)	134 000		20 000
Net primary productivity ($kJ\,m^{-2}\,year^{-1}$)	54 000	64 000	

● **Table 7.1** Energy transfer data.

ecosystems. They are passed from one organism to another, cycling round through the different living organisms, and also through the non-living parts of the ecosystem, such as the air, soil, water and rocks. The principle of recycling can be illustrated by the nitrogen cycle (*figure 7.4*).

The nitrogen cycle

Nitrogen is an essential element for all living organisms, because of its presence in proteins and nucleic acids. There is a large quantity of nitrogen in the air, which is around 78% N_2 gas. However, most organisms cannot use this nitrogen. This is because nitrogen gas exists as molecular nitrogen, in which two nitrogen atoms are linked with a triple covalent bond (N≡N). In this form, nitrogen is very unreactive. With each breath, you take in around 350 cm^3 of nitrogen gas, but this is completely useless to you. It simply passes in and

out of your body unchanged. Similarly, N_2 passes freely in and out of a plant's stomata, with the plant unable to make any use of it.

Before nitrogen can be used by living organisms it must be converted from N_2 into some more reactive form, such as ammonia (NH_3) or nitrate (NO_3^-). This conversion is called **nitrogen fixation**.

Nitrogen fixation
Nitrogen fixation can take place naturally or synthetically.

Fixation by living organisms
Only prokaryotes, including several species of bacteria, are capable of fixing nitrogen. One of the best-known nitrogen-fixing bacteria is *Rhizobium* (*figure 7.4*). This bacterium lives freely in the soil, and also in the roots of many species of plants, especially leguminous plants (belonging to the

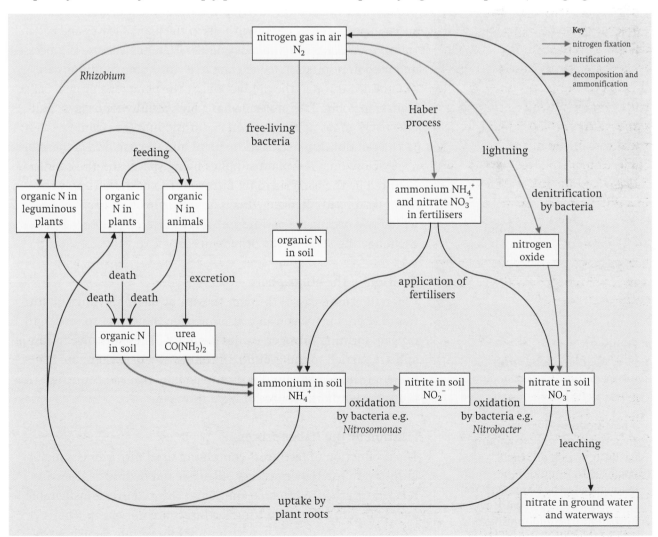

● **Figure 7.4** The nitrogen cycle.

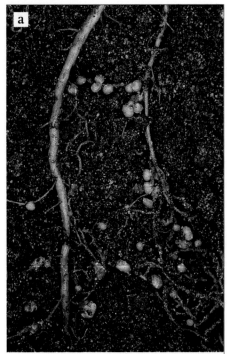

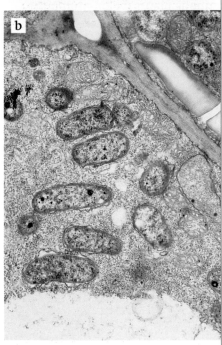

● **Figure 7.5**
a Root nodules, containing
nitrogen-fixing bacteria, on
clover roots (×1.5).
b EM (×12 000) of part of a cell in
a root nodule. The oval
structures are nitrogen-fixing
bacteria, which are each
enclosed by a membrane
belonging to the plant cell. You
can also see the cell wall, several
mitochondria, endoplasmic
reticulum and ribosomes in the
plant cell.

pea family, such as peas, beans, clover, alfalfa and acacia trees).
Rhizobium can only fix nitrogen to a very limited extent when living
freely in the soil. Most nitrogen fixation by *Rhizobium* occurs when
it is living in plant roots. The plant and the bacterium coexist in a
rather remarkable way, each benefiting from the presence of
the other.

Rhizobium is found in most soils. When a leguminous plant
germinates, its roots produce proteins called lectins which bind to
polysaccharides on the cell surface of the bacteria. The bacteria
invade the roots, spreading along the root hairs. They stimulate
some of the cells in the root to divide and develop into small lumps
or nodules, inside which the bacteria form colonies (*figure 7.5*).

The bacteria fix nitrogen with the help of an enzyme called
nitrogenase. This enzyme catalyses the conversion of nitrogen gas,
N_2, to ammonium ions, NH_4^+. To do this, it needs:

- a supply of hydrogen;
- a supply of ATP;
- anaerobic conditions, that is the absence of oxygen.

The hydrogen comes from a substance called reduced NADP which is
produced by the plant. The ATP comes from the metabolism of
sucrose, produced by photosynthesis in the plant's leaves and
transported down into the root nodules. Here the sucrose is processed
and used in respiration to generate ATP. Anaerobic conditions are
maintained through the production, by the plant, of a protein called
leghaemoglobin. This molecule has a high affinity for oxygen, and
effectively 'mops up' oxygen which diffuses into the nodules.

The relationship between the plant and the bacteria is therefore
a very close one. The plant supplies living space, and the conditions
required by the bacteria to fix nitrogen. The bacteria supply the
plant with fixed nitrogen. This is an example of **mutualism**, in
which two organisms of different species live very closely together,
each meeting some of the other's needs.

Fixation in the atmosphere

When lightning passes through the atmosphere, the huge quantities of energy involved can cause nitrogen molecules to react with
oxygen, forming nitrogen oxides (*figure 7.4*). These dissolve in rain,
and are carried to the ground. In countries where there are
frequent thunderstorms, for example many tropical countries, this
is a very significant source of fixed nitrogen.

Fixation by the Haber process

The production of fertilisers containing fixed nitrogen is a major
industry. In the Haber process, nitrogen and hydrogen gases are
reacted together to produce ammonia. This requires considerable
energy inputs, so the resulting fertilisers are not cheap. The
ammonia is often converted to ammonium nitrate, which is the
most widely used inorganic fertiliser in the world.

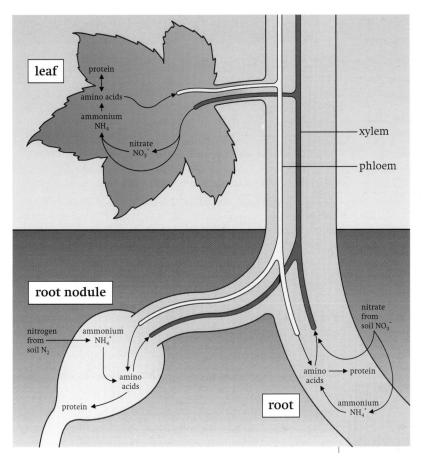

● **Figure 7.6** A summary of nitrogen metabolism and transport in plants.

Use of fixed nitrogen by plants

In legumes, the fixed nitrogen produced by *Rhizobium* in their root nodules is used to make **amino acids**. These are transported out of the nodules into xylem, distributed to all parts of the plant and used within cells to synthesise proteins (*figure 7.6*).

Other plants rely on supplies of fixed nitrogen in the soil. Their root hairs take up **nitrate ions** by active transport. In many plants, the nitrate is converted in the roots, first to nitrite (NO_2^-), then ammonia, and then amino acids which are transported to other parts of the plant in xylem. In other plant species, the nitrate ions are transported, in xylem, to the leaves before undergoing these processes. Again, most of the nitrogen ends up as part of protein molecules in the plant, especially in seeds and storage tissues.

Assimilation of nitrogen by animals

Animals, including humans, can only use nitrogen when it is part of an organic molecule. Most of our nitrogen supply comes from proteins in the diet, with a small amount from nucleic acids. During digestion, proteins are broken down to amino acids, before being absorbed into the blood and distributed to all cells in the body. Here they are built up again into proteins. Excess amino acids are **deaminated** in the liver, where the nitrogen becomes part of urea molecules. These are excreted in urine.

Return of nitrate to the soil from living organisms

When an animal or plant dies, the proteins in its cells are gradually broken down to amino acids. This is done by decomposers, especially bacteria and fungi, which produce protease enzymes. The decomposers use some of the amino acids for their own growth, while some are broken down and the nitrogen released as ammonia. Ammonia is also produced from the urea in animal urine. The production of ammonia is called **ammonification**.

Ammonia in the soil is rapidly converted to nitrite ions (NO_2^-), and then nitrate ions (NO_3^-), by a group of bacteria called **nitrifying bacteria**. They include *Nitrosomonas* and *Nitrobacter* (*figure 7.4*). These bacteria derive their energy from nitrification. In contrast to nitrogen fixation, this

● **Figure 7.7** The greater sundew, *Drosera anglica*, only grows in very wet soils where nitrates are in extremely short supply. The sticky glands on the leaves trap insects. The leaves then curl over, and digest and absorb nutrients, including amino acids, from the insect's body.

only occurs freely in well-aerated soils. Boggy soils are therefore often short of nitrates. Some plants have become adapted to growing in such soils by supplementing their nitrogen intake using animal protein. These carnivorous plants trap insects, whose proteins are digested and absorbed by the plant (*figure 7.7*).

Denitrification

Denitrifying bacteria provide themselves with energy by reversing nitrogen fixation and converting nitrate to nitrogen gas, which is returned to the air. They are common in places such as sewage treatment plants, compost heaps and wet soils. This brings the nitrogen cycle full circle.

SUMMARY

◆ Energy flows through ecosystems. All energy enters an ecosystem as sunlight, and is converted to chemical energy in organic molecules during photosynthesis in producers. Energy is transferred along food chains as one organism feeds on another. Energy is lost at each transfer within and between organisms, mostly as heat produced during respiration. This results in a decrease in biomass and energy in successive trophic levels.

◆ Matter cycles around ecosystems. Nitrogen from the air is fixed by bacteria, some of which live freely in the soil and some, especially *Rhizobium*, which live in root nodules of leguminous plants. Fixed nitrogen, in the form of nitrates, is taken up by plants and used to synthesise amino acids and proteins, on which animals feed. Decomposers convert dead organisms and their waste products to ammonia, which is then converted to nitrite and nitrate by nitrifying bacteria. Denitrifying bacteria complete the cycle, converting inorganic nitrogen compounds to nitrogen gas.

Questions

1 'Energy flows through an ecosystem, but matter cycles around it'. Discuss this statement, with reference to an ecosystem with which you are familiar.

2 Why are large carnivores rare?

3 With reference to an ecosystem you have studied, explain the difference between the following pairs of terms:

   a **ecosystem** and **habitat**
   b **population** and **community**
   c **gross primary productivity** and **net primary productivity**

4 Discuss the roles of bacteria in the cycling of nitrogen around an ecosystem.

Part 2
Transport

CHAPTER 8

The mammalian transport system

By the end of this chapter you should be able to:

1 explain why multicellular animals need transport mechanisms;

2 describe the structure of arteries, veins and capillaries, and relate their structure to their functions;

3 recognise micrographs of arteries, veins and capillaries;

4 describe the functions of tissue fluid, and its formation from blood plasma;

5 describe the functions of lymph, and its formation from tissue fluid;

6 describe the composition of blood;

7 outline the functions of white blood cells;

8 describe the role of haemoglobin in the transport of oxygen and carbon dioxide;

9 describe and explain the oxygen dissociation curve for haemoglobin;

10 describe and explain the effects of raised carbon dioxide concentrations on the haemoglobin dissociation curve (the Bohr effect);

11 describe and explain the differences between oxygen dissociation curves for haemoglobin, fetal haemoglobin and myoglobin, and explain the significance of these differences;

12 describe and explain the increase in red blood cell count at high altitude.

Why do humans have a blood system? The answer is fairly obvious even to a non-scientist: our blood system transports substances such as nutrients and oxygen around the body. However, there are many organisms which either have much less complex transport systems or do not have any kind of transport system at all. Before looking in detail at the human transport system, it is worth briefly considering why some organisms can manage without one.

A quick survey of some organisms which have very simple transport systems, or even none at all, will provide an important clue. *Table 8.1* lists six kinds of organisms, and gives a brief summary of the type of transport system that each has.

SAQ 8.1

From *table 8.1*, state whether each of the following factors appears to be important in deciding whether or not an organism needs an efficient transport system. In each case, identify the information in the table which led you to your answer.

a Size

b The surface area to volume ratio

c Level of activity

All living cells require a supply of nutrients, such as glucose. Most living cells also need a constant supply of oxygen. There will also be waste products, such as carbon dioxide, to be disposed of. Very small organisms, such as *Paramecium*, can

Type of organism	Single-celled	Cnidarians (jellyfish and sea anemones)	Insects	Green plants	Fish	Mammals
Size range	all microscopic	some microscopic, some up to 60 cm	less than 1 mm to 13 cm	1 mm to 150 m	12 mm to 10 m	35 mm to 34 m
Example	*Paramecium*	sea anemone	locust	*Pelargonium*	goldfish	human
Level of activity	move in search of food	jellyfish swim slowly; anemones are sedentary and move very slowly	move actively; many fly	no movement of whole plant; parts such as leaves may move slowly	move actively	move actively
Type of transport system	no specialised transport system	no specialised transport system	blood system with pumps	xylem and phloem make up transport system; no pump	blood system with pump	blood system with pump

● **Table 8.1** Different transport systems.

meet their requirements for the supply of nutrients and oxygen, and the removal of waste products, by means of **diffusion** (see page 54). The very small distances across which substances have to diffuse means that the speed of supply or removal is sufficient for their needs. These tiny organisms have a large surface area compared to their total volume, so there is a relativity large area of membrane across which gases can diffuse in and out of their bodies.

Even larger organisms, such as cnidarians, can manage by diffusion alone. Their body is made up of just two layers of cells, so every cell is within a very small distance of the water in which these organisms live and with which they exchange materials. They, too, have relatively large surface area to volume ratios. Moreover, cnidarians are not very active animals, so their cells do not have large requirements for glucose or oxygen, nor do they produce large amounts of waste products.

Diffusion, slow though it is, is quite adequate to supply their needs.

Larger, more active, organisms such as insects, fish and mammals, cannot rely on diffusion alone. Cells, often deep within their bodies, are metabolically very active, with requirements for rapid supplies of nutrients and oxygen, and with relatively large amounts of waste products to be removed. These organisms have well-organised transport systems, with pumps to keep fluid moving through them. Plants, although large, are less metabolically active than these groups of animals and, as you will see in chapter 10, have evolved a very different type of transport system, with no obvious pump to keep fluids moving.

The cardiovascular system

Figure 8.1 shows the general layout of the main transport system of mammals, that is the blood system or **cardiovascular system**. It is made up of a pump, the **heart**, and a system of interconnecting tubes, the **blood vessels**. The blood always remains within these vessels, and so the system is known as a **closed** blood system.

If you trace the journey of the blood around the body, beginning in the left ventricle of the heart, you will find that the blood travels twice through the heart on one complete 'circuit'. Blood is pumped out of the left ventricle into the **aorta** (*figure 8.2*), and travels from there to all parts of the body except the lungs. It returns to the right side of the heart in the **vena cava**, and is then pumped out of the right ventricle into the **pulmonary arteries**, which carry it to the lungs. The final part of the journey is along the **pulmonary veins**, which return it to the left side of the heart. This combination of pulmonary circulation and systemic circulation makes a **double circulatory system**.

SAQ 8.2 _____

Figure 8.3 shows the general layout of the circulatory system of a fish.

a How does this differ from the circulatory system of a mammal?

b Suggest the possible advantages of the design of the mammalian circulatory system over that of a fish.

The detailed structure and functions of the heart will be looked at in chapter 9. We now look at the rest of the system.

The vessels making up the blood system are of three main types. *Figure 8.4* shows these

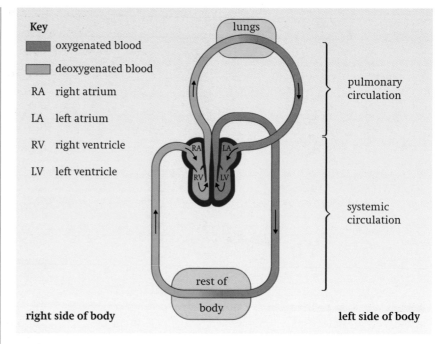

● **Figure 8.1** The general plan of the mammalian transport system, viewed as though looking at someone facing you. It is a closed double circulatory system.

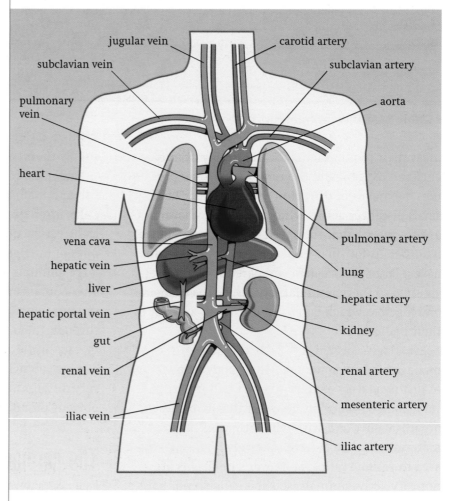

● **Figure 8.2** The positions of some of the main blood vessels in the human body.

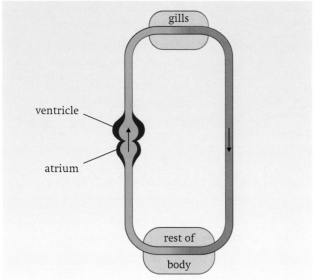

- **Figure 8.3** The general plan of the transport system of a fish.

vessels in transverse section. Vessels carrying blood *away* from the heart are known as **arteries**, while those carrying blood *towards* the heart are **veins**. Linking arteries and veins, taking blood close to almost every cell in the body, are tiny vessels called **capillaries**.

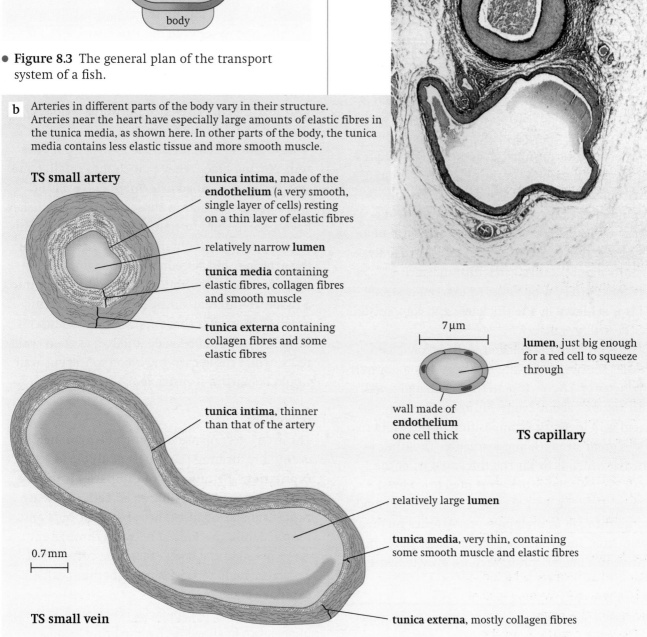

b Arteries in different parts of the body vary in their structure. Arteries near the heart have especially large amounts of elastic fibres in the tunica media, as shown here. In other parts of the body, the tunica media contains less elastic tissue and more smooth muscle.

TS small artery

tunica intima, made of the **endothelium** (a very smooth, single layer of cells) resting on a thin layer of elastic fibres

relatively narrow **lumen**

tunica media containing elastic fibres, collagen fibres and smooth muscle

tunica externa containing collagen fibres and some elastic fibres

7 µm

lumen, just big enough for a red cell to squeeze through

wall made of **endothelium** one cell thick

TS capillary

tunica intima, thinner than that of the artery

relatively large **lumen**

tunica media, very thin, containing some smooth muscle and elastic fibres

0.7 mm

TS small vein

tunica externa, mostly collagen fibres

- **Figure 8.4 a** Micrograph of an artery and a vein in TS (×15).
  b The structure of arteries, veins and capillaries.

Arteries

The function of arteries is to **transport blood, swiftly and at high pressure, to the tissues**.

The structure of the wall of an artery enables it to perform this function efficiently. Arteries and veins both have walls made up of three layers:

- an inner **endothelium** (lining tissue), made up of a layer of flat cells fitting together like jigsaw pieces (squamous epithelium, see page 19): this layer is very smooth, minimising friction with the moving blood and rests on elastic fibres;
- a middle layer called the **tunica media** ('middle coat'), containing smooth muscle, collagen and elastic fibres;
- an outer layer called the **tunica externa** ('outer coat'), containing elastic fibres and collagen fibres.

The distinctive characteristic of an artery wall is its strength. Blood leaving the heart is at a very high pressure. Blood pressure in the human aorta may be around 120 mm Hg, or 16 kPa. (Blood pressure is still measured in the old units of mm Hg even though kPa is the SI unit. It stands for 'millimetres of mercury', and refers to the distance which mercury is pushed up the arm of a U-tube as shown on page 178. 1 mm Hg is equivalent to about 0.13 kPa.) To withstand such pressure, artery walls must be extremely strong. This is achieved by the thickness and composition of the artery wall.

Arteries have the thickest walls of any blood vessel. The aorta, the largest artery, has an overall diameter of 2.5 cm close to the heart, and a wall thickness of about 2 mm. Although this may not seem very great, the composition of the wall provides great strength and resilience. The tunica media, which is by far the thickest part of the wall, contains large amounts of elastic fibres. These allow the wall to stretch as pulses of blood surge through at high pressure. Arteries further away from the heart have fewer elastic fibres in the tunica media, but have more muscle fibres.

SAQ 8.3 _____

Suggest why arteries close to the heart have more elastic fibres in their walls than arteries further away from the heart.

The elasticity of artery walls is important in allowing them to 'give', so reducing the likelihood that they will burst. This elasticity also has another very important function. Blood is pumped out of the heart in pulses, rushing out at high pressure as the ventricles contract, and slowing as the ventricles relax. The artery walls stretch as the high-pressure blood surges into them, and then recoil inwards as the pressure drops. Therefore, as blood at high pressure enters an artery, the artery becomes wider, reducing the pressure a little. As blood at lower pressure enters an artery, the artery wall recoils inwards, giving the blood a small 'push' and raising the pressure a little. The overall effect is to 'even out' the flow of blood. However, the arteries are not entirely effective in achieving this: if you feel your pulse in your wrist, you can feel the artery, even at this distance from your heart, being stretched outwards with each surge of blood from the heart.

As arteries reach the tissue to which they are transporting blood, they branch into smaller and smaller vessels, called **arterioles**. The walls of arterioles are similar to those of arteries, but they have a greater proportion of smooth muscle. This muscle can contract, narrowing the diameter of the arteriole and so reducing blood flow. This helps to control the volume of blood flowing into a tissue at different times. For example, during exercise, arterioles that supply blood to muscles in your legs would be wide (dilated) as their walls relax, while those carrying blood to the gut wall would be narrow (constricted).

Capillaries

The arterioles themselves continue to branch, eventually forming the tiniest of all blood vessels, **capillaries**. The function of capillaries is **to take blood as close as possible to all cells, allowing rapid transfer of substances between cells and blood**. Capillaries form a network throughout every tissue in the body except the cornea and cartilage. Such networks are sometimes called **capillary beds**.

The small size of capillaries is obviously of great importance in allowing them to bring blood as closely as possible to each group of cells in the body. A human capillary is approximately 7 μm in diameter, about the same size as a red blood cell (*figure 8.5*). Moreover, their walls are extremely thin, made up of a single layer of endothelial cells. As red blood cells carrying oxygen squeeze through a capillary, they are brought to within as little as 1 μm of the cells outside the capillary which need the oxygen.

SAQ 8.4

Suggest why there are no blood capillaries in the cornea of the eye. (You will have to think back to your knowledge of the eye from GCSE.). How might the cornea be supplied with its requirements?

In most capillaries, there are tiny gaps between the individual cells that form the endothelium. As we shall see later in this chapter, these gaps are important in allowing some components of the blood to seep through into the spaces between the cells in all the tissues of the body. These components form tissue fluid.

By the time blood reaches the capillaries, it has already lost a great deal of the pressure originally supplied to it by the contraction of the ventricles. As blood enters a capillary from an arteriole, it may have a pressure of around 35 mm Hg or 4.7 kPa; by the time it reaches the far end of the capillary, the pressure will have dropped to around 10 mm Hg or 1.3 kPa.

Veins

As blood leaves a capillary bed, the capillaries gradually join with one another, forming larger vessels called **venules**. These join to form **veins**. The function of veins is **to return blood to the heart**.

By the time blood enters a vein, its pressure has dropped to a very low value. In humans, a typical value for venous blood pressure is about 5 mm Hg or less. This very low pressure means that there is no need for veins to have thick walls. They have the same three layers as arteries, but the tunica media is much thinner, and has far fewer elastic fibres and muscle fibres.

The low blood pressure in veins creates a problem: how can this blood be returned to the

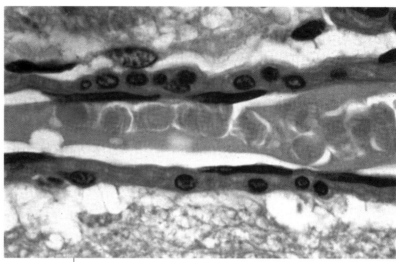

● **Figure 8.5** Micrograph of a blood capillary containing red blood cells, which are stained pink. The cells with dark purple nuclei are the endothelium of the capillary wall.

heart? The problem is perhaps most obvious if you consider how blood can return from your legs. Unaided, the blood in your leg veins would sink and accumulate in your feet. However, many of the veins run within, or very close to, several leg muscles. Whenever you tense these muscles, they squeeze inwards on the veins in your legs, temporarily raising the pressure within them.

This in itself would not help to push the blood back towards the heart; blood would just squidge up and down as you walked. To keep the blood flowing in the right direction, veins contain half-moon valves, or **semilunar valves**, formed from their endothelium (*figure 8.6*). These valves allow blood to move towards the heart, but not away

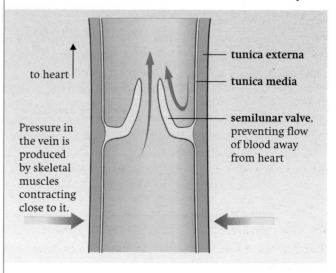

● **Figure 8.6** Longitudinal section of a small vein.

from it. Thus, when you contract your leg muscles, the blood in the veins is squeezed *up* through these valves, but cannot pass *down* through them.

SAQ 8.5
Suggest reasons for each of the following.
a Normal venous pressure in the feet is about 25 mm Hg. When a soldier stands at attention the blood pressure in their feet rises very quickly to about 90 mm Hg.
b When you breathe in, that is when the volume of the thorax increases, blood moves through the veins towards the heart.

SAQ 8.6
Construct a table comparing the structure of arteries, veins and capillaries. Include both similarities and differences, and give reasons for the differences which you describe.

SAQ 8.7
Using *figure 8.7*, describe and explain how blood pressure varies in different parts of the circulatory system.

Blood plasma and tissue fluid

Blood is composed of cells floating in a pale yellow liquid called **plasma**. Blood plasma is mostly water, with a variety of substances dissolved in it. These solutes include nutrients, such as glucose, and waste products, such as urea, that are being transported from one place to another in the body. They also include protein molecules, called **plasma proteins**, that remain in the blood all the time.

As blood flows through capillaries within tissues, some of the plasma leaks out through the gaps between the cells in the walls of the capillary, and seeps into the spaces between the cells of the tissues. Almost one-sixth of your body consists of spaces between your cells. These spaces are filled with this leaked plasma, which is known as **tissue fluid**.

Tissue fluid is almost identical in composition to blood plasma. However, it contains far fewer protein molecules than blood plasma, as these are too large to escape easily through the tiny holes in the capillary endothelium. Red blood cells are much too large to pass through, so tissue fluid does not contain these, but some white blood cells can squeeze through, and move freely around in tissue fluid. *Table 8.2* shows the sizes of the molecules of some of the substances in blood plasma, and the relative ease with which they pass from capillaries into tissue fluid.

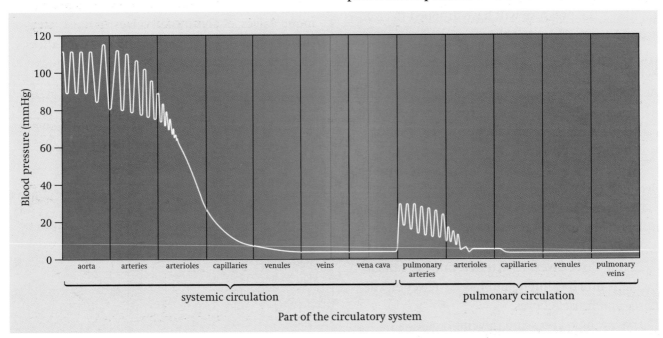

● **Figure 8.7** Blood pressure in different regions of the human circulatory system.

Substance	Relative molecular mass	Permeability
water	18	1.00
sodium ions	23	0.96
urea	60	0.8
glucose	180	0.6
haemoglobin	68 000	0.01
albumin	69 000	0.000 01

The permeability to water is given a value of 1. The other values are given in proportion to that of water.

● **Table 8.2** Relative permeability of capillaries in a muscle to different substances.

SAQ 8.8

Use the information in *table 8.2* to answer the following.

a How does relative molecular mass of a substance appear to correlate with the permeability of capillary walls to this substance?

b In a respiring muscle, would you expect the net diffusion of glucose to be *from* the blood plasma to the muscle cells, or vice versa? Explain your answer.

c Albumin is the most abundant plasma protein. Suggest why it is important that capillary walls should not be permeable to albumin.

The amount of fluid which leaves the capillary to form tissue fluid is the result of two opposing pressures. Particularly at the arterial end of a capillary bed, the blood pressure inside the capillary is enough to push fluid out into the tissue. However, we have seen that water moves by osmosis from regions of low solute concentration to regions of high solute concentration (page 56). Since tissue fluid lacks the high concentrations of proteins that exist in plasma, the imbalance leads to osmotic movement of water back into capillaries from tissue fluid. The net result of these competing processes is that fluid tends to

flow *out* of capillaries into tissue fluid at the *arterial* end of a capillary bed and *into* capillaries from tissue fluid near the *venous* end of a capillary bed. Overall, however, rather more fluid flows out of capillaries than into them, so that there is a net loss of fluid from the blood as it flows through a capillary bed.

Tissue fluid forms the immediate environment of each individual body cell. It is through tissue fluid that exchanges of materials between cells and the blood occur. Within our body, many processes take place to maintain the composition of tissue fluid at a constant level, to provide an optimum environment in which cells can work. These processes contribute to the overall process of **homeostasis**, that is the maintenance of a constant internal environment, and include the regulation of glucose concentration, water, pH, metabolic wastes and temperature.

Lymph

About 90% of the fluid that leaks from capillaries eventually seeps back into them. The remaining 10% is collected up and returned to the blood system by means of a series of tubes known as **lymph vessels** or **lymphatics**.

Lymphatics are tiny, blind-ending vessels, which are found in almost all tissues of the body. The end of one of these vessels is shown in *figure 8.8*. Tissue fluid can flow into the lymphatic through

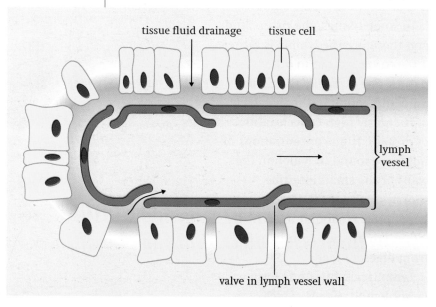

● **Figure 8.8** Drainage of tissue fluid into a lymph vessel.

tiny valves, which allow it to flow in but not out. These valves are wide enough to allow large protein molecules to pass through. This is very important, as such molecules are too big to get into blood capillaries, and so cannot be taken away by the blood. If your lymphatics did not take away the protein in the tissue fluid between your cells, you could die within 24 hours. If the protein concentration and rate of loss from plasma are not in balance with the concentration and rate of loss from tissue fluid, there can be a build up of tissue fluid, called **oedema**.

SAQ 8.9 _____

a We have seen that capillary walls are not very permeable to plasma proteins. Suggest where the protein in tissue fluid has come from.

b The disease kwashiorkor (described in chapter 12) is caused by a diet which is very low in protein. The concentration of proteins in blood plasma becomes much lower than usual. One of the symptoms of kwashiorkor is oedema. Suggest why this is so. (You will need to think about water potential.)

The fluid inside lymphatics is called **lymph**. It is virtually identical to tissue fluid: it has a different name more because it is in a different place than because it is different in composition.

In some tissues, the tissue fluid, and therefore the lymph, is rather different from that in other tissues. For example, the tissue fluid and lymph in the liver have particularly high concentrations of protein. High concentrations of lipids are found in lymph in the walls of the small intestine shortly after a meal. Here, lymphatics are found in each villus, where they absorb lipids from digested food.

Lymphatics join up to form larger lymph vessels, which gradually transport the lymph

back to the large veins which run just beneath the collarbone, the **subclavian veins** (*figure 8.9*). As in veins, the movement of fluid along the lymphatics is largely caused by the contraction of muscles around the vessels, and kept going in the right direction by valves. Lymph vessels also have smooth muscle in their walls, which can contract to push the lymph along. Lymph flow is very slow, and only about $100 \, cm^3$ per hour flows through the largest lymph vessel, the thoracic duct, in a resting human. This contrasts with the flow rate of blood of around $80 \, cm^3$ per second.

At intervals along lymph vessels, there are **lymph nodes**. These are involved in protection against disease. Bacteria and other unwanted particles are removed from lymph by some types of white blood cells as the lymph passes through a node, while other white blood cells within the nodes secrete **antibodies**. For more detail, see chapter 16.

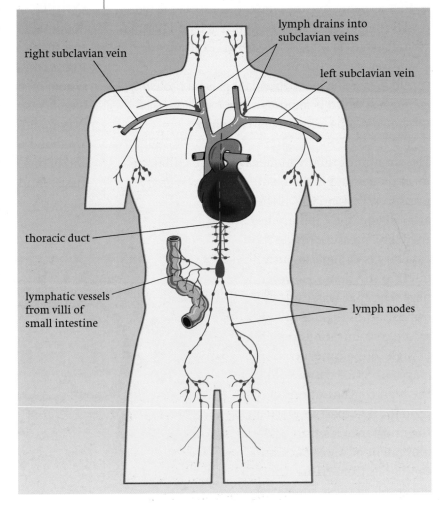

• **Figure 8.9** The human lymphatic system.

Blood

You have about $5\,dm^3$ of blood in your body, weighing about $5\,kg$. Suspended in the blood plasma, you have around 2.5×10^{13} red blood cells, 5×10^{11} white blood cells and 6×10^{12} platelets (*figure 8.10*).

Red blood cells

Red blood cells are also called **erythrocytes**, which simply means 'red cells'. Their red colour is caused by the pigment **haemoglobin**, a globular

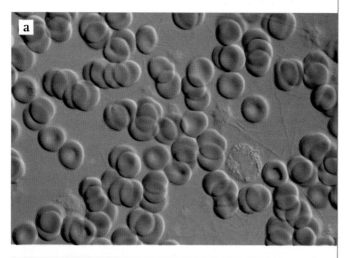

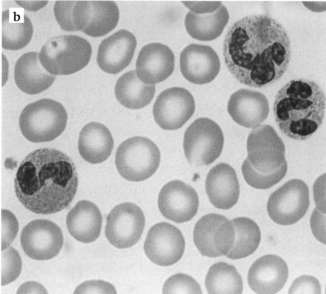

● **Figure 8.10** Micrographs of human blood.
a This photograph of unstained blood is taken with an interference contrast light microscope. Most of the cells are red blood cells. You can also see a white cell just to the right of centre (×900).
b This photograph is taken with a normal light microscope. The blood has been stained so that the nuclei of the white cells, and the platelets, are purple (×1400).

protein (see pages 34–35). The main function of haemoglobin is to transport oxygen from lungs to respiring tissues. This function is described in detail on pages 113–114.

A person's first red blood cells are formed in the liver, while still a fetus inside the uterus. By the time a baby is born, the liver has stopped manufacturing red blood cells. This function has been taken over by the bone marrow. This continues, at first in the long bones such as the humerus and femur, and then increasingly in the skull, ribs, pelvis and vertebrae, throughout life. Red blood cells do not live long; their membranes become more and more fragile and eventually rupture within some 'tight spot' in the circulatory system, often inside the spleen.

SAQ 8.10

Assuming that you have 2.5×10^{13} red blood cells in your body, that the average life of a red blood cell is 120 days, and that the total number of red blood cells remains constant, calculate how many new red blood cells must be made, on average, in your bone marrow each day.

The structure of a red blood cell (*figure 8.11*) is unusual in three ways.

■ **Red blood cells are very small**. The diameter of a human red blood cell is about $7\,\mu m$, compared with the diameter of an 'average' liver cell of $40\,\mu m$. This small size means that no

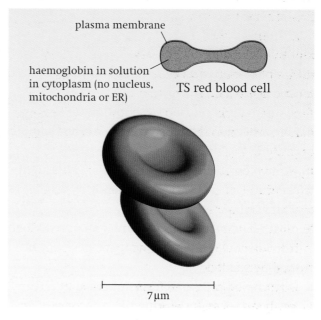

plasma membrane

haemoglobin in solution in cytoplasm (no nucleus, mitochondria or ER)

TS red blood cell

$7\,\mu m$

● **Figure 8.11** Red blood cells.

haemoglobin molecule within the cell is very far from the cell's plasma membrane, and can therefore quickly exchange oxygen with the fluid outside the cell. It also means that capillaries can be only 7 μm wide and still allow red blood cells to squeeze through them, so bringing oxygen as close as possible to cells which require it.

■ **Red blood cells are shaped like a biconcave disc.** The 'dent' in each side of a red blood cell, like its small size, increases the amount of surface area in relation to the volume of the cell, giving it a large surface area to volume ratio. This large surface area means that oxygen can diffuse quickly into or out of the cell.

■ **Red blood cells have no nucleus, no mitochondria and no endoplasmic reticulum.** The lack of these organelles means that there is more room for haemoglobin, so maximising the amount of oxygen which can be carried by each red blood cell.

SAQ 8.11

Which of these functions could, or could not, be carried out by a red blood cell? In each case, briefly justify your answer.

a Protein synthesis   b Cell division
c Lipid synthesis   d Active transport

White blood cells

White blood cells are sometimes known as **leucocytes**, which just means 'white cells'. They, too, are made in the bone marrow but are easy to distinguish from red blood cells in a blood sample because:

■ white blood cells all have a nucleus, although the shape of this varies in different types of white cell;

■ most white blood cells are larger than red blood cells, although one type, lymphocytes, may be slightly smaller;

■ white blood cells are either spherical or irregular in shape, never looking like a biconcave disc (*figures 8.10* and *8.12*).

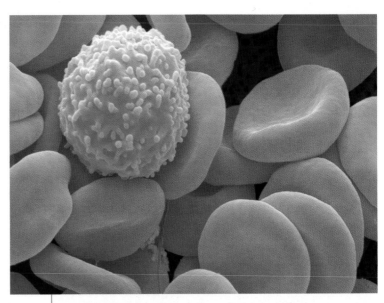

● **Figure 8.12** False-colour SEM of one human white blood cell amongst many red (×2500). Note the distinctive surface texture. Compare with *figure 6.14*.

There are many different kinds of white blood cell, with a wide variety of functions, although all are concerned with fighting disease. They can be divided into two main groups.

Phagocytes are cells that destroy invading microorganisms by phagocytosis (see page 60). The commonest type of phagocytes can be recognised by their lobed nuclei and granular cytoplasm. The three white blood cells with the dark purple nuclei in *figure 8.10b* are phagocytes.

Lymphocytes also destroy microorganisms, but not by phagocytosis. Some of them secrete chemicals called **antibodies**, which attach to and destroy the invading cells. There are different types of lymphocytes, which act in different ways, though they all look the same. Their activities are described in chapter 16. Lymphocytes are smaller than the main type of phagocyte, and they have a large round nucleus and only a small amount of cytoplasm.

Haemoglobin

A major role of the cardiovascular system is to transport oxygen from the gas exchange surfaces of the alveoli in the lungs (see page 61) to tissues all over the body. Body cells need a constant supply of oxygen, in order to be able to carry out aerobic respiration.

Oxygen is transported around the body inside red blood cells in combination with the protein **haemoglobin** (*figure 2.22*).

As we saw in chapter 2, each haemoglobin molecule is made up of four polypeptides each containing one haem group. Each haem group can combine with one oxygen molecule, O_2. Overall, then, each haemoglobin molecule can combine with four oxygen molecules (eight oxygen atoms).

$$Hb \quad + \quad 4O_2 \quad \rightleftharpoons \quad HbO_8$$

haemoglobin   oxygen   oxyhaemoglobin

SAQ 8.12

In an adult healthy human, the amount of haemoglobin in $1\,dm^3$ of blood is about 150 g.

a Given that 1 g of pure haemoglobin can combine with $1.3\,cm^3$ of oxygen at body temperature, how much oxygen can be carried in $1\,dm^3$ of blood?

b At body temperature, the solubility of oxygen in water is approximately $0.025\,cm^3$ of oxygen per cm^3 of water. Assuming that blood plasma is mostly water, how much oxygen could be carried in $1\,dm^3$ of blood if we had no haemoglobin?

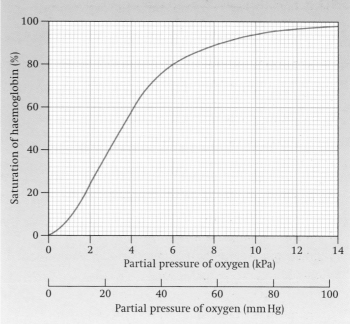

● **Figure 8.13** The haemoglobin dissociation curve.

The haemoglobin dissociation curve

A molecule whose function is to transport oxygen from one part of the body to another must be able not only to *pick up* oxygen at the lungs, but also to *release* oxygen within respiring tissues. Haemoglobin performs this task superbly.

To investigate how haemoglobin behaves, samples are extracted from blood and exposed to different concentrations, or **partial pressures**, of oxygen. The amount of oxygen which combines with each sample of haemoglobin is then measured. The maximum amount of oxygen with which a sample can possibly combine is given a value of 100%. A sample of haemoglobin which has combined with this maximum amount of oxygen is said to be **saturated**. The amounts with which identical samples combine at lower oxygen partial pressures are then expressed as a percentage of this maximum value. *Table 8.3* shows a series of results from such an investigation.

The percentage saturation of each sample can be plotted against the partial pressure of oxygen to obtain the curve shown in *figure 8.13*. This is known as a **dissociation curve**.

It shows that at low partial pressures of oxygen, the percentage saturation of haemoglobin is very low, that is the haemoglobin is combined with only a very little oxygen. At high partial pressures of oxygen, the percentage saturation of haemoglobin is very high: it is combined with large amounts of oxygen.

Partial pressure of oxygen (kPa)	1	2	3	4	5	6	7	8	9	10	11	12	13	14
Saturation of haemoglobin (%)	8.5	24.0	43.0	57.5	71.5	80.0	85.5	88.0	92.0	94.0	95.5	96.5	97.5	98.0

● **Table 8.3** The varying ability of haemoglobin to carry oxygen.

SAQ 8.13

Use the dissociation curve in *figure 8.13* to answer these questions.

a (i) The partial pressure of oxygen in the alveoli of the lungs is about 12 kPa. What is the percentage saturation of haemoglobin in the capillaries in the lungs?

 (ii) If one gram of fully saturated haemoglobin is combined with 1.3 cm^3 of oxygen, how much oxygen will one gram of haemoglobin in the capillaries in the lungs be combined with?

b (i) The partial pressure of oxygen in an actively respiring muscle is about 2 kPa. What is the percentage saturation of haemoglobin in the capillaries of such a muscle?

 (ii) How much oxygen will one gram of haemoglobin in the capillaries of this muscle be combined with?

Consider the haemoglobin within a red blood cell in a capillary in the lungs. Here, where the partial pressure of oxygen is high, this haemoglobin will be 95–97% saturated with oxygen, that is almost every haemoglobin molecule will be combined with its full complement of eight oxygen atoms. In an actively respiring muscle, on the other hand, where the partial pressure of oxygen is low, the haemoglobin will be about 20–25% saturated with oxygen, that is the haemoglobin is carrying only a quarter of the oxygen which it is capable of carrying. This means that haemoglobin coming from the lungs carries a lot of oxygen; as it reaches a muscle it releases around three-quarters. This released oxygen diffuses out of the red blood cell and into the muscle where it can be used in respiration.

The S-shaped curve

The shape of the haemoglobin dissociation curve can be explained by the behaviour of a haemoglobin molecule as it combines with or loses oxygen molecules.

Oxygen molecules combine with the iron atoms in the haem groups of a haemoglobin molecule. You will remember that each haemoglobin molecule has four haem groups. When an oxygen molecule combines with one haem group, the whole haemoglobin molecule is slightly distorted. The distortion makes it easier for a second oxygen molecule to combine with a second haem group. This in turn makes it easier for a third oxygen molecule to combine with a third haem group. It is then a little *harder* for the fourth and final oxygen molecule to combine.

The shape of the curve reflects this behaviour. Up to an oxygen partial pressure of around 2 kPa, on average only one oxygen molecule is combined with each haemoglobin molecule. Once this oxygen molecule is combined, however, it becomes successively easier for the second and third oxygen molecules to combine, so the curve rises very steeply. Over this part of the curve, a *small* change in the partial pressure of oxygen causes a *very large* change in the amount of oxygen which is carried by the haemoglobin.

The Bohr shift

The behaviour of haemoglobin in picking up oxygen at the lungs, and readily releasing it when in conditions of low oxygen partial pressure, is exactly what is needed. But, in fact, it is even better at this than is shown by the dissociation curve in *figure 8.13*. This is because the amount of oxygen it carries is affected not only by the partial pressure of *oxygen*, but also by the partial pressure of *carbon dioxide*.

Carbon dioxide is continually produced by respiring cells. It diffuses from the cells and into blood plasma, from where some of it diffuses into the red blood cells.

In the cytoplasm of red blood cells there is an enzyme, **carbonic anhydrase**. This enzyme catalyses the following reaction:

$$CO_2 + H_2O \underset{\text{carbonic anhydrase}}{\rightleftharpoons} H_2CO_3$$

carbon dioxide   water   carbonic acid

The carbonic acid dissociates:

$$H_2CO_3 \rightleftharpoons H^+ + HCO_3^-$$

carbonic acid   hydrogen ion   hydrogencarbonate ion

Haemoglobin readily combines with these hydrogen ions, forming **haemoglobinic acid, HHb**. In so doing, it releases the oxygen which it is carrying.

The net result of this reaction is two-fold:

■ The haemoglobin 'mops up' the hydrogen ions which are formed when carbon dioxide dissolves and dissociates. A high concentration of hydrogen ions means a low pH; if the hydrogen ions were left in solution the blood would be very acidic. By removing the hydrogen ions from solution, haemoglobin helps to maintain the pH of the blood close to neutral. It is acting as a **buffer**.

■ The presence of a high partial pressure of carbon dioxide causes haemoglobin to release oxygen. This is called the **Bohr effect**, after Christian Bohr who discovered it in 1904. It is exactly what is needed. High concentrations of carbon dioxide are found in actively respiring tissues, which need oxygen; these high carbon dioxide concentrations cause haemoglobin to release its oxygen even more readily than it would otherwise do.

If a dissociation curve is drawn for haemoglobin at a high partial pressure of carbon dioxide, it looks like the lower curve in *figure 8.14*. At each partial pressure of oxygen, the haemoglobin is less saturated than it would be at a low partial pressure of carbon dioxide. The curve therefore lies below, and to the right of, the 'normal' curve.

Carbon dioxide transport

The description of the Bohr effect above explains one way in which carbon dioxide is carried in the blood. One product of the dissociation of dissolved carbon dioxide is hydrogencarbonate ions, HCO_3^-. These are initially formed in the cytoplasm of the red blood cell, because this is where the enzyme carbonic anhydrase is found. Most of them then diffuse out of the red blood cell into the blood plasma, where they are carried in solution. About 85% of the carbon dioxide transported by the blood is carried in this way.

Some carbon dioxide, however, does not dissociate, but remains as carbon dioxide molecules. Some of these simply dissolve in the blood plasma; about 5% of the total is carried in this form. Others diffuse into the red blood cells, but instead of undergoing the reaction catalysed by carbonic anhydrase, combine directly with the terminal amine groups ($-NH_2$) of some of the haemoglobin molecules. The compound formed is called **carbamino-haemoglobin**. About 10% of the carbon dioxide is carried in this way (*figure 8.15*).

When blood reaches the lungs, the reactions described above go into reverse. The relatively low concentration of carbon dioxide in the alveoli compared with that in the blood causes carbon dioxide to diffuse from the blood into the air in the alveoli, stimulating the carbon dioxide of carbamino-haemoglobin to leave the red blood cell, and hydrogencarbonate and hydrogen ions to recombine to form carbon dioxide molecules once more. This leaves the haemoglobin molecules free to combine with oxygen, ready to begin another circuit of the body.

Fetal haemoglobin

A developing fetus obtains its oxygen not from its own lungs, but from its mother's blood. In the placenta, the mother's blood is brought very close to that of the fetus, allowing diffusion of various substances from mother to fetus or vice versa.

Oxygen arrives at the placenta in combination with haemoglobin, inside the mother's red blood cells. The partial pressure of oxygen in the blood vessels in the placenta is relatively low,

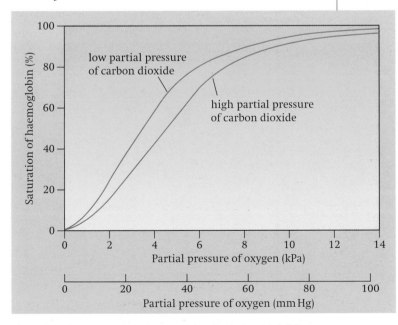

● **Figure 8.14** Dissociation curves for haemoglobin at two different partial pressures of carbon dioxide. The shift of the curve to the right when the haemoglobin is exposed to higher carbon dioxide concentration is called the Bohr effect.

because the fetus is respiring. The mother's haemoglobin therefore releases some of its oxygen, which diffuses from her blood into the fetus's blood.

The partial pressure of oxygen in the fetus's blood is only a little lower than that in its mother's blood. However, the haemoglobin of the fetus is different from its mother's haemoglobin. Fetal haemoglobin combines more readily with oxygen than adult haemoglobin does; thus, the fetal haemoglobin will pick up oxygen which the adult haemoglobin has dropped. Fetal haemoglobin is said to have a **higher affinity** for oxygen than adult haemoglobin.

A dissociation curve for fetal haemoglobin (*figure 8.16*) shows that, at each partial pressure of oxygen, fetal haemoglobin is slightly more saturated than adult haemoglobin. The curve lies *above* the curve for adult haemoglobin.

Myoglobin

Myoglobin, like haemoglobin, is a red pigment which combines reversibly with oxygen. It is not found in the blood, but inside cells in some tissues of the body, especially in muscle cells. The red colour of meat is largely caused by myoglobin.

Each myoglobin molecule is made up of only one polypeptide, rather than the four in a haemoglobin molecule. It has just one haem group, and can combine with just one oxygen molecule. However, once combined, the oxymyoglobin molecule is very stable, and will not release its oxygen unless the partial pressure

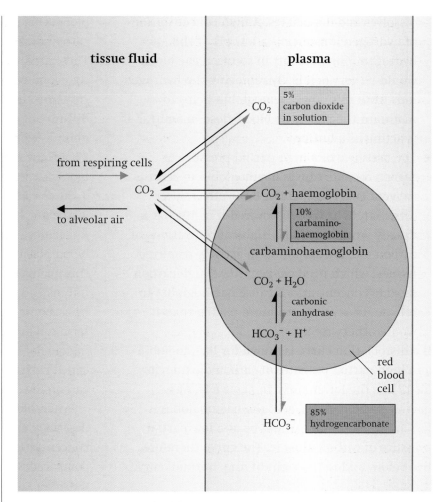

● **Figure 8.15** Carbon dioxide transport in the blood. The blood carries carbon dioxide partly as undissociated carbon dioxide in solution in the plasma, partly as hydrogencarbonate ions in solution in the plasma and partly combined with haemoglobin in the red blood cells.

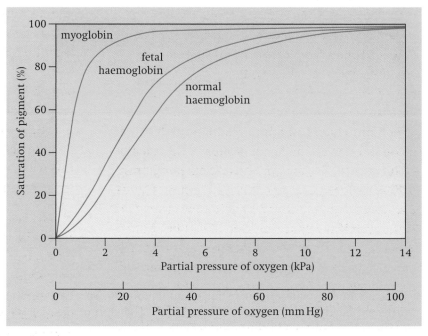

● **Figure 8.16** Dissociation curves for myoglobin and fetal haemoglobin.

of oxygen around it is very low indeed. The curve in *figure 8.16* shows this in comparison with haemoglobin. At each partial pressure of oxygen, myoglobin has a higher percentage saturation with oxygen than haemoglobin does.

This means that myoglobin acts as an **oxygen store**. At the normal partial pressures of oxygen in a respiring muscle, haemoglobin releases its oxygen. Some of this oxygen is picked up and held tightly by myoglobin in the muscle. The myoglobin will not release this oxygen unless the oxygen concentration in the muscle drops very low, that is unless the muscle is using up oxygen at a faster rate than the haemoglobin in the blood can supply it. The oxygen held by the myoglobin is a reserve, to be used only in conditions of particularly great oxygen demand (see chapter 13).

Problems with oxygen transport

The efficient transport of oxygen around the body can be impaired by many different factors. We consider some here and in chapter 14.

Carbon monoxide

Despite its almost perfect design as an oxygen-transporting molecule, haemoglobin does have one property which can prove very dangerous. It combines very readily, and almost irreversibly, with carbon monoxide.

Carbon monoxide, CO, is formed when a carbon-containing compound burns incompletely. Exhaust fumes from cars contain significant amounts of carbon monoxide, as does cigarette smoke. When such fumes are inhaled, the carbon monoxide readily diffuses across the walls of the alveoli, into blood, and into red blood cells. Here it combines with the haem groups in the haemoglobin molecules, forming **carboxyhaemoglobin**.

Haemoglobin combines with carbon monoxide 250 times more readily than it does with oxygen. Thus, even if the concentration of carbon monoxide in air is much lower than the concentration of oxygen, a high proportion of haemoglobin will combine with carbon monoxide. Moreover, carboxyhaemoglobin is a very stable compound; the carbon monoxide remains combined with the haemoglobin for a long time.

The result of this is that even relatively low concentrations of carbon monoxide, as low as 0.1% of the air, can cause death by asphyxiation. The victim looks very bright red, the colour of carboxyhaemoglobin. Treatment of carbon monoxide poisoning involves administration of a mixture of pure oxygen and carbon dioxide: high concentrations of oxygen to favour the combination of haemoglobin with oxygen rather than carbon monoxide, and carbon dioxide to stimulate an increase in the breathing rate.

Cigarette smoke contains up to 5% carbon monoxide (see pages 187–188). If you breathed in 'pure' cigarette smoke for any length of time, you would die of asphyxiation. As it is, even smokers who inhale also breathe in some normal air, diluting the carbon monoxide levels in their lungs. Nevertheless, around 5% of the haemoglobin in a regular smoker's blood is permanently combined with carbon monoxide. This considerably reduces its oxygen-carrying capacity.

High altitude

We obtain our oxygen from the air around us. At sea level, the partial pressure of oxygen in the atmosphere is just over 20 kPa, and the partial pressure of oxygen in an alveolus in the lungs is about 13 kPa. If you look at the oxygen dissociation curve for haemoglobin in *figure 8.13*, you can see that at this partial pressure of oxygen haemoglobin is almost completely saturated with oxygen.

If, however, a person climbs up a mountain to a height of 6500 metres (about 21 000 feet), then the air pressure is much less. The partial pressure of oxygen in the air is only about 10 kPa, and in the lungs about 5.3 kPa. You can see from *figure 8.13* that this will mean that the haemoglobin will become only about 70% saturated in the lungs. Less oxygen will be carried around the body, and the person may begin to feel breathless and ill.

SAQ 8.14

Mount Everest is nearly 9000 m high. The partial pressure of oxygen in the alveoli at this height is only about 2.5 kPa. Explain what effect this would have on the supply of oxygen to body cells if a person climbed to the top of Mount Everest without a supplementary oxygen supply.

If someone climbs steadily, over a period of just a few days, from sea level to a high altitude, the body does not have enough time to adjust to this drop in oxygen availability, and the person may suffer from **altitude sickness**. The symptoms frequently begin with an increase in the rate and depth of breathing, and a general feeling of dizziness and weakness. These symptoms can be easily reversed by going down to a lower altitude. Some people, however, can quickly become very ill indeed. The arterioles in their brain dilate, increasing the amount of blood flowing into the capillaries, so that fluid begins to leak from them into the brain tissues. This can cause disorientation. Fluid may also leak into the lungs, preventing them from functioning properly. Acute altitude sickness can be fatal, and a person suffering from it must be brought down to low altitude immediately, or given oxygen.

However, if the body is given plenty of time to adapt, then most people can cope well at altitudes up to at least 5000 metres. In 1979, two mountaineers climbed Mount Everest without oxygen, returning safely despite experiencing hallucinations and feelings of euphoria at the summit.

As the body gradually acclimatises to high altitude, a number of changes take place. Perhaps the most significant of these is that the number of red blood cells increases. Whereas red blood cells normally make up about 40–50% of the blood, after a few months at high altitude this rises to as much as 50–70%. However, this does take a long time to happen, and there is almost no change in the number of red blood cells for at least two or three weeks at high altitude.

SAQ 8.15

Explain how an increase in the number of red blood cells can help to compensate for the lack of oxygen in the air at high altitude.

SAQ 8.16

Athletes often prepare themselves for important competitions by spending several months training at high altitude. Explain how this could improve their performance.

● **Figure 8.18** Most high-altitude climbers, such as here on Mount Everest, breathe using oxygen carried in cylinders.

People who live permanently at high altitude, such as in the Andes or Himalayas, show a number of adaptations to their low-oxygen environment. It seems that they are not genetically different from people who live at low altitudes, but rather that their exposure to low oxygen partial pressures from birth encourages the development of these adaptations from an early age. They often have especially broad chests, providing larger lung capacities than normal. The heart is often larger than in a person who lives at low altitude, especially the right side that pumps blood to the lungs. They also have more haemoglobin in their blood than usual, so increasing the efficiency of oxygen transport from lungs to tissues.

SUMMARY

◆ Large, active organisms such as mammals need a transport system, in which fluid driven by a pump carries oxygen and nutrients to all tissues, and removes waste products from them. Mammals have a double circulatory system.

- Blood is carried away from the heart in arteries, passes through tissues in capillaries, and is returned to the heart in veins. Blood pressure drops gradually as it passes along this system.

- Arteries have thick, elastic walls, to allow them to withstand high blood pressures and to smooth out the pulsed blood flow. Capillaries are only just wide enough to allow the passage of red blood cells, and have very thin walls to allow efficient and rapid transfer of materials between blood and cells. Veins have thinner walls than arteries and possess valves, to help blood at low pressure flow back to the heart.

- Plasma leaks from capillaries to form tissue fluid. This is collected into lymphatics and returned to the blood in the subclavian veins.

- Red blood cells carry oxygen in combination with haemoglobin. Haemoglobin picks up oxygen at high partial pressures of oxygen in the lungs, and releases it at low partial pressures of oxygen in respiring tissues. It releases oxygen more easily when carbon dioxide concentration is high. Myoglobin and fetal haemoglobin have a higher affinity for oxygen than adult haemoglobin, so they can take oxygen from adult haemoglobin. Myoglobin acts as an oxygen store in the muscle.

- Carbon dioxide is mostly carried as hydrogencarbonate ions in blood plasma, but also in combination with haemoglobin in red blood cells and dissolved as carbon dioxide molecules in blood plasma.

- White blood cells aid in defence against disease.

- At high altitudes, the partial pressure of oxygen is so low that altitude sickness can be caused which can be fatal. The body can adapt to gradual changes, however, by producing more red blood cells and haemoglobin.

Questions

1 Discuss the need for transport systems in multicellular animals.

2 Discuss the ways in which a red blood cell is adapted for its functions.

3 Summarise the ways in which
  a oxygen and
  b carbon dioxide
  are transported in the body of a mammal.

4 a What is the Bohr effect?
   b Why is the Bohr effect useful?
   c The magnitude of the Bohr effect differs between species. Suggest reasons for each of the following.
     - The Bohr effect in Weddell seals, which can dive to 400 m for up to 43 minutes, is large.
     - The Bohr effect in hibernating hedgehogs is small.

5 a Explain what is meant by an *oxygen dissociation curve*.
   b Compare and contrast the oxygen dissociation curves for adult haemoglobin, fetal haemoglobin and myoglobin, discussing the reasons for the differences between them.

6 a Describe and explain the problems associated with the supply of oxygen to body cells at high altitude.
   b Describe how the blood adapts to these problems.

CHAPTER 9

The mammalian heart

By the end of this chapter you should be able to:

1 describe the external and internal structure of the human heart;

2 describe the cardiac cycle, and interpret graphs showing pressure changes during this cycle;

3 explain the reasons for the difference in thickness of the atrial and ventricular walls, and of the left and right ventricular walls;

4 describe and explain the functioning of the atrio-ventricular valves, and of the semilunar valves in the aorta and pulmonary artery;

5 explain the role of the sinoatrial node in initiating heart beat, and the roles of the atrio-ventricular node and Purkyne tissue in coordinating the actions of the different parts of the heart.

The heart of an adult human has a mass of around 300 g, and is about the size of your fist (*figure 9.1*). It is a bag of muscle, filled with blood. *Figure 9.2* shows the appearance of a human heart, looking at it from the front of the body.

The muscle of which the heart is made is called **cardiac muscle**. *Figure 9.3* shows the structure of this type of muscle. It is made of interconnecting cells, whose plasma membranes are very tightly joined together. This close contact between the muscle cells allows waves of electrical excitation

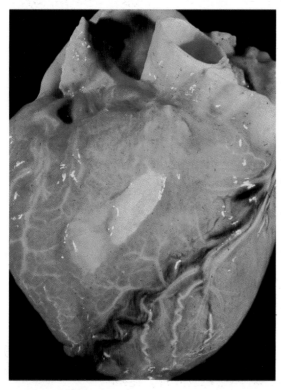

● **Figure 9.1** A human heart.

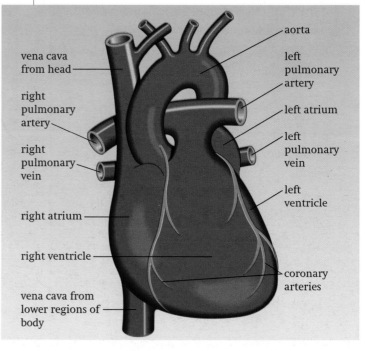

● **Figure 9.2** A human heart, seen from the front.

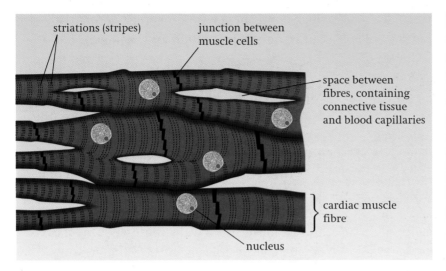

striations (stripes)

junction between muscle cells

space between fibres, containing connective tissue and blood capillaries

cardiac muscle fibre

nucleus

● **Figure 9.3** Cardiac muscle, as it appears under the high power of a light microscope (×650).

to pass easily between them, which is a very important feature of cardiac muscle, as you will see later.

Figure 9.2 also shows the blood vessels which carry blood into and out of the heart. The large, arching blood vessel is the largest artery, the **aorta**, with branches leading upwards towards the head and the main flow doubling back downwards to the rest of the body. The other blood vessel leaving the heart is the **pulmonary artery**. This, too, branches very quickly after leaving the heart, into two arteries taking blood to the right and left lungs. Running vertically on the right-hand side of the heart are the two large veins, the **venae cavae**, one bringing blood downwards from the head and the other bringing it upwards from the rest of the body. The **pulmonary veins** bring blood back to the heart from the left and right lungs.

On the surface of the heart, the **coronary arteries** can be seen (*figures 9.1* and *9.2*). These branch from the aorta, and deliver oxygenated blood to the walls of the heart itself.

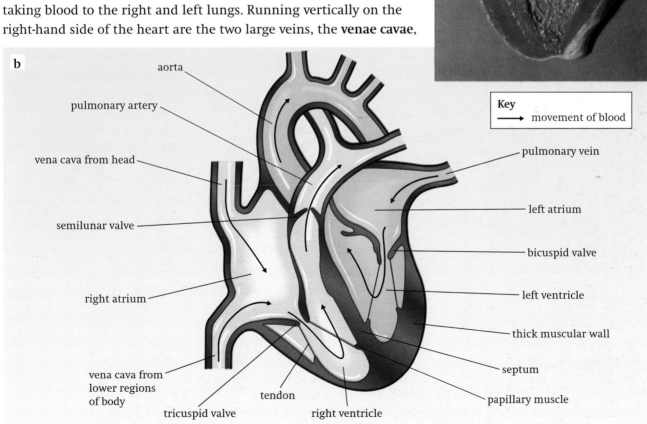

Key
→ movement of blood

aorta

pulmonary artery

vena cava from head

semilunar valve

right atrium

vena cava from lower regions of body

tendon

tricuspid valve

right ventricle

pulmonary vein

left atrium

bicuspid valve

left ventricle

thick muscular wall

septum

papillary muscle

● **Figure 9.4** Vertical sections through a human heart. **a** The heart has been cut through the left atrium and ventricle only in this photograph, whilst **b** shows both sides of the heart.

If the heart is cut open vertically (*figure 9.4*) it can be seen to contain four chambers. The two chambers on the left of the heart are completely separated from those on the right by a wall of muscle called the **septum**. Blood cannot pass through this septum; the only way for blood to get from one side of the heart to the other is to leave the heart, circulate around either the lungs or the rest of the body, and then return to the heart.

The upper chamber on each side is called an **atrium** (or sometimes an **auricle**). The two atria receive blood from the veins. You can see from *figure 9.4* that blood from the venae cavae flows into the right atrium, while blood from the pulmonary veins flows into the left atrium.

The lower chambers are **ventricles**. Blood flows into the ventricles from the atria, and is then squeezed out into the arteries. Blood from the left ventricle flows into the aorta, while blood from the right ventricle flows into the pulmonary arteries.

The atria and ventricles have valves between them, which are known as the **atrio-ventricular valves**. The one on the left is the **mitral** or **bicuspid** valve, and the one on the right is the **tricuspid valve**. We will now consider how all of these components work together so that the heart can be an efficient pump for the blood.

The cardiac cycle

Your heart beats around 70 times a minute. The **cardiac cycle** is the sequence of events which makes up one heart beat.

As the cycle is continuous, a description of it could begin anywhere. We will begin with the time when the heart is filled with blood, and the muscle in the atrial walls contracts. This stage is called **atrial systole** (*figure 9.5a*). The pressure developed by this contraction is not very great, because the muscular walls of the atria are only thin, but it is enough to force the blood in the atria down through the atrio-ventricular valves into the ventricles. The blood from the atria does not go back into the pulmonary veins or the venae cavae, because these have semilunar valves to prevent backflow.

About 0.1 second after the atria contract, the ventricles contract. This is called **ventricular systole** (*figure 9.5b*). The thick, muscular walls of the ventricles squeeze inwards on the blood,

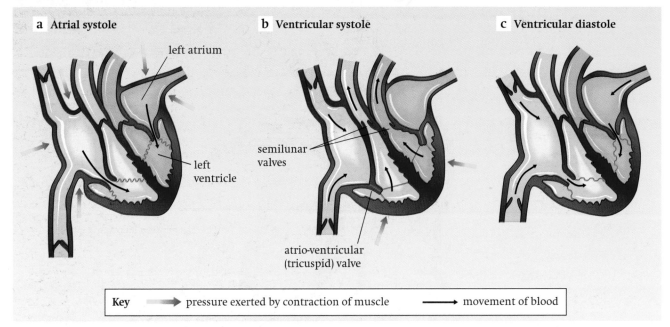

| a Atrial systole | b Ventricular systole | c Ventricular diastole |

left atrium

left ventricle

semilunar valves

atrio-ventricular (tricuspid) valve

Key ⟹ pressure exerted by contraction of muscle ⟶ movement of blood

● **Figure 9.5** The cardiac cycle. Only three stages in this continuous process are shown.
a Atrial systole Both atria contract. Blood flows from the atria into the ventricles. Backflow of blood into the veins is prevented by closure of valves in the veins.
b Ventricular systole Both ventricles contract. The atrio-ventricular valves close. The semilunar valves in the aorta and pulmonary artery open. Blood flows from the ventricles into the arteries.
c Ventricular diastole Atria and ventricles relax. Blood flows from the veins through the atria and into the ventricles.

increasing its pressure and pushing it out of the heart. As soon as the pressure in the ventricles becomes greater than the pressure in the atria, this pressure difference pushes the atrio-ventricular valves shut, preventing blood from going back into the atria. Instead, the blood rushes upwards into the aorta and the pulmonary artery, pushing open the semilunar valves in these vessels as it does so.

Ventricular systole lasts for about 0.3 second. The muscle then relaxes, and the stage called **ventricular diastole** begins (*figure 9.5c*). As the muscle relaxes, the pressure in the ventricles drops. The high-pressure blood which has just been pushed into the arteries would flow back into the ventricles, but for the presence of the semilunar valves, which snap shut as the blood fills their cusps.

During diastole, as the whole of the heart muscle relaxes, blood from the veins flows into the two atria. The blood is at a very low pressure, but the thin walls of the atria are easily distended, providing very little resistance to the blood flow. Some of the blood trickles downwards into the ventricles, through the atrio-ventricular valves. The atrial muscle then contracts, to push blood forcefully down into the ventricles, and the whole cycle begins again.

Figure 9.6 shows how the atrio-ventricular and semilunar valves work.

The walls of the ventricles are much thicker than the walls of the atria, because the ventricles need to develop much more force when they contract. Their contraction has to push the blood out of the heart and around the body. For the right ventricle, the force required is relatively small, as the blood goes only to the lungs, which are very close to the heart. The left ventricle, however, has to develop sufficient force to push blood around all the rest of the body. Therefore, the thickness of the muscular wall of the left ventricle is much greater than that of the right.

● **Figure 9.6** How the heart valves function.

a The atrio-ventricular (bicuspid and tricuspid) valves. During atrial systole (black arrow) the pressure of blood is higher in the atrium than in the ventricle and so forces the valve open. During ventricular systole (white arrow) the pressure of blood is higher in the ventricle than in the atrium. The pressure of the blood pushes up against the cusps of valve, pushing it shut. Contraction of the papillary muscles, attached to the valve by tendons, prevents the valve from being forced inside-out.

b The semilunar valves in the aorta and pulmonary arteries. During ventricular systole (white arrow) the pressure of the blood forces the valves open. During ventricular diastole (black arrows) the pressure of blood in the arteries is higher than in the ventricles. The pressure of the blood pushes into the cusps of the valves, squeezing them shut.

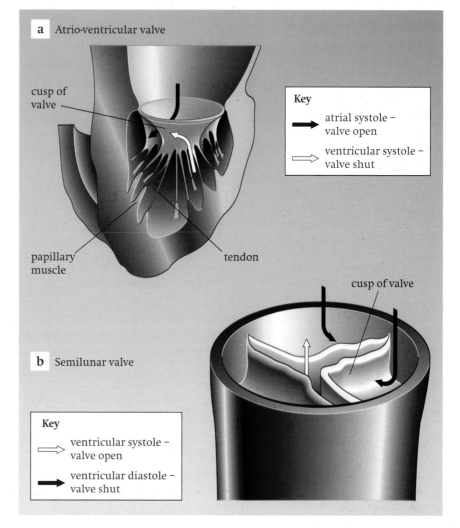

a Atrio-ventricular valve

cusp of valve

papillary muscle

tendon

Key
→ atrial systole – valve open
⇒ ventricular systole – valve shut

b Semilunar valve

cusp of valve

Key
⇒ ventricular systole – valve open
→ ventricular diastole – valve shut

SAQ 9.1

Figure 9.7 shows the pressure changes in the left atrium, left ventricle and aorta throughout two cardiac cycles. Make a copy of this diagram.

a (i) How long does one heart beat (one cardiac cycle) last?
   (ii) What is the heart rate represented on this graph, in beats per minute?

b The contraction of muscles in the ventricle wall causes the pressure inside the ventricle to rise. When the muscles relax, the pressure drops again. On your copy of the diagram, mark the following periods:
   (i) the time when the ventricle is contracting (ventricular systole);
   (ii) the time when the ventricle is relaxing (ventricular diastole).

c The contraction of muscles in the wall of the atrium raises the pressure inside it. This pressure is also raised when blood flows into the atrium from the veins, while the atrial walls are relaxed. On your copy of the diagram, mark the following periods:
   (i) the time when the atrium is contracting (atrial systole);
   (ii) the time when the atrium is relaxing (atrial diastole).

d The atrio-ventricular valves open when the pressure of the blood in the atria is greater than that in the ventricles. They snap shut when the pressure of the blood in the ventricles is greater than that in the atria. On your diagram, mark the point at which these valves will open and close.

e The opening and closing of the semilunar valves in the aorta depends in a similar way on the relative pressures in the aorta and ventricles. On your diagram, mark the point at which these valves will open and close.

f The right ventricle has much less muscle in its walls than the left ventricle, and only develops about one-quarter of the pressure developed on the left side of the heart. On your diagram, draw a line to represent the probable pressure inside the right ventricle over the 1.3 seconds shown.

Control of the heart beat

Cardiac muscle differs from the muscle in all other areas of the body in that it is **myogenic**. This means that it *naturally* contracts and relaxes: it does not need to receive impulses from a nerve to make it contract. If cardiac muscle cells are cultured in a warm, oxygenated solution containing nutrients, they contract and relax rhythmically, all by themselves.

However, the individual heart muscle cells cannot be allowed to contract at their own natural rhythms. If they did, parts of the heart would contract out of sequence with other parts; the cardiac cycle would become disordered, and the heart would stop working as a pump. The heart has its own built-in controlling and coordinating system which prevents this happening.

The cardiac cycle is initiated in a specialised patch of muscle in the wall of the right atrium, called the **sinoatrial node**. It is often

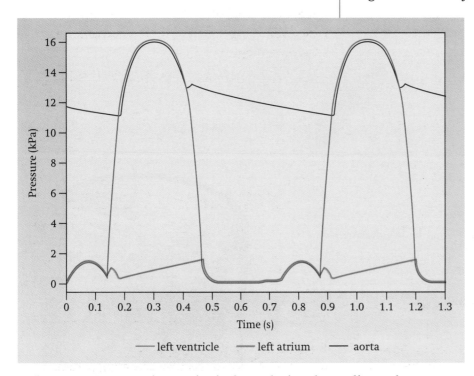

● **Figure 9.7** Pressure changes in the heart during the cardiac cycle.

called the **SAN** for short, or **pacemaker**. The muscle cells of the SAN set the rhythm for all the other cardiac muscle cells. Their natural rhythm of contraction is slightly faster than the rest of the heart muscle. Each time they contract, they set up a wave of electrical activity, which spreads out rapidly over the whole of the atrial walls. The cardiac muscle in the atrial walls responds to this excitation wave by contracting, at the same rhythm as the SAN. Thus, all the muscle in both atria contracts almost simultaneously.

As we have seen, the muscles of the ventricles do not contract until *after* the muscles of the atria. (You can imagine what would happen if they all contracted at once.) This delay is caused by a feature of the heart that briefly delays the excitation wave in its passage from the atria to the ventricles.

There is a band of fibres between the atria and ventricles which does not conduct the excitation wave. Thus, as the wave spreads out from the SAN over the atrial walls, it cannot pass into the ventricle walls. The only route through is via a patch of conducting fibres, situated in the septum, known as the **atrio-ventricular node**, or AVN (*figure 9.8*). The AVN picks up the excitation wave as it spreads across the atria and, after a delay of about 0.1 second, passes it on to a bunch of conducting fibres, called the **Purkyne tissue**, which runs down the septum between the ventricles. This transmits the excitation wave very

rapidly down to the base of the septum, from where it spreads outwards and upwards through the ventricle walls. As it does so, it causes the cardiac muscle in these walls to contract, from the bottom up, so squeezing blood upwards and into the arteries.

In a healthy heart, therefore, the atria contract and then the ventricles contract from the bottom upwards. Sometimes, this coordination of contraction goes wrong. The excitation wave becomes chaotic, passing through the ventricular muscle in all directions, feeding back on itself and restimulating areas it has just left. Small sections of the cardiac muscle contract while other sections are relaxing. The result is **fibrillation**, in which the heart wall simply flutters, rather than contracting as a whole and then relaxing as a whole. Fibrillation is almost always fatal, unless treated instantly. Fibrillation may be started by an electric shock, or by damage to large areas of muscle in the walls of the heart.

Electrocardiograms

It is relatively easy to detect and record the waves of excitation flowing through heart muscle. Electrodes can be placed on the skin over opposite sides of the heart, and the electrical potentials generated recorded with time. The result, which is essentially a graph of voltage against time, is an **electrocardiogram** (ECG).

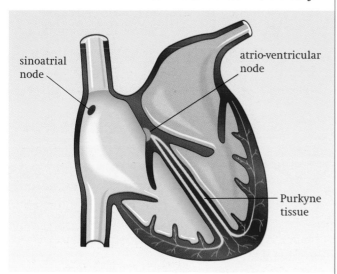

● **Figure 9.8** Vertical section of the heart to show the positions of the sinoatrial node and the atrio-ventricular node.

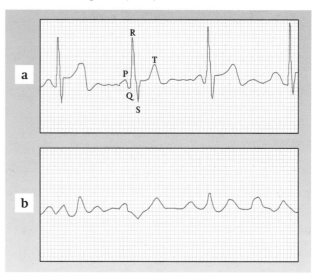

● **Figure 9.9** Electrocardiograms.
a Normal. Notice the regular, repeating pattern.
b Fibrillation.

Figure 9.9a shows a normal electrocardiogram. The part labelled **P** represents the wave of excitation sweeping over the atrial walls. The parts labelled **Q**, **R** and **S** represent the wave of excitation in the ventricle walls. The **T** section indicates the recovery of the ventricle walls.

Figure 9.9b shows an electrocardiogram from a fibrillating heart. There is no obvious regular rhythm at all. A patient in intensive care in hospital may be connected to a monitor which keeps track of the heart rhythm (*figure 9.10*). If fibrillation begins, a warning sound brings a resuscitation team running. They will attempt to shock the heart out of its fibrillation by passing a strong electric current through the chest wall. This usually stops the heart completely for up to 5 seconds, after which it often begins to beat again in a controlled way. This treatment has to be carried out within one minute of fibrillation beginning to have any real chance of success.

We consider the combined functions of heart and lungs and how they may be improved in chapter 13.

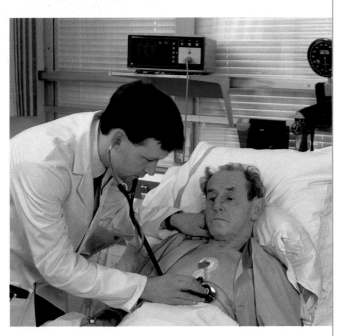

● **Figure 9.10** This patient is recovering from a heart attack in the coronary care unit of a hospital in Newcastle-upon-Tyne, England. The electrodes on his chest are connected to the heart monitor behind him, on which his heart beat is recorded.

SAQ 9.2

Figure 9.9a shows a normal ECG. The paper on which the ECG was recorded was running at a speed of $25 \, mm \, s^{-1}$.

a Calculate the heart rate in beats per minute.

b The time interval between **Q** and **T** is called the **contraction time**.
  (i) Suggest why it is given this name.
  (ii) Calculate the contraction time from this ECG.

c The time interval between **T** and **Q** is called the **filling time**.
  (i) Suggest why it is given this name.
  (ii) Calculate the filling time from this ECG.

d An adult male recorded his ECG at different heart rates. The contraction time and filling time were calculated from the ECGs. The results are shown in *table 9.1*.
  (i) Suggest how the man could have increased his heart rate for the purposes of the experiment.
  (ii) Present these results as a line graph, drawing both curves on the same pair of axes.
  (iii) Comment on these results.

Heart rate (beats per minute)	Contraction time (s)	Filling time (s)
39.5	0.37	1.14
48.4	0.39	0.82
56.6	0.39	0.66
58.0	0.38	0.60
60.0	0.38	0.57
63.8	0.40	0.54
68.2	0.42	0.45
69.8	0.38	0.46
73.2	0.38	0.44
75.0	0.38	0.39
78.9	0.38	0.36
81.1	0.39	0.33
85.7	0.37	0.32
88.2	0.39	0.30

● **Table 9.1**

SUMMARY

◆ The human heart, like that of all mammals, has two atria and two ventricles. Blood enters the heart by the atria and leaves from the ventricles. A septum separates the right side of the heart, which contains deoxygenated blood, from the left side, which contains oxygenated blood.

◆ Semilunar valves in the veins and in the entrances to the aorta and pulmonary artery, and atrio-ventricular valves, prevent backflow of blood.

◆ The heart is made of cardiac muscle and is myogenic. The sinoatrial node sets the pace of contraction for the muscle in the heart. Excitation waves spread from the SAN across the atria, causing their walls to contract. A non-conducting barrier prevents these excitation waves from spreading directly into the ventricles, thus delaying their contraction. The excitation wave travels to the ventricles via the atrio-ventricular node (AVN) and the Purkyne tissue, which runs down through the septum before spreading out into the walls of the ventricles. Both sides of the heart contract and relax at the same time. The contraction phase is called systole, and the relaxation phase diastole. One complete cycle of contraction and relaxation is known as the cardiac cycle.

◆ If damaged, the heart can contract in an uncoordinated way, known as fibrillation, which is potentially fatal.

◆ The pattern of contraction can be monitored by producing an electrocardiogram (ECG).

Questions

1 a Describe the structure of the human heart.
   b Account for the differences in the thickness of the walls of
      (i) the atria and ventricles and
      (ii) the left and right ventricles.

2 Describe the roles of the atrio-ventricular valves and the semi-lunar valves in ensuring a one-way flow of blood through the heart.

3 Outline the functions of each of the following in the coordination of the actions of different parts of the heart.
   a sinoatrial node
   b atrio-ventricular node
   c Purkyne tissue

4 Describe what happens during one heart beat. Include both a description of the way in which the beating of the different parts of the heart is synchronised, and of how the blood is moved through the heart.

CHAPTER 10

Transport in multicellular plants

By the end of this chapter you should be able to:

1 explain why plants need a transport system;

2 describe the distribution of xylem and phloem tissue in roots, stems and leaves;

3 describe the way in which water is absorbed into a root, and the pathway followed by water from root to leaf;

4 explain the mechanisms by which water moves from roots to leaves;

5 define and describe *transpiration*, and explain the effects of environmental factors on its rate;

6 explain how translocation of organic materials occurs in plants;

7 describe and compare the structure of xylem vessels, phloem sieve tube elements and companion cells;

8 relate these structures to their functions;

9 recognise xylem vessels, sieve tube elements and companion cells in light micrographs;

10 describe how the leaves of xerophytes are adapted to reduce water loss by transpiration.

Plant cells, like animal cells, need a regular supply of oxygen and nutrients. However, their requirements differ from those of animals in several ways, both in the nature of the nutrients and gases required and the rate at which these need to be supplied. Some of the particular requirements of plant cells are as follows:

■ **Carbon dioxide** Photosynthetic plant cells require a supply of carbon dioxide during daylight.

■ **Oxygen** All plant cells require a supply of oxygen for respiration, but cells which are actively photosynthesising produce more than enough oxygen for their own needs. Cells which are not photosynthesising need to take in oxygen from their environment, but they do not respire at such a high rate as mammals and therefore do

not need such a rapid oxygen supply.

■ **Organic nutrients** Some plant cells make many of their own organic food materials, such as glucose, by photosynthesis. However, many plant cells do not photosynthesise and need to be supplied with organic nutrients from photosynthetic cells.

■ **Inorganic ions and water** All plant cells require a range of different inorganic ions, and also water. These are taken up from the soil, by roots, and are transported to all regions of the plant.

The energy requirements of plant cells are, on average, far lower than those of cells in a mammal such as a human. Thus their rate of respiration, and their requirement for oxygen and glucose, is considerably less than that of mammals. They can therefore manage with a much slower transport system than the circulatory system of a mammal.

One of the main requirements of the photosynthetic regions of a plant is sunlight. In order to absorb as much sunlight as possible, plants have thin, flat leaves which present a large surface area to the Sun. In consequence, it is relatively easy for carbon dioxide and oxygen to diffuse into and out of the leaves, reaching and leaving every cell quickly enough so that there is no need for a transport system for these gases.

So, the design of a plant's transport system is quite different from that of a mammal. In fact, plants have *two* transport systems: one for carrying mainly water and inorganic ions from roots to the parts above ground, and one for carrying substances made by photosynthesis from the leaves to other areas. In neither of these systems do fluids move as rapidly as blood does in a mammal, nor is there an obvious pump such as the heart. Neither plant transport system carries oxygen or carbon dioxide, which travel to and from cells and their environment by diffusion alone.

The transport of water

Figure 10.1 outlines the pathway taken by water as it is transported through a plant. Water from the soil enters a plant through its root hairs and then moves across the root into the xylem tissue in the centre. Once inside the xylem vessels, the water moves upwards through the root to the stem and from there into the leaves.

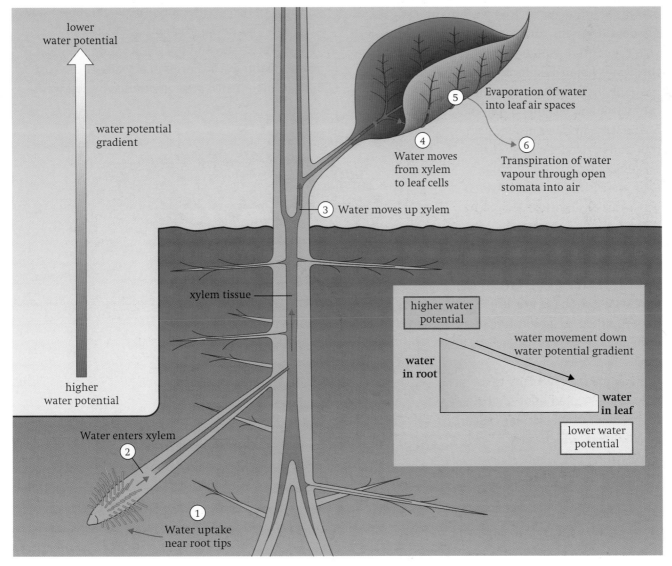

● **Figure 10.1** An overview of the movement of water through a plant. Water moves down a water potential gradient from the soil to the air.

From soil to root hair

In chapter 4 we looked at the way in which plant roots absorb water and mineral ions. *Figure 4.13a* shows a young root. The tip is covered by a tough, protective root cap and is not permeable to water. However, just behind the tip some of the cells in the outer layer, or **epidermis**, are drawn out into long, thin extensions called **root hairs**. These reach into spaces between the soil particles from where they absorb water.

Water moves into the root hairs down a water potential gradient (*figure 4.13b* and *10.1*). Although soil water contains some inorganic ions in solution, it is a relatively dilute solution and so has a relatively high water potential. However, the cytoplasm and cell sap inside the root hairs have considerable quantities of inorganic ions and organic substances, such as proteins and sugars, dissolved in them, and so have a relatively low water potential. Water, therefore, diffuses down this water potential gradient, through the partially permeable plasma membrane, into the cytoplasm and vacuole of the root hair cell.

The large number of very fine root hairs provides a large surface area in contact with soil water, thus increasing the rate at which water can be absorbed. However, these root hairs are very delicate and often only function for a few days before being replaced by new ones as the root grows. As we have seen, root hairs are also important for the absorption of mineral ions such as nitrate (pages 62–63).

Many plants, especially trees, have fungi located in or on their roots forming associations called **mycorrhizas**, which serve a similar function to root hairs. The mycorrhizas act like a mass of fine roots which absorb nutri-ents, especially phosphate, from the soil and transport them into the plant. Some trees, if growing on poor soils, are unable to

survive without these fungi. In return, the fungi receive organic nutrients from the plant.

SAQ 10.1

a What is the name given to a relationship between two different organisms in which both benefit?
b Outline one other example of this type of relationship that also involves plant roots.

From root hair to xylem

Figures 10.2 and *10.3* show transverse sections of a young root. Water taken up by root hairs crosses the cortex and enters the xylem in the centre of the root. It does this because the water potential inside the xylem vessels, for reasons to be explained later, is lower than the water potential in the root hairs. Therefore, the water moves down this water potential gradient across the root.

The water can, and does, take two possible routes through the cortex. The cells of the cortex, like all plant cells, are surrounded by cell walls

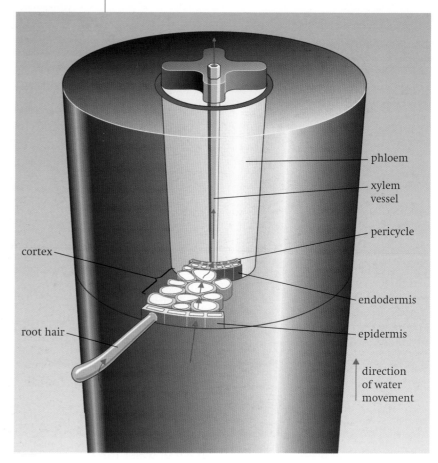

● **Figure 10.2** The pathway of water movement from root hair to xylem.

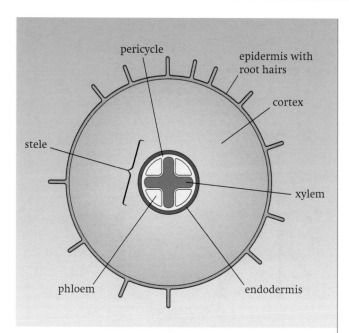

- **Figure 10.3** Transverse section of a young root to show the distribution of tissues.

made of several layers of cellulose fibres criss-crossing one another. Water can soak into these walls rather as it would soak into blotting paper, and can seep across the root from cell wall to cell wall without ever entering the cytoplasm of the cortical cells. This route is called the **apoplast pathway** (*figure 10.4a*). Another possibility is for the water to move into the cytoplasm or vacuole of a cortical cell, and then into adjacent cells

through the interconnecting plasmodesmata (see page 5). This is the **symplast pathway** (*figure 10.4b*). The relative importance of these two pathways varies from plant to plant, and in different conditions. Normally, it is probable that the symplast pathway is more important but, when transpiration rates (see page 135) are especially high, more water travels by the apoplast pathway.

Once the water reaches the stele, the apoplast pathway is abruptly barred. The cells in the outer layer surrounding the stele, the **endodermis**, have a thick, waterproof, waxy band of **suberin** in their cell walls (*figure 10.5*). This band, called the **Casparian strip**, forms an impenetrable barrier to water in the walls of the endodermis cells. The only way for the water to cross the endodermis is through the cytoplasm of these cells. As the endodermal cells get older, the suberin deposits become more extensive, except in certain cells called **passage cells**, through which water can continue to pass freely. It is thought that this arrangement gives a plant control over what inorganic ions pass into its xylem vessels, as everything has to cross plasma membranes. It may also help with the generation of root pressure (see page 137).

Once across the endodermis, water continues to move down the water potential gradient across the pericycle and towards the xylem vessels.

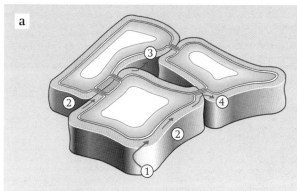

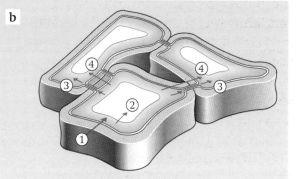

Apoplast pathway
1. Water enters the cell wall.
2. Water moves through the cell wall.
3. Water may move from cell wall to cell wall, through the intercellular spaces.
4. Water may move directly from cell wall to cell wall.

Symplast pathway
1. Water enters the cytoplasm through the partially permeable plasma membrane.
2. Water moves into the sap in the vacuole, through the tonoplast.
3. Water may move from cell to cell through the plasmodesmata.
4. Water may move from cell to cell through adjacent plasma membranes and cell walls.

- **Figure 10.4 a** Apoplast and **b** symplast pathways for movement of water from root hairs to xylem.

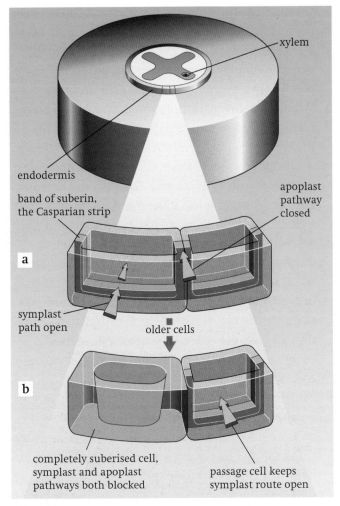

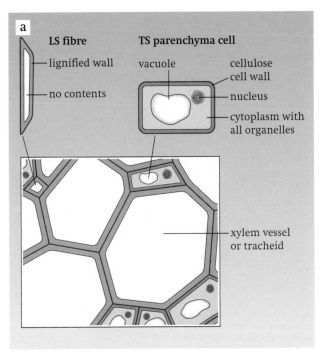

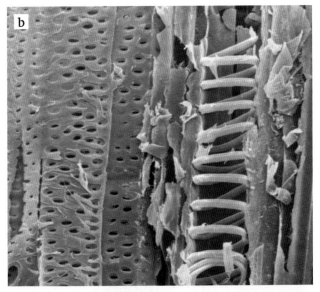

● **Figure 10.5** Suberin deposits close the apoplast pathway for water in the endodermis.

a In a young root the suberin deposits form bands in the cell walls called Casparian strips. The symplast path remains open.

b In an older root, entire cells become suberised, closing the symplast path too. Only passage cells are then permeable to water.

● **Figure 10.6** Xylem tissue.

a Diagram of a transverse section (TS) through xylem tissue. Fibres and parenchyma cells can be seen, as well as wide empty cells with lignified walls that could be either vessels or tracheids.

b Scanning electron micrograph of a longitudinal section through part of a buttercup stem, showing xylem vessels. The young vessel on the right has a spiral band of lignin around it, while those on the left are older and have more extensive coverings of lignin with many pits.

c Light micrograph of a transverse section of xylem vessels. They have been stained so that the lignin appears red. The xylem vessels are the large empty cells. You can also see smaller parenchyma cells between them; these do not have lignified walls, and contain nucleus and cytoplasm.

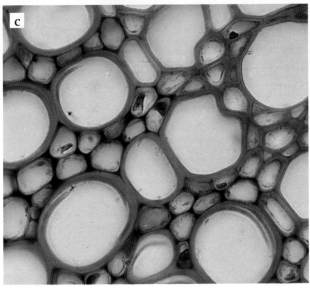

Xylem tissue

As we saw in chapter 1, a tissue is a group of cells working together to perform a particular function. Xylem tissue (*figure 10.6*) has the dual functions of support and transport. It contains several different types of cell. In angiosperms (that is, all the flowering plants except conifers), xylem tissue contains vessel elements, tracheids, fibres and parenchyma cells.

- **Vessel elements** and **tracheids** are the cells that are involved with the transport of water, and their structures and functions are described below.

- **Fibres** are elongated cells with lignified walls (see below) that help to support the plant. They are dead cells; they have no living contents at all.

- **Parenchyma cells** are 'standard' plant cells. They have unthickened cellulose cell walls and contain all the organelles you would expect a plant cell to contain (see page 15). However, the parenchyma cells in xylem tissue do not usually have chloroplasts as they are not exposed to light. They can be a variety of shapes, but are often isodiametric, that is approximately the same size in all directions.

Xylem vessels

Figure 10.7 shows the structure of a typical xylem vessel. Vessels are made up of many elongated **vessel elements** arranged end to end. Each began life as a normal plant cell in whose wall a substance called **lignin** was laid down. Lignin is a very hard, strong substance, which is imperme- able to water. As it built up around the cell, the contents of the cell died, leaving a completely empty space, or **lumen**, inside. However, in several parts of the original cell walls, where groups of plasmodesmata were, no lignin was laid down. These non-lignified areas can be seen as 'gaps' in the thick walls of the xylem vessel, and are called **pits**. Pits are not open pores; they are crossed by permeable, unthickened cellulose cell wall.

The end walls of neighbouring vessel elements break down completely, to form a continuous tube rather like a drainpipe running through the plant. This long, non-living tube is a **xylem vessel**.

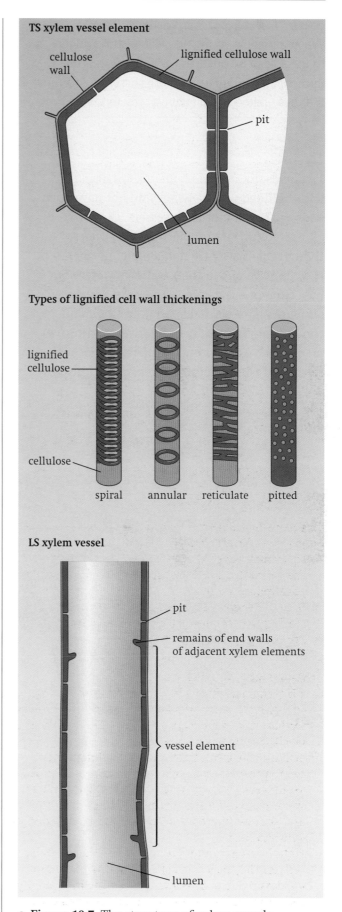

● **Figure 10.7** The structure of xylem vessels.

SAQ 10.2

When a plant is young and still growing it tends to form vessels with spiral, annular or reticulate thickening. As it matures, more vessels are formed that have pitted walls. Suggest why this is so.

Tracheids

Tracheids, like vessel elements, are dead cells with lignified walls, but they do not have open ends so they do not form vessels. They are elongated cells with tapering ends. Even though their ends are not completely open, they do have pits in their walls, so water can pass from one tracheid to the next. Although all plants have tracheids, they are the main conducting tissue only in relatively 'primitive' plants such as ferns and conifers. Angiosperms rely mostly on vessels for their water transport.

In the root, water which has crossed the cortex, endodermis and pericycle moves into the xylem vessels through the pits in their walls. It

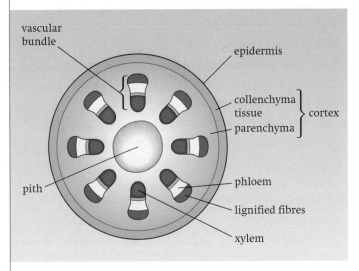

● **Figure 10.8** Transverse section of a young sunflower stem to show the distribution of tissues.

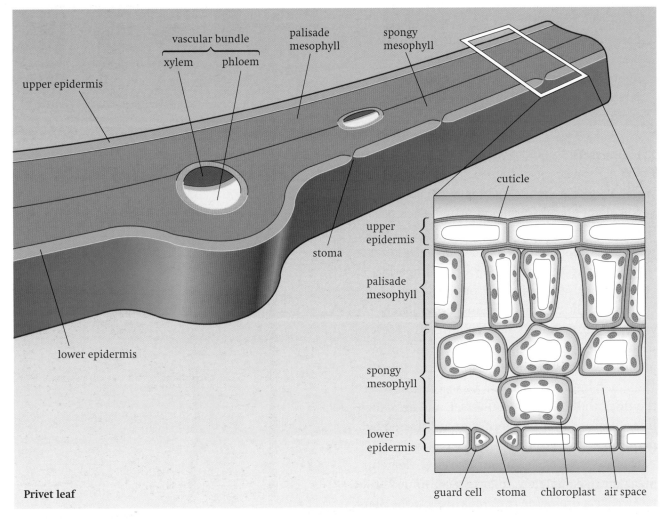

Privet leaf

● **Figure 10.9** The structure of a leaf. Water enters the leaf as liquid water in the xylem vessels, and diffuses out as water vapour through the stomata.

then moves up the vessels towards the leaves. Whereas the xylem vessels are in the centre of the root, in the stem they are nearer to the outside (*figure 10.8*).

What causes water to move up xylem vessels? In order to explain this, we must look at what happens to water in a plant's leaves.

From leaf to atmosphere – transpiration

Figure 10.9 shows the internal structure of a leaf. The cells in the **mesophyll** ('middle leaf') layers are not tightly packed, and have many spaces around them filled with air. The walls of the mesophyll cells are wet and some of this water evaporates into the air spaces (*figure 10.10*), so that the air inside the leaf is usually saturated with water vapour.

The air in the internal spaces of the leaf has direct contact with the air outside the leaf, through small pores or **stomata**. If there is a water potential gradient between the air inside the leaf and the air outside, then water vapour will diffuse out of the leaf down this gradient. This loss of water vapour from the leaves of a plant is called **transpiration**.

An increase in the water potential gradient between the air spaces in the leaf and the air outside will increase the rate of transpiration. In conditions of low humidity, the gradient is steep, so transpiration takes place more quickly than in high humidity. Transpiration may also be increased by an increase in wind speed or a rise in temperature.

SAQ 10.3

Suggest how **a** an increase in wind speed, and **b** a rise in temperature, may cause the rate of transpiration to increase.

Another factor which affects the rate of transpiration is the opening or closing of the stomata. The stomata are the means of contact between photosynthesising mesophyll cells and the external air, and must be open to allow carbon dioxide for photosynthesis to diffuse into the leaf. On a bright, sunny day, when the rate of photosynthesis is likely to be high, then demand for carbon dioxide by the

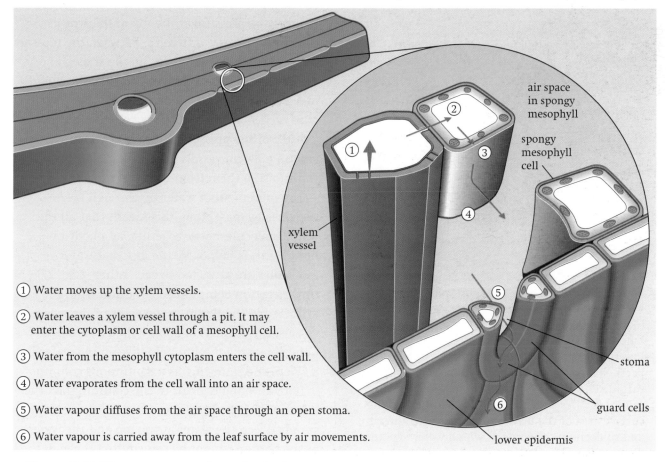

① Water moves up the xylem vessels.

② Water leaves a xylem vessel through a pit. It may enter the cytoplasm or cell wall of a mesophyll cell.

③ Water from the mesophyll cytoplasm enters the cell wall.

④ Water evaporates from the cell wall into an air space.

⑤ Water vapour diffuses from the air space through an open stoma.

⑥ Water vapour is carried away from the leaf surface by air movements.

● **Figure 10.10** Water movement through a leaf.

mesophyll cells means that stomata must be open. This inevitably increases the rate of transpiration. In especially dry conditions, when the water potential gradient between the internal air spaces and the external air is steep, a plant may have to compromise by partially closing its stomata to prevent its leaves drying out, even if this means reducing the rate of photosynthesis (*figure 10.11*).

In hot conditions, transpiration plays an important role in cooling the leaves. As water evaporates from the cell walls inside the leaf, it absorbs heat energy from these cells, thus reducing their temperature.

SAQ 10.4

How does this cooling mechanism compare with the main cooling mechanism of mammals?

The amount of water vapour lost by transpiration from the leaves of a plant can be very great. Even

● **Figure 10.11** If the rate at which water vapour is lost by transpiration exceeds the rate at which a plant can take up water from the soil, then the amount of water in its cells decreases. The cells lose turgor (page 58) and the plant wilts as the soft parts, such as leaves, lose the support provided by turgid cells. Wilting actually helps the plant to reduce further water loss, because it reduces the surface area of the leaves in contact with the air, and so decreases the rate at which water vapour diffuses out of the leaves. In this situation the plant will also close its stomata.

in the relatively cool and moist conditions of a temperate country such as Britain, a leaf may lose the volume of water contained in its leaves every 20 minutes. Thus water must move into the leaves equally rapidly to replace this lost water.

From xylem to leaf

As water evaporates from the cell walls of mesophyll cells, more water is drawn into them to replace it. The source of this water is the xylem vessels in the leaf. Water constantly moves out of these vessels, down a water potential gradient, either into the mesophyll cells or along their cell walls. Some will be used in photosynthesis, but most eventually evaporates and then diffuses out of the leaf.

The removal of water from the top of xylem vessels reduces the hydrostatic pressure. (Hydrostatic pressure is pressure exerted by a liquid.) The hydrostatic pressure at the top of the xylem vessel becomes lower than the pressure at the bottom. This pressure difference causes water to move up the xylem vessels. It is just like sucking water up a straw. Your 'suck' at the top reduces the pressure at the top of the straw, causing a pressure difference between the top and bottom which pushes water up the straw.

The water in the xylem vessels, like the liquid in a 'sucked' straw, is under tension. If you suck hard on a straw, its walls may collapse inwards as a result of the pressure differences you are creating. Xylem vessels have strong, lignified walls to stop them from collapsing in this way.

The movement of water up through xylem vessels is by **mass flow**. This means that all the water molecules move together, as a body of liquid. This is helped by the fact that water molecules are attracted to each other (page 27), the attraction being called **cohesion**. They are also attracted to the lignin in the walls of the xylem vessels, this attraction being called **adhesion**. Cohesion and adhesion help to keep the water in a xylem vessel moving as a continuous column.

If an air bubble forms in the column, then the column of water breaks and the difference in pressure between the water at the top and the water at the bottom cannot be transmitted through the vessel. We say there is an air lock. The water stops moving upwards. The small diameter of xylem vessels helps to prevent such breaks from occurring. The pits in the vessel walls also allow water to move out, which may allow it to move from one vessel to another and so bypass such an air lock. Air bubbles cannot pass through pits. Pits are also important in allowing water to move out of xylem vessels to surrounding living cells.

Root pressure

You have seen how transpiration *reduces* the water (hydrostatic) pressure at the top of a xylem vessel compared with the pressure at the base, so causing the water to flow up the vessels. Plants may also increase the pressure difference between the top and bottom by *raising* the water pressure at the *base* of the vessels.

The pressure is raised by the active secretion of solutes, for example mineral ions, into the water in the xylem vessels in the root. Cells surrounding the xylem vessels use energy to pump solutes across their membranes and into the xylem by active transport (page 59). The presence of the solutes lowers the water potential of the solution in the xylem, thus drawing in water from the surrounding root cells. This influx of water increases the water pressure at the base of the xylem vessel.

Although root pressure may help in moving water up xylem vessels, it is not essential, and is probably not significant in causing water to move up xylem in most plants. Water can continue to move up through xylem even if the plant is dead. Water transport in plants is largely a **passive** process, fuelled by transpiration from the leaves. The water simply moves down a continuous water potential gradient from the soil to the air.

SAQ 10.5 _____

Transport of water from the environment to cells occurs in both plants and mammals. For both plants and mammals, state the stages of this transport in which water moves by

a osmosis, and   **b** mass flow.

SAQ 10.6 _____

Explain how each of the following features of xylem vessels adapts them for their function of transporting water from roots to leaves.

a Total lack of cell contents

b No end walls in individual xylem elements

c A diameter of between 0.01 mm and 0.2 mm

d Lignified walls

e Pits

Comparing rates of transpiration

It is not easy to measure the rate at which water vapour is leaving a plant's leaves. This makes it very difficult to investigate directly how different factors, such as temperature, wind speed, light intensity or humidity, affect the rate of transpiration. However, it *is* relatively easy to measure the rate at which a plant stem takes up water. As a very high proportion of the water taken up by a stem is lost in transpiration, and as the rate at which transpiration is happening directly affects the rate of water uptake, this measurement can give a very good approximation of the rate of transpiration.

The apparatus used for this is called a **potometer** (*figure 10.12*). Everything must be completely water-tight and airtight, so that no leakage of water occurs, and so that no air bubbles break the continuous water column. To achieve this, it helps if you can insert the plant stem into the apparatus with everything submerged in water. It also helps to cut the end of the stem with a slanting cut, as air bubbles are less likely to get trapped against it. Potometers can be simpler than this one. You can manage without the reservoir (though this does mean it takes more time and effort to refill the potometer) and the tubing can be straight rather than bent. In other words, you can manage with a straight piece of glass tubing!

As water evaporates from the plant's leaves, it is drawn into the xylem vessels that are exposed at the cut end of the stem. Water is therefore drawn along the capillary tubing. If you record the position of the meniscus at set time intervals, you can plot a graph of distance moved against time. If you expose the plant to different conditions, then you can compare the rates of water uptake (which will have a close relationship to the rates of transpiration) under different conditions.

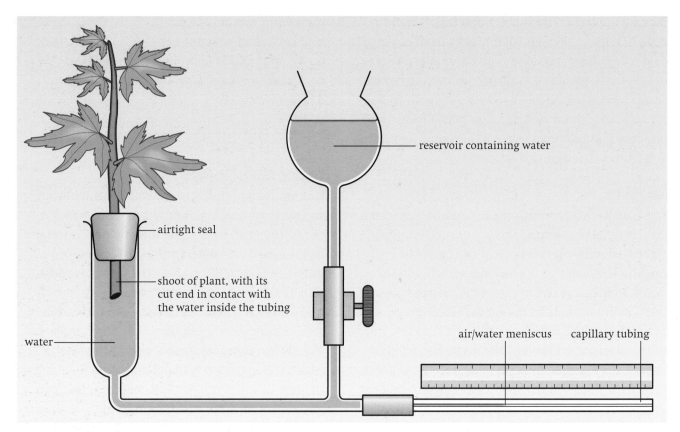

● **Figure 10.12** A potometer.

Xerophytes

Xerophytes are plants that live in places where water is in short supply. They often have adaptations to reduce the rate of transpiration.

We have already seen that plants are able to close their stomata and allow their leaves to wilt to reduce the rate of transpiration from their leaves (page 136). Many xerophytes, however, have evolved special adaptations of their leaves that keep water loss down to a minimum. Some examples are shown in *Figure 10.14*.

Translocation

Translocation is the term used to describe the transport of soluble organic substances within a plant. These are substances which the plant itself has made, for example sugars which are made by photosynthesis in the leaves. These substances are sometimes called **assimilates**.

Assimilates are transported in **sieve elements**. Sieve elements are found in **phloem tissue**, along with several other types of cells including **companion cells**, parenchyma and fibres (*figures 10.2, 10.8* and *10.13*). We will see later how the sieve

● **Figure 10.13** Light micrograph of a longitudinal section through phloem tissue. The red triangles are patches of callose that formed at the sieve plates between the sieve tube elements in response to the damage done as the section was being cut. You can see companion cells, with their denser cytoplasm, lying alongside the sieve tube elements. On the far right are some parenchyma cells.

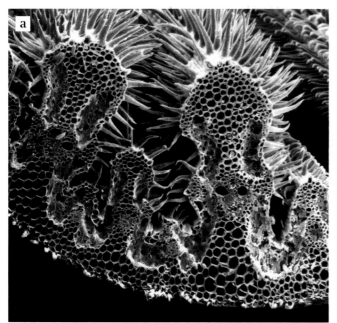

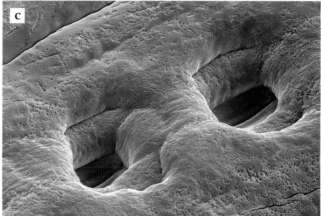

- **Figure 10.14** Some adaptations shown by xerophytes.
- **a** A scanning electronmicrograph of a transverse section through part of a rolled leaf of marram grass, *Ammophila arenaria*. This grass grows on sand dunes, where conditions are very dry. The leaves can roll up, exposing a tough, waterproof cuticle to the air outside the leaf, while the stomata open into the enclosed, humid space in the middle of the 'roll'. Hairs help to trap a layer of moist air close to the leaf surface, reducing the diffusion gradient for water vapour.
- **b** *Opuntia* is a cactus with flattened, photosynthetic stems that store water. The leaves are reduced to spines, which reduces the surface area from which transpiration can take place and protects the plant from being eaten by animals.
- **c** Falsecolour SEM of a needle from a Sitka spruce, (×1500) a large tree native to Canada and Alaska. Its leaves are in the form of needles, greatly reducing the surface area available for water loss. In addition, they are covered in a layer of waterproof wax and have sunken stomata as shown here.
- **d** TS SEM of *Phlomis italica* leaf showing its 'trichomes'. These are tiny hair-like structures that act as a physical barrier to the loss of water like the marram grass hairs. *Phlomis* is a small shrub that lives in dry habitats in the Mediterranean regions of Europe and North Africa.
- **e** The cardon, *Euphorbia canariensis*, grows in dry areas of Tenerife. It has swollen, succulent stems that store water and photosynthesise. The stems are coated with wax, which cuts down water loss. The leaves are extremely small.

elements and their companion cells work closely together to achieve translocation.

Sieve elements

Figure 10.15 shows the structure of a **sieve tube** and its accompanying companion cells. A sieve tube is made up of many elongated sieve elements, joined end to end vertically to form a continuous column. Each sieve element is a living cell. Like a 'normal' plant cell, it has a cellulose cell wall, a plasma membrane and cytoplasm containing endoplasmic reticulum and mitochondria. However, the amount of cytoplasm is very small and only forms a thin layer lining the inside of the wall of the cell. There is no nucleus, nor are there any ribosomes.

Perhaps the most striking feature of sieve elements is their end walls. Where the end walls of two sieve elements meet, a **sieve plate** is formed. This is made up of the walls of both elements, perforated by large pores. These pores are easily visible with a good light microscope. When sieve plates are viewed using an electron microscope, strands of fibrous protein can sometimes be seen passing through these pores from one sieve element to another. However, these strands have been produced by the sieve element in response to the damage caused when the tissue is cut during preparation of the specimen for viewing (see below). In living phloem the protein strands are not present; the pores are open, presenting little barrier to the free flow of liquids through them.

Companion cells

Each sieve element has at least one companion cell lying close beside it. Companion cells have the structure of a 'normal' plant cell, with a cellulose cell wall, a plasma membrane, cytoplasm, a small vacuole and a nucleus. However, the number of mitochondria and ribosomes is rather larger than normal, and the cells are metabolically very active.

Companion cells are very closely associated with their neighbouring sieve elements. Numerous plasmodesmata pass through their cell walls, making direct contact between the cytoplasms of the companion cell and sieve element.

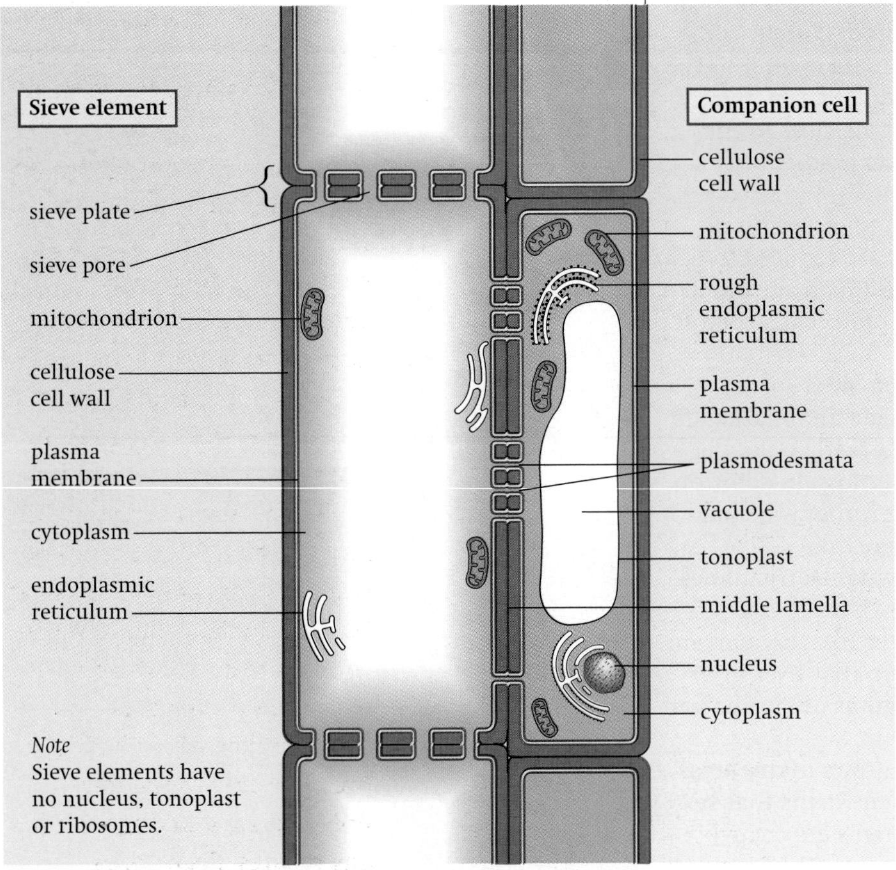

The contents of phloem sieve tubes

The liquid inside phloem sieve tubes is called **phloem sap**, or just sap. *Table 10.1* shows the composition of the sap of the castor oil plant, *Ricinus communis*.

SAQ 10.7

Which of the substances listed in *table 10.1* have been synthesised by the plant?

It is not easy to collect enough phloem sap to analyse its contents. When phloem tissue is cut, the sieve elements respond by rapidly blocking the sieve pores, in a process sometimes called 'clotting'. The pores are blocked first by plugs of phloem protein (as

Sieve element

sieve plate
sieve pore
mitochondrion
cellulose cell wall
plasma membrane
cytoplasm
endoplasmic reticulum

Note
Sieve elements have no nucleus, tonoplast or ribosomes.

Companion cell

cellulose cell wall
mitochondrion
rough endoplasmic reticulum
plasma membrane
plasmodesmata
vacuole
tonoplast
middle lamella
nucleus
cytoplasm

● **Figure 10.15** A phloem sieve tube element and its companion cell.

Solute	Concentration (mol dm^{-3})
sucrose	250
potassium ions	80
amino acids	40
chloride ions	15
phosphate ions	10
magnesium ions	5
sodium ions	2
ATP	0.5
nitrate ions	0
plant growth substances (e.g. auxin, cytokinin)	small traces

● **Table 10.1** Composition of sap.

we saw earlier) and then, within hours, by the carbohydrate **callose**. (Callose has a molecular structure very similar to cellulose. Like cellulose, its molecules are long chains of glucose units, but these are linked by β 1,3 glycosidic bonds, rather than the β 1,4 bonds of cellulose.) However, castor oil plants are unusual in that their phloem sap does continue to flow from a cut for some time, making it relatively easy to collect.

In other plants, aphids may be used to sample sap. Aphids, such as greenfly, feed using tubular mouthparts called stylets. They insert these through the surface of the plant's stem or leaves, into the phloem (*figure 10.16*). Phloem sap flows through the stylet into the aphid. If the stylet is cut near the aphid's head, the sap continues to flow; it seems that the small diameter of the stylet does not allow sap to flow out rapidly enough to switch on the plant's phloem 'clotting' mechanism.

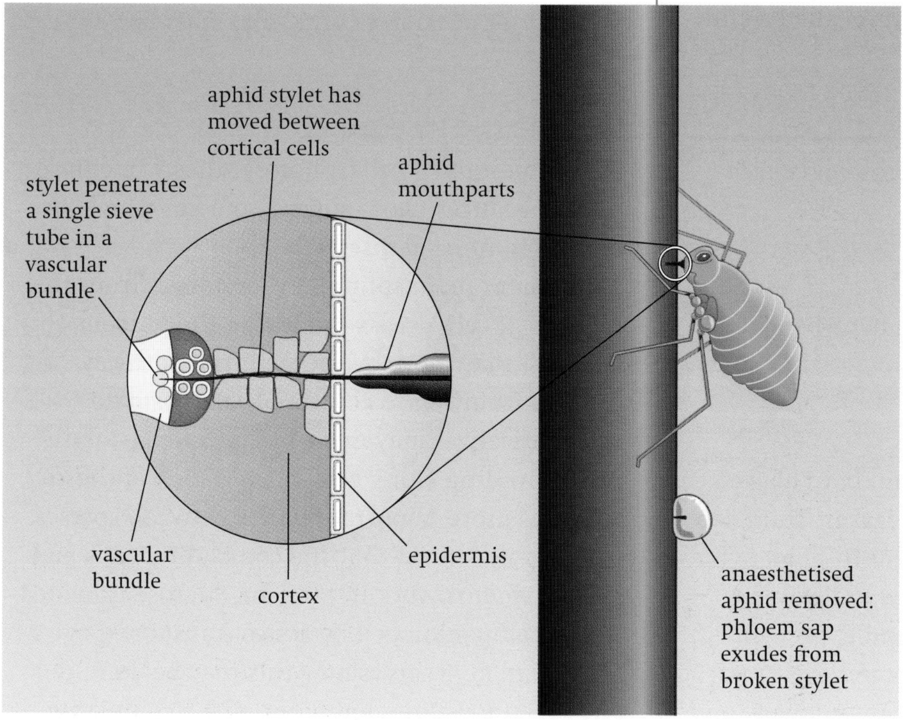

How translocation occurs

Phloem sap, like the contents of xylem vessels, moves by **mass flow**. However, whereas in xylem vessels differences in pressure are produced by a water potential gradient between soil and air, requiring no energy input from the plant, this is not so in phloem transport. To create the pressure differences needed for mass flow in phloem, the plant has to use energy. Phloem transport can therefore be considered an *active* process, in contrast to the *passive* transport in xylem.

The pressure difference is produced by **active loading** of sucrose into the sieve elements at the place from which sucrose is to be transported. This is usually in a photosynthesising leaf. As sucrose is loaded into the sieve element, this decreases the water potential in the sap inside it. Therefore, water follows the sucrose into the sieve element, moving down a water potential gradient by osmosis.

At another point along the sieve tube, sucrose may be removed by other cells, for example in the root. As sucrose is removed, water again follows by osmosis.

Thus, in the leaf, water moves into the sieve tube. In the root, water moves out of it. This creates a pressure difference; hydrostatic pressure is high in the part of the sieve tube in the leaf, and lower in the part in the root. This pressure difference causes water to flow from the high pressure area to the low pressure area, taking with it any solutes (*figure 10.17*).

● **Figure 10.16** Using an aphid to collect phloem sap.

● **Figure 10.17** The phloem sap of the sugar maple contains a high concentration of sugar and can be harvested to make maple syrup. Two or three taps are inserted into each tree and the sap runs out under its own pressure through the green and then the black plastic pipelines.

Any area of a plant in which sucrose is loaded into the phloem is called a **source**. Usually, the source is a photosynthesising leaf. Any area where sucrose is taken out of the phloem is called a **sink** (*figure 10.18*).

SAQ 10.8

Which of the following will be sources, and which will be sinks?

a A nectary in a flower.

b A developing fruit.

c The storage tissue of a potato tuber when the buds are beginning to sprout.

d A developing potato tuber.

Sinks can be anywhere in the plant, both above and below the photosynthesising leaves. Thus, sap flows both upwards and downwards in phloem (in contrast with xylem, in which flow is always upwards). Within any vascular bundle, phloem sap may be flowing upwards in some sieve tubes and downwards in others, but it can only flow one way in any particular sieve tube at any one time.

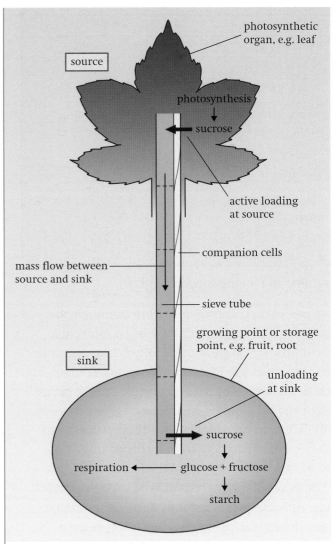

● **Figure 10.18** Sources, sinks and mass flow in phloem.

Loading of sucrose into phloem

In leaf mesophyll cells, photosynthesis in chloroplasts produces triose sugars, some of which are converted into sucrose.

The sucrose, in solution, then moves from the mesophyll cell, across the leaf to the phloem tissue. It may move by the symplast pathway, moving from cell to cell via plasmodesmata. Alternatively, it may move by the apoplast pathway, travelling along cell walls. Which of these routes is more important varies between species.

It is now known that the companion cells and sieve elements work in tandem. Sucrose is loaded into a companion cell by active transport (page 59). *Figure 10.19* shows how this may be done. Hydrogen ions are moved out of the companion cell, using ATP as an energy source. This creates a

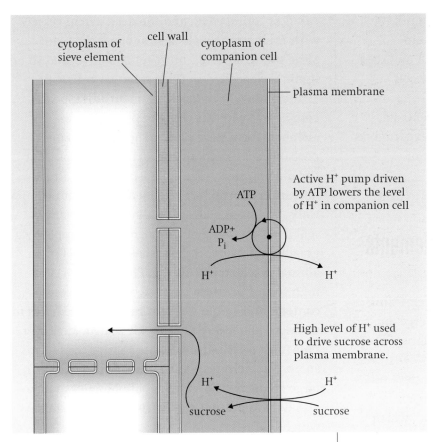

cytoplasm of sieve element

cell wall

cytoplasm of companion cell

plasma membrane

ATP

Active H$^+$ pump driven by ATP lowers the level of H$^+$ in companion cell

ADP+ P$_i$

H$^+$

H$^+$

High level of H$^+$ used to drive sucrose across plasma membrane.

H$^+$

H$^+$

sucrose

sucrose

● **Figure 10.19** A possible method by which sucrose is loaded into phloem.

large excess of hydrogen ions outside the companion cell. They can move back into the cell down their concentration gradient, through a protein which acts as a carrier for both hydrogen ions and sucrose at the same time. The sucrose molecules are carried through this **co-transporter** molecule into the companion cell, against the concentration gradient for sucrose. The sucrose molecules can then move from the companion cell into the sieve tube, through the plasmodesmata which connect them.

Unloading of sucrose from phloem

At the moment, little is known about the way in which sucrose is unloaded from phloem. Unloading occurs into any tissue which requires sucrose. It is probable that sucrose moves out of the phloem into these tissues by diffusion. Once in the tissue, the sucrose is converted into something else by enzymes, so decreasing its concentration and maintaining a concentration gradient. One such enzyme is invertase, which hydrolyses sucrose to glucose and fructose (*figure 10.18*).

Evidence for the mechanism of phloem transport

Until the late 1970s and early 1980s, there was considerable argument about whether or not phloem sap did or did not move by mass flow, in the way described above. The stumbling block was the presence of the sieve pores and phloem protein, as it was felt that these must have some important role. Several hypotheses were put forward which tried to provide a role for the phloem protein, and you may come across some of these in various textbooks. It is now known that phloem protein is not present in living, active phloem tissue, and so there is no need to provide it with a role when explaining the mechanism of phloem transport.

The evidence that phloem transport does occur by mass flow is considerable. The rate of transport in phloem is about 10 000 times faster than it would be if substances were moving by diffusion rather than by mass flow. The actual rates of transport measured match closely with those calculated from measured pressure differences at source and sink, assuming that the pores in the sieve plates are open and unobstructed.

There is also considerable evidence for the active loading of sucrose into sieve elements in sources such as leaves. Much experimental work has been done in investigating the sucrose–hydrogen ion co-transporter system in plant cells, although it has so far been very difficult to investigate this in companion cells and phloem sieve elements. Nevertheless, there is much circumstantial evidence that active loading of sucrose into phloem sieve tubes, as described above, does take place. This includes the following observations.

■ Phloem sap always has a relatively high pH, often around 8. This is what would be expected if hydrogen ions were being actively transported out of the cell.

- There is a difference in electrical potential across the plasma membrane of around −150 mV inside, again consistent with an excess of positive hydrogen ions outside the cell compared with inside.
- ATP is present in phloem sieve elements in quite large amounts. This would be expected, as it is required for the active transport of hydrogen ions out of the cell.

Differences between sieve elements and xylem vessels

From this account of translocation, several similarities with the transport of water emerge. In each case, liquid moves by mass flow along a pressure gradient, through tubes formed by cells stacked end to end. So why are phloem sieve tubes so different in structure from xylem vessels?

Unlike water transport through xylem, which occurs through dead xylem vessels, translocation through phloem sieve tubes involves active loading of sucrose at sources, thus requiring living cells.

Xylem vessels have lignified cell walls, whereas phloem tubes do not. The presence of lignin in a cell wall prevents the movement of water and solutes across it, and so kills the cell. This does not matter in xylem, as xylem vessels do not need to be alive; indeed, it is a positive advantage to have an entirely empty tube through which water can flow unimpeded, and the dead xylem vessels with their strong walls also support the plant. Sieve tubes, however, must remain alive, and so no lignin is deposited in their cellulose cell walls.

The end walls of xylem elements disappear completely, whereas those of phloem sieve elements form sieve plates. These sieve plates probably act as supporting structures to prevent the phloem sieve tube collapsing; xylem already has sufficient support provided by its lignified walls. The sieve plates also allow the phloem to seal itself up rapidly if damaged, for example by a grazing herbivore, rather as a blood vessel in an animal is sealed by clotting. Phloem sap has a high turgor pressure because of its high solute content, and would leak out rapidly if the holes in the sieve plate were not quickly sealed. Moreover, phloem sap contains valuable substances such as sucrose, which the plant cannot afford to lose in large quantity. The 'clotting' of phloem sap may also help to prevent the entry of microorganisms which might feed on the nutritious sap or cause disease.

SAQ 10.9

Draw up a comparison table between xylem vessels and sieve tubes. Some features which you could include are: cell structure (walls, diameter, cell contents, etc.), substances transported and methods of transport. Include a column giving a brief explanation for the differences in structure.

SUMMARY

◆ Water is transported through a plant in xylem vessels. This is a passive process, in which water moves down a water potential gradient from soil to air. Water enters root hairs by osmosis, crosses the root either through the cytoplasm of cells or via their cell walls, and enters the dead, empty xylem vessels. Water moves up xylem vessels by mass flow, as a result of pressure differences caused by loss of water from leaves by transpiration. Root pressure can also contribute to this pressure difference.

◆ Transpiration is an inevitable consequence of gaseous exchange in plants. Plants have air spaces within the leaf linked to the external atmosphere through stomata, so that carbon dioxide and oxygen can be exchanged with their environment. Water vapour, formed as water evaporates from wet cell walls, also diffuses through these air spaces and out of the stomata.

◆ The rate of transpiration is affected by several environmental factors, namely temperature, light intensity, wind speed and humidity. It is difficult to measure rate of transpiration directly, but water uptake can be measured using a potometer. Plants that are adapted to live in places where the environmental conditions are likely to cause high rates of transpiration, and where soil water is in short supply, are called xerophytes. They have often evolved adaptations that help to reduce the rate of loss of water vapour from their leaves.

◆ Translocation of organic solutes, such as sucrose, occurs through living phloem sieve tubes. The phloem sap moves by mass flow, as a result of pressure differences produced by active loading of sucrose at sources such as photosynthesising leaves.

Questions

1 Discuss the similarities and differences between the transport systems of plants and mammals.

2 Describe the pathway and mechanisms by which water travels through a plant, from the soil into the atmosphere.

3 Construct a table to compare and contrast the mechanisms of transport in the xylem and phloem.

4 Plants which live in environments where the soil water is very salty, such as estuaries, are called halophytes.
   a What problems might halophytes have to overcome with regard to taking up water and maintaining a suitable salt and water concentration in their cells?
   b Suggest how each of the following adaptations might help a halophyte to overcome these problems.
      ● Rapid active uptake of ions, such as Na^+ and Cl^-, by the roots.
      ● Ability to tolerate low water potentials in cell sap and cytoplasm.
      ● Ability to maintain higher salt concentrations in cell vacuoles than in cytoplasm, by active transport of Na^+ and Cl^- across the tonoplast.
      ● Salt glands in leaves, which actively excrete salt onto the surface of the leaf.

Part 3
Human Health and Disease

CHAPTER 11

Health and disease

By the end of this chapter you should be able to:

1 discuss what is meant by the terms *health* and *disease*;

2 discuss whether health is more than simply the absence of disease;

3 explain the different categories of disease and know one example of each;

4 explain the reasons for collecting health statistics;

5 describe and explain the differences between standards of health in developed and developing countries;

6 explain the terms *pandemic*, *epidemic* and *endemic*;

7 outline the aims and significance of the Human Genome Project in relation to human health and disease.

What is health?

Health is difficult to define precisely. It can be defined as **a person's physical, mental and social condition**. Health may be good or poor. Good health is often linked to happiness and a fulfilling life so it is more than just being free from disease. Someone who is healthy feels good physically and has a positive outlook on life, is well-adjusted in society and is able to undertake the physical and mental tasks they meet in everyday life without too much difficulty.

Everyone is born with a genetic potential for growth and development. People need good health to grow and realise their potential and to play a full and active part in society. They can only do this if they live in an environment free from serious hazards to health. The World Health Organisation (an agency of the United Nations) maintains that good health is a fundamental Human Right and works to reduce the serious threats from disease that overshadow human existence. To enjoy good health, a person needs proper shelter, nutrition, exercise, sleep and rest. Good hygiene reduces the chances of infection. Access to medical and social care ensures that health can be monitored and illnesses treated or prevented altogether.

What is disease?

Just as health is a broad term, so is **disease**. Put simply, a disease (or illness) is a disorder or malfunction of the mind or body which leads to a departure from good health. It can be a disorder of a specific tissue or organ due to a single cause, such as malaria, or it may have many causes, such as heart disease, in which case it is described as **multifactorial**.

Diseases are characterised by signs and symptoms that are physical, mental or both. People who are ill may report their symptoms to a doctor, who, by examining and questioning their patients and carrying out tests, can identify the signs of disease and make a diagnosis.

Some diseases are **acute**, having a sudden onset with rapid changes and lasting for a short time. For example, the symptoms of influenza appear very quickly, within a few days of being infected. The effects of long-term, or **chronic**, diseases continue for months or years. Many chronic

Category of disease	Cause of disease	Examples
physical	permanent or temporary damage to any part of the body	leprosy, multiple sclerosis
infectious	organisms which invade the body	measles, malaria
non-infectious	any cause other than invasion by an organism	stroke, sickle cell anaemia
deficiency	poor diet	scurvy, night blindness
inherited	an inherited genetic fault	cystic fibrosis, haemophilia
degenerative	gradual decline in function	coronary heart disease, Huntington's disease
mental	changes to the mind, with or without a known physical cause	schizophrenia, claustrophobia
social	social environment or behaviour, such as poor housing or drug misuse	hypothermia, drug dependence
self-inflicted	wilful damage to the body by a person's own actions	attempted suicide, lung cancer

● **Table 11.1** Different categories of disease. These categories are not mutually exclusive, so a disease may belong to more than one category.

diseases are extremely debilitating, for example tuberculosis (TB).

Apparently healthy people may not obviously be afflicted with any disease, but their living conditions, diet or personal behaviour may be putting them at risk of developing chronic diseases which only manifest themselves in later life. You will read more about an example of this in chapter 14.

Categories of disease

There are different ways of classifying disease. For example, it is possible to distinguish between physical and mental diseases, or between infectious and non-infectious ones. Nine broad categories are recognised (*table 11.1*), although some diseases fit into more than one category. For example, some mental diseases are caused by physical changes that occur in the brain. This means that they can be classified as both physical and mental diseases.

Physical diseases

Physical diseases are associated with permanent or temporary damage to part of the body. This category includes *all* the other categories, except those mental diseases where there is no sign of any physical damage to the brain.

Infectious diseases

Organisms which live in or on our bodies and gain their nutrition from us are called **parasites**. If

they cause disease they are also known as **pathogens**. **Infectious diseases** are those caused by pathogens such as viruses, bacteria, fungi, protoctists, worms and insects. They are also called 'communicable diseases', because the pathogens are transmitted from person to person or from animal to person. Some infectious diseases, such as the common cold, measles, chickenpox and athlete's foot, may be transmitted during normal social contact. Others are transmitted in particular, specialised ways such as through water, food, sexual contact or animal bite. People can be infected with a pathogen, but not have any symptoms of disease. These people are **carriers**. They can transmit the disease, but because they are not ill themselves they are often difficult to identify. Four infectious diseases are described in detail in chapter 15.

Non-infectious diseases

All the diseases that are *not* caused by pathogens are termed **non-infectious diseases** so this category includes all the categories that follow.

Some non-infectious diseases have one cause while others are more complex and are multifactorial.

Deficiency diseases

Deficiency diseases are nutritional diseases caused by an inadequate or unbalanced diet. If the diet does not supply sufficient energy for months or years, then people starve. Although most of the world's population have enough to eat, they do not all eat a balanced diet. One or more of the essential nutrients, such as proteins, vitamins and minerals can be missing or in short supply. As a consequence, people suffer from deficiency diseases, such as iron-deficiency anaemia, scurvy (deficiency of vitamin C), night blindness (vitamin A), and rickets (vitamin D). More information about deficiency diseases is given in chapter 12.

Inherited diseases

An inherited disease is one which is caused by genes and therefore can be passed from parents to children. Inherited diseases are sometimes known as genetic diseases or genetic disorders. Sickle cell anaemia (chapter 2), Huntington's disease and cystic fibrosis are all examples of inherited diseases.

In Britain the most common inherited disease is cystic fibrosis. This disease results from an abnormality in a channel protein (see chapter 4) that allows chloride ions to flow out of cells across plasma membranes. Cells with these chloride channels are found in the lungs, pancreas and testes. The movement of chloride ions is essential in the lungs as it is accompanied by outward movement of water which keeps the inner surface of the alveoli moist. If the channels do not work properly, neither the chloride ions nor the water molecules can move out and the result is a build up of thick, sticky mucus. This makes breathing difficult and is likely to form a breeding ground for bacteria, resulting in infections. The sufferer must have regular physiotherapy to loosen and remove the mucus (*figure 11.1*).

As we saw in chapters 5 and 6, the abnormal channel protein is caused by a faulty allele (version) of its gene. There are several different faulty alleles, all of which have a different base sequence from the normal gene and so do not code for the normal amino acid sequence in the protein.

You will remember that a person has two versions (alleles) of every gene in each of their body cells. The alleles that cause cystic fibrosis are **recessive** alleles, that is their effect is only seen when *both* copies of the gene in a person's cells are faulty. If we use the symbol **A** to represent the normal allele (which is **dominant**) and **a** to

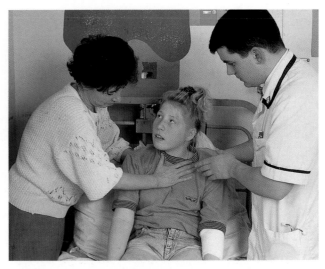

● **Figure 11.1** A physiotherapist advises a mother about giving her daughter massage to relieve the symptoms of cystic fibrosis.

represent a faulty allele, then a person's genotype (genetic makeup) for this gene could be **AA**, **Aa** or **aa**. A person with genotype **AA** or **Aa** makes the normal protein coded for by the allele **A**. Only if the genotype is **aa** will the person suffer from cystic fibrosis. A person with genotype **Aa** is a carrier because they carry the faulty allele but experience no symptoms of the disease themselves.

SAQ 11.1

Using your knowledge of genetics from your GCSE studies, draw a genetic diagram to show how two people who are carriers for the cystic fibrosis allele could have a child who has the disease. What are the chances of this happening?

Cystic fibrosis is only one of many inherited diseases. While cystic fibrosis and many others are caused by recessive alleles, some are caused by dominant alleles. Some show symptoms from birth while others develop later in life. Some faulty genes mean that a disease will always develop while others just increase the risk that it will. For example, genes are known to play a part in the likelihood that a person will develop some types of cancer, but environmental factors are important too (chapter 6). This is also the case with coronary heart disease (chapter 14).

Although many inherited diseases can be treated, it is not possible to *cure* them at the moment because we are not yet able to replace faulty alleles with normal ones. This may eventually become possible with at least some inherited diseases using a technique called **gene therapy**. (You can find out more about this if you study the A Level option *Applications of Genetics*.) The more we understand about the genes that are responsible for inherited diseases, the more likely it is that effective treatments can be developed. See the Box below for details of the **Human Genome Project**.

The Human Genome Project

This project involves scientists in many countries, including the Sanger Centre in the UK, and began in 1990. It aims to:

- determine the sequence of the four bases (adenine, cytosine, thymine and guanine) throughout all the DNA in human cells;
- identify the estimated 100 000 genes formed by the bases;
- find the locations of the genes on the 23 human chromosomes;
- store all this information on databases for future research;
- consider all the ethical, legal and social issues which arise from obtaining information about the human genome.

This is a massive undertaking. It is estimated that human DNA consists of 3000 million bases. The Project will help us to know exactly which sections of DNA, on which chromosomes, are responsible for the many different inherited diseases from which people can suffer.

There is already a practical impact. Once the sequence of bases in a gene is known it is possible to devise a reliable test to see if it is present. By 1999, diagnostic tests for several inherited diseases were available using DNA extracted from a cheek scraping or a blood sample. These tests can often identify whether a person is a carrier of a faulty allele such as that which causes cystic fibrosis or sickle cell anaemia. People who are carriers may decide not to have children or to have an antenatal genetic test to check if their child will be born with the disease. The incidence of some inherited diseases such as thalassaemia, a blood disorder common in some Mediterranean countries, is falling as a result of genetic testing.

Some genes that have been identified by the project play a contributory role in diseases that develop later in life, such as Alzheimer's disease, breast cancer and ovarian cancer. These diseases are multifactorial – genes play a part in their development but so do aspects of the environment. Genetic testing can give an idea of the probability of developing a particular disease. Those people at greatest risk can then be targeted by health authorities, screened at regular intervals and given appropriate advice about how to reduce their risks by modifying their lifestyle.

Although we do not know what many genes do, once the base sequence of a gene is discovered it should be possible to find the protein that it codes for, since the bases determine the amino acid sequence or primary structure (see page 32) of the protein. Once the 3D structure of the protein has been determined it could be possible to design drugs whose molecules would fit it perfectly. Such drugs would be much more effective than current ones that are developed in a largely trial-and-error fashion. They could also have fewer side effects. Similarly, we may be able to design drugs that act against the gene itself.

Knowing the base sequence of a normal, functioning gene may eventually make it possible to eliminate all risk of the disease by directly correcting or replacing the faulty allele in people – gene therapy. This has been done successfully in a few people with rare inherited diseases that affect their immune systems (chapter 16).

Many people are concerned about the implications of the genetic testing that has become possible as a result of the Human Genome Project. Although tests for diseases such as cystic fibrosis are useful because they inform people whether they are carriers or not, the results of other tests are not so clear cut and obvious. In some cases there is no treatment available for the diseases for which there are tests. Doctors will soon be able to carry out genetic tests on their patients for a wide range of diseases and conditions. The results may make some people anxious about their health. There are also risks of discrimination by employers, insurance companies and others when they discover that someone has had a positive result for a particular faulty gene. There are concerns about the reliability of the genetic tests themselves which may give false results. The Project is unlikely to benefit the world's poorest people who will continue to be vulnerable to infectious diseases. Some argue that the money spent on the Human Genome Project could better be spent on improving the health of these very poor people.

SAQ 11.2
Explain why there is a need for several different diagnostic tests for cystic fibrosis.

SAQ 11.3
State why the DNA for genetic testing is extracted from cheek cells or white blood cells and not red blood cells.

SAQ 11.4
Explain why people may wish to know if they are carriers of inherited diseases, such as cystic fibrosis and sickle cell anaemia.

Degenerative diseases

As we age, parts of the body work less efficiently. This may happen because the body's repair mechanisms begin to fail. These failings are associated with, for example, short-term memory loss, poor circulation and reduced mobility due to worn joints. However, degenerative diseases are not necessarily associated with growing old. Even in youth or middle age, a gradual loss of function in one or several organs or tissues can occur, associated with a progressive destruction of specialised cells. Sometimes this can happen because the defence system (the immune system – see chapter 16) begins to attack the body's own cells, as with Hashimoto's disease in which the thyroid gland is gradually destroyed. Deficiencies of nutrients during childhood can be the cause of a degenerative disease later in life, through restricting the full development of tissues.

There are three major types of degenerative disease:

■ diseases of the skeletal, muscular and nervous systems, for example osteoarthritis, muscular dystrophy (also an example of a genetic disease), multiple sclerosis, motor neurone disease and Alzheimer's disease (also an example of a mental disorder);

■ cardiovascular diseases, which are diseases of the circulatory system such as coronary heart disease and stroke (see chapter 14);

■ cancers (see chapter 6).

Mental disorders

Any disease or illness that affects a person's mind is known as a mental disorder. It may affect any combination of thoughts, emotions, memory and personal and social behaviour. There may be accompanying physical symptoms. As with most types of disease, mental disorders range, in both type and degree, from very mild to very serious. An example of a relatively mild mental illness (although it may be extremely unpleasant for the sufferer) is claustrophobia (a fear of closed spaces). Examples of serious mental disorders include Creutzfeld–Jacob disease (CJD), Alzheimer's disease, schizophrenia and manic depression.

Some mental disorders are associated with visible degeneration of brain tissue. For example, in CJD large areas of brain tissue are destroyed, resulting in a spongy appearance. This is caused by infection with a prion protein and results in loss of coordination and mental derangement; CJD is always fatal. Alzheimer's disease is caused by degeneration of certain groups of brain cells that normally secrete a substance called acetylcholine, which is a neurotransmitter (a chemical responsible for transmitting nerve impulses between cells). The brain gradually shrinks and distinctive 'plaques' of aluminium-rich protein can be seen. The symptoms of Alzheimer's include a progressive deterioration in memory, followed by a general decline in all mental faculties, which is known as **dementia**. Alzheimer's is most common in older people, but does also occur in people in younger age groups, where there is thought to be a genetic influence.

Schizophrenia and manic depression are serious mental disorders that can occur at any age but are more likely to first appear in relatively young people. It may not be obvious for some years, however, exactly what condition a person is suffering from due to the subtleties of some symptoms and the periods of apparent good health that can occur in between. Changes in brain tissue are far less obvious than in CJD or Alzheimer's but changes in patterns of blood flow can be seen in the brains of people with these conditions and there are measurable imbalances in the secretion of neurotransmitters in the brain. People with this type of mental disorder can be helped by taking drugs that mimic or inhibit these neurotransmitters as appropriate.

Social diseases

The social setting in which a person lives has a powerful effect on the amount and type of disease they may experience. Their standard of housing and sanitation, and other aspects of their physical environment such as levels of pollution and access to recreational facilities, expose them to or protect them from certain health risks. Poverty encourages disease. For example, infectious diseases tend to spread more easily in overcrowded, insanitary and unhygienic conditions. Deficiency diseases can develop when choice of food is limited by lack of money. In contrast, obesity and cardiovascular diseases, such as coronary heart disease, are more common in affluent communities and countries. But, even within these, it is people in the lower socio-economic groups who are most at risk. A person's occupation can put them at risk of developing certain acute and chronic diseases (e.g. glassblowers and silicosis).

This category of disease can be interpreted very widely to include almost all the infectious diseases and the multifactorial diseases which are influenced by people's living conditions and their personal behaviour.

Self-inflicted diseases

Self-inflicted diseases are those in which a person's health is damaged by their own decisions and behaviour.

Those who start smoking at a young age are highly likely to become addicted to nicotine. The health risks associated with smoking are described in chapter 14. Misusing other drugs, such as alcohol and heroin, can lead to drug dependence, which puts the person at risk of developing a variety of physical and mental diseases. Sunbathing can cause blistering of the skin and increases the risk of developing skin cancer. Eating large quantities of fatty food puts people at risk of putting on weight and becoming obese (see chapter 12).

Deliberate self-harm, such as taking an overdose of tablets in an attempted suicide could be considered a form of self-inflicted disease as there is often permanent damage to major body organs as a result. In most developed countries suicide is second only to accidents as a leading cause of death among young people. It is often an indication of poor mental health in which there can be a strong sense of hopelessness, failure or frustration.

SAQ 11.5

Make a table to show the classification of the following diseases (each one can be classified into more than one category): scurvy, malaria, measles, cystic fibrosis, lung cancer, sickle cell anaemia, Alzheimer's disease, schizophrenia, Creutzfeld–Jacob disease and skin cancer.

Health statistics

Epidemiology is the study of patterns of disease and the various factors that affect the spread of disease. It is concerned with how diseases affect whole populations, not just individual people. It therefore involves the collection and statistical analysis of large amounts of data.

When a new disease appears, as AIDS did in the early 1980s (chapter 15), the cause may not be immediately apparent. Collecting information on the distribution of the disease helps to identify its underlying cause. If it turns out to be an infectious disease, such data may indicate the way in which it is transmitted.

Epidemiology also provides useful information about non-infectious diseases. It was epidemiologists who first identified the link between smoking and lung cancer in the 1950s. They looked for common factors amongst people who developed the disease (chapter 14).

Epidemiologists collect data on the number of people who are ill (**morbidity**) and on the number who have died (**mortality**). These data are always particular to a given population under study, for example that of a city, county or country.

To make comparisons between different places or between different years, the data are adjusted in some way. For example, you may find deaths from heart disease expressed as 'per 100 000 population aged between 35 and 74' (see page 196). When data are expressed in this way, fair comparisons can be made which are not possible with simple, unadjusted, death rates.

Three types of data provide information on the spread of disease:
- **incidence** – the number of new cases in a population occurring per week, month or year;
- **prevalence** – the number of people in a population with a disease within any given week, month or year;
- **mortality** – the number of people who have died of a certain disease per week, month or year.

When these three types of data are collected for all categories of disease they provide good indicators of a nation's health.

Who uses health statistics?

Governments collect health statistics so that medical authorities and politicians can identify trends in the health of their own country's population and make priorities for allocating financial and human resources to different health programmes. For example, in the UK over recent years there has been an increase in deaths from bronchial asthma (see pages 232–233). As a result, asthma is now the subject of research to find the cause for its recent increase and advice is made more readily available for sufferers.

Statistics also reveal differences *within* a country, for example between geographical regions, ethnic groups and socio-economic groups. This allows health authorities to target resources for treatment and prevention at those people who are most at risk.

Mass screening of whole populations may take place to find who is at risk and to catch the early stages of disease (for example cervical cancer) or screening may be directed at that part of the population already known to be at greatest risk, such as people with a family history of heart disease or breast cancer.

National governments and local authorities are not the only organisations that are interested in health statistics. The World Health Organisation (WHO) also collects such data and identifies common trends so that it can initiate global health programmes and coordinate the responses of national governments according to the changing patterns of disease. International statistics collected by WHO help to identify regions where there are special problems, for example the high mortality rate from heart disease in Finland and the prevalence of high blood pressure in many Eastern European countries.

Statistics can be used to monitor the effectiveness of health provision. For example, 31 countries reported cases of smallpox in 1967 but in 1978 there were no reported cases of smallpox in the world. This demonstrated the effectiveness of WHO's programme to eradicate the disease (see page 230–231).

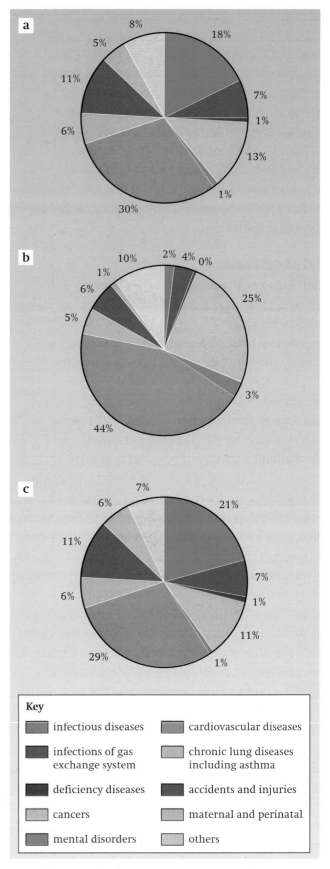

Key

- infectious diseases
- cardiovascular diseases
- infections of gas exchange system
- chronic lung diseases including asthma
- deficiency diseases
- accidents and injuries
- cancers
- maternal and perinatal
- mental disorders
- others

● **Figure 11.2** The causes of death in 1998
a worldwide.
b in developed countries only.
c in developing countries only.

Endemic, epidemic or pandemic?

If an infectious disease is always present in a population it is described as being **endemic**. Tuberculosis (TB) is endemic in most parts of the world (chapter 15). Many people have, or have had at some stage, the bacteria in their lungs that cause the disease. They can carry the bacteria but not show any symptoms of TB because they have an efficient immune system that prevents the bacteria doing any harm.

An **epidemic** occurs when a disease suddenly spreads rapidly to affect many people. Every few years there are epidemics of influenza that spread across a country.

When a disease spreads over a very large area, such as a continent or even the whole world, it is called a **pandemic**. There are pandemics of AIDS and TB at present.

SAQ 11.6

a When does a disease become an epidemic?
b What is the difference between an **epidemic** and a **pandemic**?

SAQ 11.7

A disease is spreading rapidly through a community. Explain why it is useful to know the **incidence** and **prevalence** of the disease in the community and the **mortality** from the disease.

Global patterns of disease

What is the pattern of disease around the world and how does it change with time? A study of mortality data collected by WHO is one way of comparing standards of health in different countries.

Figure 11.2a shows the main causes of death worldwide in 1998. Most deaths were due to degenerative diseases, such as cardiovascular diseases and cancers, and infectious diseases. But the pattern of mortality is not even. *Figure 11.2b* shows that in developed countries there are very few deaths from infectious diseases unlike the situation in developing countries (*figure 11.2c*). There are two reasons for this difference. Firstly, the *incidence* of serious infectious diseases, such as measles, polio, TB and malaria, is low in developed countries. Secondly, if someone does become infected, **antibiotics** can be administered, providing a cure for most bacterial infections. The low incidence and rates of mortality from infectious diseases in developed countries have only come about relatively recently. In contrast, 1901 saw about 9000 deaths from measles in England and Wales. The change is partly due to medical advances, particularly **vaccination** and antibiotics, and partly to improved standards of hygiene, sanitation and nutrition. These social factors alone are thought to have brought about the decline in deaths from whooping cough that began well before vaccination was widely used (*figure 11.3*).

Great improvements have been made in the developing world, too. For example, polio has been nearly eradicated from the world by the use of a vaccination programme similar to that used for the eradication of smallpox.

Globally, the health of many people is improving. The data reveal that many countries are in transition from high death rates (particularly among children and young people), low life expectancy and high incidence of infectious diseases to lower death rates, few deaths among children and young people and an increasing

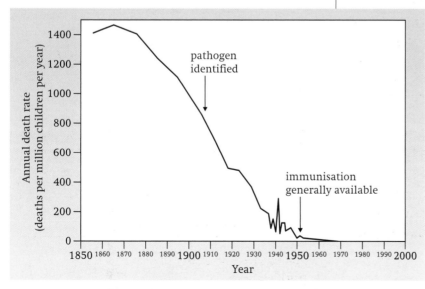

● **Figure 11.3** Rates of death from whooping cough of children aged under 15 years in England and Wales.

life expectancy. This means that a larger proportion of the world's population dies of degenerative diseases associated with longer life and lifestyles that put people at risk of heart disease and cancers. *Figures 11.2b* and *11.2c* show that, while the incidence of these diseases is high in developed countries, they cause a large proportion of deaths in developing countries too. Smoking is associated with these diseases and WHO considers smoking an epidemic that is now spreading throughout the developing world as manufacturers meet more legal restrictions in the developed world.

This should not be allowed to hide the fact, however, that there are still many poor people in the world and it is poverty that is responsible for the highest death rates in some countries. When mortality data are adjusted for richest and poorest countries, 59% of deaths in the poorest 20% of countries are caused by infectious, maternal, perinatal and deficiency diseases compared with only 8% in the richest 20% of countries. Here, 85% of deaths are due to degenerative diseases whereas these only account for 32% in the poorest. It is the young who make up a large proportion of deaths in the poorest nations, infectious diseases being responsible for more than 13 million deaths a year.

SAQ 11.8

Use the information in *figures 11.2a, b* and *c* to make three lists to show the leading causes of death in the world, in developed countries and in developing countries. Comment on the similarities and differences that you find.

SUMMARY

♦ Good health is more than freedom from disease. A healthy person enjoys good mental and physical health and plays a full role in society.

♦ Disease is a disorder or malfunctioning of the mind or body. Each disease presents a certain set of signs and symptoms that can be used to make a diagnosis.

♦ Nine different categories of disease are often recognised. Most diseases, however, can be classified into more than one category.

♦ Physical diseases involve damage to part of the body. This category includes all the other categories except the less severe mental diseases where there is no sign of any physical damage to the brain.

♦ Infectious diseases are caused by pathogenic organisms which parasitise the body. These are viruses, bacteria, fungi, protoctists, worms and insects.

♦ Non-infectious diseases are those that are not caused by pathogens. They can be due to dietary deficiency, an inherited faulty gene, degeneration of specific tissues, social conditions or personal behaviour.

♦ Mental disorders are diseases of the mind which may or may not be associated with physical damage to the brain.

♦ Epidemiology is the study of disease patterns. Statistics collected on disease (morbidity) and death (mortality) reveal patterns that can indicate what causes diseases, how they are spread, where to target health education and care and whether such programmes are successful.

♦ Patterns of disease differ between developed and developing countries. Degenerative diseases kill a larger proportion of people in developed countries than any other type of disease does. In developing countries, deaths from infectious diseases are far more common.

◆ When a disease spreads rapidly through a population it is an epidemic. When this is worldwide it is a pandemic. Diseases that are always present in a population, even though they may not cause much ill health or death, are endemic.

◆ The Human Genome Project aims to identify all human genes and determine the sequence of bases in the DNA of these genes. This will allow people to find out if they are at risk of developing certain diseases and will help in the design of new drugs targeted at the genes or the proteins for which they code.

Questions

1 Discuss the statement that health is more than the absence of disease.

2 With reference to named diseases, discuss the problem of classifying diseases into different categories.

3 Explain the differences between the following pairs of categories used to classify diseases: a physical and mental, b infectious and non-infectious, c inherited and deficiency.

4 Explain the advantages of collecting health statistics.

5 Discuss the factors that influence the differences in prevalence of disease in developed and developing countries.

6 Discuss the significance of the Human Genome Project.

7 Knowing what a person's genotype is may not always be in their best interests. Discuss the ethical, moral and social implications of being able to find out what alleles people carry for particular genes.

CHAPTER 12

Diet

By the end of this chapter you should be able to:

1 list the components of a balanced diet;

2 explain what is meant by the term *Dietary Reference Value* (*DRV*) and describe how these values should be used;

3 discuss the energy and nutrient requirements of people with reference to gender, age, activity, pregnancy and lactation;

4 describe the functions of essential amino acids, essential fatty acids and vitamins A and D in the body;

5 describe the consequences of malnutrition with reference to starvation, protein deficiency, anorexia nervosa, deficiencies of vitamins A and D, and obesity.

Our diet is everything we eat and drink. A **balanced diet** is one which provides an adequate intake of energy and nutrients needed for the maintenance of our body and thus our good health. We need complex molecules to provide energy and materials for growth, repair, movement and the functioning of our vital organs. As we saw in chapter 7, carbohydrates, fats (lipids) and proteins fulfil this role. Each day, they are supplied in large quantities in our diet and so are called **macronutrients**. We also need very much smaller quantities of other nutrients, such as vitamins and minerals. These are called **micronutrients**.

Cells can convert some compounds into others; for example glucose can be converted into fat for storage, proteins are synthesised from amino acids, and phospholipids are made from glycerol and fatty acids (chapter 2). However, there are some organic compounds that our cells cannot make from anything else. These compounds have to be provided in our diet. They are:

- essential amino acids;
- essential fatty acids;
- most vitamins.

The diet must also provide water, enough to replace what we lose every day, and dietary fibre, material that we cannot digest but which helps the movement of food along the gut by peristalsis. *Table 12.1* shows all the components of a balanced diet and their functions in the body's metabolism (chemical processes).

Malnutrition results from an **unbalanced diet**, one in which some nutrients are absent or not in the right quantities to meet our needs. In some cases, too much can be as bad for us as too little. Whilst deficiency diseases are diseases of want, some diet-related diseases are the result of eating more than we need.

How much and what *actually* eat is often dictated by considerations other than health such as cultural, social and economic factors. Designers of diet-related health promotion programmes must bear these powerful forces in mind.

How much and what *do* we need? Everybody needs some of every nutrient but individual people require different amounts and proportions, depending on their height, weight, age, gender, level of physical activity and even the climate they live in. Pregnancy, lactation (breast-feeding) and fighting infection create their own dietary requirements. In this chapter, we look in detail at these varying needs, how they are assessed and what the effect is on health when they are not met.

Nutrient	Function
Macronutrients	
carbohydrates	provide energy
fats (lipids)	provide energy and essential fatty acids for plasma membranes, some hormones
protein	provide energy and essential amino acids for making: structural proteins (e.g. collagen in bone, keratin in hair); metabolic proteins (enzymes); communication proteins (e.g. some hormones) and protective proteins (e.g. antibodies)
Micronutrients	
fat-soluble vitamins:	
A (retinol)	proper functioning of the retina in the eye and epithelial tissues
D	stimulates calcium uptake from the gut and its deposition in bone
E	antioxidant
K	formation in the liver of substances that promote blood clotting
water-soluble vitamins:	
vitamin B complex, including folic acid and B_{12}	required for respiration, protein synthesis, nucleic acid synthesis, red cell production, nerve function
C	formation of collagen, proper functioning of skin and mucous membranes, antioxidant, stimulates absorption of iron from the gut, aids healing of wounds
minerals:	
calcium	strengthening of bones and teeth; required for muscle contraction
phosphorus	strengthening of bones and teeth; ATP, DNA and RNA synthesis
iron	component of haemoglobin and myoglobin
iodine	formation of thyroid hormones
potassium	conduction of nerve impulses, muscle function
sodium	osmotic balance, muscle function, conduction of nerve impulses
chloride	osmotic balance, hydrochloric acid in stomach
magnesium	development of bones and teeth, enzyme activity
zinc	constituent of some enzymes, involved in wound healing and functioning of insulin
copper, manganese and cobalt	required for enzyme function
fluoride	component of tooth enamel, reduces risk of tooth decay
Dietary fibre (non-starch polysaccharides)	aids peristalsis, prevents constipation, gives protection against gut diseases and lowers blood cholesterol
Water	solvent, hydrolysis of food in gut, transport medium (e.g. blood), coolant (sweat), removal of excretory waste in urine

● **Table 12.1** The components of a balanced diet and their functions.

Calculating dietary requirements

Our body mass is one indicator of the appropriateness of our diet. If our body mass increases and no growth is occurring, our intake is exceeding demand. Conversely, a decreasing body mass shows that demand is exceeding intake. If our body mass stays fairly constant and we are not suffering from any disease of deficiency or excess, then we must be eating just the right quantity and balance of food to meet our needs for all the basic metabolic processes, maintenance of our body temperature, growth and repair and physical activity.

In such a situation, it should be possible to judge how much energy and nutrients we need by recording what we eat and analysing its chemical composition. (*Table 12.2* shows the energy values of the main components of food.) However, people

Nutrient	Energy (kJ g^{-1})
carbohydrate	16
fat	37
protein	17
alcohol	29

● **Table 12.2** Energy values of some dietary components.

are not very good at accurately remembering everything they have eaten. Studies suggest that we probably underestimate our food intake by as much as 25%. Surveys of household expenditure (what goods and services people buy) give an indication of the diet of the nation as a whole, but within that there will be much individual variation. Studies of the intake of specific nutrients such as proteins or vitamins are difficult with human subjects and generalisations from animal studies may not be relevant. It is possible to measure an individual's energy consumption by monitoring their oxygen absorption. It is estimated that 21.2 kJ are made available when 1 dm³ of oxygen is used in respiration. Experiments show that adults need about 8000–9000 kJ every day as a minimum to stay alive.

Dietary Reference Values

We saw in chapter 11 that local, national and international organisations are involved in monitoring patterns of health and disease and investigating their causes. The role of diet is no exception. In 1943, the US Government published **Recommended Dietary Allowances (RDAs)** to help plan diets for military personnel in the Second World War. The first comprehensive set of RDAs in Britain was published in 1950 and the latest revision was in 1991, when the Committee on Medical Aspects of Food Policy (COMA) surveyed all the available data on nutrition and health and published a report of their findings. This proved very influential.

The COMA report introduced the term **Dietary Reference Values (DRVs)** to avoid the suggestion that there was one recommended diet for everyone. DRVs reflect the fact that, for example, not everyone of the same age needs the same intake of energy or nutrients. For example, two 14-year-olds may have different rates of metabolism or growth.

There are two different kinds of DRV as a result of the varying amounts of data for particular nutrients that were available for analysis by

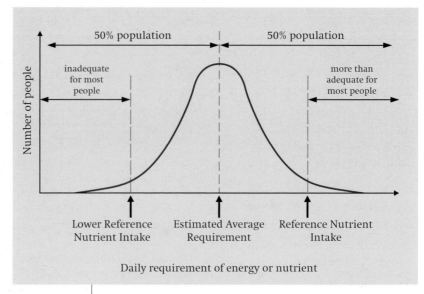

● **Figure 12.1** The requirements for energy and nutrients of a survey group show a normal distribution. Three Dietary Reference Values (DRVs) are shown.

COMA. Where there were sufficient data, COMA constructed graphs similar to that in *figure 12.1*. No figures are shown in *figure 12.1* as they would depend on which specific nutrient and group of people the data referred to, but notice the *shape* of the graph – it applies in all cases. It shows that most people in the group require a daily intake that is near the mean for the group. Very few people require either a much larger or a much smaller intake. This type of distribution of data is known as a **normal distribution**. Also note that, instead of just one RDA for a nutrient, up to three DRVs can be calculated for each component of the diet as follows.

■ **Estimated Average Requirement** (for energy and nutrients). This is an estimate of the average requirement of a population: 50% of the group will need more than this DRV, 50% will need less.

■ **Reference Nutrient Intake** (for nutrients only). This represents enough or more than enough to meet the needs of almost all the population, even those with high needs.

■ **Lower Reference Nutrient Intake** (for nutrients only). This is the amount that is sufficient for people with low needs. Most people need more than this.

Note that there are no Reference or Lower Reference Nutrient Values for energy, as individual requirements within an age group vary so much. For example, an athlete clearly needs higher levels than the population average but the precise amount will depend on a variety of other factors such as body mass and training regimen.

The second group of DRVs are known as **Safe Intakes**. These are for the nutrients for which there were insufficient data available to construct graphs similar to *figure 12.1*, for example vitamins E and K and minerals such as fluoride. As you would expect, too low an intake risks deficiency, but some micronutrients are toxic when taken in large amounts (e.g. vitamin A), hence the term Safe Intake. These DRVs are set well below such dangerous levels.

We have seen that the requirements for energy and nutrients vary *within* an age group. They also vary *between* age groups and with gender. DRVs for males and females of different age groups are shown in *tables 12.3* and *12.4*. We also know that requirements change when there are extra demands on the body. We will look at DRVs for women who are pregnant or lactating later in this chapter.

Age	Estimated Average Requirement (MJ day^{-1})	
	males	females
0–3 months (formula-fed)	2.28	2.16
4–6 months	2.89	2.69
7–9 months	3.44	3.20
10–12 months	3.85	3.61
1–3 years	5.15	4.86
4–6 years	7.16	6.46
7–10 years	8.24	7.28
11–14 years	9.27	7.92
15–18 years	11.51	8.83
19–49 years	10.60	8.10
50–59 years	10.60	8.00
60–64 years	9.93	7.99

● **Table 12.3** Estimated Average Requirements for energy for different age groups and sexes, all with low activity levels.

SAQ 12.1
Suggest likely outcomes of eating a diet with a daily energy intake greater than required.

Age	Protein (g day^{-1})	Calcium (mg day^{-1})	Iron (mg day^{-1})	Zinc (mg day^{-1})	Vitamin A (μg day^{-1})	Folic acid (μg day^{-1})	Vitamin C (mg day^{-1})
males and females:							
0–3 months*	12.5	525	1.7	4.0	350	50	25
4–6 months	12.7	525	4.3	4.0	350	50	25
7–9 months	13.7	525	7.8	5.0	350	50	25
10–12 months	14.9	525	7.8	5.0	350	50	25
1–3 years	14.5	350	6.9	5.0	400	70	30
4–6 years	19.7	450	6.1	6.5	500	100	30
7–10 years	28.3	550	8.7	7.0	500	150	30
males:							
11–14 years	42.1	1000	11.3	9.0	600	200	35
15–18 years	55.2	1000	11.3	9.5	700	200	40
19–50 years	55.5	700	8.7	9.5	700	200	40
50+ years	53.3	700	8.7	9.5	700	200	40
females:							
11–14 years	41.2	800	14.8	9.0	600	200	35
15–18 years	45.0	800	14.8	7.0	600	200	40
19–50 years	45.0	700	14.8	7.0	600	200	40
50+ years	46.5	700	8.7	7.0	600	200	40

*formula-fed

● **Table 12.4** Reference Nutrient Intakes for protein and six micronutrients. All the values assume a well-balanced diet in which DRVs for energy and all other nutrients are met. Note that μg = microgram and 1000 μg = 1 mg.

SAQ12.2

Looking at *table 12.4*, suggest reasons for the variations in Reference Nutrient Intakes given for different age groups for protein, calcium and iron.

Proteins and amino acids

We have already seen the roles of proteins in the human body (chapters 2 and 3 and *table 12.1*). When we eat proteins, the protein molecules are broken down into their constituent amino acids in the digestive system. The amino acids are absorbed into the blood and then taken via the liver and other parts of the body to individual cells. Here they are used to synthesise whichever particular proteins are required in those cells, interacting with tRNA and ribosomes, as we saw in chapter 5.

There are 20 different amino acids and we must have supplies of all 20 if we are to make every type of protein in our body. We can change some amino acids into others, if required. For example, if we have plenty of methionine but not enough cysteine, then our cells can convert some of the methionine molecules into cysteine. But some amino acids cannot be made in this way. The only way we can get them is through our food. These are therefore known as **essential amino acids** and there are eight of them (*table 12.5*). You can see their chemical structures in appendix 1.

A balanced diet will therefore contain all of the essential amino acids and a good supply of the non-essential ones. There are *no* DRVs for individual amino acids as the British diet usually contains enough protein to supply all the essential amino acids in sufficient quantities. This is not always the case in the developing world. In 1985 the Food and Agriculture Organisation and WHO jointly suggested target amounts of essential amino acids for adults and infants. These are the values shown in *table 12.5*. Most foods of animal origin (meat, eggs and milk) contain all the different amino acids we need. Many foods of plant origin, however, may be deficient in one or more essential amino acid. For example, wheat is deficient in lysine, maize in tryptophan and soya beans in methionine. A growing proportion of the British population eats a vegetarian or vegan diet. They need to ensure that this includes a wide variety of protein-containing foods in order to obtain an adequate supply of all the amino acids they need.

Fats and sugars

Triglycerides and phospholipids are fats (lipids) and their use in the human body is summarised in *table 12.1*. They all contain fatty acids which can be saturated or unsaturated, as we saw in chapter 2. Their chemical structures are described on pages 28–30.

To make all the different fats we need, we must have a supply of a variety of fatty acids. We are able to make many of these inside our cells from other molecules but some cannot be synthesised in this way and so must be present in our diet. They are termed **essential fatty acids**. There are just two, **linoleic acid** and **linolenic acid** and both are unsaturated.

Essential amino acid	Estimated daily amino acid requirements (mg kg^{-1} body mass day^{-1})			
	3–4 months	2 years old	10–12 years	adult
isoleucine	70	31	28	10
leucine	161	73	44	14
lysine	103	64	44	12
methionine	58	27	22	13
phenylalanine	125	69	22	14
threonine	87	37	28	7
tryptophan	17	12	3	3
valine	93	38	25	10

● **Table 12.5** Estimates of daily essential amino acid requirements.

We need only very small quantities of essential fatty acids in the diet. Well-nourished people probably have a year's supply in their fat stores. Nevertheless, there are DRVs for them.

A major role of fats is the provision of energy, but the high levels of fat in the average British diet are implicated in diet-related diseases such as heart disease. This is especially true of saturated fats which may raise blood cholesterol levels. COMA therefore set DRVs for fats as percentages of total energy intake rather than in terms of mass of nutrient. The DRV for total fat intake is 33–35% of total energy intake. In Britain, this is lower than the average *actual* intake (39.2% in 1997). The DRV for saturated fat is no more than 10% of total dietary energy (again, lower than the 15% actual consumption in 1997). The DRV for linoleic acid is 1% and for linolenic acid 0.2% of total energy intake. Most vegetable oils and some fish oils are good sources of essential fatty acids.

SAQ 12.3

Calculate the mass of fat in a diet that provides 35% of the daily energy intake for 17-year-old males and females.

SAQ 12.4

Explain why reducing fat intake in particular can significantly reduce total energy intake.

The role of carbohydrates is summarised in *table 12.1* and in chapter 2. The average British diet contains high levels of simple carbohydrates (sugars) which can lead to disease such as diabetes and dental caries. As with fats, COMA set DRVs for carbohydrates in terms of % total energy: 10–11% for non-milk sugars such as sucrose and 37–39% for starch (a complex carbohydrate) and milk sugars such as lactose. Taken together, COMA recommended that no more than 85% of the energy in a diet should come from fats and carbohydrates. The remainder will come from protein.

Fibre

Dietary fibre is provided by structural polysaccharides such as cellulose, hemicellulose and pectins, found in the cell walls of plants (see chapters 1, 2 and 10). Humans do not have enzymes to digest these large, complex compounds so they pass straight through the gut. Fibre does not provide any energy or nutrients, but it gives bulk to food so that peristalsis in the intestines occurs efficiently. Fibre absorbs water and makes sure that some of it is retained when the food reaches the large intestine. This makes it easier to pass faeces and so helps prevent constipation. Fibre may have a protective role in reducing the risk of diseases of the gut such as colon cancer and in lowering blood cholesterol. The DRV for fibre in the adult diet is an average of 18 g per day with a range of 12–24 g per day.

Water

The daily water turnover in the body is about 4% of the body mass of an adult. Water intake must balance this or else dehydration occurs. Water is needed to replace that lost in the breath, faeces and sweat. It is essential as a solvent to enable absorption of nutrients in the gut and excretion of waste such as urea by the kidneys. Other important features of water are described in chapter 2. Excess water in the body is lost in the urine. The minimum quantity of water needed by a 70 kg male is about 1.5–2.0 dm^3 per day. A cyclist in the Tour de France requires up to 6 dm^3 a day. If there is no water in the diet, death occurs from dehydration within a few days. Even sedentary people are recommended to drink water freely and regularly, at a rate of about a glass an hour.

SAQ 12.5

State the functions of water in the body.

Vitamins

Vitamins are organic compounds that are needed in very small quantities in the diet. Only vitamins D and K can be made in the body, so the majority are essential dietary components. The Reference Nutrient Intakes for vitamins A and C and folic acid (one of the B vitamins) are shown in *table 12.4*. Vitamins have a very wide range of roles in the body (*table 12.1*). We will look at vitamins A and D in detail later in the chapter.

DRVs for pregnancy and lactation

During pregnancy, a woman's metabolism goes through considerable changes. There is an increase in the metabolic demand to support growth of the uterus, placenta and fetus. This is met by using stores of fat and micronutrients more efficiently than usual. In practice, it is often not necessary for a mother to increase her intake of energy significantly until the last three months of pregnancy as she will use fat stores and may be less active than usual. Women who are planning to become pregnant are strongly recommended to supplement their diet with folic acid tablets (400 µg per day) to protect against neural tube defects such as spina bifida in the developing embryo. It is advisable to start supplementing the diet with folic acid *before* conception since by the time pregnancy is confirmed the embryo may have already developed a neural tube. Other recommended changes to diet are shown in *table 12.6*. Note that most women have a dietary requirement for vitamin D during pregnancy and lactation only. This explains why vitamin D appears in *table 12.6* but not in *table 12.4*.

Infants fed on breast milk utilise nutrients very efficiently. Breast milk meets the exact nutritional needs of most babies including supplying all the energy for growth, development and metabolism. Infants who are fed on formula (powdered) milk do not use nutrients as efficiently. As a result the DRVs for infants fed on formula milk shown in *tables 12.3* and *12.4* give values which are a little higher than the equivalent values for breast milk. There are other advantages of breast feeding; for example, the colostrum produced during the first few days of lactation is rich in antibodies (see chapter 16).

SAQ 12.6

a From *table 12.6*, state the Estimated Average Requirements for energy for 25-year-old women during pregnancy and during their first and fourth months of lactation.

b Explain the differences between these values during pregnancy and lactation.

c State the Reference Nutrient Intakes for the seven micronutrients given in *table 12.6* for 25-year-old women during pregnancy.

d Explain why women are advised to supplement their diet with folic acid before they become pregnant rather than starting when pregnancy is confirmed.

The uses of Dietary Reference Values

DRVs refer to groups of people; they are not daily recommended quantities for individuals. However, we have seen that they do provide a guide to the adequacy of individual diets. If you are eating at, or above, the Reference Nutrient Intake for nutrients, then it is unlikely that you are deficient since so few people in the population have very high requirements (*figure 12.1*). No harm is done by eating just above the values. The Estimated Average Requirements for energy show the average energy intake for the population; but there may be many reasons for people having intakes above or below this DRV, which is just a guide to how much food energy people require.

DRVs are useful in assessing information from dietary surveys, especially if it is suspected that a population is suffering from a dietary disease such as anaemia. For example, a survey of the

Component of diet (DRV)	Pregnancy	Lactation	
		1st month	4–6 months
energy (MJ day^{-1})	+0.8^a	+1.9	+2.4^b
protein (g day^{-1})	+6.0	+11.0	+11.0
calcium (mg day^{-1})	–	+550	+550
iron (mg day^{-1})	–	–	–
zinc (mg day^{-1})	–	+6.0	+2.5
vitamin A (µg day^{-1})	+100	+350	+350
folic acid (µg day^{-1})	+100	+60	+60
vitamin C (mg day^{-1})	+10	+30	+30
vitamin D (mg day^{-1})	+10	+10	+10

(^{a} last three months only; ^{b} if breast milk is infants' main source of energy.)

● **Table 12.6** Increase in DRVs for energy (Estimated Average Requirement) and some selected nutrients (Reference Nutrient Intake) during pregnancy and lactation. These quantities should be added to a woman's normal intake for her age as given in *tables 12.3* and *12.4*.

nutrition of young children in the UK in the 1990s found that 84% of those under four years old were consuming less than the Reference Nutrient Intake for iron (6.9 mg a day). As many as 16% were consuming less than the Lower Reference Intake (3.7 mg a day).

SAQ 12.7

Suggest why there is concern about iron deficiency in children.

As DRVs apply to groups of people, they are useful for caterers and dietitians devising meals for institutions such as hospitals, schools, military bases, prisons and old people's homes. However, DRVs cannot be used to assess the dietary requirements of people suffering from diseases which affect the absorption or use of nutrients. For example in disorders of the gut certain nutrients may not be absorbed efficiently, such as vitamin B_{12} in pernicious anaemia. People with such disorders will therefore need higher levels in their diets than the RNIs or even have supplementary injections to bypass the gut.

Food labels

Consumers often like to monitor what the food they are buying contains, either for ethical reasons or to ensure a balanced diet for themselves. To help them, food manufacturers print nutritional information on packets of food. There is a minimum legal requirement, and any information given must be presented in a standard form as defined by European Directive 90/496 and the UK's 1996 Food Labelling Regulations. Any food manufacturer in the United Kingdom who declares that a food is a **source** of a micronutrient, such as vitamin C or folic acid, must show on the label that a normal daily serving of the food supplies at least 17% of the Recommended Daily Allowance. If a manufacturer claims that the food is a **rich source** (e.g. 'rich in vitamin C'), the label must then show that a normal daily serving supplies at least 50% of the RDA. This explains why you will find RDAs given on labels for foods such as breakfast cereals and fruit juices.

Note that RDAs are quoted, not DRVs. The figures (*table 12.7*) are derived from World Health

Micronutrient	European RDA
vitamin A	800 µg
vitamin B_1	1.4 mg
vitamin C	60 mg
vitamin D	5 µg
folic acid	200 µg
calcium	800 mg
iron	14 mg
zinc	15 mg

● **Table 12.7** The European RDAs for eight of the micronutrients for which regulations governing food labels exist in the UK.

Organisation recommendations and differ from COMA's. For example, the Reference Nutrient Intake for vitamin C for adults is 40 mg, the European RDA is 60 mg. The RDAs apply to adults and the quantities are sufficient for the needs of the population as a whole.

The nutritional contents of produce that is not sold in packets can be found by consulting tables such as those published by the Ministry of Agriculture, Fisheries and Food (see their *Manual of Nutrition*).

When dietary requirements go unmet

We will now look in detail at the effects on health when a person's diet does not match their body's requirements.

Starvation

A shortage or complete lack of food leads to starvation. There is a lack of both energy and nutrients. During starvation, or semi-starvation, the body adapts by reducing the rate of metabolism so that less energy is used to maintain the normal functions of the body. Some people have survived for up to 70 days without food, so long as they have access to water, because they use their reserves of carbohydrate, fat and protein to provide energy. People who were well fed before starvation began often do not suffer from any micronutrient deficiencies as most of them are stored in the body. Those on a poor diet before starvation may well show symptoms, particularly

Kwashiorkor	Marasmus
underweight	very underweight
oedema	no oedema
'moon face'	'old man's face'
muscle wasting	muscle wasting
dry, brittle and thin, reddish hair	little change to hair
fatty enlarged liver	little fat
bloated appearance	wrinkled skin
apathetic	mentally alert
loss of appetite	no loss of appetite

● **Table 12.8** The features of kwashiorkor and marasmus. Children with marasmus probably adapt better to a shortage of energy than those with kwashiorkor. Some show signs of both forms.

those of vitamin A deficiency. Both groups suffer from energy malnutrition, sometimes called **protein energy malnutrition**. The worst form of this is seen in young children, especially when they are weaned from milk onto poor, starchy foods. Such children grow slowly and have high mortality rates. Two extreme forms of protein energy malnutrition are **kwashiorkor** and **marasmus** (see *figure 12.2* and *table 12.8*).

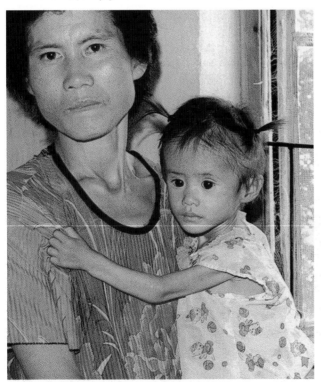

● **Figure 12.2** A severely malnourished child photographed during a famine in North Korea in 1997.

As starvation proceeds the body adapts by using:
■ glycogen stores in the liver (these last less than a day);
■ fat stores (lasting between four and six weeks, depending on the amount stored, the physical activity and the temperature);
■ protein in muscles and other tissue (lasting between one and two weeks).

In kwashiorkor the shortage of protein means that the body cannot make all of the proteins it needs. Those proteins already in the body are broken down to supply energy. This includes proteins in muscle tissue and blood plasma. The loss of these **plasma proteins** decreases the concentration of solutes in the blood plasma, increasing its water potential (see page 110). One consequence is that water is not absorbed into the blood from tissue fluid by osmosis, causing the tissue to swell. The characteristic bloated abdomen of a child with kwashiorkor is a result of a swollen liver and the accumulation of fluid in the tissues, a condition known as **oedema** (page 110). More common symptoms of protein energy malnutrition are the conditions of wasting and stunting.
■ **Wasting** is characteristic of acute protein energy malnutrition as there is rapid weight loss or a failure to put on weight.
■ **Stunting** is characteristic of chronic protein energy malnutrition as there is an inability to grow in height. This is difficult to reverse even if the diet improves later because it is often caused by prolonged malnutrition over a long time.

It used to be thought that these symptoms were caused only by a lack of protein and that they could be reversed with a very protein-rich diet. This probably did more harm than good. People recovering from starvation need about 8% of the energy they consume as protein. Cereals, such as maize and wheat, contain 8–11%. What malnourished people therefore require is an increase in staple foods and intake of energy. As food quantity increases, protein content increases in proportion. 'Unimix' is an example of a food used in emergency feeding programmes in famine areas (*table 12.9*). Supplementary feeding (*figures 12.3* and *12.5*) may be required if diets do not provide enough micronutrients, as during famines when

Nutrient	Mass per 100 g Unimix	Nutrient	Mass per 100 g Unimix
protein	6.82 g	potassium	145.8 mg
fat	21.80 g	vitamin A	231.0 µg
carbohydrate	62.50 g	vitamin B$_1$	0.39 mg
calcium	92.4 mg	vitamin B$_2$	0.23 mg
phosphorus	113.10 mg	vitamin B$_3$	3.17 mg
iron	3.08 mg		

● **Table 12.9** Nutritional value per 100 g of dry 'Unimix'. Each child receives about 350 g per day.

children suffer from nutritional deficiencies. Children whose staple diet is starchy root crops such as cassava, which contains only about 2% protein, should also be given supplementary protein.

Although most people in developed countries usually have sufficient energy intakes this is not the case during or immediately after a prolonged war (*figure 12.4*). A few people also have problems with digestion and absorption of food, or specific nutrient deficiencies such as anaemia. There is also the eating disorder, anorexia nervosa.

SAQ. 12.8

a From *tables 12.2* and *12.9*, calculate the total energy content in a day's supply of Unimix.

b Compare the result with the Estimated Average Requirements for energy for children of different ages as given in *table 12.3*.

c Compare the daily provision of protein, iron, calcium and vitamin A in Unimix with the Reference Nutrient Intakes given in *table 12.4* for children between one and ten years of age.

● **Figure 12.3** Food given to starving children must provide sufficient energy, proteins, vitamins and minerals.

SAQ. 12.9

During the famine in the Netherlands in 1945, women tended to survive for several weeks longer than men. Suggest a reason for this.

● **Figure 12.4** These children photographed in Amsterdam in 1945 survived the famine in Holland caused by the disruption at the end of the Second World War and severe flooding. Over one thousand people died in the city, and many more in the rest of the Netherlands.

● **Figure 12.5** Unimix being distributed at a mission in Kenya.

Anorexia nervosa

Anorexia nervosa is a wasting disease. The physical signs of semi-starvation reflect an underlying psychological distress. Most

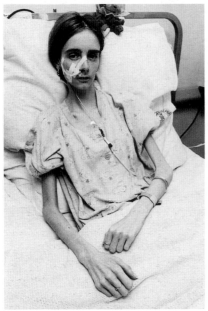

● **Figure 12.6** An anorexic girl. When weight falls below 75% of an acceptable level, anorexics are often admitted to a hospital or clinic to establish a normal eating pattern. Psychological support is often given. Some may be force fed.

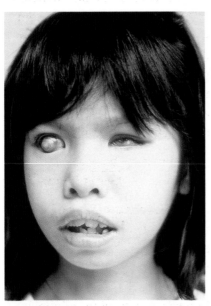

● **Figure 12.7** This girl from Thailand is blind from scarring of the cornea as a result of vitamin A deficiency.

anorexics are teenagers, and 90% of diagnosed cases are female. The causes are complex, but most are to do with anxiety over growing up, sexuality and poor self-image or low self-esteem. Up to half of girls and a third of boys responding to surveys in Britain say that they are concerned about their body image. Many admire the 'supermodels' (sometimes called 'superwaifs') and attempt to copy them.

Anorexia develops from reducing weight by extreme dieting. Even anorexics who have lost a considerable amount of weight consider themselves to be too fat. They become obsessive about food and eat less and less. They resist the pangs of hunger and may be obsessed with diet, exercise and death. The physical symptoms are equivalent to marasmus in younger children and include muscle wasting (including heart muscle), loss of body fat, thin sparse hair, cold hands and feet and low blood pressure (*figure 12.6*). There is limited sexual development and the menstrual cycle stops. Anorexics are highly susceptible to infections and they may lose so much weight that they die of starvation.

Vitamin deficiencies

As we have seen, a diet may provide sufficient energy but lack particular nutrients. We now look in detail at the effects on health of two vitamin deficiencies.

Vitamin A

Vitamin A (retinol) is not widely distributed in food. It is in some animal foods, such as milk, eggs, liver and fish-liver oils as well as in some fruit (mango and papaya). Related compounds, such as carotenoids (e.g. β carotene), are in a wide variety of vegetables such as cabbage, carrots and spinach. β carotene is converted in the body into retinol. In well-nourished people the liver stores enough vitamin A to last one or two years. It is stored in the liver because in high blood concentrations the vitamin is toxic.

Children with vitamin A deficiency often have dry, rough skin, inflammation of the eyes, **xerophthalmia** – a drying or scarring of the cornea (*figure 12.7*) – and cannot see in dim light (**night blindness**). Rod cells in the retina of the eye detect light of low intensity, for example in late evening and at night. They convert vitamin A into a pigment, rhodopsin, which is bleached when light enters the eye. Rod cells resynthesise rhodopsin, but if there is a deficiency of the vitamin, rod cells can no longer function and night blindness is the result. Adults, too, may suffer from night blindness if their diet lacks vitamin A for long periods of time.

Epithelial cells (chapter 1) use retinol to make retinoic acid, a chemical that aids cell development and growth. Without retinoic acid epithelia are not maintained properly and the body becomes susceptible to infections, particularly measles and infections of the gas exchange system and gut.

Children are at risk of vitamin A deficiency if they are fed diets based mainly on cereals (maize, rice or wheat) with small quantities of meat or fresh vegetables. This disease is thought to be responsible for half a million cases of childhood blindness worldwide (40–50% of the total). Millions more children receive just enough vitamin A to stave off blindness but not enough to maintain either their immune system (chapter 16) or their epithelia.

Vitamin D

This is sometimes known as the 'sunshine vitamin'. If the skin receives sufficient sunlight then the body can make enough vitamin D, so it is not always needed in the diet. Even though many people in Britain do not receive much sunlight in the winter, the amount made in the summer months (mainly between May and July) is usually enough to last the rest of the year because vitamin D is stored in muscles and fat. However, people confined indoors and those whose religion requires them to wear completely enveloping clothes may not be able to make enough vitamin D, and for them the Reference Nutrient Intake is 10 μg per day. Dark skin produces little vitamin D, so dark-skinned people in temperate countries must also ensure that they receive enough vitamin D in their diet. Eggs and oily fish are rich in vitamin D, and margarine and low fat spreads are fortified with it by law. Meat and meat products are also good sources.

Enzymes in the liver and kidney convert vitamin D into 'active vitamin D' which acts as a hormone to stimulate epithelial cells in the intestine to absorb calcium.

Vitamin D also acts on bone cells to regulate the deposition of calcium. Deficiency of vitamin D in children leads to **rickets** (*figure 12.8*). In adults it causes **osteomalacia**, a progressive softening which makes the bones susceptible to fracture. Women, especially in developing countries, who have a large number of children and breastfeed them are at risk of developing osteomalacia.

SAQ. 12.10
A study in Holland during the Second World War showed that nuns were particularly susceptible to osteomalacia. Suggest why this was so.

SAQ. 12.11
Suggest which groups of people in the UK are most at risk of rickets and osteomalacia.

Obesity

Overeating is a form of malnutrition. If people regularly eat more energy than they use, then they put on weight. This is more likely to happen if the diet is rich in fat and carbohydrate. Any carbohydrate that is not used in metabolism is converted into fat

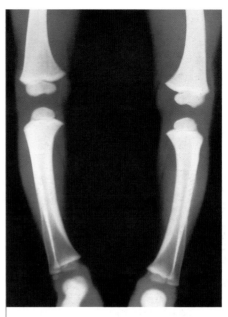

● **Figure 12.8** An X-ray of weakened bones and bowed legs of a child with rickets. The long bones are severely deformed because they lack the strengthening that calcium salts provide.

and stored around the major organs, such as the heart and kidneys, and (in women) under the skin. There is little danger in being slightly overweight, but risks to health increase as body weight increases. When someone is 20% or more above the recommended weight for their height they are **obese** (*figure 12.8*).

The **body mass index** (BMI) is used to find out whether people are underweight, overweight or obese. This is calculated as:

$$\frac{\text{body mass}}{\text{index}} = \frac{\text{body mass (in kg)}}{\text{height (in metres)}^2}$$

The body mass index of a man who is 1.73 m (5'8") tall with a mass of 70 kg is 23. This falls in the 'acceptable' category (*table 12.10*). Note that the body mass index is only used for adults. It is difficult to measure obesity in children and adolescents as they store fat as part of their growth.

BMI	Category
< 20	underweight
20–24	acceptable
25–30	overweight
>30	obese

● **Table 12.10** Body mass indexes.

SAQ 12.12

Three people have the following heights: 1.65 metres (5'5"), 1.73 m (5'8") and 1.83 m (6'0"). They each have a BMI of 30. Calculate their individual body masses.

People who are obese are at risk of suffering from a variety of diseases. They tend to have high concentrations of cholesterol in their blood and high blood pressure. This puts them at risk of developing coronary heart disease (see page 194). Obese people often develop diabetes as they cannot control the concentration of sugar in their blood. They are also at increased risk of several cancers, especially of the colon, rectum and prostate in men and uterus, cervix and breast in women. Supporting a large body mass puts a strain on the skeleton and obese people often suffer from arthritis. Obese people are also likely to develop hernias, varicose veins and gallstones. Since body organs are surrounded by large quantities of fat, surgical operations also carry more risk in people who are obese.

One long-term investigation showed that women with waists greater than 80 cm (31.4 inches) and men with waists greater than 94 cm (36.9 inches) were twice as likely to develop cardiovascular diseases than the rest of the population. Although taking measurements of the circumference of the waist is easier than calculating the body mass index, it does not indicate *where* most of the fat is stored. Taking the hip measurement as well and calculating the waist to hip ratio gives this information. Studies show that men with a high ratio are at a greater risk of cardiovascular diseases and diabetes. Most of their fat is deposited around the waist (creating the 'apple shape') rather than around the hips ('pear shape'), which is often the case in women. However, women with fat distributed in the 'apple shape' have the same risk of developing serious disease as men of this shape.

Obesity is an increasing health problem in North America, Europe and Australasia. It is quite rare in the rest of the world. It is associated with a 'Western-style' way of life as people are not physically active and have diets rich in fat. All diets providing more energy than people need can lead to weight gain, but as fat provides more than twice as much energy per gram as carbohydrate or protein do, then a fat-rich diet increases the chance of gaining weight (see *table 12.2*). Samples of the population in the UK show that there has been an increase in the percentage of men and women who are overweight and obese (*table 12.11*). Amongst children, too, obesity is becoming a problem. 10% of secondary school age children in the UK are very much heavier than they should be for their age and height.

	Percentage of sample					
	1980	1986/87	1991/92	1993	1995	1997
Men						
Obese	6	7	13	13	15	17
Overweight	33	38	40	43	43	43
Acceptable	51	49	41	39	38	35
Underweight	10	6	6	5	5	4
Women						
Obese	8	12	15	16	17	19
Overweight	24	24	26	30	30	30
Acceptable	54	53	50	46	46	43
Underweight	14	11	9	8	7	7

● **Table 12.11** Samples of the population since 1980 showing an increase in the percentage of people who are overweight and obese in the UK.

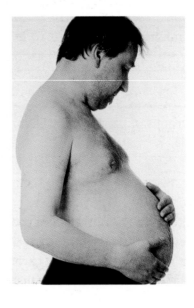

● **Figure 12.9** An obese person.

SUMMARY

- A balanced diet must provide: sufficient energy for metabolism, growth and physical activity; essential amino acids and essential fatty acids; micronutrients: (vitamins and minerals); water and fibre.

- Dietary Reference Values (DRVs) describe the required energy and nutrient intakes of the British population. When plotted on a graph these intakes show a normal distribution. The Estimated Average Requirement is the population average, the Reference Nutrient Intake is a value that includes most of the population; the Lower Reference Nutrient Intake provides enough for only a very small proportion of the population. These values provide useful standards for analysing dietary surveys and for planning diets for groups of people.

- The DRV for energy is the Estimated Average Requirement. The DRVs for protein and most of the micronutrients are Estimated Average Requirements, Reference Nutrient Intakes and Lower Reference Nutrient Intakes. Safe Intakes are the DRVs for two vitamins (E and K) and several minerals (e.g. fluoride).

- Amino acids are required for protein synthesis; fatty acids are required for making phospholipids. The amino acids and fatty acids that the body cannot synthesise are termed essential and must be provided by the diet.

- Vitamin A is needed for proper functioning of the retina and epithelia; vitamin D is needed for bone growth and development.

- Malnutrition is any disorder of nutrition resulting from eating an unbalanced diet. Starvation is caused by a lack of food and leads to exhaustion of body reserves of carbohydrate, fat and protein. Marasmus, kwashiorkor and anorexia nervosa are forms of protein energy malnutrition.

- Specific deficiency diseases, for example rickets, occur when there are micronutrient deficiencies.

- Overeating is a form of malnutrition which can lead to obesity and increase the risk of developing many diseases such as cardiovascular disease and diabetes.

Questions

1. **a** Explain the term *balanced diet*.
   b Discuss the importance of diet in preventing disease.

2. Explain the term *Dietary Reference Values* and discuss the advantages of publishing these values for energy, protein and micronutrients.

3. Describe and explain the dietary advice that a nutritionist might give to the following groups of people: **a** pregnant women, **b** athletes, **c** elderly people, **d** Arctic explorers.

4. Discuss the functions of the following in the body: **a** essential amino acids, **b** essential fatty acids, **c** vitamin A, **d** vitamin D.

5. Discuss the impact of malnutrition on developed and developing countries.

6. Describe the health risks of anorexia nervosa and obesity.

CHAPTER 13

Gaseous exchange and exercise

By the end of this chapter you should be able to:

1 describe the distribution of alveoli and blood vessels in lung tissue;

2 describe the distribution of cartilage, ciliated epithelium, goblet cells and smooth muscle in the trachea, bronchi and bronchioles;

3 describe the functions of cartilage, cilia, goblet cells, smooth muscle and elastic fibres in the gaseous exchange system;

4 explain the meanings of the terms *tidal volume* and *vital capacity*;

5 describe how to measure a person's pulse rate;

6 understand that pulse rate is a measure of heart rate and explain the significance of resting pulse rate in relation to physical fitness;

7 explain the terms *systolic blood pressure*, *diastolic blood pressure* and *hypertension*;

8 describe the immediate effects of exercise on the body, including the concept of oxygen debt and the production of lactate by anaerobic respiration;

9 explain the meaning of the term *aerobic exercise*;

10 describe how much exercise needs to be taken for significant sustained improvement in aerobic fitness;

11 discuss the long-term consequences of exercise on the body and the benefits of maintaining a physically fit body, relating these benefits to the concept that health is more than the absence of disease.

In this chapter we consider how the structure and functions of our gaseous exchange and cardiovascular systems are linked, how they are affected by physical activity and the contribution this makes to our overall level of health.

The gaseous exchange system

The gaseous exchange system links the circulatory system (chapter 8) with the atmosphere. It is adapted to:

■ clean and warm the air that enters during breathing;

■ maximise the surface area for diffusion of oxygen and carbon dioxide between the blood and atmosphere;

■ minimise the distance for this diffusion;

■ maintain adequate gradients for this diffusion.

Lungs

As we saw in chapter 4, the lungs are the site of gaseous exchange between air and blood and they present a huge surface area to the air that flows in and out. They are in the thoracic (chest) cavity surrounded by an airtight space between the pleural membranes. This space contains a small

Airway	Number	Approximate diameter	Cartilage	Goblet cells	Smooth muscle	Cilia	Site of gas exchange
trachea	1	1.8 cm	yes	yes	yes	yes	no
bronchus	2	1.2 cm	yes	yes	yes	yes	no
terminal bronchiole	48 000	1.0 mm	no	no	yes	yes	no
respiratory bronchiole	300 000	0.5 mm	no	no	no	yes	no
alveolar duct	9×10^6	400 μm	no	no	no	no	yes
alveoli	3×10^9	250 μm	no	no	no	no	yes

● **Table 13.1** The structure of the airways from the trachea to the alveoli. The various airways are shown in *figure 4.12*.

quantity of fluid to allow friction-free movement as the lungs are ventilated by the movement of the diaphragm and ribs. The structure and contents of the thorax are shown in *figure 4.12* on page 61.

Trachea, bronchi and bronchioles

The lungs are ventilated with air which passes through a branching system of airways (*figure 4.12* and *table 13.1*). Leading from the throat to the lungs is the **trachea**. At the base of the trachea are two **bronchi** (singular **bronchus**), which subdivide and branch extensively forming a bronchial 'tree' in each lung. **Cartilage** in the trachea and bronchi keeps these airways open and air resistance low, and prevents them from collapsing or bursting as the air pressure changes during breathing. In the trachea there is a regular arrangement of C-shaped rings of cartilage; in the bronchi there are irregular blocks of cartilage instead (*figure 13.1*). The small bronchioles are surrounded by smooth muscle which can contract or relax to adjust the diameter of these tiny airways. During exercise they relax to allow a greater flow of air to the alveoli. The absence of cartilage makes these adjustments possible.

Warming and cleaning the air

As air flows through the nose and the trachea it is warmed to body temperature and moistened by evaporation from the lining, so protecting the delicate surfaces inside the lungs from desiccation (drying out). Protection is also needed against the suspended matter carried in the air, which may include dust, pollen, bacteria, fungal spores, sand and viruses. All are a potential threat to the proper functioning of the lungs. Particles larger than about 5–10 μm are caught on the hairs inside the nose and the **mucus** lining the nasal passages and other airways.

In the trachea and bronchi, the mucus is produced by the **goblet cells** of the ciliated epithelium (page 19). Using a microscope, the epithelium looks as if it is made of several separate layers of cells, but this is deceptive. Each cell reaches the basement membrane and so it is a pseudostratified epithelium. The upper part of each goblet cell is swollen with **mucin** droplets which have been secreted by the cell. Mucus is a slimy solution of mucin, which is composed of glycoproteins with many carbohydrate chains that make them sticky and able to trap inhaled particles. The rest of the cell, which contains the nucleus, is quite slender like the stem of a goblet. Mucus is also made by glands beneath the epithelium. Some chemical pollutants, such as sulphur dioxide and nitrogen dioxide, can dissolve in mucus to form an acid solution that irritates the lining of the airways.

Between the goblet cells are the ciliated cells (*figure 13.2*). The continual beating of their cilia carries the carpet of mucus upwards towards the larynx at a speed of about 1 cm per minute. When mucus reaches the top of the trachea it is usually swallowed so that pathogens are destroyed by the acid in the stomach.

Phagocytic white blood cells known as **macrophages** (see chapters 4 and 16) patrol the surfaces of the airways scavenging small particles such as bacteria and fine dust particles. During an infection they are joined by other phagocytic cells which leave the capillaries to help remove pathogens.

Figure 13.1

a A light micrograph of part of the trachea in transverse section (×150). The lining is comprised of ciliated epithelium which rests on a basement membrane made of protein fibres. In between the ciliated cells are goblet cells (here stained blue). Beneath the epithelium is an area of loose tissue with blood vessels and glands that secret mucus. The trachea as a whole is supported by C-shaped rings of cartilage, a portion of which appears as the thick layer running across the bottom of the picture. Compare with figure 1.26 on page 19.

b A light micrograph of part of a bronchus in transverse section (×1300). Between the ciliated epithelial cells, the goblet cells are stained pink. There are fewer goblet cells per cm^2 than in the trachea and the epithelial cells are not as tall. Beneath the epithelium there are elastic fibres. Blocks of cartilage, not rings, support the bronchus and part of one can be seen, also stained pink, stretching from top to bottom of the picture.

c A light micrograph of a small bronchiole in transverse section (×135). Surrounding the epithelium is smooth muscle. There is no cartilage. Around the bronchiole are some alveloli.

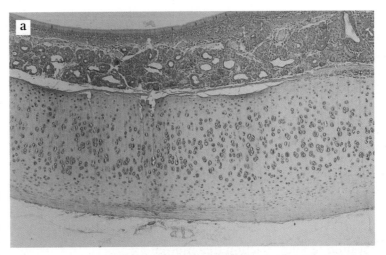

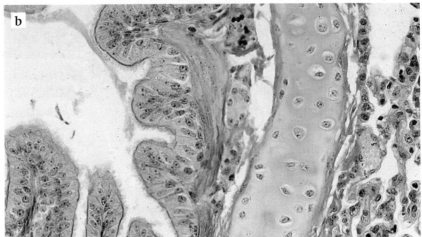

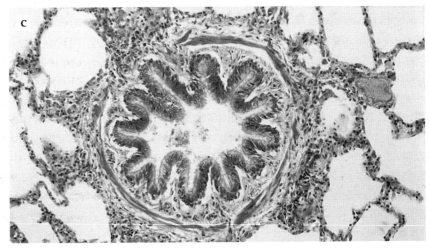

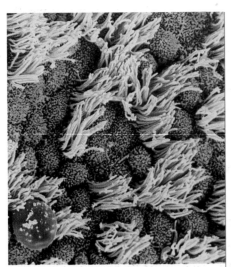

● **Figure 13.2** False-colour SEM of the surface of the trachea, showing large numbers of cilia (yellow) and some mucus-secreting goblet cells (red) (×2300).

Alveoli

At the end of the pathway between the atmosphere and the blood-stream are the **alveoli** (*figures 13.1c and 13.3*). These have a very thin epithelial lining and are surrounded by many blood capillaries carrying deoxygenated blood. The short distance between air and blood means that oxygen and carbon dioxide can be exchanged efficiently by diffusion (chapter 4). Alveolar walls contain **elastic fibres** which stretch during breathing and recoil during expiration

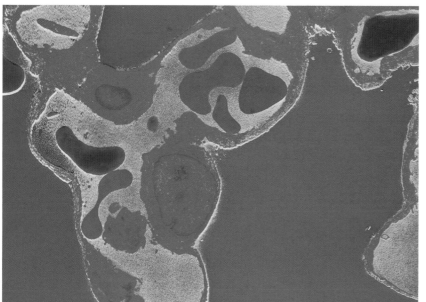

- **Figure 13.3** False-colour TEM of the lining of an alveolus. Red blood cells fill the blood capillaries (yellow) which are separated from the air (blue) by a thin layer of cells (pink).

to help force out air. This elasticity allows alveoli to expand according to the volume of air breathed in. When fully expanded during exercise the surface area available for diffusion increases, and the air is expelled efficiently when the elastic fibres recoil.

SAQ 13.1
Describe the pathway taken by a molecule of oxygen as it passes from the atmosphere to the blood in the lungs.

SAQ 13.2
Explain how alveoli are adapted for gaseous exchange. (It may help to look back to chapter 4.)

SAQ 13.3
Explain the advantage of being able to adjust the diameter of bronchioles.

Breathing rate and heart rate

As the body varies its level of activity so the rate at which the cells use oxygen also varies. The rate of supply of oxygen to the cells is determined by the rate and depth of breathing and by the rate at which the heart pumps blood around the body.

Breathing rate and depth

Breathing refreshes the air in the alveoli so that the concentrations of oxygen and carbon dioxide within them remain constant whatever our level of activity. Changing the depth and rate of breathing achieves this. (See the Box on page 176 for details of how lung volumes and depth of breathing are measured.)

At rest we need to ventilate our lungs with about $6.0\,dm^3$ of air per minute. About $0.35\,dm^3$ of new air enters the alveoli with each breath, representing only about one seventh of the total volume of air in the alveoli. This means that large changes in the composition of alveolar air never occur. In any case, it is impossible to empty the lungs completely and, even when the chest is compressed during forced exhalation, about $1.0\,dm^3$ of air still remains in the alveoli and the airways. This volume is the **residual volume**. A much larger volume (approximately $2.5\,dm^3$) remains in the lungs after breathing out normally. When breathing deeply the lungs can increase in volume by as much as $3\,dm^3$.

As exercise becomes harder the depth of breathing increases. Often the breathing rate increases too. This gives us the ability to respond to changes in demand for gaseous exchange during exercise. The effect of exercise on breathing is measured by calculating the **ventilation rate**. This is the total volume of air moved into the lungs in one minute. Ventilation rate (expressed as $dm^3\,min^{-1}$) is calculated as:

$$\text{tidal volume} \times \text{breathing rate}$$

A well-trained athlete can achieve adequate ventilation by increasing the tidal volume with only a small increase in the rate of breathing when taking moderate exercise. This is possible because training improves the efficiency of the muscles involved with breathing.

Measuring lung volumes

Ventilation brings about changes in lung volume, and these changes can be measured by a **spirometer**. In the spirometer shown in *figure 13.4* a person breathes from a tube connected to an oxygen-containing chamber that floats on a tank of water. The chamber falls during inhalation and rises during exhalation. A canister of soda lime absorbs all the carbon dioxide in the exhaled air. The chamber does not rise to the same height with each breath because oxygen is absorbed in the lungs. The movements of the chamber are recorded on a kymograph trace (*figure 13.5*).

Two measurements can be obtained from the trace.

■ **Tidal volume** is the volume of air breathed in and then breathed out during a single breath. The tidal volume at rest is about $0.5\,dm^3$ ($500\,cm^3$).

■ **Vital capacity** is the maximum volume of air that can be breathed in and then breathed out of the lungs by movement of the diaphragm and ribs. In young men the average is about $4.6\,dm^3$; in young women it is about $3.1\,dm^3$. In trained athletes the figures may be as much as $6.0\,dm^3$ for men and $4.5\,dm^3$ for women.

SAQ 13.4

a Looking at the trace in *figure 13.5*, measure the tidal volume and vital capacity;

b and, looking at the part labelled A, calculate:

   (i) the rate of breathing in breaths per minute;

   (ii) the ventilation rate (tidal volume × breathing rate);

   (iii) the volume of oxygen absorbed per minute.

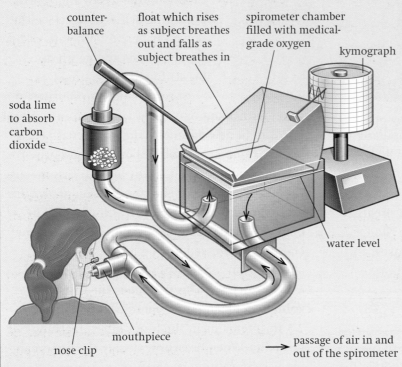

counter-balance

float which rises as subject breathes out and falls as subject breathes in

spirometer chamber filled with medical-grade oxygen

kymograph

soda lime to absorb carbon dioxide

water level

mouthpiece

nose clip

passage of air in and out of the spirometer

● **Figure 13.4** A spirometer.

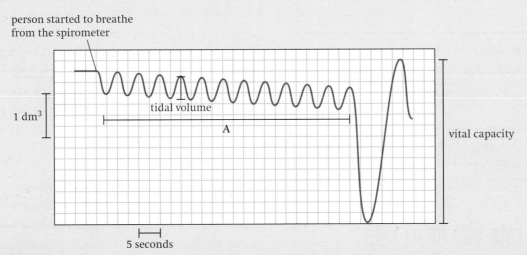

person started to breathe from the spirometer

tidal volume

A

$1\,dm^3$

vital capacity

5 seconds

● **Figure 13.5**
A kymograph trace of a 17-year-old male with a mass of 70 kg who breathed normally, took a deep breath and breathed out as much as possible. The kymograph drum revolves at a speed of $2.5\,mm\,s^{-1}$.

Pulse rate

When the heart contracts, a surge of blood flows into the aorta and the pulmonary arteries under pressure, as we saw in chapter 9. The volume of blood pumped out from each ventricle during each contraction is the **stroke volume**. The total volume pumped out per minute is the **cardiac output**. The surge of blood distends arteries, which contain elastic tissue. The stretch and subsequent recoil of the aorta and the arteries travels as a wave along all the arteries. This is the **pulse**. The **pulse rate** is identical to the heart rate. It is usually measured at the wrist where the radial artery passes over a bone, or at the carotid artery in the neck. It is counted for 30 seconds with the person sitting still and the result doubled to give the resting pulse rate in beats per minute. The resting pulse rate is an indication of fitness.

At rest, the cardiac output is about 5 dm^3 of blood every minute. This can be achieved by having either a large stroke volume with a low pulse rate, or a small stroke volume with a high pulse rate. However it is more efficient to pump slowly as the heart uses less energy than when pumping at a high rate. During exercise, the heart rate increases, providing a faster supply of oxygenated blood to the muscles and of deoxygenated blood to the lungs. If the resting pulse is low and the stroke volume high, only a small increase in pulse is necessary to achieve the required blood supply. People who are physically fit often have a low resting pulse and their pulse rates return to this level quickly after exercise (see page 183). Endurance athletes in particular usually have large hearts with low pulse rates.

The normal range of resting pulse rates is 60 to 100 beats per minute (*table 13.2*). The average in fit young adults is about 70, and falls with age. The pulse rate is higher during and after exercise, and also after eating or smoking. It is at its lowest when people are asleep.

Blood pressure

During systole in the cardiac cycle both ventricles contract. Contraction of the left ventricle forces oxygenated blood out of the heart to supply the body (chapter 9). The maximum arterial pressure during this active stroke is the **systolic pressure** and this is the pressure at which blood leaves the heart through the aorta. As the heart relaxes, the pressure in the left ventricle falls, so that the high pressure in the aorta closes the semilunar valve. Elastic recoil of the aorta and the main arteries provides a head of pressure to maintain a steady flow of blood in the arteries towards the capillaries.

The minimum pressure in the arteries is the **diastolic pressure**. The value of the diastolic pressure reflects the resistance of the small arteries and capillaries to blood flow and therefore the load against which the heart must work. If the resistance is high, so is the diastolic pressure. This can be the result of arteries not stretching very well because they have hardened.

Blood pressures are determined using a **sphygmomanometer** (see Box on page 178); it is conventional to give the values in millimetres of mercury (mm Hg) even if the equipment is digital and computerised. Typical blood pressures are:

- systolic – 120 mm Hg (equivalent to 15.8 kPa);
- diastolic – 80 mm Hg (equivalent to 10.5 kPa).

This is often written as 120/80 (120 over 80). Both pressures rise and fall during the day and change in the longer term with age: for a young adult they may be 110/75, but by age 60 years they could be 130/90. At any age, blood pressures may vary slightly from these typical values without causing any health problems.

Pulse rate at rest	Level of fitness
less than 50	outstanding
50–59	excellent
60–69	good
70–79	fair
80 and over	poor

● **Table 13.2** Resting pulse rates and levels of fitness

SAQ 13.5

Suggest some factors that might affect blood pressure during the day.

SAQ 13.6

Explain why blood pressure increases with age.

Measuring blood pressure

The traditional way to measure blood pressure is with a mercury sphygmomanometer (*figure 13.6*). The rubber cuff of the sphygmomanometer is inflated to give a pressure of 200 mm Hg. This stops the flow of blood into the brachial artery. A stethoscope is placed over the artery and the cuff deflated gradually. The systolic pressure is the pressure when the heart beat is first heard as a soft tapping sound. The cuff is deflated further until the sounds disappear. The diastolic pressure is the pressure when sounds can no longer be heard. Dual blood pressure and pulse rate monitors with digital displays are available for untrained people to use.

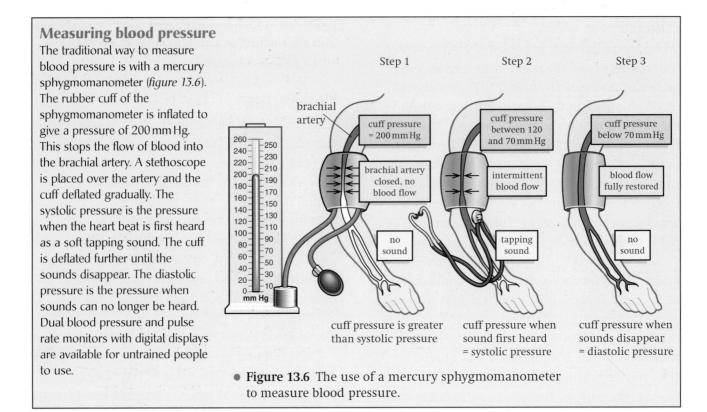

● **Figure 13.6** The use of a mercury sphygmomanometer to measure blood pressure.

Hypertension

Blood pressure is a measure of how hard the heart is working to pump blood around the body. Systolic pressure may rise during exercise to 200 mm Hg; diastolic pressure rarely changes very much in healthy people, even during strenuous exercise. If systolic and diastolic blood pressures are high at rest, this indicates that the heart is working too hard at pumping blood. This condition is known as **hypertension**.

Population surveys show that there is a **normal distribution** of blood pressure (a bell-shaped curve like *figure 12.1*). There is no sharp distinction between 'normal' and 'high' blood pressure. However, the risks of cardiovascular diseases such as stroke and coronary heart disease increase considerably with blood pressures in excess of 140/90 (see pages 194–195). The World Health Organisation classifies the resting blood pressures of adults into four groups (*table 13.3*). Hypertension is taken as a blood pressure higher than 160/95. In Britain 15–20% of adults may be hypertensive.

The causes of high blood pressure are generally unknown. In the short term it occurs because of contraction of smooth muscle in the walls of small arteries and arterioles (page 106). This may happen because of an increase in the concentration of the hormone noradrenaline in the blood, which stimulates arterioles to contract. This increases the resistance of the blood vessels and so the heart works harder to force blood through the circulatory system. However, this does not explain long-term hypertension.

Long-term hypertension imposes a strain on the cardiovascular system. If this is not corrected it can lead to heart failure, which occurs when heart muscles weaken and are unable to pump properly. Hypertension is known as the 'silent killer' as there are often no prior symptoms to give a warning of impending heart failure, heart attack or stroke (page 195). In 90% of cases the exact cause of hypertension is unknown, but the

Category	Blood pressure (mm Hg)	
	systolic	diastolic
below normal	< 100	< 60
normal	100–139	60–89
borderline	140–159	90–94
hypertension	> 159	> 94

● **Table 13.3** The World Health Organisation classification of adult blood pressures.

condition is known to be closely linked to:
- moderate to excessive alcohol intake;
- smoking;
- obesity;
- salt in the diet;
- genetic factors (people who have close relatives who are hypertensive may also be at risk even if they are not in any of the other high risk categories).

Energy and exercise

ATP is the energy currency of cells, as discussed in chapter 7. Muscles use ATP to provide the energy they need to contract but muscle cells cannot store large quantities of ATP. Their small store of ATP is soon exhausted during exercise, although there may be enough for an 'explosive' event, such as the shot put or a tennis serve. For exercise that lasts longer than this, muscles must release the chemical potential energy in other molecules to synthesise more ATP.

There are several sources of energy available to muscles:
- a small amount of **ATP** already present in muscle cells;
- **glycogen** stored in muscle cells that can be broken down to glucose;
- **glucose** supplied in the blood from stores of glycogen in the liver;
- **fatty acids** supplied in the blood from fat stores in the body.

The energy in glucose and fatty acids can be released to supply the muscles with the necessary amounts of ATP by **respiration**.

Respiration

There are two forms of respiration that occur in cells. If there is sufficient oxygen available **aerobic respiration** occurs. In this process, glucose and fatty acids are broken down to form carbon dioxide and water with the release of much energy. Some of this energy is converted to energy in ATP; the rest is released as heat. Most aerobic respiration occurs in mitochondria (page 13), using oxygen that diffuses from the blood.

If there is very little oxygen available, the mitochondria cannot function efficiently. Fatty acids cannot be respired in these conditions but ATP continues to be made available by **anaerobic respiration** of glucose. Glucose is only partially broken down in this process. The end product of anaerobic respiration is **lactate**, which is a compound still rich in energy.

Oxygen for aerobic respiration comes from two sources:
- oxyhaemoglobin in the blood;
- oxymyoglobin stored in muscle.

You have seen that haemoglobin inside the red blood cells combines with oxygen to form oxyhaemoglobin (chapters 2 and 8). Oxygen is transported in this form from the lungs to tissues, such as muscle. Oxyhaemoglobin dissociates and releases oxygen which diffuses from the capillaries into muscle tissue. Some is used immediately by mitochondria; the rest combines with myoglobin to form oxymyoglobin. Myoglobin holds on to oxygen more strongly than haemoglobin – it has a higher affinity than haemoglobin (page 116). As a result it acts as a store of oxygen, releasing it for the mitochondria only when the concentration of oxygen in muscle cells is very low, such as during sustained activity.

Aerobic exercise

When you take exercise that is powered by aerobic respiration in your muscles, then you are taking aerobic exercise. This is any type of exercise that takes place when you supply your muscles with oxygen. To do this you must use your lungs, heart and blood vessels efficiently. Aerobic exercise includes everything from brisk walking to cycling, swimming and marathon running. If you take this type of exercise regularly, the body adapts so the supply of energy becomes more efficient. The ability of the circulation to deliver blood to the tissues improves and cells produce more of the enzymes involved in respiration so that they supply ATP more effectively. With training, the lungs and heart become more efficient at oxygen-ating the blood and pumping it around the body.

On your marks

Imagine you are about to take part in an athletic event – a run, swim or cycle race. Before starting your body anticipates the increase in demand for energy that will happen as soon as you begin. The hormone adrenaline flows into the blood causing the heart and ventilation rates to increase. Arterioles in your skin and gut constrict and those in your muscles dilate, thereby diverting the blood supply to the area of most need. Glucose is released from the liver and fatty acids are released from fat stores. The race begins. The demand for energy increases very steeply. Your muscles quickly use up their stores of ATP so that their rate of respiration increases to make more ATP. It is unlikely that there is enough oxygen for all the ATP to be formed by aerobic respiration. The limited supply of oxygen means that your muscles carry out anaerobic respiration as well. This produces lactate, which diffuses from the muscle cells into the blood.

The flow of lactate and carbon dioxide into the tissue fluid stimulates the arterioles to dilate further and increases blood flow to the muscles. We have already seen that the depth and rate of breathing increases. **Adrenaline** stimulates your bronchioles to widen so that the resistance to air flow in the lungs decreases. The output of blood from your heart also increases. These adjustments improve the supply of oxygen to muscles so that the rate of aerobic respiration increases.

During exercise more oxyhaemoglobin dissociates to release oxygen than at rest due to the Bohr effect (chapter 8). This is stimulated by the following conditions in the muscle tissue during exercise:

- low oxygen concentration;
- high carbon dioxide concentration;
- low pH (due to accumulation of lactate);
- high temperature.

Time to stop

Muscle cells produce very little lactate if there is an efficient supply of oxygen. However, if you undertake strenuous exercise it is unlikely that aerobic respiration alone will supply enough energy. Most of the energy for some 'sprint' events, such as a 100 m swim or a 400 m run, is provided by anaerobic respiration. This means that anaerobic respiration occurs as well and lactate builds up in the body. Lactate is like an early warning device. As it accumulates in muscle cells, the pH decreases and enzymes become less efficient. Less energy is

released and you find it difficult to continue and become fatigued, maybe experiencing some pain in the muscles. This may cause you to stop exercising. Lactate is not excreted since it is a rich source of energy. It is absorbed by the liver and converted back to glucose. Some of the glucose leaves the liver to maintain the concentration in the blood. The rest is stored as glycogen. This conversion of lactate in the liver requires oxygen.

In training

Figure 13.7 shows an athlete running on a treadmill while his ventilation rate, pulse rate, stroke volume and oxygen uptake are measured. The treadmill can be adjusted to operate so that the athlete runs at different speeds. *Figure 13.8* shows what happens to oxygen uptake before, during and after taking strenuous exercise. Standing still, he absorbs oxygen at the resting rate of $0.2 \, \text{dm}^3 \, \text{min}^{-1}$. (This is a measure of his **metabolic rate**.) At a slow speed oxygen uptake increases to $0.8 \, \text{dm}^3 \, \text{min}^{-1}$. When exercise begins, he needs an extra $2.3 \, \text{dm}^3 \, \text{min}^{-1}$ to support the aerobic respiration in his muscles. This increases his overall demand to $2.5 \, \text{dm}^3 \, \text{min}^{-1}$. However, it takes four minutes for his heart and lungs to adjust to meet this demand. The response of his heart to increasing levels of exercise is recorded as changes in pulse rate and volume of blood pumped out with each beat

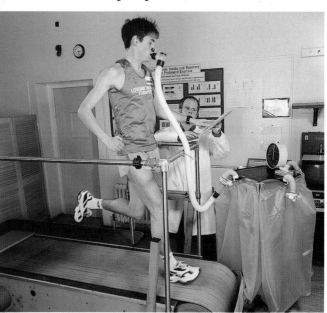

● **Figure 13.7** An athlete running on a treadmill while various physiological measurements of his heart and lungs are taken.

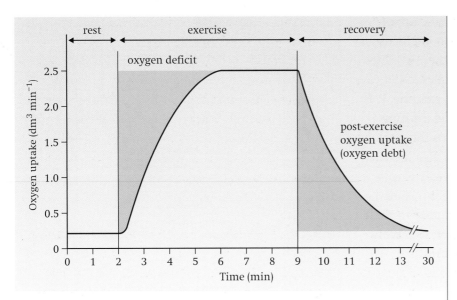

● **Figure 13.8** Oxygen uptake before, during and after strenuous exercise. The post-exercise oxygen uptake (oxygen debt) is that amount over and above the resting uptake (unshaded area) during recovery.

(stroke volume) and the response of his lungs is recorded as the ventilation rate (*figure 13.9*). During this time anaerobic respiration occurs in his muscles. Thus he builds up an **oxygen deficit**. For the next three minutes he supplies enough oxygen. When exercise stops, he continues to breathe deeply so that he absorbs oxygen at a higher rate than at rest. This post-exercise uptake of extra oxygen is sometimes called the **oxygen debt**. It is required for:

- respiration of lactate in the liver;
- reoxygenation of myoglobin in the muscles;
- reoxygenation of haemoglobin in the blood;
- a high metabolic rate, as many organs are operating at above resting levels.

SAQ 13.7

a Use *figure 13.9a* to calculate the total cardiac output at the following metabolic rates:
   (i) $0.8\,dm^3\,min^{-1}$;
   (ii) $1.6\,dm^3\,min^{-1}$;
   (iii) $2.4\,dm^3\,min^{-1}$.

b Calculate the cardiac output at the remaining metabolic rates and plot a graph to show the effect on cardiac output of exercising at different intensities.

c Describe the adjustments that are made in the cardiovascular and gaseous exchange systems at the beginning of exercise.

To sustain exercise over the long-term, such as during middle to long distance running, cycling and swimming, oxygen demand must equal oxygen uptake. This is what happens between 6 and 9 minutes in *figure 13.8*. An athlete's success depends upon the efficiency with which the heart, lungs and blood vessels can supply oxygen to the muscles to support high rates of aerobic respiration. During

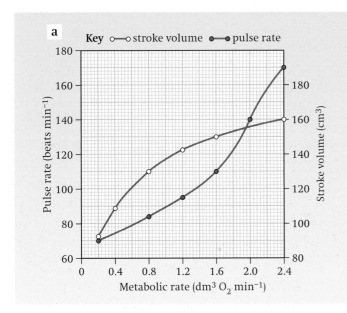

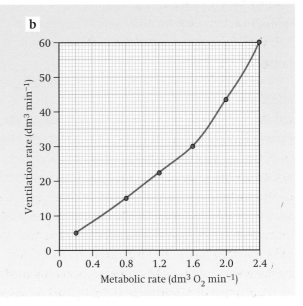

● **Figure 13.9** Increases in **a** pulse rate and stroke volume, and **b** ventilation rate during exercise.

endurance events athletes respire a mixture of glucose and fatty acids. When the blood glucose is low and glycogen stores exhausted, these athletes 'hit the wall'. All athletes have enough fat and can supply enough oxygen for long-term exercise. It is the store of carbohydrate which is the limiting factor. This explains why marathon runners take glucose drinks at intervals. They can also increase the glycogen content of their muscles by eating food rich in carbohydrates, such as pasta, shortly after a training session. The carbohydrate in their diet is converted into muscle glycogen to replenish the stores exhausted during training.

Aerobic fitness

Aerobic fitness is a measurement of the uptake, transport and use of oxygen. People who have good aerobic fitness are good at supplying oxygen to their muscles. One way of measuring aerobic fitness that is used in laboratories, such as that depicted in *figure 13.7*, is to find the maximum rate at which the body can absorb and utilise oxygen. This is known as $\dot{V}_{O_2}$**max** and can be expressed in $dm^3\ min^{-1}$ or $cm^3\ kg^{-1}$ of body mass min^{-1}. It is measured by recording a person's oxygen uptake with a gas analyser while they exercise on a treadmill. By increasing the speed and gradient of the treadmill, the intensity of exercise is increased. As the treadmill becomes faster and steeper, the person has to use more energy and the rate of aerobic respiration increases. Oxygen uptake increases until it reaches a peak (*figure 13.10*) or the person stops from exhaustion. The better the person's aerobic fitness, the higher the intensity of the exercise at $\dot{V}_{O_2}$max.

Few people have access to the equipment necessary to measure $\dot{V}_{O_2}$max. However, there is a strong correlation between pulse rate and $\dot{V}_{O_2}$max. Taking the pulse rate during or immediately after exercise is a much simpler method of assessing someone's aerobic fitness than using the method shown in *figure 13.7*. For example, studies show that their $\dot{V}_{O_2}$max correlates well with their pulse rates taken at the moment they finish exercising. People with a low pulse during recovery from exercise had a large $\dot{V}_{O_2}$max. Young women with a recovery pulse rate of 170 beats per minute had a $\dot{V}_{O_2}$max of $34.0\ cm^3\ kg^{-1}\ min^{-1}$, whereas those with

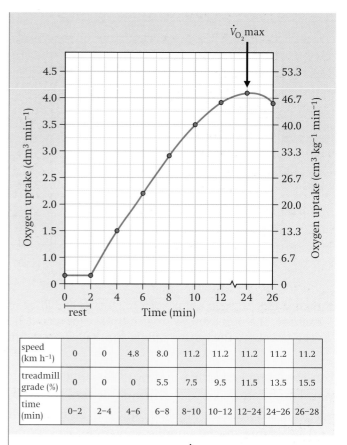

● **Figure 13.10** Finding the $\dot{V}_{O_2}$max. The table provides the speed, treadmill grade (slope) and duration values for each record plotted.

speed (km h⁻¹)	0	0	4.8	8.0	11.2	11.2	11.2	11.2	11.2
treadmill grade (%)	0	0	0	5.5	7.5	9.5	11.5	13.5	15.5
time (min)	0–2	2–4	4–6	6–8	8–10	10–12	12–24	24–26	26–28

a pulse rate of 130 beats per minute had a $\dot{V}_{O_2}$max of $40\ cm^3\ kg^{-1}\ min^{-1}$. At your $\dot{V}_{O_2}$max your heart rate is near its maximum. To calculate your maximum safe heart rate, deduct your age from 220.

SAQ 13.8
a Suggest the factors that influence the $\dot{V}_{O_2}$max.
b Suggest what would happen if you were to exercise beyond your $\dot{V}_{O_2}$max.

If you want to study the effects of exercise on people's aerobic fitness, you can use pulse rates as a measure of fitness. (You will see most change if you investigate the fitness of people who have a sedentary lifestyle – normally take little exercise – as those who already have good aerobic fitness will show little improvement.) Aerobic fitness can be assessed before the subject starts any training. The safest type of test for this is a **step test**. This involves stepping on and off a bench, box or stair.

There are a variety of ways of carrying out a step test, but the one described in the box below requires no specialised equipment and can be done easily at home or college.

You can use a pulse meter or a data logger with an appropriate sensor to record your heart rate before, during and after performing a step test. When the results are plotted on a graph, they will look similar to those in *figure 13.11*. Notice that the pattern is very similar to that shown in *figure 13.8*.

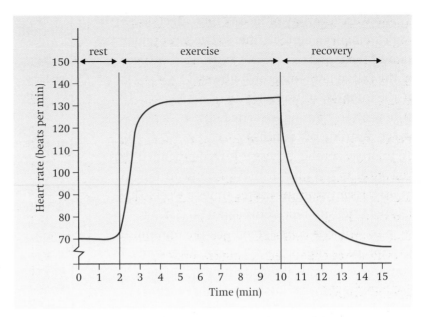

● **Figure 13.11** Heart rate before, during and after eight minutes of exercise such as step-ups. The heart rate of people with good aerobic fitness returns to their resting value quite quickly during recovery.

A step test

Before doing this test, walk up and down a flight of stairs with 12 to 15 steps. This is to check that it is safe for you to do this test. Walk up and down the stairs normally three times without resting. Take your pulse for 15 seconds. If it is over 40, or you are out of breath, or you feel pain (especially in the chest) or if you feel numb or dizzy do not continue with this test.

To continue, find a stair, box or stool that is about 25 cm high. The stepping movement is in four stages:
1 step up;
2 put both feet on the step;
3 step down;
4 put both feet on the floor.
Each cycle begins and ends with both feet on the floor. You must now practise stepping up and down so that you can complete one cycle in two seconds. Practise stepping up and down in a regular fashion. When you can keep a regular rhythm of stepping, stop and rest.

The test is to step on and off the object at the pace you have practised for four minutes without stopping. When you have finished:
■ rest for one minute and then take your pulse for 15 seconds;
■ rest for another 45 seconds and take your pulse again for 15 seconds;
■ rest another 45 seconds and take your pulse for 15 seconds.
Write your results in a table like the one here. Multiply each pulse rate by four to calculate the beats per minute and then add the three results together.

Time (minutes)	Pulse (beats per 15 seconds)	Pulse (beats per minute)
1		
2		
3		
Total beats =		

To calculate your aerobic fitness rating, use this formula

$$\text{Aerobic fitness rating} = \frac{24\,000}{\text{Total beats}}$$

If your rating is less than 61, then your aerobic fitness is poor. If it is between 61 and 70 it is average; 71 to 80 is very good and over 90 is excellent.

There are many variations on this test, such as the Harvard step test that gives you a fitness score based on your age and weight.

The test can be taken at intervals during a training programme to assess the improvement in your aerobic fitness. It can also be used in *advance* of a training programme to assess how much exercise should be taken to see an improvement in fitness whilst staying within safe limits.

A word of warning. Although this test is designed for people to do without undue exertion, if you feel unwell when doing this test stop immediately. You should check with a responsible person before starting any tests of aerobic fitness as part of your course. People who are not used to taking strenuous exercise or have a medical condition should check with a doctor before starting any fitness programme.

There are a variety of factors that affect improvement in aerobic fitness. The most important of these are:

- the initial level of aerobic fitness;
- the intensity of training;
- how often training is carried out;
- the duration of training.

To improve aerobic fitness it is recommended that you work at 70% of your maximum heart rate for at least twenty minutes three times a week. This level of intensity represents about 50–55% of $\dot{V}_{O_2}$max, which is considered to be the minimum to improve aerobic fitness. You can achieve this by running, cycling, jogging, swimming, doing aerobics, dancing or taking any other sort of exercise that uses your heart and lungs. More intense exercise can be more effective, but no extra improvement is achieved by exercising for more than four or five times a week. Exercising below the threshold is equally effective if the duration is correspondingly longer. As fitness improves during training, the intensity of exercise must increase to maintain the desired training heart rate as cardiac output increases. Even mild exercise can be beneficial. The US Public Health Service guidelines recommend a half-hour walk every day. This uses about 650 kJ and confers some protection against heart disease.

Aerobic exercise benefits the cardiovascular and gaseous exchange systems and the muscles and, in the longer term, it also has a variety of benefits for health in the wider sense. Some of these benefits are listed in the Box here.

Benefits of exercise

Cardiovascular fitness
- fall in resting heart rate (may be by as much as 20 beat min^{-1})
- increase in stroke volume
- increase in cardiac output
- increase in heart size, slight thickening of left ventricle wall
- decrease in resting systolic and diastolic pressures
- improved supply of blood to muscles during exercise
- more powerful heart beat

Respiratory fitness
- increase in tidal volume
- increase in vital capacity
- steady rate of oxygen uptake during exercise reached more quickly

Muscles
- increase in muscle size
- increase in capillary density, so shorter diffusion distance for oxygen from blood to muscle cells
- increase in size of muscle fibres
- increase in number and size of mitochondria
- more glycogen and fat stored in muscles
- increase in quantities of respiratory enzymes
- enhanced ability to transfer energy to ATP from fatty acids
- increase in myoglobin stored in muscles

Health benefits
- decrease in blood pressure for people with hypertension
- increased use of body fat (increase in lipase in adipose tissue)
- loss in weight
- improved resistance to infection
- reduced risk of osteoporosis in females
- reduced risk of coronary heart disease and stroke
- decrease in plasma cholesterol concentration
- slowing down of atherosclerosis
- improvement in balance, coordination, strength and flexibility
- strengthening of ligaments, tendons and bones
- reduced chance of lower back pain
- psychological benefits, such as a more positive mood and greater self-esteem

SUMMARY

◆ Air passes down the trachea and through a branching system of airways in the lungs to reach the alveoli. The airways are lined by a ciliated epithelium with mucus-secreting goblet cells. The epithelium protects the alveoli by moving a carpet of mucus towards the throat where it can be swallowed. The alveoli are the site of gaseous exchange.

◆ A spirometer measures the tidal volume and vital capacity of the lungs. Tidal volume is the volume of air breathed in and then out. At rest it is about $0.5\,dm^3$. Vital capacity is the maximum volume of air that can be breathed out after fully inflating the lungs.

◆ The pulse rate is identical to the heart rate. Resting pulse rate is used as a measurement of aerobic fitness since a low rate is associated with a large volume of blood expelled by the heart with each beat.

◆ Blood in the arteries is under pressure which can be measured using a sphygmomanometer. When the heart contracts, this pressure rises. The maximum pressure which corresponds to the emptying of the left ventricle is the systolic pressure. The minimum pressure in the arteries occurs when the left ventricle is relaxed and filling with blood. This is the diastolic pressure.

◆ Hypertension is high blood pressure. The causes of this are unknown, but appear to be related to genetic factors, a diet rich in salt, consumption of alcohol and obesity. High blood pressure is a contributory factor to coronary heart disease.

◆ The lungs and heart make adjustments during exercise to deliver oxygen to respiring tissues. The ventilation rate (tidal volume × rate of breathing) and cardiac output (stroke volume × heart rate) both increase during exercise.

◆ Aerobic exercise is any form of exercise that uses the heart and lungs to provide oxygen for aerobic respiration in muscles. Explosive events, such as weight lifting, do not require energy from aerobic respiration during exercise; all the energy is provided by anaerobic respiration. Aerobic exercise includes everything from brisk walking to endurance events such as long-distance cycling, running and swimming.

◆ $\dot{V}_{O_2}$ max is a measure of aerobic fitness, and is found by measuring oxygen uptake or by taking the recovery pulse rate. A low pulse rate during recovery and at rest indicates a high level of aerobic fitness.

◆ Aerobic exercise has many benefits. The performance and health of the heart and lungs improve and the supply of oxygen to the muscles is more efficient. Everyday tasks can be carried out without fatigue and there are long-term benefits for general health, both physical and mental.

Questions

1 a Describe how the structure of the lungs is adapted to absorb oxygen.

   b Describe how the lung surfaces are protected from damage.

2 Describe how measurements of lung volumes are made.

3 Explain the term **aerobic exercise** and describe how aerobic fitness can be assessed.

4 Describe the adjustments made in the body at the beginning of strenuous exercise.

5 Explain the differences between aerobic and anaerobic respiration.

6 Explain why you keep breathing deeply when you finish a run.

7 Describe an investigation to find out how much exercise is required to achieve a significant improvement in aerobic fitness.

8 Discuss the importance of aerobic exercise in maintaining good health.

CHAPTER 14

Smoking and disease

By the end of this chapter you should be able to:

1 describe the symptoms of chronic bronchitis and emphysema (chronic obstructive pulmonary disease) and lung cancer;

2 describe the effects of tar and carcinogens in tobacco smoke on the gaseous exchange system;

3 evaluate the epidemiological and experimental evidence linking cigarette smoking to disease and early death;

4 describe the effects of nicotine and carbon monoxide in tobacco smoke on the cardiovascular system with reference to atherosclerosis, coronary heart disease and strokes;

5 discuss the possible links between diet and coronary heart disease;

6 discuss the reasons for the global distribution of coronary heart disease;

7 discuss the difficulty in achieving a balance between prevention and cure with reference to coronary heart disease, coronary by-pass surgery and heart transplant surgery.

The World Health Organisation considers smoking to be a disease (see page 156). Until the end of the nineteenth century, tobacco was smoked almost exclusively by men and in pipes and cigars, involving little inhalation. Then manufacture of cigarettes began. Smoking cigarettes became fashionable for European men during the First World War and in the 1940s women started smoking in large numbers too. In the following decades, the vast majority of the UK population smoked. Towards the end of the twentieth century a slow decline in smoking rates began but, contrary to this overall trend, the practice grew amongst young people.

Tobacco smoke

The tobacco companies do not declare the ingredients in their products, but it is known by analysis that there are over 4000 different chemicals in cigarette smoke, many of which are toxic. Tobacco smoke is composed of 'mainstream'

smoke (from the filter or mouth end) and 'sidestream' smoke (from the burning tip). When a person smokes, about 85% of the smoke that they release is sidestream smoke. Many of the toxic ingredients are in a higher concentration in sidestream than in mainstream smoke and any other people in the vicinity are also exposed to them. Breathing someone else's cigarette smoke is called **passive smoking**.

Three main components of cigarette smoke pose a threat to human health, damaging in particular either the gaseous exchange or cardiovascular system.

■ **Tar** (a mixture of aromatic compounds) settles on the lining of the airways in the lungs and stimulates a series of changes that may lead to obstructive lung diseases and lung cancer (see below). This connection was recognised in the 1950s.

■ **Carbon monoxide** diffuses across the walls of the alveoli and into the blood in the lungs. It diffuses into red blood cells where it combines with haemoglobin to form the stable compound carboxyhaemoglobin (see page 117). This means that haemoglobin does not become fully oxygenated. The quantity of oxygen transported in the blood may be 5–10% smaller in a smoker than in a non-smoker. Less oxygen is supplied to the heart muscle, putting a strain on it especially when the heart rate increases during exercise (see chapter 13). Carbon monoxide also damages the lining of the arteries.

■ **Nicotine** is the drug in tobacco. It is absorbed very readily by the blood and travels to the brain within a few seconds. It stimulates the nervous system to reduce the diameter of the arterioles and to release the hormone adrenaline from the adrenal glands. As a result, heart rate and blood pressure increase (page 178) and there is a decrease in blood supply to the extremities of the body, such as hands and feet, reducing their supply of oxygen. Nicotine also increases the 'stickiness' of blood platelets, so increasing the risk of blood clotting.

Both carbon monoxide and nicotine increase the risk of developing cardiovascular disease (see pages 193–200), a link that was discovered in the latter half of the twentieth century.

Lung disease

We saw in chapter 13 how naturally efficient and adaptable the gaseous exchange system is and how training can improve its function and, thereby, our general health. Healthy people breathe with little conscious effort; for people with lung diseases every breath may be a struggle.

The lungs' large surface area of delicate tissue is constantly exposed to moving streams of air that may carry potentially harmful gases and particles. Despite the filtering system in the airways, very small particles (< 2 μm in diameter) can reach the alveoli and stay there. The air that flows down the trachea with each breath fills the huge volume of tiny airways. The small particles settle out easily because the air flow in the depths of the lungs is very slow.

Such deposits make the lungs susceptible to airborne infections such as influenza and pneumonia and, in some people, can cause an allergic reaction. **Allergens** (substances that cause allergies), such as pollen and the faeces of house dust mites, trigger a defence mechanism in the cells lining the airways. If this is very bad it may cause an asthmatic attack in which the smooth muscles in the airways contract, obstructing the flow of air and making breathing difficult. The body's defence mechanisms may react with the production of more mucus and the collection of white blood cells in the airways. This can block the airways and cause severe bouts of coughing, which can damage the alveoli. Continuous damage can lead to the replacement of the thin alveolar surface by scar tissue, so reducing the surface area for diffusion. This replacement also happens when particles of coal dust or asbestos regularly reach the alveoli.

Chronic (long-term) **obstructive lung diseases**, such as asthma, chronic bronchitis and emphysema, are now prevalent as a result of atmospheric pollution from vehicle and industrial emissions and smoking. After heart disease and strokes, lung diseases are the most common cause of illness and death in the UK. It is estimated that one in seven children in the UK suffers from asthma. You can read more about asthma on page 233. There are increasing legal controls in the UK on emissions of pollutants from industrial, domestic and transport fuels and on the condition of the work place, but as yet none regarding tobacco smoke.

Chronic bronchitis

Tar in cigarette smoke stimulates goblet cells and mucous glands to enlarge and secrete more mucus (page 173). Tar also inhibits the cleaning action of the ciliated epithelium that lines the airways. It destroys many cilia and weakens the sweeping action of those that remain. As a result mucus accumulates in the bronchioles and the smallest of these may become obstructed. As mucus is not moved, or at best only moved slowly, dirt, bacteria and viruses collect and block the bronchioles. This stimulates 'smoker's cough' which is an attempt to move the mucus up the airways. With time the damaged epithelia are replaced by scar tissue and the smooth muscle surrounding the bronchioles and bronchi becomes thicker. This thickening of the airways causes them to narrow and makes it difficult to move air into and out of the lungs.

Infections such as pneumonia easily develop in the accumulated mucus. When there is an infection in the lungs the linings become inflamed and this further narrows the airways. This damage and blocking of the airways is **chronic bronchitis**. Sufferers have a severe cough, producing large quantities of phlegm, which is a mixture of mucus, bacteria and some white blood cells.

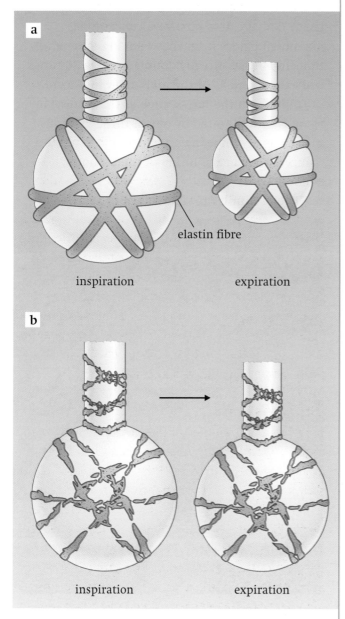

• **Figure 14.1** The development of emphysema.
a Healthy alveoli partially deflate when breathing out due to the recoil of elastin fibres.
b Phagocytes from the blood make pathways through alveolar walls by digesting elastin and, after many years of this destruction, the alveoli do not deflate very much.

Emphysema

The inflammation of the constantly infected lungs causes phagocytes to leave the blood and line the airways. Phagocytes are white blood cells that remove bacteria from the body (see chapters 4 and 16). To reach the lining of the lungs from the capillaries, phagocytes release the protein-digesting enzyme elastase. This enzyme destroys elastin in the walls of the alveoli so making a pathway for the phagocytes to reach the surface and remove bacteria. Elastin is responsible for the recoil of the alveoli when we breathe out. With much smaller quantities of elastin in the alveolar walls the alveoli do not stretch and recoil when breathing in and out (*figure 14.1*). As a result, the bronchioles collapse during exhalation trapping air in the alveoli, which often burst. Large spaces appear where they have burst and this reduces the surface area for gaseous exchange. This condition is called **emphysema**.

The loss of elastin makes it difficult to move air out of the lungs. Non-smokers can force out about $4\,dm^3$ of air after taking a deep breath; someone with emphysema may manage to force out only $1.3\,dm^3$ of air. The air remains in the lungs and is not refreshed during ventilation. Together with the reduced surface area for gaseous exchange, this means that many people with emphysema do not oxygenate their blood very well and have a rapid breathing rate.

As the disease progresses the blood vessels in the lungs become more resistant to the flow of blood. To compensate for this increased resistance, the blood pressure in the pulmonary artery increases and, over time, the right side of the heart enlarges.

As lung function deteriorates, wheezing occurs and breathlessness becomes progressively worse. It may become so bad in some people that they cannot get out of bed. People with severe emphysema often need a continuous supply of oxygen through a face mask to stay alive. In *figure 14.2*, you can compare the appearance of diseased and relatively unaffected lung tissue in a computed tomography (CT) scan.

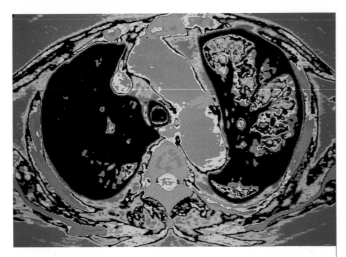

● **Figure 14.2** A computerised tomography scan (CT scan) of a horizontal section through the thorax. The two black regions are the lungs. The right lung is diseased with emphysema, (blue-green areas). The left lung is relatively unaffected at the level of this scan. You can see a cross section of a vertebra at the bottom.

Chronic obstructive pulmonary disease

Chronic bronchitis and emphysema often occur together and constitute a serious risk to health. The term **chronic obstructive pulmonary disease** refers to the overall condition, which is a progressively disabling disease. The gradual onset of breathlessness only becomes troublesome when about half of the lungs is destroyed. Only in very rare circumstances is it reversible. If smoking is given up when still young, lung function can improve. In older people recovery from chronic obstructive pulmonary disease is not possible.

Chronic obstructive pulmonary disease is responsible for over 30 000 deaths in the UK each year. The UK has the highest death rate for this disease in the world.

SAQ 14.1

Summarise the changes that occur in the lungs of people with chronic bronchitis and emphysema.

Lung cancer

Tar in tobacco smoke contains several substances that have been identified as carcinogens (see chapter 6). These react, directly or via breakdown products, with DNA in epithelial cells to produce mutations, which are the first in a series of

changes that lead to the development of a malignant tumour (*figures 6.16* and *14.3*).

As the cancer develops, it spreads through the bronchial epithelium and enters the lymphatic tissues (see page 109) in the lung. Cells may break away and spread to other organs (metastasis) so that secondary tumours become established.

Lung cancer takes 20–30 years to develop. Most of the growth of a tumour occurs before there are any symptoms. The most common symptom of lung cancer is coughing up blood, as a result of tissue damage. It is rare for a cancer to be diagnosed before it reaches 1 cm in diameter. By that time it has already doubled in size 30 times from the moment of the malignant mutation.

Tumours in the lungs, such as that shown in *figure 14.3*, are located by one of three methods:
■ bronchoscopy, using an endoscope to allow a direct view of the lining of the bronchi;
■ chest X-ray;
■ CT scan (similar to that shown in *figure 14.2*).

● **Figure 14.3** A scanning electron micrograph of a bronchial carcinoma – a cancer in a bronchus. Cancers often develop at the base of the trachea where it divides into the bronchi as this is where most of the tar is deposited. The disorganised malignant tumour cells at the bottom right are invading the normal tissue of the ciliated epithelium (× 1000).

By the time most lung cancers are discovered they are well advanced and the only hope is to remove them by surgery. If the cancer is small and in one lung, then either a part, or all, of the lung is removed. However, metastasis has usually happened by the time of the diagnosis so, if there are secondary tumours, surgery will not cure the disease. Chemotherapy with anti-cancer drugs or radiotherapy with X-rays (or other form of radiation) will be used.

Proving the links between smoking and lung disease

As we have seen, cigarette smoking was not widespread until the first half of the twentieth century. In the UK, doctors started noticing cases of lung cancer from the 1930s onwards, and then from the 1950s there was an epidemic (*figure 14.4*). In 1912 there were 374 cases of lung cancer; now there are over 35 000 deaths each year in the UK from the disease.

Epidemiological evidence

Epidemiologists discovered a correlation between lung cancer and cigarette smoking. *Table 14.1* shows the correlation between the number of cigarettes smoked per day and the risk of early death. Epidemiological data link smoking and lung diseases including cancer in the following ways.

General

- Up to 50% of smokers may die of smoking-related diseases.
- Smokers are three times more likely to die in middle age than are non-smokers.

Chronic obstructive pulmonary disease

- Chronic obstructive pulmonary disease is very rare in non-smokers.
- 90% of deaths from chronic obstructive pulmonary disease are attributed to smoking.
- 98% of people with emphysema are smokers.
- 20% of smokers suffer from emphysema.
- Deaths from pneumonia and influenza are twice as high among smokers.

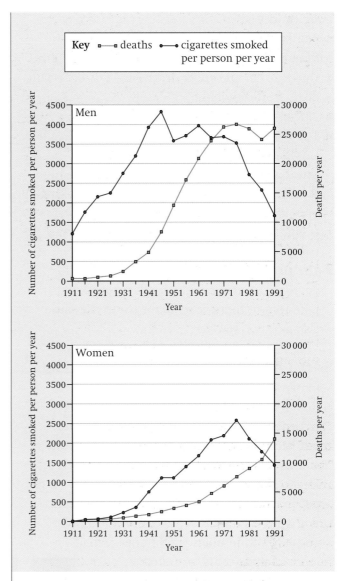

- **Figure 14.4** The smoking epidemic. The correlation between the consumption of cigarettes and deaths from lung cancer in the UK from 1911 to 1991.

Number of cigarettes smoked per day	Annual death rate per 100 000 men
0	10
1–14	78
15–24	127
>25	251

Note that these are deaths from all causes not just lung cancer.

- **Table 14.1** Results of a study carried out on male doctors in Britain, showing that the risk of early death increases with the number of cigarettes smoked per day.

Lung cancer

■ Smokers are 18 times more likely to develop lung cancer than non-smokers.

■ One-third of all cancer deaths are a direct result of cigarette smoking.

■ 25% of smokers die of lung cancer.

■ The risk of developing lung cancer increases if smokers inhale; start young; increase the number of cigarettes smoked per day; use high tar cigarettes; smoke for a long time (smoking one packet of cigarettes per day for forty years is eight times more hazardous than smoking two packets for twenty years).

■ The risk of developing lung cancer starts to decrease as soon as smoking is stopped, but it takes ten or more years to return to the same risk as a non-smoker.

SAQ 14.2

Summarise the trends shown in *figure 14.4*.

Conclusions drawn from epidemiological data about the risks of developing lung cancer could be criticised because they only show that there is an *association* between the two, not a *causal link* between them. There may be another common factor which is the causative one. For example, exposure to atmospheric pollutants such as sulphur dioxide could be a cause. However, epidemiological studies have ruled out these other factors – comparably close correlations with them cannot be found. With smoking, on the other hand, it is possible to show a direct link with lung cancer because smoking is the common factor in almost all cases. (Reports by the Royal College of Physicians published in 1962, 1971, 1977, 1983 and 1992 reviewed the epidemiological evidence for the link.)

Cigarette smoking is linked with other cancers. It is a major cause of cancers of the mouth, oesophagus and larynx. It is a cause of bladder cancer and a contributory factor in the development of cancers of the pancreas, kidney and cervix.

Experimental evidence

Experimental evidence shows a direct causative link between smoking and lung cancer. There are two lines of evidence.

■ Tumours similar to those found in humans develop in animals exposed to cigarette smoke.

■ Carcinogens have been identified in tar.

In the 1960s experimental animals were used to investigate the effect of cigarette smoke on the lungs (*figure 14.5*). In one study 48 dogs were divided into two groups. One group was made to smoke filter-tipped cigarettes and did not develop cancer. The other group smoked plain (unfiltered) cigarettes and developed abnormalities similar to those in human lung cancer patients. The animals also showed changes similar to those caused by chronic obstructive pulmonary disease. The fact that the group smoking filter-tipped cigarettes remained healthy does not show that the filters remove all the carcinogens from smoke. In fact some of the dogs developed pre-cancerous changes in the cells lining their airways.

Smoking machines, which copy the inhaling pattern of smokers, extract the chemicals contained in smoke. Chemical analysis of the black, oily liquid that accumulates in these machines shows that tar contains a variety of

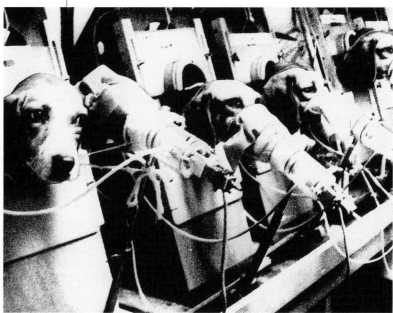

● **Figure 14.5** Beagles used in experiments in the 1960s to investigate the link between smoking and lung cancer. When the results were published they convinced many smokers to change to low tar, filter-tipped brands.

carcinogens and co-carcinogens. The latter are compounds which increase the likelihood that carcinogens will cause mutations in DNA. The most potent carcinogen is benzpyrene. When carcinogens from tar are painted onto the skin of mice, cancerous growths develop. Experiments like this not only confirm the link between smoking and lung cancer, they also help to show how tumours develop in the lungs.

The connection between cigarette smoking and lung cancer is irrefutable. The mechanisms by which carcinogens cause mutations and the factors that influence the growth of cancers are still being investigated. As the popularity of smoking decreases in developed countries, the smoking epidemic is spreading to the developing world, which, it is predicted, will see a rise in smoking-related diseases in the 21st century.

SAQ 14.3

Summarise the effects of tobacco smoke on the gaseous exchange system.

Cardiovascular diseases

Cardiovascular diseases are degenerative diseases of the heart and circulatory system, such as coronary heart disease and stroke. They are a major cause of death and disability. They are responsible for 20% of all deaths worldwide and up to 50% of deaths in developed countries. Cardiovascular diseases are **multifactorial**, meaning that many factors contribute to the development of these diseases. Smoking is just one among several **risk factors** that increase the chances of developing one of the cardiovascular diseases.

Atherosclerosis

The main process that leads to cardiovascular diseases is the accumulation of fatty material in artery walls. This reduces the flow of blood to the tissues and may also increase the chance of blood clots forming within the artery, obstructing the flow of blood altogether. If blood cannot flow into capillaries, the surrounding tissue does not receive enough nutrients and oxygen, and may die. This build-up of **atheroma**, which contains cholesterol, fibres, dead muscle cells and platelets, is termed **atherosclerosis**.

The inside of a healthy artery is pale and smooth but yellow fatty streaks can start appearing at any time from childhood. These start with damage to the lining of the arteries. In response to the damage, there is an invasion of phagocytes whose secretions stimulate the growth of smooth muscle cells (to aid repair) and the accumulation of cholesterol.

Cholesterol is a lipid (see page 28) which is needed for the synthesis of vitamin D in the skin, steroid hormones in the ovaries, testes and adrenal glands and, in all cells, plasma membranes (see page 52). It is therefore an essential biochemical. Problems arise, however, if excessive cholesterol collects in tissues.

Cholesterol is insoluble in water and so is transported in the blood plasma in tiny balls of lipid and protein called **lipoproteins** (*figure 14.6*). There are two groups of lipoproteins, **low density** lipoproteins and **high density** lipoproteins. Low density lipoproteins transport cholesterol from the liver to the tissues, including the artery walls.

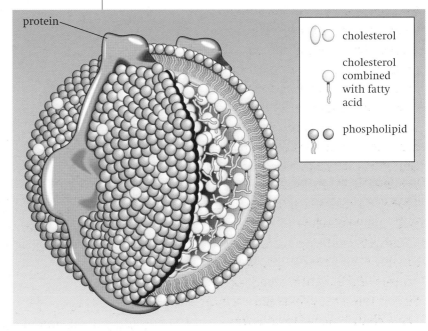

protein

cholesterol

cholesterol combined with fatty acid

phospholipid

● **Figure 14.6** A low density lipoprotein (LDL). High density lipoproteins (HDLs) have a lower content of cholesterol than LDLs.

They tend to deposit their cholesterol at any damaged sites, in particular. In contrast, high density lipoproteins remove cholesterol from tissues and transport it to the liver to be excreted. High density lipoproteins therefore help to protect arteries against atherosclerosis.

The cholesterol-rich atheroma forms **plaques** in the lining of the arteries, making them less elastic and restricting the flow of blood (*figures 14.7* and *14.8*). Plaques grow within the artery wall and then push inwards reducing or blocking the passage of blood. The plaque may break through the lining of the artery to give a rough surface. The blood can no longer flow smoothly and tends to clot, forming a **thrombus**. This process of **thrombosis** interrupts blood flow even more, so tissues are starved of oxygen and nutrients. When this happens in a coronary artery, heart muscle may die, causing a heart attack (see chapter 9 and below). If it happens in an artery in the brain the result is a stroke.

Coronary heart disease

Two coronary arteries branch from the aorta to supply all the muscles of the atria and the ventricles (see *figure 9.2*). **Coronary heart disease** is a disease of these arteries that causes damage to, or malfunction of, the heart.

When atherosclerosis occurs in the lining of the coronary arteries they become narrow, restricting the flow of blood. As a result, the heart has to work harder to force blood through

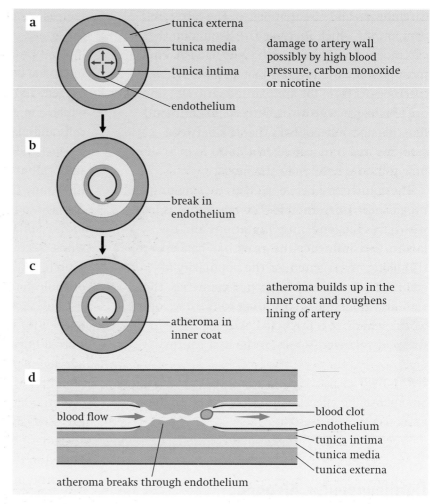

● **Figure 14.7** How damage to artery walls promotes the development of fatty plaques and blood clots. **a–c** Cross sections of an artery showing the development of a plaque; **d** longitudinal section of an artery with a blood clot forming at the site of a plaque.

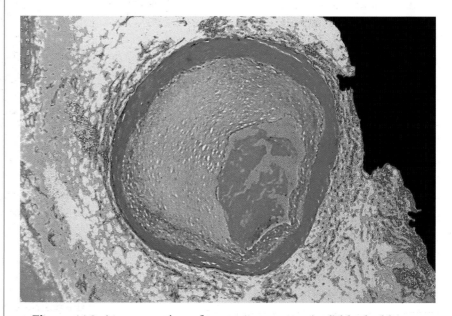

● **Figure 14.8** A cross section of a coronary artery (red) blocked by plaque (orange). Some blood (red) can flow through the lumen of the artery, but is restricted by the plaque.

the coronary arteries and this may cause blood pressure to rise. It also means that it is more difficult to supply heart muscle with extra oxygen and nutrients when it has to respond during exercise (chapter 13).

Coronary heart disease develops if the blood supply to the heart muscle is reduced. There are three forms of coronary heart disease.

- **Angina pectoris**, the main symptom of which is severe chest pain brought on by exertion. The pain starts when exercising, but goes when resting. The pain is caused by a severe shortage of blood to the heart muscle, but there is no death of heart tissue.
- **Heart attack** which is also known as **myocardial infarction**. When a moderately large branch of a coronary artery is obstructed by a blood clot, part of the heart muscle is starved of oxygen and dies. This causes sudden and severe chest pain. A heart attack may be fatal, but many people survive if they are treated immediately.
- **Heart failure** due to the blockage of a main coronary artery and the resulting gradual damage of heart muscle. The heart weakens and fails to pump efficiently.

Stroke

A **stroke** occurs when an artery in the brain bursts so that blood leaks into brain tissue (a brain haemorrhage) or, more commonly, when there is a blockage in a brain artery due to atherosclerosis or a thrombus. The brain tissue in the area supplied by the artery is starved of oxygen and dies (**cerebral infarction**). A stroke may be fatal or cause mild or severe disability. The degree of disability depends on the amount of the brain affected by shortage or lack of oxygen. As a result of a stroke, some people are unable to control part of their body; others may lose their ability to speak or some of their memory. Even personality can change. Some of these faculties can be taken over by other parts of the brain

naturally and treatment can restore others. A comparison of healthy and dead brain tissue is shown in *figure 14.9*.

SAQ 14.4

a Describe the changes that occur in the heart that lead to a heart attack.

b Explain the likely effects on the brain of a stroke.

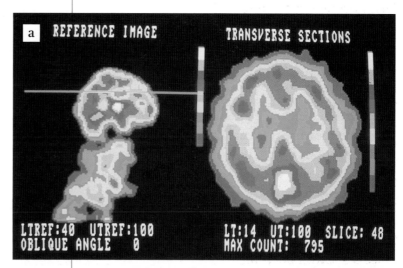

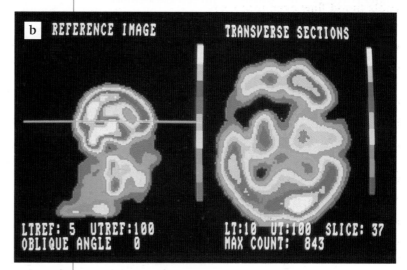

● **Figure 14.9** Scintigram scans of a normal brain and a brain following a stroke. Scintigram scanning shows the pattern of γ rays emitted by a radioactive tracer introduced into the body. The tracer is taken up by different tissues producing a distinct image in organs and tissues which are functioning correctly. **a** Scan of a normal brain in vertical and horizontal section. The green line on the left shows the position of the horizontal section. **b** Scan of a brain following a stroke. The black area in the front of the horizontal section shows where tissue has died as a result of an infarction.

Global distribution of coronary heart disease

Death rates for coronary heart disease are not evenly distributed across the world. The rate is highest in northern Europe and lowest in Japan and France (*figure 14.10*). Coronary heart disease is the major cause of premature death in developed countries and responsible for much ill health and disability.

Coronary heart disease was almost unknown before the twentieth century and until recently it has mainly been confined to developed countries. It is considered to be a disease associated with affluence, but as it is a degenerative disease it is possible that the incidence of coronary heart disease is high simply because people now live longer. High death rates from infectious diseases in earlier centuries obscured the degenerative changes that may have been occurring in people's coronary arteries. In other words, people did not die from coronary heart disease because they died of something else first. As death rates from infectious diseases decrease in the developing world, death rates from cardiovascular diseases, especially coronary heart disease, increase. Coronary heart disease has become the leading cause of death in Argentina, Cuba, Chile, Uruguay and Trinidad and Tobago which have rising standards of living and good public health systems.

In just the same way that death rates for coronary heart disease are not the same over the whole world, so they differ *within* countries. In the UK, the incidence of the disease is highest:

- in Scotland, Northern Ireland and the north and north-west of England;
- among poorer people;
- among certain ethnic groups including south Asians;
- among men.

These epidemiological data suggest that people are not equally at risk of developing coronary heart disease.

Epidemiological evidence

The evidence for links between smoking and cardiovascular diseases is not as clear cut as it is for smoking and lung cancer. Although many smokers die of coronary heart disease and stroke, so do many non-smokers.

It is known that smoking increases the chances of both the development of atherosclerosis and blood clotting. Both nicotine and carbon monoxide speed up the development of plaques, although it is not known how they do this. They also stimulate the production of one of the blood clotting factors (fibrinogen) and reduce the production of enzymes that remove clots. Nicotine increases blood pressure and heart rate and thus the body's demand for oxygen, but carbon monoxide reduces the blood's ability to carry it.

Smoking also interacts with other risk factors. It increases blood pressure and increases the concentration of cholesterol in the blood; high blood cholesterol is a risk factor for coronary heart disease and hypertension is the major risk factor for stroke.

Smokers not only increase their own risk of developing coronary heart disease or stroke, but also that of other people. Passive smoking is

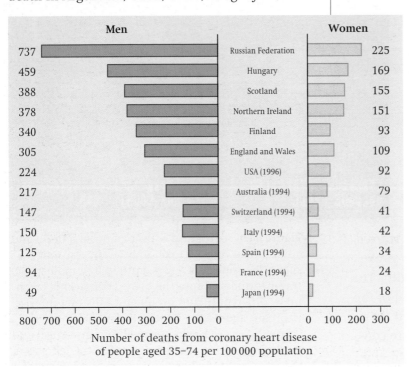

Men		Women
737	Russian Federation	225
459	Hungary	169
388	Scotland	155
378	Northern Ireland	151
340	Finland	93
305	England and Wales	109
224	USA (1996)	92
217	Australia (1994)	79
147	Switzerland (1994)	41
150	Italy (1994)	42
125	Spain (1994)	34
94	France (1994)	24
49	Japan (1994)	18

800 700 600 500 400 300 200 100 0   0 100 200 300

Number of deaths from coronary heart disease of people aged 35–74 per 100 000 population

- **Figure 14.10** Death rates from coronary heart disease for men and women aged 35–74 per 100 000 population for selected countries. Unless stated otherwise the figures are for 1997.

believed to be responsible for many deaths from cardiovascular disease and those most at risk are those who live, work or socialise with smokers.

SAQ 14.5
Describe the effects of tobacco smoke on the cardiovascular system.

Table 14.2 shows the risk factors that are associated with coronary heart disease. Some of these are fixed, since there is nothing anyone can do about their sex, age or the genes that they have inherited. Others are modifiable. People can take steps to change their way of life to reduce the risks of developing coronary heart disease by giving up smoking, eating less saturated fat, losing weight and taking more exercise.

These factors were identified in long-term epidemiological studies with large groups of people in which information about their way of life, illnesses and causes of death were recorded. A study of the population of Framingham in Massachusetts, USA and a study of civil servants in the UK (the Whitehall study) showed that:

- hypertension, high cholesterol concentrations in the blood, cigarette smoking and diabetes were common factors among inhabitants of Framingham who developed coronary heart disease;
- British civil servants who took regular exercise had half the incidence of coronary heart disease than their less active colleagues.

To find the reasons for the global distribution of coronary heart disease, the World Health Organisation set up a multinational monitoring

Factor	Effect
age	Risk increases with increasing age: about 80% of people who die of coronary heart disease are 65 or older.
gender	Men are more at risk than women: protection is given by oestrogen which occurs either naturally or by hormone replacement therapy (HRT).
heredity	Children of parents with heart disease are at greater risk than others: genes are involved in developing high blood cholesterol concentrations, high blood pressure and diabetes mellitus.
body mass	Being overweight or obese increases risk: excess weight puts a strain on the heart and blood pressure rises.
diet	Risk increases with high intake of saturated fat and salt (most prevalent in meat and processed foods): development of atherosclerosis and high blood pressure are more likely. Risk decreases with high intake of antioxidants (such as vitamins E and C, found mostly in fruit and vegetables) and soluble fibre and moderate intake of unsaturated fats (mainly from fish and vegetables).
blood cholesterol	There is a direct relationship between concentration of cholesterol in the blood and risk of coronary heart disease: above 250 mg cholesterol per 100 cm^3 of blood is considered to be high.
high blood pressure	Risk increases with increasing blood pressure.
smoking	Combines with all other risk factors to multiply the chances of developing coronary heart disease.
exercise	Risk decreases as more exercise is taken: aerobic activity helps to control blood cholesterol, diabetes mellitus and obesity and, in some people, lowers blood pressure.
diabetes	There is an increased risk for people with diabetes.
alcohol	Risk increases with high intake: blood pressure rises and atherosclerosis is more likely. Risk may decrease with moderate intake.
social class	Risk increases with poverty.

● **Table 14.2** Factors associated with coronary heart disease.

project (known as MONICA) in 1979. Death rates from coronary heart disease were compared with death rates from all causes in a number of different countries. *Table 14.3* shows some results for two European countries, Finland and Spain, with markedly different death rates for coronary heart disease. These rates tend to decline in a north-east to south-west direction across Europe, being particularly high in Finland and low in Spain. Data were collected from two regions within these countries, North Karelia, a region of Finland which used to have the highest death rate from coronary heart disease in the world, and Catalonia in Spain, which has one of the lowest. The MONICA project also collected data on the risk factors associated with coronary heart disease. The results showed that the Finns tended to have much higher blood pressures and blood cholesterol concentrations than the Catalonians. The incidence of obesity was similar in the two populations and more Catalonians smoked. This evidence pointed to the importance of blood pressure and blood cholesterol as key factors in predicting whether someone would suffer from coronary heart disease.

SAQ 14.6

Looking at *table 14.3*,

a suggest why data were collected for the 35-64 year age group and not for all age groups;

b compare the populations of North Karelia and Catalonia in terms of the proportions of deaths due to (i) all cardiovascular diseases, (ii) coronary heart disease, and (iii) strokes;

c suggest which members of the population of the two regions are most at risk of developing cardiovascular diseases.

It is important to realise that each of the factors listed in *table 14.2* is *associated* with heart disease. None by itself predicts that heart disease will develop. For example, there are many smokers who do not develop heart disease or have a stroke. However, smokers increase their risk of developing heart disease. A smoker who is overweight and eats a diet rich in saturated fat is even more at risk. Recent research suggests that genetic factors are important. Those most at risk have inherited a genetic condition which leads to a very high concentration of blood cholesterol. The disease affects 1 in 500 people in the UK. These people have a very high risk of developing coronary heart disease early in life and they should take special care about controlling other risk factors such as weight, diet and blood pressure. Recent research shows that people can inherit genes that dispose them to high blood pressure and diabetes and increase the risk of heart disease.

The role of diet in coronary heart disease

Dietary factors have been implicated in heart disease for a long time. People with high levels of saturated fat and cholesterol in their diet tend to have high blood cholesterol levels. The blood cholesterol concentration in the body is not dependent solely on the intake of cholesterol in foods such as meat and eggs; it depends mainly on the saturated fat derived from animal foods. Red meat and dairy products, such as milk and butter, are especially rich in saturated fat. This helps to explain the high incidence of heart disease in countries such as Finland, where the traditional diet is mainly composed of foods rich in animal fat. Some of the lowest rates of heart

Country or region	Annual mortality (deaths per 100 000 population in age group 35–64 between 1984 and 1986)							
	total number of deaths (all causes)		deaths from all cardiovascular diseases		deaths from coronary heart disease		deaths from stroke	
	men	women	men	women	men	women	men	women
Finland	894	314	427	103	317	52	57	32
North Karelia	1111	364	600	140	456	75	82	40
Spain	634	277	193	77	89	20	43	25
Catalonia	536	237	138	49	68	16	32	18

● **Table 14.3** Data on death rates collected from Finland and Spain as part of the World Health Organisation MONICA project

disease are found in countries with high fat intakes, such as Spain and Italy, but the fat is mainly unsaturated. Increasing the intake of unsaturated fats in the diet tends to cause the blood cholesterol concentration to go down so long as saturated fat intake is low.

However, the link between diet and coronary heart disease is not so easily explained. France has one of the lowest rates of heart disease in the world. The consumption of animal fat is as high as it is in the USA where the rate of heart disease is nearly three times greater. This suggests that saturated fat and cholesterol intake alone are not important. The MONICA project found that vitamin E, which is an antioxidant and protects artery walls against atherosclerosis, was much higher in the blood in people from countries with low rates of heart disease.

For a heart attack to occur, blood must clot in the coronary artery – thrombosis must occur. There appears to be no link between fat intake and the risk of thrombosis. Other blood factors, which may or may not be diet-related, are now considered to be important in increasing the risk of thrombosis and therefore deserve as much attention as fat in the diet.

Prevention and cure of coronary heart disease

The governments of many developed countries have taken steps to reduce the incidence and prevalence of heart disease. They encourage people to reduce the risk of developing the disease by taking more exercise, giving up smoking and decreasing the intake of animal fat in their diet. Death rates in these countries have fallen over the past 25 years, but whether this is as a result of these changes is uncertain. The USA and Australia in particular have seen significant reductions in death rates.

The death rate from coronary heart disease in the UK is one of the highest in the world. Coronary heart disease accounts for a third of all deaths of people between the ages of 45 and 64. Although the death rate is decreasing in the UK, partly as a result of better screening and treatment, it is still higher than in most other countries.

Reducing the incidence of coronary heart disease was the first target listed in the UK Government's long-term health strategy, *Health of*

the Nation, published in 1992. The reasons for this are that coronary heart disease is:

- the major cause of premature death in the UK;
- one of the main causes of avoidable ill health;
- a major cost to the National Health Service and to the community.

Treatment for coronary heart disease involves using drugs to lower blood pressure, decrease the risk of blood clotting, prevent abnormal heart rhythms, reduce the retention of fluids and decrease the cholesterol concentration in the blood. If these drug treatments are not successful then a coronary artery **by-pass** operation may be carried out. This involves using a blood vessel from the leg to replace the diseased vessel. The by-pass carries blood from the aorta to a place on the heart beyond the blockage in the coronary artery. Sometimes two or three by-passes are necessary. The number of by-pass operations carried out in the UK increased threefold during the 1980s. In 1997 there were over 24 000 operations, compared with only a few hundred transplants to treat coronary heart disease.

A complete heart transplant is the method of last resort. The costs of the operation are very high and there are difficulties in finding enough donor hearts. Before the operation can be carried out the tissues of the donor and the recipient must be matched so that the new heart is not rejected by the body's immune system. Often heart–lung transplants are more successful than heart-only transplants as the immune system seems to be 'overwhelmed' by the new organs and does not mount such a vigorous defence (chapter 16). Drugs are used to suppress the immune system after the transplant, but these often have unpleasant side-effects and may not prevent rejection. With limited resources, there is the problem of deciding who receives a transplant. In some cases doctors have refused surgery to people who have ignored advice to give up smoking.

Treating coronary heart disease is hugely expensive. There are two ways in which this cost may be reduced. Both involve primary health care, that is advising people to take precautions to avoid developing disease in the first place.

One way is to screen the population to find individuals who are at risk of developing coronary heart disease and target health care to them. The best methods are screening for high blood pressure, high blood cholesterol concentration and monitoring the behaviour of the heart during exercise. Screening can be done by doctors on a regular basis and can be followed with advice to those at risk to give up smoking, adopt a healthier diet and take more exercise. Studies show that methods of lowering blood pressure, such as reducing salt intake and using drugs, are effective. Attempts to change diet are not always so successful, but new drugs that lower blood cholesterol are proving beneficial and are prescribed to those at risk of having a heart attack. It is therefore probably effective to screen the population for the risk factors outlined in *table 14.2* and concentrate on those at highest risk of dying prematurely of heart disease.

The second way is to encourage the population as a whole to adopt a healthy lifestyle to reduce the risks of developing heart disease. Advertising and health education may be able to play a large part in reducing illness and deaths from coronary heart disease by encouraging a healthy way of life from an early age. Encouraging people to engage in different forms of aerobic exercise is seen as an important aspect of the 'population approach' as it often encourages people to change their diet, lose weight, stop smoking and reduce their alcohol intake in the process. Exercise is also one way of decreasing blood pressure. In 1997 the UK Government published its health strategy *Our Healthier Nation*. This includes the target of reducing deaths rates from cardiovascular diseases in people under 75 by at least 40% by 2010. If this reduction is achieved then the health of, and quality of life for, many people should improve. However, in 1996 only £11.6 million was spent on *prevention* of coronary heart disease, less than 1% of the total spending on *treatment* of the disease by the National Health Service. A major problem

with health campaigns is that many people resist the advice they are given until it is too late. As coronary heart disease is a long-term degenerative disease this advice should be provided early in life. Degenerative changes in arteries have been seen in children as young as seven.

The mortality rate from heart disease and strokes in the UK began to decrease in the 1970s. This may have something to do with changing ways of life, for example decreasing the intake of saturated fat and giving up smoking. It may also have much to do with better equipped casualty departments in hospitals and improvements in the treatment of heart attack patients. However, some studies suggest that it might have more to do with better maternal nutrition. These studies show that:

- higher birth weight is associated with lower blood pressure in middle age;
- high weight at one year of age is associated with a lower risk of diabetes and a low level in the blood of low density lipoproteins.

It appears from this epidemiological evidence that better maternal nutrition in the early and middle part of the twentieth century meant that later generations were better protected against heart disease. It may also explain why coronary heart disease is more common among poor people than among the affluent.

SAQ 14.7

It is estimated that smoking is responsible for 90% of all deaths from lung cancer, 76% of deaths from chronic obstructive pulmonary disease and 16% of deaths from stroke and coronary heart disease. Use the data in *table 14.4* to calculate:

a the number of deaths in 1993 in (i) men and (ii) women that were attributable to smoking;

b the percentage of deaths of (i) men and (ii) women that were attributable to smoking.

Disease	Men		Women		All
	Number of deaths	Percentage of total deaths	Number of deaths	Percentage of total deaths	
lung cancer	24 963	7.87	12 757	3.75	37 720
chronic obstructive pulmonary disease	18 826	5.93	11 848	3.48	30 674
stroke	26 310	8.29	44 976	13.21	71 286
coronary heart disease	90 774	28.62	76 831	22.57	167 605
all diseases	317 194	100.00	340 373	100.00	657 567

● **Table 14.4** Deaths from lung cancer, chronic obstructive pulmonary disease, stroke and coronary heart disease for all ages in the UK in 1993.

SUMMARY

◆ Damage to the bronchioles and alveoli occurs in chronic obstructive pulmonary diseases. In chronic bronchitis the airways are blocked by inflammation and infection; in emphysema the alveoli are destroyed, reducing the surface area for gaseous exchange.

◆ Tobacco smoke contains tar, carbon monoxide and nicotine.

◆ Tar contains carcinogens which cause changes in DNA in bronchial epithelial cells leading to the development of a bronchial carcinoma. This is lung cancer.

◆ Carbon monoxide combines irreversibly with haemoglobin, reducing the oxygen-carrying capacity of the blood.

◆ Nicotine stimulates the nervous system, increasing heart rate and blood pressure.

◆ Epidemiological and experimental evidence show a strong correlation between smoking and lung cancer; smoking damages the cardiovascular system, multiplying the risks of developing coronary heart disease.

◆ Diet is thought to be a contributory factor in the development of coronary heart disease. Saturated fat in the diet is linked with high blood cholesterol concentrations.

◆ Coronary heart disease is most prevalent in Eastern Europe and the United Kingdom. France and Japan have a very low prevalence of the disease and death rates are low. The reasons for this global distribution are unclear, although high blood cholesterol concentration and high blood pressure are two risk factors that are implicated in countries where coronary heart disease is a major cause of illness and death.

◆ Coronary heart disease may be treated with drugs to lower blood cholesterol and blood pressure. Coronary artery by-pass surgery involves using a vein from the leg to replace the part or parts of a coronary artery that are damaged. A heart transplant may be necessary, but it is an expensive operation and difficult to find donor hearts so very few are performed.

◆ Primary health care can reduce morbidity and mortality from coronary heart disease and strokes. Screening people for risk factors of coronary heart disease and stroke allows early intervention. Advertising and education can promote the benefits of exercise, not smoking, avoiding an excessive consumption of alcohol and eating a diet low in saturated fat. These alternatives to treatment and surgery may be more cost effective in the long-term, but they depend on people being willing and able to change their lifestyle.

Questions

1 Describe the likely appearance of the bronchial epithelium of a long-term heavy smoker. Explain the appearance you describe.

2 Describe how the lung tissue of a person suffering from emphysema would differ from healthy lung tissue.

3 Explain why lung cancers are rarely found in young people.

4 Discuss the short-term and long-term effects of tar and carcinogens on the gaseous exchange system.

5 Summarise the evidence which links smoking with lung cancer.

6 Discuss how you would try to convince someone of the benefits of giving up smoking.

7 Describe the effects of smoking on the cardiovascular system.

8 Discuss the role of diet in the development of coronary heart disease.

9 Discuss the screening methods that could be used to identify people at risk of developing coronary heart disease.

10 Discuss the likely reasons for the global distribution of coronary heart disease.

11 Explain why governments are actively promoting ways of reducing coronary heart disease.

12 Suggest ways in which health promotion may be improved.

13 Explain why lung cancer, coronary heart disease and stroke are categorised as degenerative diseases.

CHAPTER 15

Infectious diseases

By the end of this chapter you should be able to:

1 describe the causes of cholera, malaria, AIDS and TB;

2 explain how these diseases are transmitted and assess the importance of these diseases worldwide;

3 discuss the roles of social, economic and biological factors in the prevention and control of these diseases;

4 outline the role of antibiotics in the treatment of infectious disease.

Infectious diseases are transmissible, or communicable, diseases as we saw in chapter 11. This means that these diseases are caused by pathogens that can spread from infected people to uninfected people. Some diseases can only spread from one person to another by direct contact, as the pathogen cannot survive outside the human body. Others can survive in water, human food, faeces or animals (including insects) and so are transmitted indirectly from person to person. Some people may spread a pathogen even though they do not have the disease themselves. Such people are symptomless **carriers** and it can be very difficult to trace them as the source of an infection.

The way in which a pathogen passes from one host to another is called the **transmission cycle**. Control methods for disease attempt to break transmission cycles by removing the conditions that favour the spread of the pathogen. This is only possible once the cause of the disease and its method of transmission are known and understood.

Worldwide importance of infectious diseases

The four diseases described in the following pages are of current concern as they have increased in prevalence in recent years. They are all of worldwide importance, posing serious public health problems now and for the foreseeable future.

A new strain of **cholera** appeared in 1992 to begin the eighth pandemic of the disease. **Malaria** has been on the increase since the 1970s and constitutes a serious risk to health in many tropical countries. **AIDS** was officially recognised in 1981, but the infective agent (**HIV**) was in human populations for many years before it was identified. The spread of HIV infection since the early 1980s has been exponential. **Tuberculosis (TB)**, once thought to be nearly eradicated, has shown a resurgence and poses a considerable health risk in both developed and developing countries.

These diseases know no boundaries. As a result of easily accessible international travel it is possible for a person to become infected one day and be half way round the world the next. Tourists, business travellers, migrants, refugees and asylum seekers all represent a challenge to health authorities. There are few effective barriers to disease transmission and the means of treating and curing diseases are rapidly becoming obsolete. For example, since 1940 much of the success in treating bacterial infectious diseases has been due to antibiotics. Now, due to their overuse, some bacteria are resistant to these antibiotics.

Cholera

The features of cholera are given in *table 15.1*. It is caused by the bacterium *Vibrio cholerae* (*figure 15.1*).

Pathogen	*Vibrio cholerae*
Methods of transmission	food-borne, water-borne
Global distribution	Asia, Africa, Latin America
Incubation period	1–5 days
Site of action of pathogen	wall of small intestine
Clinical features	severe diarrhoea ('rice water'), loss of water and salts, dehydration, weakness
Method of diagnosis	microscopical analysis of faeces
Annual incidence worldwide	5.5 million
Annual mortality worldwide	120 000

● **Table 15.1** The features of cholera

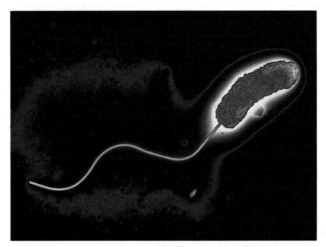

● **Figure 15.1** An electron micrograph of *Vibrio cholerae*. The faeces of a cholera victim are full of these bacteria with their distinctive flagella (× 13 400).

As the disease is water-borne, it occurs where people do not have access to proper sanitation, a clean water supply or uncontaminated food. Infected people, three-quarters of whom may be symptomless carriers, pass out large numbers of bacteria in their faeces. If these contaminate the water supply, or if infected people handle food or cooking utensils without washing their hands, then bacteria are transmitted to uninfected people.

To reach their site of action, the small intestine, bacteria have to pass through the stomach. If the contents are sufficiently acidic (< pH4.5) the bacteria are unlikely to survive. If bacteria do reach the small intestine they multiply and secrete a toxin,

choleragen, which disrupts the functions of the epithelium so that salts and water leave the blood causing severe diarrhoea. This loss of fluid can be fatal if not treated within 24 hours.

Almost all people with cholera who are treated make a quick recovery. A death from cholera is an avoidable death. The disease can be controlled by giving a solution of salts and glucose intravenously to rehydrate the body (*figure 15.2*). If people can drink, they are given **oral rehydration therapy**. Glucose is effective because it is absorbed into the blood and takes salts (e.g. Na$^+$ and K$^+$) with it. It is important to make sure that a sufferer's fluid intake equals fluid losses in urine and faeces and to maintain the osmotic balance of the blood and tissue fluids (chapter 4).

In developing countries, especially those with large cities which have grown considerably in recent years but as yet have no sewage treatment or clean water, there exist perfect conditions for the spread of the disease. Increasing quantities of untreated faeces from a growing population

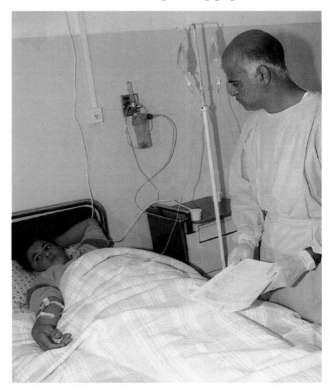

● **Figure 15.2** A Palestinian boy being given intravenous rehydration therapy for cholera in a Gaza Strip hospital, the Middle East, 1994. The drip contains a solution of salts to replace those lost through severe diarrhoea. Cholera causes many deaths when normal life is disrupted by war and other catastrophes.

favour cholera's survival. Many countries, saddled with huge debts, do not have the financial resources to tackle large municipal projects such as providing drainage and a clean water supply to large areas of substandard housing. In many countries raw human sewage is used to irrigate vegetables. (This was the source of a cholera outbreak in Santiago, Chile in 1991.) Inadequate cooking or washing in contaminated water are other common causes. Areas of the world where cholera is endemic are West and East Africa and Afghanistan. In Kabul, the capital of Afghanistan, there were 10 000 cases in 1998. A similar situation was seen in large British cities in the nineteenth century until the water-borne nature of the disease was understood. Cholera is now almost unknown in the developed world as a result of sewage treatment and the provision of clean piped water, which is chlorinated to kill bacteria. The transmission cycle has been broken.

Travellers from areas free of cholera to those where cholera is endemic used to be advised to be vaccinated, although the vaccine only provides short-term protection. This recommendation has now largely been dropped. The reasons for this are explained on page 230.

There are 60 different strains of *V. cholerae*. Until the 1990s only the strain known as 01 caused cholera. Between 1817 and 1923 there were six pandemics of cholera. Each originated in what is now Bangladesh and they were caused by the 'classical' strain of cholera 01. A seventh pandemic began in 1961 when a variety of 01, named 'El Tor', originated in Indonesia. El Tor soon spread to India, then to Italy in 1973, reaching South America in January 1991 where it caused an epidemic in Peru. The discharge of a ship's sewage into the sea may have been responsible. Within days of the start of the epidemic the disease had spread 2000 km along the coast and within four weeks had moved inland. In February and March of that year, an average of 2550 cases a day were being reported. People in neighbouring countries were soon infected. In Peru many sewers discharge straight onto shellfish beds. Seafood, especially filter-feeders such as oysters and mussels, become contaminated because they concentrate cholera bacteria when sewage is pumped into the sea. Fish and shellfish are often

eaten raw. As the epidemic developed so rapidly in Peru, the disease probably spread through contaminated seafood.

A new strain, known as *V. cholerae* 0139, originated in Madras in October 1992 and has spread to other parts of India and Bangladesh. This strain threatens to be responsible for an eighth pandemic. It took El Tor 2 years to displace the 'classical' strain in India; 0139 replaced El Tor in less than two months suggesting that it may be more virulent. Many adult cases have been reported, and this may be because previous exposure to El Tor has not given them immunity to 0139.

SAQ 15.1
List the ways in which cholera is transmitted from person to person.

SAQ 15.2
One person can excrete 10^{13} cholera bacteria a day. An infective dose is 10^6. How many people could one person infect in one day?

SAQ 15.3
Explain why there is such a high risk of cholera in refugee camps.

SAQ 15.4
Describe the precautions that a visitor to a country where cholera is endemic can take to avoid catching the disease.

Malaria
The features of this disease are summarised in *table 15.2*. Malaria is caused by one of four species of the protoctist *Plasmodium*, whose life cycle is shown in *figure 15.3*.

Female *Anopheles* mosquitoes feed on human blood to obtain the protein they need to develop their eggs. If the person they bite is infected with *Plasmodium*, they will take up some of the pathogen's gametes with the blood meal. These gametes fuse and develop in the mosquito's gut to form infective stages, which move to the

Pathogen	*Plasmodium falciparum*, *P. vivax*, *P. ovale*, *P. malariae*
Method of transmission	insect vector: female *Anopheles* mosquito
Global distribution	throughout the tropics and sub-tropics (endemic in 91 countries)
Incubation period	from a week to a year
Site of action of pathogen	liver, red blood cells, brain
Clinical features	fever, anaemia, nausea, headaches, muscle pain, shivering, sweating, enlarged spleen
Method of diagnosis	microscopical examination of blood
Annual incidence worldwide	300 million (90% of cases are in Africa)
Annual mortality worldwide	1.5–2.7 million; in tropical Africa malaria kills 1 million children under the age of 5

● **Table 15.2** The features of malaria.

mosquito's salivary glands. When the mosquito feeds again, it injects an anticoagulant that prevents the blood meal from clotting so that it flows out of the host into the mosquito. The infective stages pass out into the blood together with the anticoagulant in the saliva, and the parasites enter the red blood cells, where they multiply (*figure 15.4*). The female *Anopheles* mosquito is therefore a **vector** of malaria and she transmits the disease when she passes the infective stages into an uninfected person. Malaria may also be transmitted during blood transfusion and when unsterile needles are reused. *Plasmodium* can also pass across the placenta from mother to fetus.

Plasmodium multiplies in both hosts, the human and the mosquito; at each stage there is a huge increase in the number of parasites and this improves the chances of infecting another mosquito or human host.

If people are continually reinfected they become **immune** to malaria (chapter 16). However, this only happens if they survive the first five years of

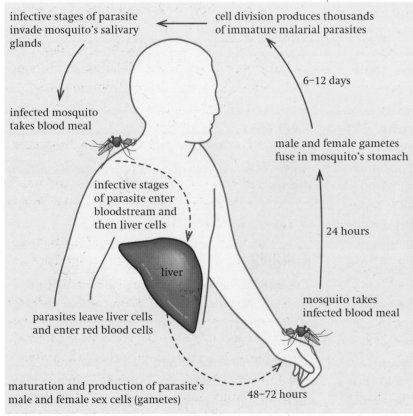

infective stages of parasite invade mosquito's salivary glands

cell division produces thousands of immature malarial parasites

6–12 days

infected mosquito takes blood meal

infective stages of parasite enter bloodstream and then liver cells

male and female gametes fuse in mosquito's stomach

24 hours

liver

mosquito takes infected blood meal

parasites leave liver cells and enter red blood cells

maturation and production of parasite's male and female sex cells (gametes)

48–72 hours

● **Figure 15.3** The life cycle of *Plasmodium*. The parasite has two hosts: the sexual stage occurs in mosquitoes, the asexual stage in humans. The time between infection and appearance of parasites inside red blood cells is 7–30 days in *P. falciparum*; longer in other species.

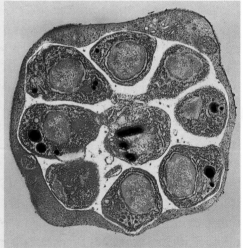

● **Figure 15.4** A transmission electron micrograph of a section through a red blood cell packed tightly with malarial parasites. *Plasmodium* multiplies inside red blood cells; this cell will soon burst, releasing parasites which will infect other red blood cells.

life when mortality from malaria is very high. The immunity only lasts as long as they are in contact with the disease. This explains why epidemics in places where malaria is not endemic can be very serious, and why it is more dangerous in those areas where it only occurs during and after the rainy season. This often coincides with the time of maximum agricultural activity so the disease has a disastrous effect on the economy: people cannot cultivate the land when they are sick.

There are three main ways to control malaria:

- reduce the number of mosquitoes;
- avoid being bitten by mosquitoes;
- use drugs to prevent the parasite infecting people.

It is possible to kill the insect vector and break the transmission cycle. Mosquitoes lay their eggs in water. Larvae hatch and develop in water but breathe air by coming to the surface. Oil can be spread over the surfaces of water to make it impossible for mosquito larvae and pupae to breathe. Marshes can be drained and vegetation cleared. Two biological control measures that can be used are:

- stocking ponds, irrigation and drainage ditches and other permanent bodies of water with fish which feed on mosquito larvae;
- spraying a preparation containing the bacterium *Bacillus thuringiensis*, which kills mosquito larvae, but is not toxic to other forms of life.

Mosquitoes will lay their eggs in small puddles or pools and this makes it impossible to eradicate breeding sites, especially in the rainy season.

The best protection against malaria is to avoid being bitten. People are advised to sleep beneath mosquito nets and use insect repellents. Soaking mosquito nets in insecticide every six months has been shown to reduce mortality from malaria. People should not expose their skin when mosquitoes are active at dusk. Villagers in New Guinea recommend sleeping with a dog or a pig. They say that mosquitoes much prefer animal blood to human blood.

Anti-malarial drugs such as quinine and chloroquine are used to treat infected people. They are also used as **prophylactic** (preventative) drugs, stopping an infection occurring if a person is bitten by an infected mosquito. They are taken before,

during and after visiting an area where malaria is endemic. Chloroquine inhibits protein synthesis and prevents the parasite spreading within the body. Another prophylactic, proguanil, has the added advantage of inhibiting the sexual reproduction of *Plasmodium* inside the biting mosquito. Where anti-malarial drugs have been used widely there are strains of drug-resistant *Plasmodium*. Chloroquine resistance is widespread in parts of South America, Africa and New Guinea. Newer drugs, such as mefloquine, are used in these areas. However, mefloquine is expensive and sometimes causes unpleasant side effects such as restlessness, dizziness, vomiting and disturbed sleep.

People visiting many parts of the tropics are at great risk of contracting malaria. There were between 1500 and 2300 cases of malaria a year in the UK between 1984 and 1993. Doctors in developed countries, who see very few cases of malaria, often misdiagnose it as influenza since the initial symptoms are similar. Many of these cases are settled immigrants who have been visiting relatives in Africa or India. They do not take prophylactic drugs because they do not realise that they have lost their immunity.

In the 1950s the World Health Organisation coordinated a worldwide eradication programme. Although malaria was cleared from some countries, it was not generally successful. There were two main reasons for this:

- *Plasmodium* became resistant to the drugs used to control it.
- Mosquitoes became resistant to DDT and the other insecticides that were used at the time, such as dieldrin.

This programme was also hugely expensive and often unpopular. People living in areas where malaria was temporarily eradicated by the programme lost their immunity and suffered considerably, even dying, when the disease returned. Some villagers in South-East Asia lost the roofs of their houses because dieldrin killed a parasitic wasp that controlled the numbers of thatch-eating caterpillars. Some spray teams were set upon and killed by angry villagers in New Guinea. The programme could have been more successful if it had been tackled more sensitively, with more involvement of the indigenous people. In the

1970s, war and civil unrest destroyed much of the infrastructure throughout Africa and South-East Asia, making it impossible for mosquito control teams to work effectively.

The reasons for the worldwide concern over the spread of malaria are:

- an increase in drug-resistant forms of *Plasmodium*;
- an increase in the proportion of cases caused by *P. falciparum*, the form that causes severe, often fatal malaria;
- difficulties in developing a vaccine;
- an increase in the number of epidemics because of climatic and environmental changes that favour the spread of mosquitoes;
- the migration of people as a result of civil unrest and war.

Malaria is still one of the world's biggest threats to health. 40% of the world's population live in areas where there is a risk of malaria. In recent years there has been a resurgence of the disease in Africa. Control methods now concentrate on working within the health systems to improve diagnosis, improve the supply of effective drugs and promote appropriate methods to prevent transmission. These methods have proved successful in South America where the death rate from malaria

decreased by 60% between 1994 and 1997 in some countries. Several recent advances give hope that malaria may one day be controlled. The introduction of simple 'dipstick'-type tests for diagnosing malaria means that diagnosis can be done quickly without the need for laboratories. The whole genome of *Plasmodium* is being sequenced and this may lead to the development of effective vaccines. Several vaccines are being trialled, but it is not likely that a successful vaccine will be available for some time. Several drugs are being used in combination to reduce the chances of drug resistance arising.

SAQ 15.5
Describe how malaria is transmitted.

SAQ 15.6
Describe the factors that make malaria a difficult disease to control.

SAQ 15.7
Describe the precautions that people can take to avoid catching malaria.

Pathogen	Human Immunodeficiency Virus
Methods of transmission	in semen and vaginal fluids during sexual intercourse, infected blood or blood products, contaminated hypodermic syringes, mother to fetus across placenta, mother to infant in breast milk
Global distribution	worldwide, especially in sub-Saharan Africa and South-East Asia
Incubation period	initial incubation a few weeks, but up to ten years or more before symptoms of AIDS may develop
Site of action of pathogen	T helper lymphocytes, macrophages, brain cells
Clinical features	HIV infection – flu-like symptoms and then symptomless; AIDS – opportunistic infections including pneumonia, TB, and cancers; weight loss, diarrhoea, fever, sweating, dementia
Method of diagnosis	blood test for antibodies to HIV
Estimated total number of people infected with HIV worldwide in 1998	33.4 million
Estimated number of new cases of HIV infection worldwide in 1998	6 million
Estimated number of deaths from AIDS-related diseases worldwide in 1998	2.5 million (one third due to TB)

● **Table 15.3** The features of HIV/AIDS.

Acquired Immune Deficiency Syndrome (AIDS)

Features of AIDS and HIV are listed in *table 15.3*. AIDS is caused by the human immunodeficiency virus (HIV) (*figure 15.5*). The virus infects and destroys cells of the body's immune system (*figure 15.6*) so that their numbers gradually decrease. These cells, known as **T helper lymphocytes** (see page 226), control the **immune system**'s response to infection. When the numbers are low, the body is unable to defend itself against infection so allowing a range of pathogens to cause a variety of **opportunistic infections**. AIDS is not a disease. It is a collection of these rare opportunistic diseases associated with immunodeficiency caused by HIV infection. Since HIV is an infective agent, AIDS is called an 'acquired' immunodeficiency to distinguish it from other types, for example an inherited form.

After initial uncertainties in the early 1980s surrounding the emergence of an apparently new disease, it soon became clear that an epidemic

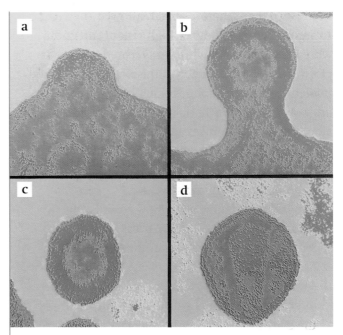

● **Figure 15.6** A series of transmission electron micrographs showing HIV budding from the surface of an infected lymphocyte, becoming surrounded by a membrane derived from the plasma membrane of the host cell. **a** The viral particle first appears as a bump, **b** which then buds out and **c** is eventually cut off. **d** The outer shell of dense material and less dense core are visible in the released virus. (× 176 000)

and then a pandemic was underway. The World Health Organisation estimated that 47 million people had been infected with HIV by 1998 and that 14 million of them had died.

HIV is a virus that is spread by intimate human contact: there is no vector (unlike in malaria) and the virus is unable to survive outside the human body (unlike cholera or malaria pathogens). Transmission is only possible by direct exchange of body fluids. In practice this means that HIV can be spread most easily through sexual intercourse, blood donation, the sharing of intravenous needles and across the placenta from mother to fetus.

The initial epidemic in North America and Europe was amongst those male homosexuals who practised anal intercourse and had many sex partners, two forms of behaviour that put them at risk. The mucous lining of the rectum is not as thick as that of the vagina and there is less natural lubrication. As a result it is easily damaged during intercourse and the virus can pass from semen to blood. Multiple partners, both

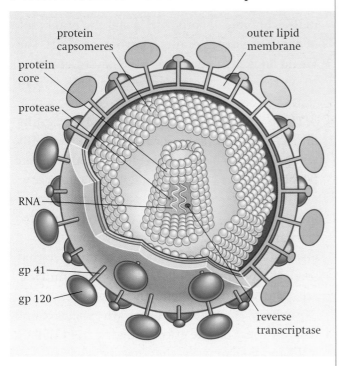

● **Figure 15.5** Human immunodeficiency virus (HIV). The outer envelope contains two glycoproteins gp120 and gp 41. The protein core contains genetic material (RNA) and two enzymes, a protease and reverse transcriptase. Reverse transcriptase uses the RNA as a template to produce DNA (page 77) once the virus is inside a host cell.

homosexual and heterosexual, allowed the virus to spread more widely. At high risk of infection were haemophiliacs who were treated with a clotting substance (factor VIII) isolated from blood pooled from many donors. Such blood products are now largely synthetic (page 77). The transmission of HIV by heterosexual intercourse is rising worldwide. This is particulary rapid in some African states where equal numbers of males and females are now 'HIV positive'.

The statistics below show how serious the pandemic is in sub-Saharan Africa.

- 80% of the world's deaths from AIDS occur in Africa.
- 34 million people are estimated to have been infected with HIV in sub-Saharan Africa since the start of the pandemic and 11.4 million are estimated to have died.
- One-quarter of the population of Zimbabwe is infected with HIV.
- Between 20% and 25% of people aged between 15 and 49 in Botswana and Zimbabwe are infected with HIV.
- 5.9 million children are estimated to have been orphaned by AIDS; in some places this is 25% of the population under 15.
- The prevalence of HIV among women attending antenatal clincs in Zimbabwe was between 20% and 50% in 1997.
- A large proportion of women in Rwanda are HIV positive following the use of rape as a genocidal weapon in the civil war of the early 1990s.
- The average life expectancy in South Africa dropped from 65 to 55 during 1995–1999.

HIV is a slow virus and after infection there may not be any symptoms until years later. Some people who have the virus even appear not to develop any initial symptoms, although there are often flu-like symptoms for several weeks after becoming infected. At this stage a person is HIV positive but does not have AIDS. The infections that can opportunistically develop to create AIDS tend to be characteristic of the condition. Two of these are caused by fungi: oral thrush caused by *Candida albicans*, and a rare form of pneumonia caused by *Pneumocystis carinii*. During the early years of the AIDS epidemic people in developed countries died within twelve hours of contracting

this unusual pneumonia. Now this condition is managed much better and drugs are prescribed to prevent the disease developing. As and when the immune system collapses further, it becomes less effective in finding and destroying cancers. A rare form of skin cancer, Kaposi's sarcoma caused by a herpes-like virus, is associated with AIDS. Kaposi's sarcoma and cancers of internal organs are now the most likely causes of death of people with AIDS in developed countries, along with degenerative diseases of the brain, such as dementias.

At about the same time that AIDS was first reported on the west coast of the USA and in Europe, doctors in Central Africa reported seeing people with similar opportunistic infections. We have seen that HIV/AIDS is now widespread throughout sub-Saharan Africa from Uganda to South Africa. It is a serious public health problem here because HIV infection makes people more vulnerable to existing diseases such as malnutrition, TB and malaria. AIDS is having an adverse effect on the economic development of countries in the region as it affects sexually active people in their 20s and 30s who are also potentially the most economically productive and the purchase of expensive drugs drains government funds. The World Bank estimated that AIDS had reversed 10–15 years of economic growth for some African states by the end of the twentieth century.

There is as yet no cure for AIDS and no vaccine for HIV. No-one knows how many people with HIV will progress to developing full-blown AIDS. Some people think it is 100% although a tiny minority of HIV positive people do appear to have immunity (chapter 16) and can live as entirely symptomless carriers. Drug therapy can slow down the onset of AIDS quite dramatically, so much so that some HIV positive people in developed countries are adjusting to a suddenly increased life expectancy. However, the drugs are expensive and have a variety of side effects ranging from the mild and temporary (rashes, headaches, diarrhoea) to the severe and permanent (nerve damage, abnormal fat distribution). If used in combination, two or more drugs which prevent the replication of the virus inside host cells can prolong life, but they do not offer a cure. The drugs are similar to DNA nucleotides (e.g.

zidovudine is similar to the nucleotide that contains the base thymine). Zidovudine binds to the viral enzyme reverse transcriptase and blocks its action. This stops the replication of the viral genetic material and leads to an increase in some of the body's lymphocytes. A course of combination therapy can be very complicated to follow. The pattern and timing of medication through the day must be strictly followed. People who are unable to keep to such a regimen can become susceptible to strains of HIV that have developed resistance to the drugs.

The spread of AIDS is difficult to control. The virus's long latent stage means it can be transmitted by people who are HIV positive but who show no symptoms of AIDS and do not know they are infected. The virus changes its surface proteins, which makes it hard for the body's immune system to recognise it (see chapter 16). This also makes the development of a vaccine very difficult.

For the present, public health measures are the only way to stop the spread of HIV. People can be educated about the spread of the infection and encouraged to change their behaviour so as to protect themselves and others. Condoms, femidoms and dental dams are the only effective methods of reducing the risk of infection during intercourse as they form a barrier between body fluids, reducing the chances of transmission of the virus. Uganda and the Philippines are unique in the developing world in their concerted health programmes to promote the use of condoms. As a result, infection rates in these countries have slowed.

SAQ 15.8
Suggest why the true total of AIDS cases worldwide may be much higher than reported.

SAQ 15.9
Suggest why condoms are not fully effective at preventing HIV infection.

SAQ 15.10
Suggest the types of advice which might be offered as part of an AIDS education programme.

Contact tracing is an important part of HIV control in the UK. If a person who is diagnosed as HIV positive is willing and able to identify the people who they have put at risk of infection by sexual intercourse or needle sharing, then these people will be offered an HIV test. This test identifies the presence of antibodies to HIV, though antibodies only appear several weeks after the initial infection.

Injecting drug users are advised to give up their habit, stop sharing needles or take their drug in some other way. Needle exchange schemes operate in some places to exchange used needles for sterile ones to reduce the chances of infection with HIV and other blood-borne diseases.

In developed countries, blood collected from blood donors is routinely screened for HIV and heat-treated to kill any viruses. People who think they may have been exposed to the virus are strongly discouraged from donating blood. Both methods are expensive and unlikely to be implemented throughout the developing world for some time. In these countries, people about to have an operation are recommended to donate their own blood before surgery to reduce the risk of infection.

SAQ 15.11
Children in Africa with sickle cell anaemia or malaria often receive blood transfusions. Explain how this puts them at risk of HIV infection.

Widespread testing of a population to find people who are HIV positive is not expensive, but governments are reluctant to introduce such testing because of the infringement of personal freedom. In the developed world, HIV testing is promoted most strongly to people in high risk groups, such as male homosexuals, prostitutes, injecting drug users and their sexual partners. If tested positive they can be given the medical and psychological support they need. Despite this, people in Britain tend to have an HIV test at a far later stage than any other Europeans. In Africa and South-East Asia the epidemic is not restricted to such easily identifiable groups and widespread testing is not feasible due to the expense of reaching the majority of the population and the difficulty of organising it. People in these regions find out that they are HIV positive when they develop the symptoms of AIDS.

SAQ 15.12

Explain why the early knowledge of HIV infection is important in transmission control.

HIV positive women in developed countries are advised not to breast feed their children because of the risk of transmitting the virus to their child. Both viral particles and infected lymphocytes are found in breast milk. In developing countries the benefits of breast feeding, such as the protection this gives against other diseases and the lack of clean water to make up supplements, outweigh the risks of transmitting HIV.

Tuberculosis (TB)

Table 15.4 gives the main features of this disease. TB is caused by two bacteria, *Mycobacterium tuberculosis* (*figure 15.7*) and *M. bovis*. These are pathogens that live inside human cells, particularly in the lungs. This is the first site of infection, but the bacteria can spread throughout the whole body and even infect the bone tissue. Some people become infected and develop TB quite quickly, whilst in others the bacteria remain inactive for many years. It is estimated that 30% of the world's population is infected with TB without showing any symptoms of the infection; people with this inactive infection do not spread the disease to others. However, the bacteria can later become active and this is most likely to happen when people are weakened by other diseases, suffer from malnutrition or become infected with HIV. Those who have the active form of TB often suffer from debilitating illness for a long time. They have a persistent cough and, as part of their defence, cells release hormone-like compounds which cause fever and suppress the appetite. As a result sufferers lose weight and often look emaciated (*figure 15.8*).

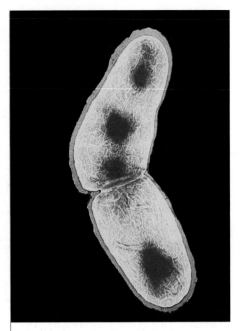

● **Figure 15.7** False-colour transmission electron micrograph of *Mycobacterium tuberculosis* dividing into two. It may multiply like this inside the lungs and then spread throughout the body or lie dormant, becoming active many years later.

TB is often the first opportunistic infection to strike HIV-positive people. HIV infection may reactivate dormant infections of *M. tuberculosis* which may have been present from childhood or, if people are uninfected, make them susceptible to infection. TB is now the

Pathogen	*Mycobacterium tuberculosis*; *M. bovis*
Methods of transmission	airborne droplets; via unpasteurised milk
Global distribution	worldwide
Incubation period	few weeks or months
Site of action of pathogen	primary infection in lungs; secondary infections in lymph nodes, bones and gut
Clinical features	racking cough, coughing blood, chest pain, shortness of breath, fever, sweating, weight loss
Methods of diagnosis	microscopical examination of sputum for bacteria, chest X-ray
Annual incidence worldwide in 1998	8 million (more than 6000 cases in UK)
Annual mortality worldwide in 1998	2 million

● **Table 15.4** The features of tuberculosis.

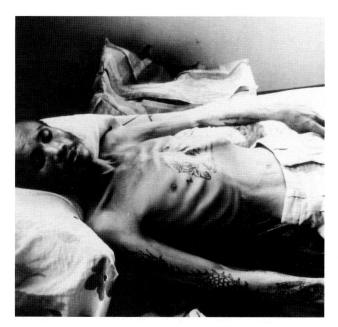

● **Figure 15.8** A TB patient in Thailand. Health workers or members of his family may supervise his drug treatment which can last for up to a year.

leading cause of death of HIV-positive people. The HIV pandemic has been followed very closely by a TB pandemic.

TB is spread when infected people with the active form of the illness cough or sneeze and the bacteria are carried in the air in tiny droplets of liquid. Transmission occurs when people who are uninfected inhale the droplets. TB spreads most rapidly among people living in overcrowded conditions. People who sleep close together in large numbers are particularly at risk. The disease primarily attacks the homeless and people who live in poor, substandard housing; those with low immunity, because of malnutrition or being HIV positive, are also particularly vulnerable.

The form of TB caused by *M. bovis* also occurs in cattle and is spread to humans in meat and milk. It is estimated that there were about 800 000 deaths in the UK between 1850 and 1950 as a result of TB transmitted from cattle. Very few now acquire TB in this way in developed countries for reasons explained later, although this still remains a source of infection in some developing countries.

The incidence of TB in the UK decreased steeply well before the introduction of a vaccine in the 1950s, because of improvements in housing conditions and diet. The antibiotic streptomycin was introduced in the 1940s and this hastened the decrease in the incidence of TB. This pattern was repeated throughout the developed world.

Once thought to be practically eradicated, TB is now showing a resurgence. There are high rates of incidence all across the developing world and in the countries of the former Soviet Union (*figure 15.9*). Very high rates are found in areas of destitution in inner cities such as New York. The incidence in such areas is as high as in developing countries. The resurgence is due in part to the following factors:

- some strains of TB bacteria which are resistant to drugs;
- the AIDS pandemic;
- poor housing in inner cities in the developed world and rising homelessness;
- the breakdown of TB control programmes, particularly in the USA; partial treatment for TB increases the chance of drug resistance in *Mycobacterium*;
- migration from Eastern Europe and developing countries to large cities such as London and New York.

When a doctor first sees a person with the likely symptoms of TB, samples of the sputum (mucus and pus) from their lungs are collected for analysis. The identification of the tuberculosis bacteria can be done very quickly by microscopy. If TB is confirmed, then sufferers should be isolated while they are in the most infectious stage (which is at two to four weeks). This is particularly the case if they are infected with a drug-resistant strain of the bacterium. The treatment involves using several drugs to ensure that all the bacteria are killed. If not, drug-resistant forms remain to continue the infection. The treatment is a long one (nine months to one year) because it takes a long time to kill the bacteria as they are slow growing and are not very sensitive to the drugs used. Unfortunately, many people do not complete their course of drugs as they think that when they feel better they are cured. Anyone who does not complete their treatment may be harbouring drug-resistant bacteria and may spread these to others if the bacteria become active.

Strains of drug-resistant *M. tuberculosis* were identified when treatment with antibiotics began in the 1950s. Antibiotics act as selective agents

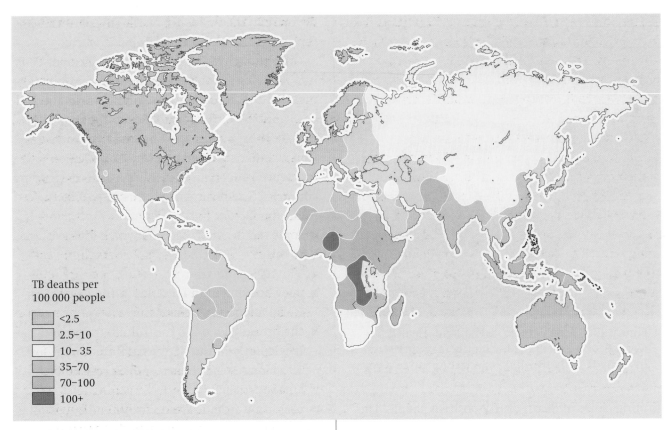

TB deaths per
100 000 people

<2.5
2.5–10
10–35
35–70
70–100
100+

● **Figure 15.9** The global distribution of TB.

killing drug-sensitive strains and leaving resistant ones behind. Drug resistance occurs as a result of mutation in the bacterial DNA. Mutation is a random event and occurs with a frequency of about one in every thousand bacteria. If three drugs are used in treatment then the chance of resistance arising by mutation to all three of them is reduced to 1 in a thousand million. If four drugs are used the chance is reduced to 1 in a billion. If TB is not treated or the person stops the treatment before the bacteria are completely eliminated, they spread throughout the body, increasing the likelihood that mutations will arise as the bacteria survive for a long time and multiply. Stopping treatment early can mean that *M. tuberculosis* develops resistance to all the drugs being used. People who do not complete a course of treatment are highly likely to infect others with drug-resistant forms of TB. It is estimated that one person can easily infect ten to fifteen others, especially if they live in overcrowded conditions.

Multiple drug resistant forms of TB (MDR-TB) now exist. In 1995, an HIV unit in London reported an outbreak of MDR-TB with a form of

M. tuberculosis that was resistant to five of the major drugs used to treat the disease including isoniazid, which is the most successful drug.

The World Health Organisation now promotes a scheme to ensure that patients complete their course of drugs. DOTS (Direct Observation Treatment, Short Course), involves health workers, or responsible family members, making sure that patients take their medicine regularly for six to eight months. The drugs widely used are isoniazid and rifampicin, often in combination with others. This drug therapy cures 95% of all patients, is twice as effective as other strategies and is helping to reduce the spread of MDR strains.

Contact tracing (see page 211) and their subsequent testing for the bacterium is an essential part of controlling TB. Contacts are screened for symptoms of TB infection, but the diagnosis can take up to two weeks. The spread of the disease among children is prevented, to a large extent, by vaccination. In the UK, teenagers are routinely vaccinated at the age of 13 or 14. The BCG vaccine is derived from *M. bovis* and protects up to 70 to 80% of teenagers in the UK, its effectiveness decreasing with age unless there is exposure to

TB. Studies of the effectiveness of BCG in protecting adults and children give conflicting results. It also appears that the vaccine is effective in some parts of the world (e.g. UK), but less effective in others (e.g. India). Many of the world's victims were not vaccinated.

TB can be transmitted between humans and cattle. To prevent people catching TB in this way, cattle are routinely tested for TB and any found to be infected are destroyed. TB bacteria are killed when milk is pasteurised. These control methods are very effective and have reduced the incidence of human TB caused by *M. bovis* considerably so that it is virtually eliminated in countries where these controls operate. In 1995, there were just eleven cases of TB caused by *M. bovis* in the UK.

SAQ 15.13
Describe the global distribution of TB and explain the reasons for the distribution you have described.

Antibiotics

Antibiotics are drugs that are used to treat or cure infections. Effective antibiotics show **selective toxicity**, killing or disabling the pathogen but having no effect on host cells. There is a wide range of antibiotics to treat bacterial and fungal infections, but only very few for viral infections. Antibiotics are derived from living organisms, although other antimicrobial drugs, such as isoniazid used for the treatment of tuberculosis, are synthetic.

Antibiotics interfere with some aspect of growth or metabolism of the target organism such as:

■ synthesis of bacterial walls (chapter 1);
■ protein synthesis (transcription and translation, chapter 5);
■ plasma membrane function (chapter 4);
■ enzyme action (chapter 3).

The main sites of action of antibiotics are shown in *figure 15.10*.

Different diseases are treated with different antibiotics. Some kinds of bacteria are completely resistant to particular antibiotics (for example, all strains of *M. tuberculosis* are resistant to penicillins) whilst other bacteria have certain strains that are resistant. **Broad spectrum** antibiotics are effective against a wide range of bacteria, while **narrow spectrum** antibiotics are active only against a few.

One type of antibiotic, penicillins, function by preventing the synthesis of the cross-links between the peptidoglycan polymers in the cell walls of bacteria. This means that they are only active against bacteria and only while they are growing. Many types of bacteria have enzymes for destroying penicillins (penicillinases) and are therefore resistant to these antibiotics.

As a result of all these variables, antibiotics should be chosen carefully. Screening antibiotics against the strain of the bacterium or fungus isolated from sufferers ensures that the most effective antibiotic can be used in treatment. *Figure 15.11* shows the results of an antibiotic sensitivity test carried out on a pathogenic strain of the human gut bacterium *E. coli* (O157). Bacteria are collected from faeces, food or water, and grown on an agar medium. Various antibiotics are absorbed onto discs of filter paper and placed on

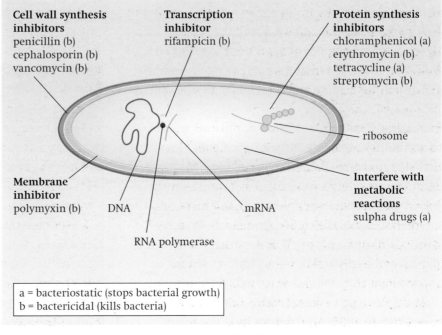

Cell wall synthesis inhibitors
penicillin (b)
cephalosporin (b)
vancomycin (b)

Transcription inhibitor
rifampicin (b)

Protein synthesis inhibitors
chloramphenicol (a)
erythromycin (b)
tetracycline (a)
streptomycin (b)

ribosome

Membrane inhibitor
polymyxin (b)

DNA

mRNA

Interfere with metabolic reactions
sulpha drugs (a)

RNA polymerase

a = bacteriostatic (stops bacterial growth)
b = bactericidal (kills bacteria)

● **Figure 15.10** The sites of action of antibiotics in bacteria.

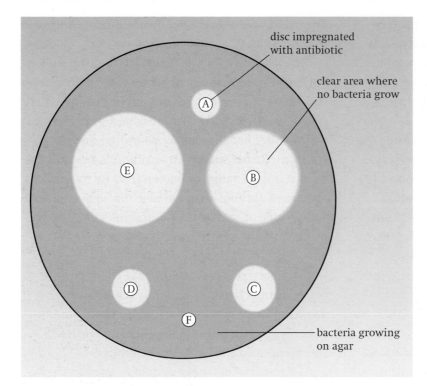

| Antibiotic | Inhibition zone diameter (mm) | |
	Resistant	Sensitive
A	≤ 11	≥ 14
B	≤ 12	≥ 18
C	≤ 9	≥ 14
D	≤ 11	≥ 22
E	≤ 12	≥ 15
F	≤ 14	≥ 19

● **Table 15.5** Inhibition zone diameters for the antibiotics of *figure 15.11*.

If the diameter of the inhibition zone for an antibiotic is equal to or less than the figure given in the first column, the bacteria are resistant to it. If the diameter is equal to or greater than the figure in the right hand column, the bacteria are sensitive and the antibiotic may be chosen for treatment.

● **Figure 15.11** An antibiotic sensitivity test for a pathogenic strain of *Escherichia coli*. *Table 15.5* shows the inhibition zone diameters for the six antibiotics.

the agar plate. The plate is incubated and the diameters of the **inhibition zones** where no bacteria are growing are measured. The diameters are compared with a table similar to *table 15.5* and the most effective antibiotics chosen to treat infected people.

SAQ 15.14

Which of the antibiotics in *figure 15.11* and *table 15.5* would be chosen to treat the patient with the pathogenic strain of *E. coli* (O157)? Explain your answer.

Increasingly, bacteria which were once susceptible to antibiotics are becoming resistant, meaning that sick individuals cannot be treated. This has a great impact on disease control as it prolongs the period of time when people are ill and increases the risk of higher mortality rates. Some British hospitals harbour Methicillin Resistant *Staphylococcus aureus* (**MRSA**), which is resistant to at least four antibiotics due to their previous inappropriate and widespread use. It is advisable to keep some antibiotics for use as a 'last resort', when everything else has failed, so as to lessen the

chances of more such resistant organisms. Meanwhile, drug companies are continuing to invest in research for new antibiotics, even though they too may quickly become redundant. You can find more information about antibiotics in two of the A Level option texts in this series: *Applications of Genetics* and *Microbiology and Biotechnology*.

SUMMARY

◆ Cholera is caused by the bacterium *Vibrio cholerae* and is transmitted in water or food contaminated by the faeces of infected people.

◆ Cholera can be controlled by treating patients with oral rehydration therapy and making sure that human faeces do not reach the water supply. The disease is prevented by providing clean, chlorinated, water and good sanitation. There is no effective vaccine.

◆ Malaria is caused by four species of *Plasmodium*. The most dangerous is *P. falciparum*. The disease is transmitted by female *Anopheles* mosquitoes that transfer *Plasmodium* from infected to uninfected people.

◆ Malaria is controlled in three main ways: reducing the number of mosquitoes by insecticide spraying or draining breeding sites; using mosquito nets (more effective if soaked in insecticide); using drugs to prevent *Plasmodium* infecting people. There is no effective vaccine.

◆ AIDS is a set of diseases caused by the destruction of the immune system by infection with human immunodeficiency virus (HIV). HIV is transmitted in certain body fluids: blood, semen, vaginal secretions and breast milk. It also crosses the placenta. It primarily infects economically active members of populations in developing countries and has an extremely adverse effect on social and economic development.

◆ The transmission of HIV can be controlled by using barrier methods (e.g. condom and femidom) during sexual intercourse. Educating people to practise safer sex is the only control method currently available to health authorities. Contact tracing is used to find people who may have contracted HIV so that they can be tested and counselled. Life expectancy can be greatly extended by the use of combination drug therapy which interferes with the replication of the virus. However, such treatment is expensive, difficult to adhere to and has unpleasant side-effects. There is no vaccine for HIV and no cure for AIDS.

◆ TB is caused by the bacterium *Mycobacterium tuberculosis* (in developing countries, it may also be caused by *M. bovis*, which also causes a related disease in cattle).

◆ *M. tuberculosis* is spread when people infected with the active form of the disease release bacteria in droplets of liquid when they cough or sneeze. Transmission occurs when uninfected people inhale the bacteria. This is most likely to happen where people live in overcrowded conditions and especially where many sleep close together. Many people have the inactive form of TB in their lungs, but they do not have the disease and do not spread it. The inactive bacteria may become active in people who are malnourished or who become infected with HIV.

◆ Drugs are used to treat people with the active form of TB. The treatment may take nine months or more as it is difficult to kill the bacteria. Contact tracing is used to find people who may have caught the disease. These people are tested for TB and treated if found to be infected. The BCG vaccine provides some protection against TB, but its effectiveness varies in different parts of the world.

◆ Cholera, malaria, AIDS and TB are all increasing in prevalence and pose severe threats to the health of populations in developed and developing countries.

◆ Public health measures are taken to reduce the transmission of these diseases, but to be effective they must be informed by a knowledge of the life cycle of each pathogen.

◆ Antibiotics are used to inhibit the growth of pathogenic organisms. Most are only effective against bacteria. The widespread and indiscriminate use of antibiotics has led to the growth of resistant strains of bacteria. This poses a serious challenge to the maintenance of health services in the twenty-first century.

Questions

1. Describe the transmission of cholera, malaria, tuberculosis and HIV/AIDS.

2. Discuss the public health measures that should be taken during a cholera epidemic.

3. Explain how a knowledge of the life cycle of the malarial parasite is important in devising methods to control the spread of the disease.

4. Describe how you would attempt to prevent the spread of malaria in a rural community in the tropics.

5. Explain the value of the following in disease control: contact tracing, DOTS for TB, antibiotic sensitivity tests, isolation of patients and health education.

6. Discuss the social, biological and economic problems associated with controlling the spread of HIV infection.

7. Make a table to compare the causes, transmission and methods of prevention and control for the diseases described in this chapter.

8. Outline the role of antibiotics in controlling disease.

9. Discuss the social, medical and economic problems of controlling the spread of disease in sub-Saharan Africa.

CHAPTER 16

Immunity

By the end of this chapter you should be able to:

1 describe the structure, origin, maturation and mode of action of phagocytes and lymphocytes;

2 explain the meaning of the term *immune response*;

3 distinguish between the actions of B lymphocytes and T lymphocytes in fighting infection;

4 explain the role of memory cells in long-term immunity;

5 relate the molecular structure of antibodies to their functions;

6 distinguish between active and passive, natural and artificial immunity;

7 explain how vaccination can control disease;

8 discuss the reasons why vaccination has eradicated smallpox but not measles, TB, malaria or cholera;

9 outline the role of the immune system in allergies, with reference to asthma and hay fever.

We now consider in detail something that was mentioned in chapter 15: the body's varying ability to resist infection by pathogens. We have seen that some people experience few or no symptoms when exposed to certain infectious diseases. Even though they may be a carrier of disease to other people, they have **immunity** themselves. How is this possible? The disease measles is used as an example here.

Measles is caused by a virus which enters the body and replicates inside human cells. There are no symptoms for about 8 to 14 days and then a rash appears and a fever develops. Amongst poor people, especially those living in overcrowded conditions, measles can be a serious disease and a major cause of death, especially among infants. Amongst others, after about ten days the disease clears up and there are rarely any complications. Measles used to be a common childhood disease in the UK that most people had only once. In most cases it is very unlikely that anyone surviving the disease will suffer from it again. They are

immune. While suffering from the symptoms of the disease the body's defence system has developed a way of recognising the virus and preventing it from doing any harm again. Immunity is the protection against disease provided by the body's defence or **immune system**.

Defence against disease

We have a variety of mechanisms to protect ourselves against infectious diseases, such as measles and those described in the previous chapter. Many pathogens do not harm us because, if we are healthy, we have physical, chemical and cellular defences that prevent them entering, or if they do enter, from spreading through the body. For example, the epithelia that cover the airways are an effective barrier to the entry of pathogens (see page 173); hydrochloric acid in the stomach kills many bacteria that we ingest with our food and drink; blood clotting is a defence mechanism that stops the loss of blood and prevents the entry of pathogens through wounds in the skin. If pathogens do successfully enter the body, white blood cells (chapter 8) can recognise them as something foreign and destroy them.

White blood cells are part of the immune system and they recognise pathogens by the distinctive, large molecules that cover their surfaces, such as proteins, glycoproteins, lipids and polysaccharides, and the waste materials which some pathogens produce. Any molecule which the body recognises as foreign is an **antigen**.

Lymphocytes are one type of white blood cell. (Their structure and functions are described in detail below.) They play an important role in the **immune response**, as follows. We have many different kinds of lymphocytes each capable of producing a type of protein, termed an **antibody**, that acts against a particular antigen. The antigen and antibody are specific for each other and the lymphocyte's antibodies are only secreted when the appropriate antigen is encountered. The first time this happens in a person's life, the production of antibodies is slow. It may take several weeks to build up enough antibodies to destroy the pathogen. Subsequent encounters, however, see a very rapid response with the result that symptoms can be entirely prevented and the host remains well.

SAQ 16.1

Explain the terms *antigen, antibody* and *immune response*.

Cells of the immune system

The cells of the immune system originate from the bone marrow. There are two groups of these cells involved in defence:
- phagocytes (neutrophils and macrophages);
- lymphocytes.

All of these cells are visible among red blood cells when a blood smear is stained to show nuclei as shown in *figure 16.1*.

SAQ 16.2

Looking at *figure 16.1*, **a** describe the differences between the neutrophil and lymphocyte and **b** calculate the actual size of the neutrophil.

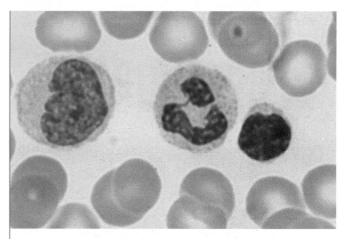

● **Figure 16.1** A monocyte (left), which will develop into a macrophage, a neutrophil (centre) and a lymphocyte (right) together with red blood cells in a blood smear which has been photographed through a light microscope. The cytoplasm of the neutrophil contains vacuoles full of hydrolytic enzymes (×2200).

Phagocytes

Phagocytes are produced throughout life by the bone marrow. They are stored there before being distributed around the body in the blood. They are scavengers, removing any dead cells as well as invasive microorganisms.

Neutrophils are a kind of phagocyte and form about 60% of the white cells in the blood (*figure 16.2*). They travel throughout the body often leaving the blood by squeezing through the walls of capillaries to 'patrol' the tissues. During an infection they are released in large numbers from their stores but they are short-lived cells.

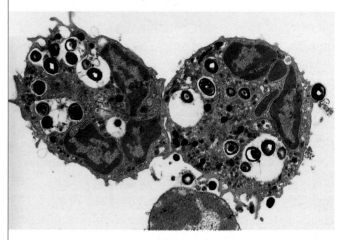

● **Figure 16.2** TEM of two neutrophils that have ingested several *Staphylococcus* bacteria. Notice at the extreme right one bacterium being engulfed. Compare this photograph with *figure 16.3* (×7500).

Macrophages are also phagocytes but are larger then neutrophils and tend to be found in organs, such as the lungs, liver, spleen, kidney and lymph nodes, rather than remaining in the blood. They leave the bone marrow and travel in the blood as **monocytes**, which develop into macrophages once they leave the blood and settle in the organs, removing any foreign matter found there.

Macrophages are long-lived cells and play a crucial role in *initiating* immune responses since they do not destroy pathogens completely, but cut them up to display antigens that can be recognised by lymphocytes.

Phagocytosis

If pathogens invade the body and cause an infection, some of the cells under attack respond by releasing chemicals such as **histamine**. These, with any chemicals released by the pathogens themselves, attract passing neutrophils to the site. The neutrophils destroy the pathogens by phagocytosis (*figures 4.11a* and *16.3*).

The neutrophils move towards the pathogens, which may be clustered together and covered in antibodies. This further stimulates the neutrophils to attack them. This is because neutrophils have receptor proteins on their surfaces that recognise antibody molecules and attach to them. When this happens the neutrophil's plasma membrane engulfs the pathogen and traps it within a vacuole. Digestive enzymes are secreted into the vacuole so destroying the pathogen.

Neutrophils have a short life – after killing and digesting some pathogens, they die. Dead neutrophils often collect at a site of infection to form pus.

Lymphocytes

Lymphocytes are smaller than phagocytes. They have a large nucleus that fills most of the cell (*figure 16.1*). There are two types of lymphocyte, both of which are produced before birth in bone marrow.

- **B lymphocytes (B cells)** remain in the bone marrow until they are mature and then spread throughout the body concentrating in lymph nodes and the spleen.
- **T lymphocytes (T cells)** leave the bone marrow and collect in the **thymus** where they mature. The thymus is a gland that lies in the chest just beneath the sternum. It doubles in size between birth and puberty, but after puberty it shrinks. Only mature lymphocytes can carry out immune responses. During the

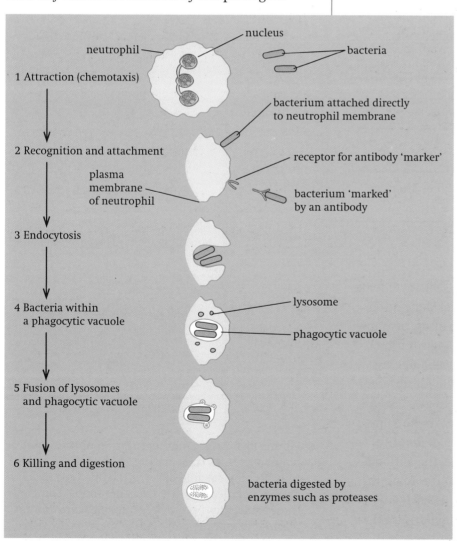

● **Figure 16.3** The stages of phagocytosis.

1 Attraction (chemotaxis)
2 Recognition and attachment
3 Endocytosis
4 Bacteria within a phagocytic vacuole
5 Fusion of lysosomes and phagocytic vacuole
6 Killing and digestion

neutrophil — nucleus — bacteria
bacterium attached directly to neutrophil membrane
plasma membrane of neutrophil — receptor for antibody 'marker'
bacterium 'marked' by an antibody
lysosome — phagocytic vacuole
bacteria digested by enzymes such as proteases

maturation process many different types of B and T lymphocyte develop, perhaps many millions. As we have seen, each type is specialised to respond to one antigen, giving the immune system as a whole the ability to respond to almost any type of pathogen that enters the body. When mature, all these B and T cells circulate between the blood and the lymph (chapter 8). This ensures that they are distributed throughout the body so that they come into contact with any pathogens *and* with each other. Immune responses depend on B and T cells interacting with each other to give an effective defence. We will look in detail at the roles of B and T cells and how they interact in the following section. Briefly, however, some T cells coordinate the immune response, stimulating B cells to divide and then secrete antibodies into the blood; these antibodies destroy the antigenic pathogens. Other T cells seek out and kill any of the body's own cells that are infected with pathogens. To do this they must make direct contact with infected cells.

SAQ 16.3

State the sites of origin and maturation of B lymphocytes (B cells) and T lymphocytes (T cells).

SAQ 16.4

Suggest why the thymus gland becomes smaller after puberty.

B lymphocytes

As each B cell matures it gains the ability to make just one type of antibody molecule. Many different types of B cell develop in each of us, perhaps as many as 10 million. During the maturation process, the genes that code for antibodies are changed in a variety of ways to code for different antibodies. Each cell then divides to give a small number of cells that are able to make the same type of antibody. Each small group of identical cells is called a **clone**. At this stage, the antibody molecules do not leave the B cell but remain in the plasma membrane. Here, part of each antibody forms a protein **receptor**, which can combine specifically with one type of antigen. If that antigen enters the body, there will be some

mature B cells with cell surface receptors that will recognise it (*figure 16.4*).

Figure 16.5 shows what happens to B cells during the immune response when an antigen enters the body on two separate occasions. When the pathogens first invade the body, some of them are taken up by macrophages in lymph nodes (chapter 8) and elsewhere. The macrophages expose the antigens from the pathogen on their surfaces. Any B lymphocytes whose cell surface receptors fit the antigens respond by dividing repeatedly by mitosis (chapter 6). Huge numbers of identical B cells are produced over a few weeks.

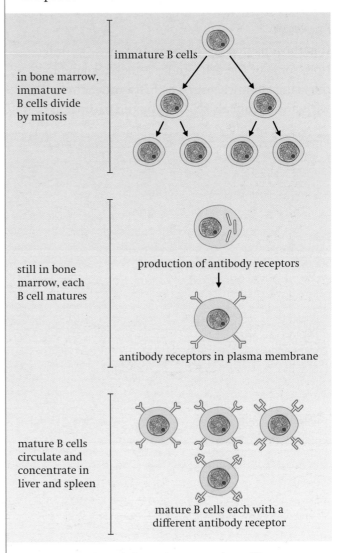

immature B cells

in bone marrow, immature B cells divide by mitosis

still in bone marrow, each B cell matures

production of antibody receptors

antibody receptors in plasma membrane

mature B cells circulate and concentrate in liver and spleen

mature B cells each with a different antibody receptor

● **Figure 16.4** Origin and maturation of B lymphocytes. As they mature in bone marrow, the cells become capable of secreting one type of antibody molecule with a specific shape. Some of these molecules become receptor proteins in the plasma membrane and act like markers. By the time of birth, there are millions of different B cells, each with a specific antibody receptor.

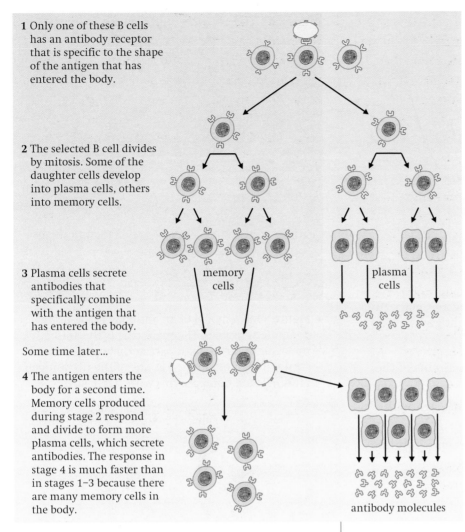

1 Only one of these B cells has an antibody receptor that is specific to the shape of the antigen that has entered the body.

2 The selected B cell divides by mitosis. Some of the daughter cells develop into plasma cells, others into memory cells.

3 Plasma cells secrete antibodies that specifically combine with the antigen that has entered the body.

Some time later...

4 The antigen enters the body for a second time. Memory cells produced during stage 2 respond and divide to form more plasma cells, which secrete antibodies. The response in stage 4 is much faster than in stages 1–3 because there are many memory cells in the body.

memory cells

plasma cells

antibody molecules

● **Figure 16.5** The function of B lymphocytes during an immune response. Compare with *figure 16.7*.

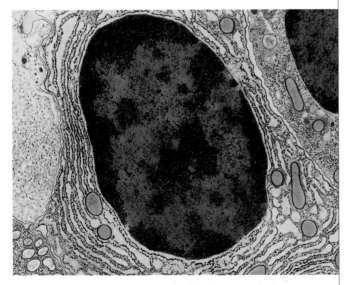

● **Figure 16.6** TEM of the contents of a plasma cell. There is an extensive network of RER (green) in the cytoplasm for the production of antibody molecules, which plasma cells secrete into blood or lymph by exocytosis (chapter 4).

Some of these activated B cells become **plasma cells** that produce antibody molecules very quickly – up to several thousand a second. Plasma cells secrete antibodies into the blood, lymph or onto the linings of the lungs and the gut (*figure 16.6*). These cells do not live long: after several weeks their numbers decrease. The antibody molecules they have secreted stay in the blood for longer, however, until they too eventually decrease in concentration.

Other B cells become **memory cells**. These cells remain circulating in the body for a long time. If the same antigen is reintroduced a few weeks or months after the first infection, memory cells divide rapidly and develop into plasma cells and more memory cells. This is repeated on every subsequent invasion by the same antigen, meaning that the infection can be destroyed and removed before any symptoms of disease develop.

Figure 16.7 shows the changes in the concentration of antibody molecules in the blood when the body encounters an antigen. The first or **primary response** is slow because, at this stage, there are very few B cells that are specific to the antigen. The **secondary response** is faster because there are now many memory cells, which quickly divide and differentiate into plasma cells. Many more antibodies are produced in the secondary response.

Memory cells are the basis of **immunological memory**; they last for many years, often a lifetime. This explains why someone is very unlikely to catch measles twice. There is only one strain of the virus that causes measles and each time it infects the body there is a fast secondary response. However, we do suffer repeated infections of the common cold and influenza because

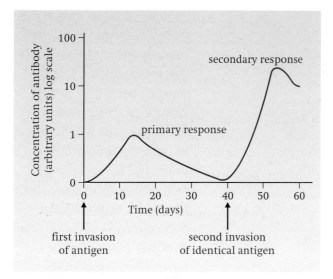

● **Figure 16.7** The changes in antibody concentration in the blood during a primary and secondary response to the same antigen.

there are many different and new strains of the viruses that cause these diseases, each one having different antigens. Each time a pathogen with different antigens infects us, the primary response must occur before we become immune and during that time we often become ill.

Antibodies

Antibodies are all globular glycoproteins (chapter 2) and form the group of plasma proteins called **immunoglobulins**. The basic molecule common to all antibodies consists of four polypeptide chains: two 'long' or 'heavy' chains and two 'short' or 'light' chains (*figures 16.8* and *16.9*). Disulphide bridges hold the chains together. Each molecule has two identical antigen binding sites which are formed by both light and heavy chains. The sequences of amino acids in these regions make the specific three-dimensional shape which binds to just one type of antigen. This is the **variable region** which is different on each type of antibody molecule produced. The 'hinge' region gives the flexibility for the antibody molecule to bind around the antigen.

Figure 16.10 shows the different ways in which antibodies work to protect the body from pathogens. As we saw earlier, some antibodies act as labels to identify antigens as appropriate targets for phagocytes to destroy. A special group of antibodies are **antitoxins** which block the

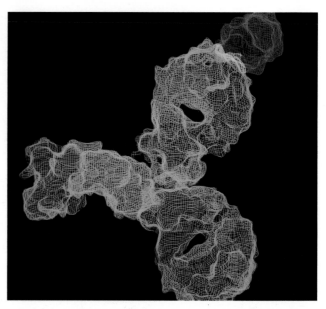

● **Figure 16.8** A model of an antibody made using computer graphics. The main part is the antibody molecule and the small part in the top right-hand corner (red) is an antigen at one of the two antigen binding sites. Compare this with *figure 16.9*.

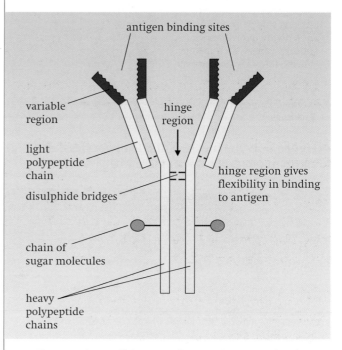

● **Figure 16.9** A diagram of an antibody molecule. Antigen–antibody binding occurs at the variable regions. An antigen fits into the binding site like a substrate fitting into the active site of an enzyme.

toxins released by bacteria such as those that cause diphtheria and tetanus.

Table 16.1 shows the four classes of antibody. Even though they have different structures, these different classes of antibody share common sub-units in their structure. The variable regions

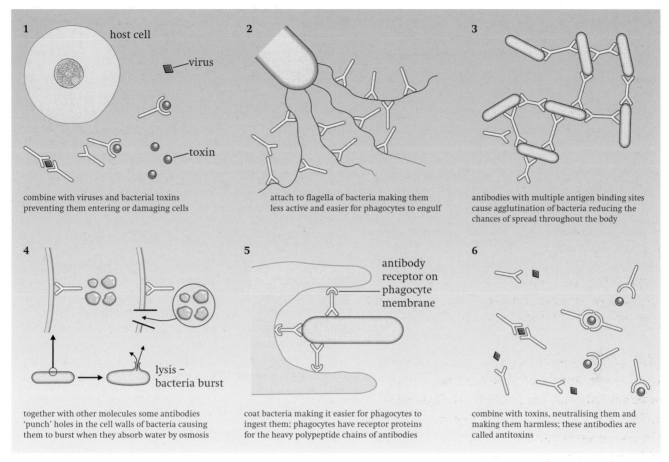

1 host cell — virus — toxin

combine with viruses and bacterial toxins preventing them entering or damaging cells

2

attach to flagella of bacteria making them less active and easier for phagocytes to engulf

3

antibodies with multiple antigen binding sites cause agglutination of bacteria reducing the chances of spread throughout the body

4

lysis – bacteria burst

together with other molecules some antibodies 'punch' holes in the cell walls of bacteria causing them to burst when they absorb water by osmosis

5 antibody receptor on phagocyte membrane

coat bacteria making it easier for phagocytes to ingest them; phagocytes have receptor proteins for the heavy polypeptide chains of antibodies

6

combine with toxins, neutralising them and making them harmless; these antibodies are called antitoxins

● **Figure 16.10** The functions of antibodies. Antibodies have different functions according to the type of antigen to which they bind.

show great diversity, but the constant regions of the heavy chains in each class are the same and carry out the same functions. For example, the heavy chains of IgE bind to receptors on some of our cells, especially a type known as **mast cells**, triggering them to release histamine and cause inflammation (page 233).

SAQ 16.5

Explain how plasma B cells are adapted to secrete large quantities of antibody molecules.

SAQ 16.6

Explain why B cells divide by mitosis during an immune response.

SAQ 16.7

Explain why polysaccharides would not be suitable for making antibody molecules.

SAQ 16.8

Explain why only some B cells respond during an immune response to a pathogen.

SAQ 16.9

There are many different strains of the rhinovirus, which causes the common cold. Explain why people can catch several different colds in the space of a few months.

T lymphocytes

Mature T cells have specific cell surface receptors called T cell receptors (*figure 16.11*). These have a structure similar to antibodies and they are each specific to one antigen. T cells are activated when they encounter this antigen in contact with another host cell. Sometimes this is a macrophage that has engulfed a pathogen and cut it up to expose the pathogen's surface molecules or it may be a body cell that has been invaded by a

Antibody class	Relative molecular mass	Number of antigen binding sites	Sites of action	Functions
Immunoglobulin G (IgG)	150 000	2	blood tissue fluid (can cross placenta)	• enhances activity of macrophages • act as antitoxins • causes agglutination
Immunoglobulin M (IgM)	970 000	10	blood tissue fluid (cannot cross placenta)	• causes agglutination
Immunoglobulin A (IgA)	160 000 or 320 000	2 or 4	saliva, tears bronchial secretions mucus secretions of small intestine prostate and vaginal secretions nasal fluid colostrum/breast milk	• inhibits bacteria adhering to host cells • prevents bacteria forming colonies on mucous membranes
Immunoglobulin E (IgE)	180 000	2	tissues	• heavy chains of IgE activate mast cells to release histamine • involved in response to infections by worms, and allergic responses to harmless substances, e.g. pollen (hay fever)

● **Table 16.1** The four different classes of antibody and their functions. Whatever the class of antibody, each antibody molecule produced by a single clone of plasma cells possesses just one type of variable region and binds to one antigen.

pathogen and is similarly displaying the antigen on its plasma membrane as a kind of 'help' signal. Those T cells that have matching receptors respond to the antigen by dividing.

There are two main types of T cell:

■ **T helper cells**;
■ **killer T cells** (or T cytotoxic cells).

When T helper cells are activated they release hormone-like **cytokines** that stimulate appropriate B cells to divide, develop into plasma cells and secrete antibodies. Some T helper cells secrete cytokines that stimulate macrophages to carry out phagocytosis more vigorously. Killer T cells search the body for cells that have become invaded by pathogens and are displaying foreign antigens from the pathogens on their plasma membranes. Killer T cells recognise the antigens, attach themselves to the surface of infected cells and secrete toxic

substances, such as hydrogen peroxide, killing the body cells and the pathogens inside (*figure 16.12*).

In addition to the helper cells and killer cells, **memory** T cells are produced which remain in the body and become active very quickly during the secondary response to antigens.

SAQ 16.10

Explain why people are often ill for several weeks after they catch a disease, even though they can make antibodies against the disease.

SAQ 16.11

Outline the functions of B lymphocytes and T lymphocytes and describe how they interact during an immune response.

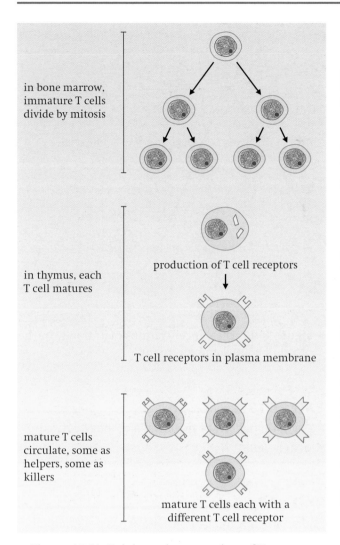

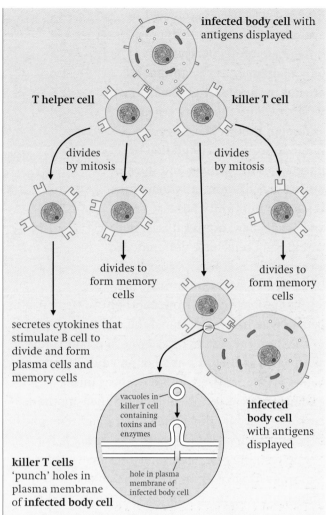

● **Figure 16.11** Origin and maturation of T lymphocytes. As T cells mature in the thymus gland they produce T cell receptor proteins. Each cell has a specific receptor. Some cells become T helper cells, others become killer T cells.

● **Figure 16.12** The functions of T lymphocytes during an immune response. T helper cells and killer T cells with T cell receptor proteins specific to the antigen respond and divide by mitosis. Activated T helper cells stimulate B cells to divide and develop into plasma cells (*figure 16.5*). Killer T cells attach themselves to infected cells and kill them.

Active and passive immunity

The type of immunity described so far occurs during the course of an infection. This form of immunity is **active** because lymphocytes are activated by antigens on the surface of pathogens that have invaded the body. As this activation occurs naturally during an infection it is called **natural active immunity**. The immune response can also be activated artificially either by injecting antigens into the body or taking them by mouth. This is the basis of **artificial active immunity**, more commonly known as **vaccination**. The immune response is similar to that following an infection, and the effect is the same – long-term immunity. In both natural and artificial active immunity anti-

body concentrations in the blood follow patterns similar to those shown in *figure 16.7*.

In both forms of active immunity, it takes time for sufficient active B and T cells to be produced to give an effective defence. If a person becomes infected with a potentially fatal disease such as tetanus, a more immediate defence is needed for survival. Tetanus kills quickly, before the body's natural primary response can take place. So people who have a wound that may be infected with the bacterium that causes tetanus are given an injection of **antitoxin**. This is a preparation of human antibodies against the tetanus toxin. The antibodies are collected from blood donors who have recently been vaccinated against tetanus. Antitoxin provides immediate protection but this is only temporary as the antibodies are not produced by the body's own B cells and are therefore regarded as foreign themselves. They are removed from the circulation by phagocytes in the liver and spleen.

This type of immunity to tetanus is **passive immunity** because the B and T cells have not been activated and plasma cells have not produced any antibodies. More specifically, it is **artificial passive immunity**: the antibodies have come from another person who has encountered the antigen.

The immune system of a newborn infant is not as effective as that of a child or an adult. However, babies are not entirely unprotected against pathogens because antibodies from their mothers cross the placenta during pregnancy and remain in the infant for several months (*figure 16.13*). For example, antibodies against measles may last for four months or more in the infant's blood. **Colostrum**, the thick yellowish fluid produced by a mother's breasts for the first four or five days after birth, is rich in IgA. Some of these antibodies remain on the surface of the infant's gut wall while others pass into the blood undigested. IgA acts in the gut to prevent the growth of bacteria and viruses and also circulates in the blood. This is **natural passive immunity**. The features of active and passive immunity are compared in *table 16.2*.

SAQ 16.12

Explain the difference between artificial active immunisation (vaccination) and artificial passive immunisation.

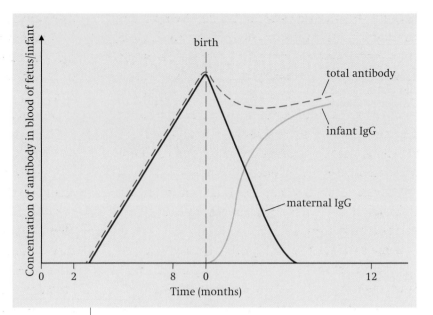

● **Figure 16.13** The concentrations of antibody in the blood of a fetus and an infant.

SAQ 16.13

Explain the pattern of maternal and infant IgG shown in *figure 16.13*.

SAQ 16.14

Explain the advantages of natural passive immunity for newborn infants.

Vaccination

A **vaccine** is a preparation containing antigenic material, which may be a whole live micro-organism, a dead one, a harmless version (known as an attenuated organism), a harmless form of a toxin (toxoid) or a preparation of surface antigens. Vaccines are either given by injection into a vein or muscle, or are taken orally.

Immunity derived from a natural infection is often extremely good at providing protection

Immunity		Features			
	antigen encountered	immune response	time before antibodies appear in blood	production of memory cells	protection
Active	yes	yes	several weeks during primary response	yes	permanent
Passive	no	no	immediate	no	temporary

● **Table 16.2** Features of active and passive immunity.

because the immune system has met living organisms which persist inside the body for some time, so that the immune system has time to develop an effective response. When possible, vaccination tries to mimic this. Sometimes this works very well, when vaccines contain live microorganisms. The microorganisms reproduce, albeit rather slowly, so that the immune system is continually presented with a large dose of antigens. Less effective are those vaccines that do not mimic an infection because they are made from dead bacteria or viruses.

Some vaccines are highly effective and one injection may well give a lifetime's protection. Less effective ones need booster injections to stimulate secondary responses that give enhanced protection (*figure 16.7*). It is often a good idea to receive booster injections if you are likely to be exposed to a disease, even though you may have been vaccinated as a child.

Problems with vaccines

Poor response

Some people do not respond at all, or not very well, to vaccinations. This may be because they have a defective immune system and as a result do not develop the necessary B and T cell clones. It may also be because they suffer from malnutrition, particularly protein energy malnutrition (chapter 12), and do not have enough protein to make antibodies or clones of lymphocytes. These people are at a high risk of developing infectious diseases and transmitting them to people who have no immunity.

People vaccinated with a live virus may pass it out in their faeces during the primary response and may infect others. This is why it is better to vaccinate a large number of people at the same time to give **herd immunity**, or to ensure that all children are vaccinated within a few months of birth. Herd immunity interrupts transmission in a population, so that those who are susceptible never encounter the infectious agents concerned.

Antigenic variation

In spite of years of research, there are no vaccines for the common cold. The type of rhinovirus that causes most colds has at least 113 different strains. It may be impossible to develop a vaccine that protects against all of these.

The influenza virus mutates regularly to give different antigens. When there are only minor changes in the viral antigen, memory cells will still recognise them and start a secondary response. These minor changes are called **antigenic drift**. More serious are major changes in antigen structure – known as **antigenic shift** – when influenza viruses change their antigens considerably and the protective immunity given by vaccination against a previous strain is ineffective against the new one. The World Health Organisation (WHO) recommends the type of vaccine to use according to the antigens that are common at the time. The vaccine is changed almost every year.

There are, as yet, no effective vaccines against the diseases which are caused by protoctists such as malaria and sleeping sickness. This is because these pathogens are eukaryotes with many more genes than bacteria and viruses. They can have many hundreds, or even thousands, of antigens on their cell surfaces. *Plasmodium* passes through three stages in its life cycle while it is in the human host. Each stage has its own specific antigens. This means that effective vaccines would have to contain antigens to all three stages or be specific to the infective stage. The latter would only work if the immune system can give an effective response in the short period of time (a few hours) between the mosquito bite and the infection of liver cells (*figure 15.3*). *Trypanosoma*, the causative agent of sleeping sickness, has a total of about a thousand different antigens and changes them every four or five days. This makes it impossible for the immune system to respond effectively. After several weeks the body is completely overwhelmed by the parasite, with fatal consequences.

SAQ 16.15
Explain why malnourished children give very weak responses to vaccines.

SAQ 16.16
Explain why humans cannot produce an effective immune response to an infection by *Trypanosoma*.

Antigenic concealment

Some pathogens evade attack by the immune system by living inside cells. For example when *Plasmodium* enters liver cells or red blood cells, it is protected against antibodies in the plasma. Some parasitic worms conceal themselves by covering their bodies in host proteins, so they remain invisible to the immune system. Other pathogens suppress the immune system by parasitising cells such as macrophages and T cells. It is very difficult to develop effective vaccines against these pathogens because there is such a short period of time for an immune response to occur before the pathogen 'hides'.

Another example is *Vibrio cholerae* (the causative agent of cholera), which remains in the intestine where it is beyond the reach of many antibodies. The cholera vaccine is injected rather than taken orally and so it is unable to stimulate antibody production in the intestine, nor can it stimulate the production of an antitoxin against choleragen. An oral vaccine against cholera is currently being developed.

SAQ. 16.17

Name one pathogen that parasitises
a macrophages and **b** T helper cells.

The eradication of smallpox

Smallpox was an acute, highly infectious disease caused by the variola virus and transmitted by direct contact. It was a terrible disease. Red spots containing a transparent fluid would appear all over the body (*figure 16.14*). These then filled with thick pus. Eyelids became swollen and could become 'glued' together. Sufferers often had to be prevented from tearing at their flesh. Many people who recovered were permanently blind and disfigured by scabs left when the pustules dried out. Smallpox killed between 12 and 30% of its victims.

WHO started an eradication programme in 1956; in 1967 it stated its intention to rid the world of the disease within ten years. There were two main aspects of the programme: vaccination and surveillance. Successful attempts were made across the world to vaccinate in excess of 80% of populations at risk of the disease. When a case of

● **Figure 16.14** A parent and child of the Kampa people of the Amazon region, South America. They clearly show the characteristic pustules of smallpox.

smallpox was reported, everyone in the household and the 30 surrounding households, as well as other relatives and possible contacts in the area, were vaccinated. This **ring vaccination** protected everyone who could possibly have come into contact with a person with the disease, reduced the chances of transmission and contained the disease. The last strongholds of smallpox were in East Africa, Afghanistan and the Indian subcontinent. Eradication was most difficult in Ethiopia and Somalia, where many people lived in remote districts well away from main roads which were no more than dirt tracks. In the late 1970s the two countries went to war and, even though large parts of Ethiopia were overrun by the Somalis, the eradication programme continued. The last case of smallpox was reported in Somalia in 1977. WHO finally declared the world free of smallpox in 1980.

The eradication programme was successful for a number of reasons.

■ The variola virus was stable; it did not mutate and change its surface antigens. This meant that the same vaccine could be used everywhere in the world throughout the campaign.

It was therefore cheap to produce.

- The vaccine was made from a harmless strain of a similar virus (vaccinia) and was effective because it was a 'live' vaccine.
- The vaccine was freeze-dried and could be kept at high temperatures for as long as 6 months. This made it suitable for use in the tropics.
- Infected people were easy to identify.
- The vaccine was easy to administer and was even more effective after the development of a stainless steel, reusable needle for its delivery. This 'bifurcated needle' had two prongs, which were used to push the vaccine into the skin.
- The smallpox virus did not linger in the body after an infection to become active later and form a reservoir of infection.
- The virus did not infect animals, which made it easier to break the transmission cycle.
- Many 16- to 17-year-olds became enthusiastic vaccinators and suppliers of information about cases; this was especially valuable in remote areas.

The eradication of smallpox is a medical success story. It has been more difficult to repeat this success with other infectious diseases. This is partly because of the more unstable political situation in the late 1970s and 1980s particularly in Africa, Latin America and parts of Asia such as Afghanistan. Public health facilities are difficult to organise in developing countries with poor infrastructure, few trained personnel and limited financial resources. They are almost impossible to maintain during periods of civil unrest or during a war. Nevertheless, WHO declared the Americas to be free of polio in 1991 and vaccination programmes have been organised in Asia to try to eradicate the disease from the world (figure 16.15).

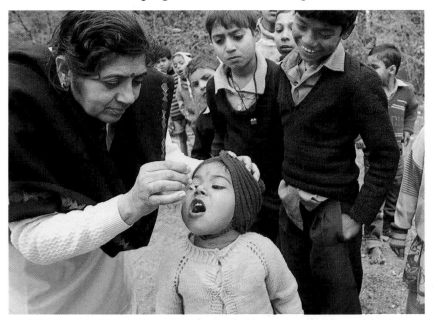

- **Figure 16.15** Indian children queuing to be given an oral vaccine against polio on 17th January 1999. The Indian government organised a programme to vaccinate 130 million children during the day in an attempt to eradicate the disease.

Measles

Measles is caused by a virus which is spread by airborne droplets. As we saw at the beginning of this chapter, it causes a rash and fever. There can be fatal complications. The disease rarely affects infants under eight months of age as they have passive immunity in the form of antibodies that have crossed the placenta from their mother. Measles used to be a common childhood disease in the UK and other developed countries, but is now quite rare because most children are vaccinated. However, epidemics do occur in the developed world, for example in the USA in 1989–90 when there were 55 000 cases and 132 deaths.

Measles is a major disease in developing countries, particularly in cities where people live in overcrowded, insanitary conditions and where there is a high birth rate. The measles virus is transmitted easily in these conditions and it infects mainly malnourished infants suffering from vitamin A deficiency. Measles is responsible for many cases of childhood blindness and it also causes severe brain damage, which can be fatal. In 1993 it was estimated that there were over 45 million cases of measles and 1.16 million deaths making it the ninth leading cause of death worldwide. Most of those who die from measles are young malnourished children who do not have the resistance to fight it.

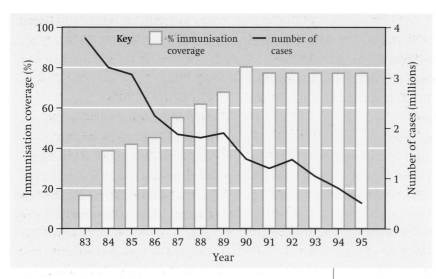

- **Figure 16.16** The global measles immunisation programme coordinated by WHO has increased the immunisation coverage to about 80% of young children. As a result, the number of cases reported each year has decreased significantly.

Measles is a preventable disease and one that can be eradicated by a worldwide surveillance and vaccination programme. However, a programme of one-dose-vaccination has not eliminated the disease in any country despite high coverage of the population. This is explained by the poor response to the vaccine shown by some children who need several boosters to develop full immunity. In large cities with high birth rates and shifting populations, it can be difficult to give boosters, follow up cases of measles and trace contacts. Migrants and refugees can form reservoirs of infection, experiencing epidemics within their communities and spreading the disease to surrounding populations. This makes measles a very difficult disease to eliminate even with high vaccination coverage.

Measles is highly infectious and it is estimated that herd immunity of 93–95% is required to prevent transmission in a population. As the currently available vaccine has a success rate of 95%, this means that the whole population needs to be vaccinated and infants must be vaccinated within about eight months of birth. Many countries achieve up to 80% or more coverage with measles vaccination (*figure 16.16*), and it is hoped to declare the Americas free of the disease early in the twenty-first century. With coverage of under 50% in Africa, it is likely that the disease will still persist there for many years to come.

Allergies

So far we have considered what happens when the immune system responds appropriately. Unfortunately, there are occasions when the immune system responds to harmless substances. Often the responses are exaggerated and lead to severe illness. Such overreactions of the immune system to a harmless antigen are known as **allergies**. Asthma, hay fever and eczema are allergic reactions which happen when the immune system responds to substances known as **allergens** that are antigenic, but do no real harm (chapter 14).

Allergens include such things as house dust, tiny particles of animal skin, pollen and the house-dust mite and its faeces (*figure 16.17*). When these particles are inhaled into the lungs the immune system recognises them as foreign and initiates an immune response. B cells produce antibodies belonging to the class IgE (*table 16.1*). These antibodies are normally involved in the body's defence against large parasites such as worms. IgE antibodies coat the surfaces of **mast cells** that are found in the lining of the airways. The body is now **sensitised** to these allergens.

When the allergen enters the body for a second time it binds to the IgE antibody molecules on the mast cells and stimulates them to release

- **Figure 16.17** The house-dust mite and its faeces: a common allergen for people with asthma. (×350)

histamine, which causes blood vessels to widen and become leaky. Fluid and white blood cells leave capillaries. The area affected becomes hot and red and is inflamed. This is similar to what happens when you have a cut that becomes infected. In hay fever the **inflammation** is restricted to the eyes, nose and throat. People who suffer badly from hay fever may have quite severe symptoms; however, the symptoms are not life-threatening and only occur at certain times of the year. In the UK, grass pollen is responsible for most attacks and so the hay fever season usually lasts from May to July. Asthma, however, is much more severe: attacks can occur at any time and may be fatal. Over a thousand people die from the disease every year in the UK.

People with asthma have airways that are nearly always inflamed. During an asthmatic attack this inflammation worsens. Fluid leaks from the blood into the airways and the goblet cells and mucous glands secrete large quantities of mucus (chapter 13). The smaller airways may become blocked with fluid. Muscles surrounding the trachea, bronchi and bronchioles contract, which narrows the airways and increases the resistance to air flow. Breathing becomes very difficult and sufferers experience wheezing, coughing, a tightness about the chest and shortage of breath (*figures 16.18* and *16.19*).

At present there is no cure for asthma. However, vaccines are being developed to make the allergic response less severe. These will work in a different way to the vaccines described earlier in this chapter. The vaccines will be designed to desensitise people so that they do not produce antibodies to allergens. Asthma appears to run in families, so genes play a part in determining who develops this disease. It may be possible to develop genetic

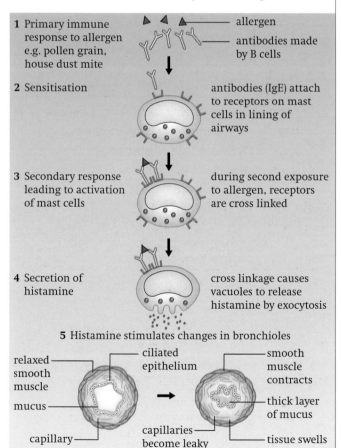

● **Figure 16.18** The sequence of events when a person becomes sensitised to an allergen and the subsequent allergic reaction during an asthmatic attack. The airways become very narrow so that breathing is difficult.

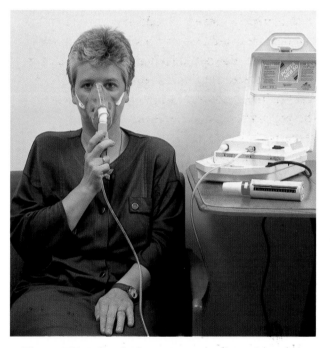

● **Figure 16.19** During an acute attack, asthmatics may relieve the symptoms by using a nebuliser to deliver a large dose of a bronchodilator drug into the lungs. The drug relaxes the muscles so that the airways widen and breathing becomes easier. This patient has a peak flow meter on the table next to her. Asthmatics blow into a peak flow meter to find out how well they are managing their condition. A high peak flow score means that air flows easily through the airways. This indicates that the airways are clear and unobstructed and that asthma is under control. A low score shows that treatment is not working well and that an asthmatic attack may be likely.

tests to identify those children who are at risk of developing asthma and offer a vaccine to prevent this happening.

Allergies are an emerging health problem. One in seven children in the UK has asthma and the number is increasing. It is estimated that 10% of the world's population suffer from this disease.

The reasons for this increase are complex, but environmental factors such as air pollution by sulphur dioxide and diesel fumes trigger asthma attacks. Studies have shown that passive smoking is closely linked to the development of asthma (chapter 14).

SUMMARY

◆ Phagocytes and lymphocytes are the cells of the immune system.

◆ Phagocytes originate in the bone marrow and are produced there throughout life. There are two types: neutrophils circulate in the blood and enter infected tissues; macrophages are more stationary inside tissues. They destroy bacteria and viruses by phagocytosis.

◆ Lymphocytes also originate in bone marrow, but migrate just before and after birth to other sites in the body. There are two types: B lymphocytes (B cells) and T lymphocytes (T cells).

◆ Antigens are 'foreign' macromolecules that stimulate the immune system.

◆ During an immune response, those B and T cells that have receptors specific to the antigen are activated.

◆ When B cells are activated they form plasma cells which secrete antibodies.

◆ T lymphocytes do not secrete antibodies; their surface receptors are similar to antibodies and identify antigens. They mature in the thymus and develop into either T helper cells or killer T cells (cytotoxic T cells). T helper cells secrete cytokines that control the immune system, activating B cells and killer T cells, which kill infected host cells.

◆ During an immune response, memory cells are formed which retain the ability to divide rapidly and develop into active B or T cells on a second exposure to the same antigen (immunological memory).

◆ Antibodies are globular glycoproteins. They all have one or more pairs of identical heavy polypeptides and of identical light polypeptides. Each type of antibody interacts with one antigen via the specific shape of its variable region. Each molecule of the simplest antibody (IgG) can bind to two antigen molecules. Larger antibodies (IgM and IgA) have more than two antigen binding sites.

◆ Antibodies agglutinate bacteria; prevent viruses infecting cells; coat bacteria and viruses to aid phagocytosis; act with plasma proteins to burst bacteria; neutralise toxins.

◆ Active immunity is the production of antibodies and active T cells during a primary immune response to an antigen acquired either naturally by infection or artificially by vaccination. This gives permanent immunity.

◆ Passive immunity is the introduction of antibodies either naturally across the placenta or in breast milk, or artificially by injection.

◆ Vaccination confers artificial active immunity by introducing a small quantity of an antigen by injection or by mouth. This may be a whole living organism, a dead one, a harmless version of a toxin (toxoid) or a preparation of surface antigens.

◆ It is difficult to develop successful vaccines against diseases caused by organisms that have many different strains, or express different antigens during their life cycle within humans (antigenic variation), or infect parts of the body beyond the reach of antibodies (antigenic concealment).

◆ Smallpox was eradicated by a programme of surveillance, contact tracing and 'ring' vaccination, using a 'live' vaccine against the only strain of the smallpox virus.

◆ Measles is a common cause of death amongst infants in poor communities. It is difficult to eradicate because a wide coverage of vaccination has not been achieved and malnourished children do not respond well to just one dose of the vaccine.

◆ Allergies are caused by immune responses to harmless substances known as allergens, such as dust, the house-dust mite and its faeces, and pollen. Once sensitised to an allergen, a person's mast cells are stimulated to release histamine. This chemical triggers inflammation, narrowing the airways and making breathing difficult. Inhalers and nebulisers can ease asthmatic symptoms. Desensitisation by vaccine is the long-term aim for treatment.

Questions

1 Explain the difference between the following pairs of terms:
   a **antigen** and **antibody**;
   b **active** and **passive immunity**;
   c **natural** and **artificial immunity**.

2 Discuss the roles of phagocytes and lymphocytes in defence against pathogens.

3 Describe the events that occur during an immune response.

4 Explain how the immune system recognises many thousands of different antigens.

5 Explain why someone may be injected with a preparation of antibodies.

6 Explain how a new vaccine might be tested before becoming generally available.

7 Explain how vaccination was used in the programme to eradicate smallpox.

8 Explain what is meant by herd immunity.

9 Discuss the problems involved in developing vaccines for cholera, malaria, AIDS and TB.

10 Discuss the social and economic problems involved in using vaccination to eradicate measles.

11 Explain why some people suffer from allergies such as hay fever and asthma.

Amino acid R groups

The general formula for an amino acid is shown in *figure 2.15*. In the list below, only the R groups are shown; the rest of the amino acid molecule is represented by a block.

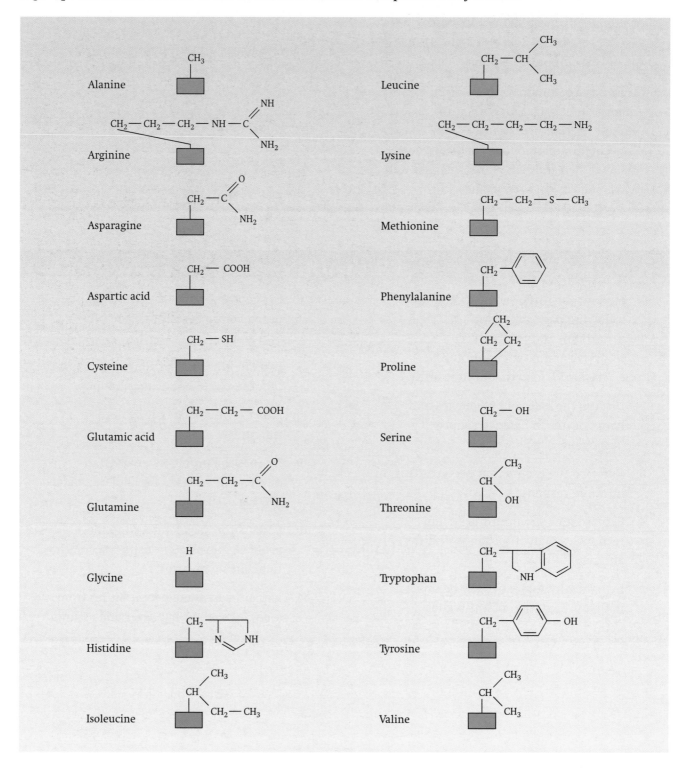

DNA triplet codes

The table shows all the possible triplets of bases in a DNA molecule and what each codes for. The 3-letter abbreviations for each amino acid are, in most cases, the first three letters of their full name – see Appendix 1.

first position	Second position				Third position
	A	G	T	C	
A	Phe	Ser	Tyr	Cys	A
	Phe	Ser	Tyr	Cys	G
	Leu	Ser	STOP	STOP	T
	Leu	Ser	STOP	Trp	C
G	Leu	Pro	His	Arg	A
	Leu	Pro	His	Arg	G
	Leu	Pro	Gln	Arg	T
	Leu	Pro	Gln	Arg	C
T	Ile	Thr	Asn	Ser	A
	Ile	Thr	Asn	Ser	G
	Ile	Thr	Lys	Arg	T
	Met	Thr	Lys	Arg	C
C	Val	Ala	Asp	Gly	A
	Val	Ala	Asp	Gly	G
	Val	Ala	Glu	Gly	T
	Val	Ala	Glu	Gly	C

Answers to self-assessment questions

Chapter 1

1.1 Structures found in both animal and plant cells: nucleus with nucleolus and chromatin; cytoplasm containing mitochondria, Golgi apparatus and other small structures; plasma membrane. Structure found only in animal cells: centriole. Structures found only in plant cells: chloroplasts, large central vacuole, cell wall with middle lamella and plasmodesmata.

1.2   **a** Actual diameter = 20 μm (see caption)
Diameter on diagram = 60 mm = 60 000 μm
Magnification = size of image ÷ size of specimen = 60 000 ÷ 20
Therefore magnification = ×3000
  b Magnification = ×80 000 (see caption)
Length on micrograph = 65 mm = 65 000 μm
Size of specimen = size of image ÷ magnification = 65 000 ÷ 80 000
Therefore actual size of chloroplast = 0.8125 μm

1.3 Resolution of a microscope is limited by the radiation used to view the specimen. Resolution equals half the wavelength of the radiation used. Shortest wavelength of light is 400 nm; therefore resolution of a light microscope is 200 nm. Diameter of ribosome is much smaller than this, namely 22 nm.

1.4 Detail seen with electron microscope: in the **nucleus**, chromatin can be distinguished; the nucleus is seen to be surrounded by a double membrane with **pores** in it; **mitochondria** have surrounding double membrane, the inner layer forming folds pointing inwards; **endoplasmic reticulum** is extensive throughout cell, some with **ribosomes** and some without; small structures seen under the light microscope can be distinguished as **lysosomes** and **vesicles**; free **ribosomes** seen throughout cell; **centriole** consists of two structures. (The microvilli seen on *figure 1.11* are not characteristic of all cells.)

1.5 Details seen with electron microscope: in the **nucleus**, chromatin can be distinguished; **nuclear membrane** can be seen as a double structure, continuous with rough endoplasmic reticulum, and with pores in it; there is extensive **rough** and **smooth endoplasmic reticulum** throughout cell; free **ribosomes** in cytoplasm; **mitochondria** have double membrane, the inner layer having folds into matrix in middle; **chloroplasts** have double outer membrane; **grana** can be seen as stacks of double membrane sacs connected to other grana by longer sacs.

1.6 **plasma membrane**: essential because it forms a partially permeable barrier between the cell and its environment, regulating movement of materials into and out of the cell. This is necessary to maintain an environment inside the cell which is different from that outside the cell.
cytoplasm: site of metabolic activity; contains biochemicals in solution.
ribosomes: sites of protein synthesis, an essential activity of all cells. (DNA controls cells by controlling which proteins are made.) Protein synthesis is a complex process involving the interaction of many molecules – the ribosome provides a site where this can happen in an organised way.
DNA: the genetic material. Contains the information which controls the activities of the cell. Has the ability to replicate itself, enabling new cells to be formed.
cell wall (absent in animal cells): prevents the cell from bursting if it is exposed to a solution of higher water potential.

1.7 a The cilia sweep mucus, secreted by goblet cells also present in the epithelium, up towards the throat where it is swallowed. The mucus traps bacteria and other particles that may be present in air that is breathed in, and so reduces the chance of infection in, or damage to, the lungs.

b The cilia sweep the egg, and also the zygote if the egg is fertilised, along the oviduct towards the uterus.

Chapter 2

2.1 a $C_3H_6O_3$ or $(CH_2O)_3$ b $C_5H_{10}O_5$ or $(CH_2O)_5$

2.2 a To ensure that *all* of the sugar reacts with the Benedict's.

b FIrst, carry out the test, using excess Benedict's solution, on a range of samples of known concentration of reducing sugar. Each sample must be of the same volume, and the test carried out in exactly the same way. If you have a colorimeter, take a reading for each concentration and plot reading against concentration a graph. If you do not have a colorimeter, line the tubes up in a rack.

Then carry out the test in exactly the same way on your unknown sample. If using a colorimeter, obtain a reading for it and use the graph to read off the concentration. If not, hold against the row of samples and judge which is the closest match by eye.

Alternatively, you can filter the contents of the tube, and dry and mass the precipitate obtained. Once again, you can compare the results from your unknown solution with those from a range of known ones.

2.3 First, carry out the test for reducing sugar. If this is negative, then test for non-reducing sugar.

If it is positive, ensure that you have added excess Benedict's reagent, that is, ensure that *all* of the reducing sugar has reacted. Then filter the contents of the tube, and save the filtrate. If there is any non-reducing sugar present, this is where it will be. Test the filtrate for non-reducing sugar.

2.4 Hydrolysis

2.5 1 macromolecules/polymers
2 polysaccharides
3 made from α-glucose
4 glucose units held together by 1, 4 links (glycosidic bonds formed by condensation)
5 branches formed by 1, 6 links

2.6

amylose	cellulose
made from α-glucose	made from β-glucose
all glucose units have the same orientation	successive glucose units are at 180° to each other
molecule is not fibrous – chains not attracted to each other	fibrous molecule – chains held together by hydrogen bonds to form microfibrils and fibres.

2.7 At one end of the chain of amino acids; also in the R groups of many of the amino acids in the chain.

2.8

	property	importance
a	Water requires a relatively large amount of heat energy to evaporate, that is water has a high heat of vapourisation.	Heat energy which is transferred to water molecules in sweat allows them to evaporate from the skin, which cools down, helping to prevent the body from overheating. A relatively large amount of heat can be lost with mimimal loss of water from the body.
b	The solid form of water (ice) is less dense than the liquid form and so floats.	Bodies of water such as lakes start to freeze from the top down. Ice insulates the water below it, increasing the chance of survival of organisms in the water.
c	High surface tension.	Small insects can land on, or live on, water without drowning. This increases the range of habitats available for feeding, reproduction (especially if aquatic larvae), etc.
d	Solvent.	Needed for transport by diffusion or active transport into, out of, or within cells. Also for circulation in blood so that nutrients can reach the sites where they are needed. Chemical reactions take place in aqueous solution.

Chapter 3

3.1 In case of inaccuracy of measurement at 30 seconds. The shape of the curve is more likely to give an accurate value.

3.2 See figure.

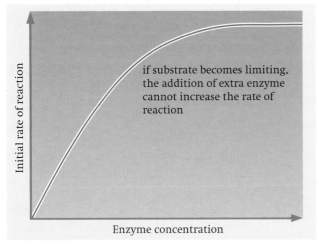

if substrate becomes limiting, the addition of extra enzyme cannot increase the rate of reaction

Initial rate of reaction (vertical axis)

Enzyme concentration (horizontal axis)

● **Answer for** SAQ 3.2

3.3 a See figure.

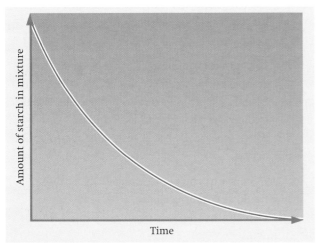

Amount of starch in mixture (vertical axis)

Time (horizontal axis)

● **Answer for** SAQ 3.3a

  b Calculate the slope of the curve right at the beginning of the reaction.

3.4 Measure the volume of oxygen given off over time for several hydrogen peroxide–catalase reactions at different temperatures. In each case, all conditions other than temperature must remain constant. In particular, the same volume of hydrogen peroxide and of catalase solutions should be used each time. Plot total volume of oxygen against time for each reaction. Calculate the slope of the line at the beginning of the reaction in each case to give the initial reaction rate. Then plot initial reaction rate against time.

3.5 a Haemoglobin colours blood stains. Protein-digesting enzymes hydrolyse haemoglobin to amino acids, which are colourless. They are also soluble, so will wash away in water.

  b Many protein-digesting enzymes have an optimum temperature of around 40 °C.

  c Other components of washing powders, such as the oil-removing detergents, work best at high temperatures.

3.6 One possible answer is as follows; other answers might be equally acceptable.

  Set up two sets of five tubes containing equal volumes of the same concentration of milk suspension. Make up five buffer solutions of varying pH. Add equal volumes of buffer solution to the milk suspension, two of each pH. To one set of tubes, add equal volumes of trypsin solution. To the other set of tubes, add the same volume of water; these act as controls. Time the disappearance of cloudiness in each tube. Plot rate of reaction (1/time taken) against pH.

Chapter 4

4.1 Large number of possible reasons, e.g. gain nutrients, remove waste products, gain oxygen for respiration, secrete hormones, secrete enzymes, maintain constant pH and ionic concentration.

4.2 Water potentials are equal.

4.3 a The pure water or dilute solution.

  b The concentrated solution.

  c The solution with the same concentration as the red cell.

4.4 a From A to B.

  b Water molecules can move from A to B and from B to A, but more move from A to B in a given time period. Overall therefore, A loses water and B gains water – the overall movement is the net movement.

  c A has a higher water potential than B (−250 is less negative than −400) and water always moves from regions of higher to lower water potential. Water crosses a partially permeable plasma membrane every time it enters or leaves a cell – this process is called osmosis.

  d (i) Pure water has a water potential of zero, which is higher than that of cells A and B. There is therefore a net movement of water into cells A and B by osmosis through their partially permeable plasma membranes. As water enters, the volume of the protoplasts will increase, exerting pressure on the cell walls and raising the pressure potential of the cells. This increases the water potential of the cells. This will continue until an equilibrium is reached when the contents of the cell reach the same water potential as the water, namely zero. The cells will then be turgid.

(ii) A $1 \, mol \, dm^{-3}$ sucrose solution has a lower water potential than that of cells A and B. There is therefore a net movement of water out of cells A and B by osmosis through their partially permeable plasma membranes. As water leaves the cells, the protoplasts shrink and the pressure they exert on the cell walls drops; in other words the pressure potential of the cells decreases. This decreases the water potential of the cells. Eventually the pressure potential drops to zero and the cells are at incipient plasmolysis. As shrinkage continues, the protoplasts pull away from the cell walls – this is plasmolysis. The sucrose solution can pass freely through the permeable cell walls and remains in contact with the protoplasts. As water leaves the cells, the contents of the protoplasts get more and more concentrated and their water potential gets lower and lower (more and more negative). Equilibrium is reached when the water potential of the cells equals that of the sucrose solution.

4.5 The animal cell does not have a cell wall. Plasmolysis is the pulling away of cytoplasm from the cell wall.

4.6 Five – into and then out of a cell in the alveolar wall, into and then out of a cell in the capillary wall, and then into a red blood cell.

4.7 Large surface area – increases the number of molecules or ions that can cross the surface in a given time.

Thin barriers across which substances cross – decreases the time taken for the molecules or ions to cross them.

Chapter 5

5.1 a ATP, which phosphorylates the nucleotides, providing energy to drive the reaction.
DNA polymerase, which catalyses the linkage of adjacent nucleotides once they have correctly base-paired.
   b The nucleus.

5.2 a The DNA in tube 2 is less dense than that in tube 1. In tube 1, all the N in the DNA molecules is ^{15}N. In tube 2, each DNA molecule is made up of one strand containing ^{14}N and one containing ^{15}N.
   b One band in the original position (the 'old' DNA containing only ^{15}N), and another band higher up (the 'new' DNA containing only ^{14}N).
   c Assuming that most strands ended up with a mix of ^{14}N and ^{15}N – which you would expect if the bits of each kind were scattered randomly – then there would be a single band, like the one shown in tube 2.
   d Tube 3. If the DNA had replicated dispersively, then instead of two distinct bands there would be a single, wide one because each strand of DNA would contain a mix of ^{14}N and ^{15}N. The band would be higher than that in tube 2, because there would now be more ^{14}N and less ^{15}N in the DNA molecules.
   As it is, the two bands contain molecules with one strand containing ^{14}N and the other ^{15}N (the bottom band) and molecules in which all the N is ^{14}N (the top band).

5.3 a 64
   b For 'punctuation marks', that is for starting or stopping the synthesis of a polypeptide chain. Also, some amino acids could be coded for by two or three different base triplets.
   c A two-letter code could only code for 16 amino acids.

5.4 DNA contains the pentose sugar deoxyribose, while RNA contains ribose.
DNA contains the base thymine, while RNA has uracil.
DNA is made up of two polynucleotide strands, whereas RNA has only one.
DNA molecules are much longer than RNA molecules.

5.5 There are various possible flow diagrams, but a suitable one might be as follows:

DNA unwinds and the two strands separate → complementary mRNA molecule built up against one DNA strand (transcription) → mRNA molecule attaches to ribosome → complementary tRNA loaded with appropriate amino acid pairs with one codon on mRNA (translation) → peptide bond forms between adjacent amino acids

Chapter 6

6.1   The chromosomes are arranged in order of size in the karyotype.

6.2   **a** (i) 92 (at this stage the cell is, technically, 4n)
(ii) 92 (each chromatid contains one)
(iii) 46 (the diploid number)
(iv) 92

b (i)   (ii)

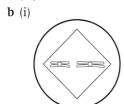   

metaphase   anaphase

c nucleotides

d C, H, O, N, P (deoxyribose and bases contain C, H and O; bases also contain N; phosphate contains P and O).

e To hold chromatids together and to attach chromosomes to spindle.

f Nine cells out of 75 000 were undergoing mitosis. Therefore mitosis occupies 9/75 000 of the cell cycle. Mitosis lasts 1 hour. Therefore cell cycle = 75 000/9 hours long, = 8333 hours = 8333/24 days = 347 days. (Cell cycles vary in length in adult animals from less than 8 hours to more than 1 year.)

Chapter 7

7.1   These animals are homeothermic, generating heat within their cells to keep their body temperature constant. This body temperature is normally above the environmental temperature, and so large quantities of heat are lost from their bodies.

7.2   **a** 38 000 kJ m^{-2} year^{-1}, 31 000 kJ m^{-2} year^{-1}
b 54 000 kJ m^{-2} year^{-1}
c For example, higher light intensity, higher temperatures and higher rainfall allow photosynthesis to take place at a greater rate; there are few seasonal variations in these factors, so photosynthesis can continue all the year round; coniferous trees in the pine forest must be adapted to withstand cold and water shortage in winter, so have narrow needles, limiting maximum rates of light absorption even when environmental conditions are ideal for photosynthesis; tropical rain forest has a greater density of plants.

d Alfalfa plants are young and growing, so much of the carbon they fix in photosynthesis is incorporated into new cells rather than being respired. In the rain forest, the trees are mostly mature and amounts of growth will be small. Alfalfa is a nitrogen-fixer and this, together with the probable application of fertiliser to the crop, could allow greater rates of growth than in the rain forest or pine forest.

Chapter 8

8.1   **a** Size is important, but is not the only factor. Microscopic organisms such as *Paramecium* do not have transport systems, whereas all large organisms such as green plants, fish and mammals do. However, cnidarians do not have transport systems even though some of them are considerably larger than insects, which do.

b Surface area to volume ratio is important. Small organisms have large surface area to volume ratios, and as explained in **a**, these generally do not have a transport system. Organisms with branching bodies, such as plants, can have large surface area to volume ratios even if they are large; they do have transport systems, but (as you will see) these are not used for transporting gases, and they do not have pumps.

c Level of activity is important. Animals such as fish and mammals have a transport system containing a pump; plants, most of which are less active than most animals, do not have a pump. Insects have pumps in their transport system, even though they are smaller than the less active cnidarians, which do not have a pump.

8.2   **a** The fish has a single circulatory system, whereas the mammal has a double circulatory system. In the fish, blood leaves the heart and travels to the gills, where it picks up oxygen, before continuing around the body. In the mammal, the blood returns to the heart after picking up oxygen at the lungs, and is then pumped around the body.

b Oxygenated blood can be pumped around the body at a higher pressure, and therefore faster, in a mammal than in a fish, because pressure is lost in the capillaries in the gills. This can provide a more efficient oxygen supply to mammalian cells than to fish cells.

8.3 a Elastic fibres allow the artery to stretch and recoil as blood pulses through. Nearer the heart, the pressure changes between systole and diastole will be greater, and the maximum systolic pressure greater, than anywhere else in the circulatory system. Thus more elastic fibres are needed to cope with these large pressures and pressure changes.

8.4 Blood cells, and haemoglobin in red blood cells, would cause scattering and absorption of light before it reached the retina. The aqueous humour supplies the cornea with its requirements.

8.5 a Gravity pulls blood downwards. Normally, contraction and relaxation of leg muscles squeezes in on leg veins; valves in them ensure blood moves upwards and not downwards. When standing to attention, these muscles are still, so blood accumulates in the feet.

b As thoracic volume increases, pressure inside the thorax decreases. This decreases the pressure in the blood vessels in the thorax. The effect is very small in the arteries, but more significant in the veins. The relatively low pressure of the blood in the veins in the thorax, compared with the pressure in veins elsewhere in the body, produces a pressure difference causing blood movement towards the thorax.

8.6 Answers to this may be found in the text.

8.7 Answers should include reference to: the fluctuating pressure in arteries; why the fluctuations become gradually less as the blood passes through the arterial system; the rapid drop in pressure as the blood flows along the arterioles and capillaries and reasons for this; the rise of pressure as blood enters the pulmonary circulation via the right-hand side of the heart, but not so high as the pressure in the aorta, and reasons for this.

8.8 a The larger the relative molecular mass, the lower the permeability.

b Net diffusion for glucose would be into the muscle. Respiration within the muscle requires glucose, so that its concentration within the muscle cells is lower than in the blood plasma.

c Albumin in the blood plasma raises its solute concentration (osmotic pressure), thus helping to draw water back from the tissue fluid into capillaries. If albumin could diffuse out of capillaries into tissue fluid, more water would accumulate in the tissue fluid. (This is called oedema.)

8.9 a Protein in tissue fluid comes from the cells making up the tissues, many of which secrete proteins.

b If plasma protein concentrations are low, then, as explained in SAQ 8.8c above, water will not be drawn back into capillaries from tissue fluid.

8.10 2.1×10^{11}

8.11 a Protein synthesis – no; there is no DNA, so no mRNA can be transcribed.

b Cell division – no; there are no chromosomes, so mitosis cannot occur, nor are there centrioles for spindle formation.

c Lipid synthesis – no; this occurs on the smooth endoplasmic reticulum, and there is none.

d Active transport – yes; this occurs across the plasma membrane, and can be fuelled by ATP produced by anaerobic respiration.

8.12 a $195 \, cm^3$

b $25 \, cm^3$

8.13 a (i) 96.5%

(ii) $1.25 \, cm^3$

b (i) 24.0%

(ii) $0.31 \, cm^3$

8.14 Less oxygen would enter the blood by diffusion, and therefore less oxygen would be carried to the body cells. The percentage saturation of haemoglobin will be only about 30% saturated (*figure 8.13*).

8.15 At these heights, the percentage saturation of the haemoglobin is relatively low. If the number of red blood cells is increased, then the number of haemoglobin molecules is also increased. Even though the percentage saturation of the haemoglobin is low, the fact that that there is more of it can increase the actual quantity of oxygen carried in the blood.

8.16 Spending a length of time at high altitude stimulates the body to produce more red blood cells. When the athlete returns to sea level, these 'extra' red blood cells remain in the body for some time, and can supply extra oxygen to muscles enabling them to work harder and for longer than they would otherwise be able to do.

Chapter 9

9.1 **a** (i) 0.7–0.8 seconds

(ii) 60/0.8 = 75 beats per minute

For **b**, **c**, **d**, **e** and **f**, see figure below.

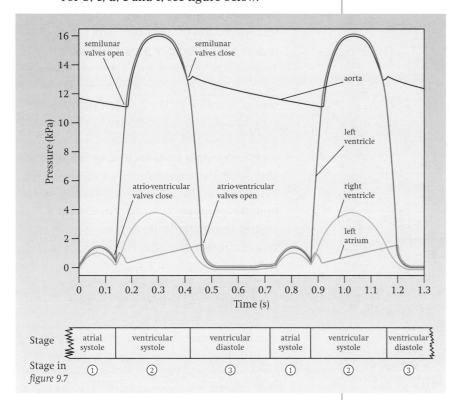

Stage	atrial systole	ventricular systole	ventricular diastole	atrial systole	ventricular systole	ventricular diastole
Stage in figure 9.7	①	②	③	①	②	③

● **Answer for** SAQ 9.1

9.2 **a** 1 beat = about 20 mm on the grid.

25 mm on the grid represents 1 second.

So 20 mm represents $\frac{20}{25}$ seconds = 0.8 seconds.

If one beat lasts 0.8 seconds, then in 1 second there are $\frac{1}{0.8}$ beats.

So in 1 minute there are $\frac{1 \times 60}{0.8}$ = 75 beats.

b (i) This is the time during which the ventricles are contracting.

(ii) On the grid, the distance betweeen Q and T is about 7 mm.

This represents $\frac{7}{25}$ = 0.28 seconds.

c (i) This is the time when the ventricles are relaxed, and are filling with blood.

(ii) On the grid, the distance between T and Q is about 13 mm.

This represents $\frac{13}{25}$ = 0.52 seconds.

A quicker way of working this out is to subtract your answer to b(ii) from 0.8 seconds.

d (i) By performing varying levels of exercise.

(ii) See figure.

(iii) As heart rate increases, contraction time remains constant, but filling time decreases. This indicates that the increase in heart rate is produced by a shorter time interval between ventricular contractions, rather than by a faster ventricular contraction.

The more frequent contractions increase the rate of circulation of blood around the body, providing extra oxygen to exercising muscles. If this was done by shortening the time over which the ventricles contract, much of the advantage would be lost, as less blood would probably be forced out by each contraction. By shortening the time *between* contractions, the amount of blood pumped out of the heart per unit time is increased.

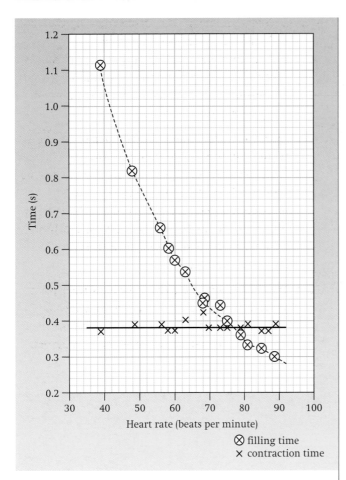

Heart rate (beats per minute)

⊗ filling time
✕ contraction time

● **Answer for** SAQ 9.2d(ii)

Chapter 10

10.1   a Mutualism.

   b The relationship between *Rhizobium* and leguminous plants. The bacterium stimulates the roots to form nodules, in which the bacteria live and where they fix nitrogen. The plant uses the fixed nitrogen to make amino acids and proteins. The bacteria obtain organic nutrients and a source of energy from the plant.

10.2   Spiral, annular or reticulate walls can all stretch and lengthen as the plant grows. The walls of pitted vessels cannot do this.

10.3   a Increased wind speed moves water vapour away from the leaf more rapidly, thus maintaining a steeper water potential gradient between the air spaces of the leaf and the surrounding air.

   b Rise in temperature increases the kinetic energy of water molecules which move, and therefore diffuse, more rapidly. High temperatures may also decrease the humidity of the air (as warm air can hold more water), so increasing the diffusion gradient.

10.4   Mammals use the evaporation of water in sweat for cooling purposes; the water evaporates from the skin surface, absorbing heat energy. Thus the two processes are very similar.

10.5   a In plants, osmosis is involved in the uptake of water from soil into the root hair. It may also be involved in movement from cell to cell across the root, but only if the water moves through the cell surface membranes of the cells. If it travels by the apoplast pathway, or via plasmodesmata between cells, then osmosis is not involved. Movement across the root endodermis does involve crossing cell surface membranes, so osmosis is again involved here. In the leaf, osmosis is involved if water moves into the cytoplasm of a cell across the cell surface membrane, but not if it moves by the apoplast pathway or plasmodesmata, as in the root.

   In animals, osmosis is involved in the movement of water from the ileum and colon into the cells lining these parts of the alimentary canal, and then out of these cells into the blood. The water again moves by osmosis when leaving the blood and entering cells in body tissues. Osmosis is also involved in the reabsorption of water from nephrons.

   b In plants, mass flow is involved in the movement of water up the xylem vessels.

   In animals, mass flow is involved in the movement of blood plasma (containing water) along the blood vessels.

10.6   a The total lack of cell contents provides an uninterrupted pathway for the flow of water.

   b Lack of end walls also provides an uninterrupted pathway for the flow of water.

   c The wider the diameter, the more water can be moved up through a xylem vessel per unit time. However, if the vessels are too wide, there is an increased tendency for the water column to break. The diameter of xylem vessels is a compromise between these two requirements.

   d The lignified walls provide support, preventing the vessels from collapsing inwards.

   e Pits in the walls of the vessels allow water to move into and out of them.

10.7   Sucrose, amino acids, ATP and plant growth substances.

10.8 Sources: storage tissue of a potato tuber when the buds are beginning to sprout.
Sinks: nectary, developing fruit, developing potato tuber.

10.9 All the required contents of this comparison table are in the text on pages 132–143. Care should be taken that equivalent points are kept opposite each other.

Chapter 11

11.1 Both parents are carriers (Aa):

Parents: Aa × Aa

Gametes: $\textcircled{A}$, $\textcircled{a}$ + $\textcircled{A}$, $\textcircled{a}$

	$\textcircled{A}$	$\textcircled{a}$
$\textcircled{A}$	AA	Aa
$\textcircled{a}$	Aa	aa

Child with cystic fibrosis is aa.

11.2 There are different mutations in the gene and one test does not identify all of them.

11.3 Red blood cells do not have nuclei and do not contain DNA.

11.4 So they can make informed decisions about whether to have children. Also whether they should request antenatal genetic tests to see if their children will be born with cystic fibrosis.

11.5 These are suggestions. You may disagree with some of these.

11.6 **a** Epidemic: when many people develop the disease in a short period of time.
b Pandemic: when a disease spreads across a continent or even the whole world. An epidemic affects a much smaller population, e.g. a town or a country.

11.7 Incidence: how many new cases of a disease are reported (useful in determining whether control measures are proving successful). Prevalence: the number of people who have the disease (an indication of the number of people who require treatment from the medical services). Mortality: how many people die from the disease (an indication of its severity).

11. 8 The lists should show that degenerative diseases are the leading cause of death worldwide and in developed countries. Infectious diseases are a leading cause of death in developing countries.

Disease	Category of disease								
	physical	infectious	non-infectious	deficiency	inherited	degenerative	mental	social	self-inflicted
scurvy	✓	✗	✓	✓	✗	✓	✗	✓	✗
malaria	✓	✓	✗	✗	✗	✗	✗	✗	✗
measles	✓	✓	✗	✗	✗	✗	✗	✓	✗
cystic fibrosis	✓	✗	✓	✗	✓	✓	✗	✗	✗
lung cancer	✓	✗	✓	✗	✗	✓	✗	✓	✓
sickle cell anaemia	✓	✗	✓	✗	✓	✓	✗	✗	✗
Altzeimer's disease	✓	✗	✓	✗	✗	✓	✓	✗	✗
schizophrenia	✓	✗	✓	✗	?	✗	✓	✗	✗
Creutzfeld–Jacob disease	✓	✓	✗	✗	?	✓	✓	✗	✗
skin cancer	✓	✗	✓	✗	✗	✓	✗	✓	✓

Chapter 12

12.1 An increase in body fat; outcomes associated with becoming overweight or obese.

12.2 Requirement for protein increases as body mass increases during growth, then the requirement remains fairly constant when fully grown. Protein is needed for growth of muscles and skeleton and other tissues. Calcium is needed for growth of skeleton: main periods of growth are in infancy and during adolescence. Less calcium is required after growth is complete. Iron is needed for haemoglobin and myoglobin. Women need larger quantities of iron because of menstrual loss. After the menopause their requirement becomes the same as that of men.

12.3 The EAR for men is $11.51\,\text{MJ day}^{-1}$; energy from fat $= 0.35 \times 11.51 = 4.03\,\text{MJ day}^{-1}$. Each gram of fat provides $37\,\text{kJ}$, so
$$\frac{4.03 \times 1000}{37} = 108.9\,\text{g};$$
$108.9\,\text{g}$ of fat provides 35% of the daily energy intake.
The EAR for women is $8.83\,\text{MJ day}^{-1}$; energy from fat $= 0.35 \times 8.83 = 3.09\,\text{MJ day}^{-1}$.
$$\frac{3.09 \times 1000}{37} = 83.5\,\text{g};$$
$83.5\,\text{g}$ of fat provides 35% of the daily energy intake.

12.4 Fat provides $37\,\text{kJ g}^{-1}$, which is about twice as much as the same mass of carbohydrate. Reducing fat intake will reduce energy intake significantly.

12.5 Solvent in blood plasma and lymphatic systems; solvent in urine; required in tears, and in saliva and other digestive juices; hydrolysis reactions in digestion (e.g. starch $\longrightarrow$ maltose $\longrightarrow$ glucose); heat loss in sweating; solvent for all biochemical reactions.

12.6 **a** Pregnancy: $8.1\,\text{MJ day}^{-1}$ for first 6 months; 8.9 for last 3 months
Lactation: $10\,\text{MJ day}^{-1}$ for first month; 10.5 MJ day^{-1} for 4–6 months (if breast milk is main energy source)
b During pregnancy, mothers may use stores of fat to provide energy for growth of the fetus, and will not need to eat extra energy-containing foods until the last 3 months, when the fetus increases in size. After birth, infants grow rapidly and require a high input of energy from mothers' breast milk.

c

Nutrient	RNI
calcium	$700\,\text{mg day}^{-1}$
iron	$14.8\,\text{mg day}^{-1}$
zinc	$7.0\,\text{mg day}^{-1}$
vitamin A	$700\,\mu\text{g day}^{-1}$
folic acid	$300\,\mu\text{g day}^{-1}$
vitamin C	$50\,\text{mg day}^{-1}$
vitamin D	$10\,\text{mg day}^{-1}$

d There could be as much as 14 days between conception and the first missed period. There may be an even longer delay before pregnancy is confirmed. The nervous system of the fetus begins developing during these first few weeks so it is advisable to supplement the diet with folic acid before pregnancy is confirmed to reduce the chances of spina bifida.

12.7 Iron is required for the synthesis of haemoglobin and myoglobin; a deficiency of haemoglobin limits the supply of oxygen to the tissues, leading to slow physical and mental development.

12.8 **a** $6.72\,\text{MJ day}^{-1}$
b This compares well with EARs for 4- to 6-year-olds: $7.16\,\text{MJ day}^{-1}$ (males) and $6.46\,\text{MJ day}^{-1}$ (females), and is considerably higher than the requirements of 1- to 3-year-olds.
c

Nutrient	350 g Unimix	RNI for children between the ages of 1 and 10 years
protein (g day^{-1})	23.87	14.5–28.3
iron (mg day^{-1})	10.78	6.9–8.7
calcium (mg day^{-1})	323.40	350–550
vitamin A (μg day^{-1})	808.50	400–500

Unimix provides enough protein and iron and almost enough calcium. It provides more than enough vitamin A to protect children from infections and to make up for any deficiency that existed before they needed food aid.

12.9 Women have a larger proportion of body fat than men.

12.10 The nuns' diet was probably deficient in vitamin D. Very little of their skin would have been exposed to sunlight.

2.11 The housebound and the elderly. People who wear completely enveloping clothing (e.g. Asian girls and women) are also at risk, as are people whose skin is too dark to absorb enough light to synthesise much vitamin D.

12.12 1.65 m = 81.7 kg; 1.73 m = 89.8 kg; 1.83 m = 100.5 kg.

Chapter 13

13.1 Mouth/nostril; nasal cavity; pharynx; trachea; bronchus; terminal and respiratory bronchioles; alveolar duct; alveolus; epithelium; connective tissue; endothelium of capillary; plasma; red blood cell.

13.2 Large surface area; thin epithelium, therefore short diffusion distance between air and blood; well supplied with many blood capillaries.

13.3 During exercise the bronchioles are wider to allow more air to reach the alveoli to supply the large quantities of oxygen needed during exercise and to remove carbon dioxide.

13.4 **a** tidal volume = 0.5 dm^3
vital capacity = 3.75 dm^3
  b (i) 12 breaths per minute;
  (ii) 6.0 $dm^3 min^{-1}$
  (iii) 0.38 $dm^3 min^{-1}$

13.5 Exercise; smoking; excitement; release of adrenaline; sleep; fear; meditation.

13.6 With age, the arteries do not stretch as well and there is an increased resistance to the flow of blood. The heart needs to beat harder to overcome this resistance.

13.7 **a** 10.92 $dm^3 min^{-1}$ at MR = 0.8;
16.50 $dm^3 min^{-1}$ at MR = 1.6;
27.20 $dm^3 min^{-1}$ at MR = 2.4.

b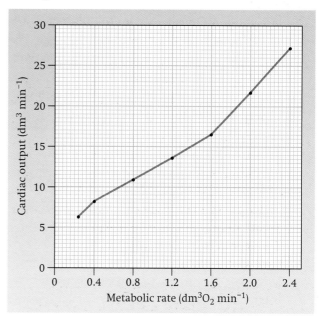

Metabolic rate ($dm^3 O_2 min^{-1}$)	Cardiac output ($dm^3 min^{-1}$)
0.2	6.3
0.4	8.2
0.8	10.9
1.2	13.6
1.6	16.5
2.0	21.7
2.4	27.2

● **Answer for** SAQ 13.7a

c All of the following increase: heart rate, stroke volume, cardiac output, systolic blood pressure, tidal volume, breathing rate and ventilation rate. Blood is diverted away from skin and gut to the muscles. Bronchioles widen.

13.8 **a** Level of aerobic fitness, size, age, gender, smoker/non-smoker.
  b Lactate accumulates, fatigue sets in and this will force you to stop.

Chapter 14

14.1 Bronchitis: enlargement of mucus glands in airways; increased secretion of mucus; narrowing/obstruction of airways; inflammation; severe coughing; coughing-up of phlegm. Emphysema: digestion by phagocytes of pathways through alveolar walls; loss of elastin; overextension and bursting of alveoli to form large air spaces; decrease in surface area for gaseous exchange; lack of recoiling of air spaces when breathing out; decrease in volume of air forced out from lungs; shortness of breath.

14.2 Deaths from lung cancer lag behind increase in cigarette smoking by some 20 years or more in both men and women. Women began smoking later than men, so rise in death rate did not begin until later. More men than women smoke, and more men than women die of lung cancer. The male death rate started to decrease in 1975, roughly twenty years after the fall in cigarette consumption. Fall in consumption by women began about 1975, but by 1991 this had yet to be reflected in a decrease in mortality from lung cancer.

14.3 Tar: paralyses or destroys cilia; stimulates oversecretion of mucus; leads to the development of bronchitis and emphysema (see SAQ 14.1). Carcinogens: cause changes in the DNA of cells in the bronchial epithelium, leading to the development of bronchial carcinoma – lung cancer.

14.4 **a** A break in the wall of the coronary artery; invasion by phagocytes; build-up of cholesterol; growth of smooth muscle; atherosclerosis; blood flow through artery is reduced; blood clots at site of atheroma; blood cannot supply oxygen and nutrients to heart muscle; heart muscle dies; myocardial infarction (heart attack).

b As blood does not supply oxygen and nutrients to part of the brain, the nerve cells in that area die. This may be fatal; if not, the part of the brain affected may not function properly or at all. As a result, a stroke may lead to loss of e.g. memory, movement or the ability to speak.

14.5 Carbon monoxide: combines with haemoglobin to form stable compound carboxyhaemoglobin, with the result that less oxygen is transported in the blood.
Nicotine: raises blood pressure; raises heart rate; makes platelets sticky and therefore increases likelihood of thrombosis; decreases blood supply to the extremities.

14.6 **a** Cardiovascular diseases are degenerative diseases; deaths in this age range are premature deaths.

b (i) The death rates are much higher in North Karelia than Catalonia for all cardiovascular diseases in both men and women. They are higher in North Karelia than the national figures for finland, but lower in Catalonia than the national figures for Spain.
(ii) CHD accounts for over half of all deaths in this category in North Karelia, less than half in Catalonia.
(iii) Strokes are responsible for the lowest number of deaths, but the death rate is still more than twice as high in North Karelia than in Catalonia.

c men

14.7 **a** total number of deaths attributable to smoking: men = 55 508; women = 39 975.

b percentages: men = 17.5%; women = 11.74%; total = 14.5%.

Chapter 15

15.1 Faeces from infected person contain *Vibrio cholerae*. These bacteria are transmitted to uninfected people in drinking water, contaminated food (e.g. vegetables irrigated with raw sewage or food prepared by a symptomless carrier), or when washing or bathing in contaminated water.

15.2 $\dfrac{10^{13}}{10^{6}} = 10$ million

15.3 Refugees rarely have access to proper sanitation, clean water, or uncontaminated food.

15.4 The visitor can drink bottled or boiled water; and avoid eating salads and raw vegetables.

15.5 When a female *Anopheles* mosquito bites an infected person she takes up some gametes of the parasite. These develop into infective stages which enter an uninfected person when the same mosquito takes another blood meal.

15.6 The resistance of mosquitoes to insecticides such as DDT and dieldrin; the difficulty of controlling the breeding of mosquitoes because they lay eggs in small bodies of water; the resistance of some strains of *Plasmodium* to anti-malarial drugs such as chloroquine.

15.7 People can avoid being bitten by mosquitoes, sleep under nets impregnated with insecticide, use repellents; and use anti-malarial drugs as prophylactics (but not those to which *Plasmodium* is resistant).

15.8 Many cases of AIDS are not diagnosed or reported.

15.9 Condoms can split when in use or may not be put on correctly.

15.10 Practise safer sex (e.g. use condoms); do not use unsterile needles; have one sexual partner; do not donate blood if at risk of HIV infection; do not use prostitutes (male or female); have a blood test to find out if you are HIV+.

15.11 HIV is a blood-borne virus; blood donations may not be screened or heat-treated for HIV.

15.12 It is important for people to know whether they are HIV+ so that they can make sure they reduce the chances of transmitting the virus to others.

15.13 Highest incidence/prevalence in South-East Asia, sub-Saharan Africa, countries of old Soviet Union, India, China, Mexico, Peru, Bolivia.
Poor nutrition; HIV infection; poor disease control; large cities with poor housing and homeless people; countries with limited health facilities and large numbers of displaced people (e.g. migrants and refugees).

15.14 B and E. These have inhibition zones larger than the minimum required to be in the sensitive range. These antibiotics could be used together.

Chapter 16

16.1 Antigen: any large molecule (e.g. protein) recognised by the body as foreign.
Antibody: a protein made by the immune system in response to the presence of an antigen and targeted specifically at it.
Immune response: lymphocytes respond to the presence of a pathogen in the body by producing antibodies.

16.2 **a** The lymphocyte nucleus takes up most of the cell; there is very little cytoplasm. Neutrophils have a lobed nucleus, with a larger amount of cytoplasm. The neutrophil is larger.
b 10 μm.

16.3 B lymphocytes originate and mature in bone marrow. T lymphocytes originate in bone marrow, but mature in the thymus gland.

16.4 By puberty, T cells have matured and left the thymus gland. The thymus has no further use, so decreases in size.

16.5 The cytoplasm of plasma cells is full of rough endoplasmic reticulum where protein is made. There are also Golgi bodies for packaging antibodies in vacuoles for secretion.

16.6 The plasma cells will be identical to the original B cell and will therefore all produce exactly the same antibody molecules. Also the memory cells will be identical so that the same antibody molecules are produced during any subsequent immune response to the same antigen.

16.7 Polysaccharides are made from only a small number of different sugars unlike proteins that are made from twenty different amino acids. Polysaccharides would not give the same huge number of different molecular shapes as is achieved with proteins in the variable region of antibodies.

16.8 Only some B and T cells have receptors of the correct specificity.

16.9 Immunity to one strain does not provide immunity to all of them as they do not all share the same antigens.

16.10 The primary response to an antigen is slow. It takes several weeks to produce enough antibody molecules to fight the infection effectively. During this time we usually show the symptoms of the disease concerned.

16.11 B lymphocytes with antibody receptors specific to the invading antigen divide by mitosis to form plasma cells and memory cells. The short-lived plasma cells secrete antibody molecules.
T helper lymphocytes and killer T lymphocytes with T cell receptors specific to the invading antigen also divide by mitosis. The T helper cells secrete cytokines to activate appropriate B lymphocytes to divide and macrophages to carry out phagocytosis. The killer T cells search for any infected cells in the body and kill them.

16.12 Active: antigens are introduced into the body by injection or by mouth, and stimulate an immune response by B and T cells. This provides long-term immunity but is not immediate as the immune response takes several weeks to become effective. Passive: antibodies are injected into the body to give immediate protection against a pathogen or toxin. Antibodies are soon removed from circulation and no immune response has occurred, so this is a temporary form of immunity.

16.13 Maternal IgG increases during pregnancy as it crosses the placenta; it decreases after birth as it is removed from the circulation. This is natural passive immunity. The fetus does not produce its own antibodies because it does not have any mature T or B cells and develops in a sterile environment. The infant produces its own antibodies shortly after birth as it begins to encounter infections.

16.14 The infant is protected against diseases which are endemic and which the mother has caught or been vaccinated against. For example, measles is a serious childhood infection; the infant is protected for several months by its mother's antibodies. (Note that the infant will not gain passive immunity to any diseases the mother has not encountered.)

16.15 Antibodies are proteins. If children have protein energy malnutrition (see chapter 12) they may not have the ability to produce many antibodies or develop T and B cell clones during an immune reponse.

16.16 Every time the parasite changes its antigens a new primary response will be activated. As soon as there are some antibodies in the blood, the parasite exposes different antigens, so making the antibodies ineffective.

16.17 a *Mycobacterium tuberculosis, M. bovis*
b HIV

Glossary

activation energy the energy that must be provided to make a reaction take place; enzymes reduce the activation energy required for a substrate to change into a product.

active immunity immunity gained when an antigen enters the body, an immune response occurs and antibodies are produced by plasma cells.

active site an area on an enzyme molecule where the substrate can bind.

active transport the movement of molecules or ions through transport proteins across a cell membrane, against their concentration gradient, involving the use of energy from ATP.

acute illness one that has a sudden onset and lasts for relatively short time, e.g. influenza.

aerobic exercise any exercise that uses the heart and lungs to provide oxygen for aerobic respiration in muscles, e.g. cycling, long-distance running.

aerobic fitness a measure of the ability of the heart and lungs to respond to the demands of aerobic exercise. A low resting pulse rate is a good indicator of a high standard of aerobic fitness.

allergen an otherwise harmless substance that sensitises the immune system to give an immune response.

allergy a response by the immune system to a harmless substance; asthma and hay fever are examples of allergies.

anorexia nervosa a disease characterised by severe loss of weight following failure to eat due to psychological problems.

antibiotic a substance produced by a living organism that is capable of destroying or inhibiting the growth of a microorganism.

antibody a protein (immunoglobulin) made by plasma cells derived from B lymphocytes, secreted in response to an antigen; the variable region of the antibody molecule is complementary in shape to its specific antigen.

antigen a substance that is foreign to the body and stimulates an immune response.

artery a blood vessel with a relatively thick wall containing large amounts of elastic fibres and that carries blood away from the heart.

artificial immunity immunity gained either by vaccination (**active**) or by injecting antibodies (**passive**).

assimilates substances, such as sucrose, that have been made within a plant.

asthma a chronic disease in which the airways in the lungs become inflamed and congested as a result of an exaggerated response by the immune system to harmless substances. *See also* **allergen**

atherosclerosis progressive build-up of fatty material in the lining of arteries.

atrio-ventricular node a patch of tissue in the septum of the heart, through which the wave of electrical excitation is passed from the atria to the Purkyne tissue.

B lymphocyte a type of lymphocyte that gives rise to plasma cells, which secrete antibodies.

base pairing the pairing, held by hydrogen bonds, between the nitrogenous bases cytosine and guanine, and between thymine and adenine or uracil, that occurs in the polynucleotides DNA and RNA.

Benedict's test a test for the presence of reducing sugars; the unknown substance is heated with Benedict's reagent, and a change from a clear blue solution to the production of a yellow or red precipitate indicates the presence of reducing sugars such as glucose.

biuret test a test for the presence of amine groups, and thus for the presence of proteins; biuret reagent is added to the unknown substance, and a change from pale blue to purple indicates the presence of proteins.

Bohr effect the decrease in affinity of haemoglobin for oxygen that occurs when carbon dioxide is present.

bronchitis a disease in which the airways in the lungs become inflamed and congested with mucus; chronic bronchitis is often associated with smoking.

cancer a disease, often but not always treatable, that results from a breakdown in the usual control mechanisms that regulate cell division; certain cells divide uncontrollably and form tumours, from which cells may break away and form secondary tumours in other areas of the body (metastasis).

capillary the smallest type of blood vessel, whose function is to facilitate exchange of substances between the blood and the tissues; capillary walls are made up of a single layer of squamous epithelium, and their internal diameter is only a little larger than that of a red blood cell.

carcinogen a substance that can cause cancer.

cardiac cycle the sequence of events taking place during one heart beat.

cardiovascular diseases degenerative diseases of the heart and circulatory system, for example coronary heart disease, stroke.

cell a structure bounded by a plasma membrane, containing cytoplasm and organelles.

cell cycle the sequence of events that takes place from one cell division until the next; it is made up of interphase, mitosis and cytokinesis.

chromatid one of two identical parts of a chromosome, held together by a centromere, formed during interphase by the replication of the DNA strand.

chromosome a structure made of DNA and histones, found in the nucleus of a eukaryotic cell. The term **bacterial chromosome** is now commonly used for the circular strand of DNA present in a prokaryotic cell.

chronic illness one that lasts for a relatively long time and usually has a gradual onset, e.g. coronary heart disease.

chronic obstructive pulmonary disease a disease of the lungs characterised by bronchitis and emphysema.

closed circulation a circulatory system in which the blood is always contained within vessels, as in mammals.

community all of the living organisms, of all species, that are found in a particular habitat at a particular time.

companion cell a cell with an unthickened cellulose wall and dense cytoplasm that is found in close association with a phloem sieve element to which it is directly linked via many plasmodesmata.

consumer a heterotrophic organism; an organism that obtains its food in organic form, either directly or indirectly from that which has been synthesised by producers.

coronary heart disease a disease of the heart caused by damage to the coronary arteries, often as a result of atherosclerosis.

deficiency disease a disease caused by the lack of energy or nutrients (e.g. vitamin A) in the diet.

degenerative disease a progressive deterioration of part of the body.

diastolic blood pressure the minimum pressure of blood in the arteries when the ventricles of the heart are relaxing; it is usually about 80 mmHg.

dietary reference values four indications of the requirements for energy and nutrients of all healthy people in the UK, not intended as recommendations for individuals: Reference Nutrient Intake, Lower Reference Nutrient Intake, Estimated Average Requirement and Safe Intake.

diffusion the net movement, as a result of random motion of its molecules or ions, of a substance from an area of relatively high concentration to an area of relatively low concentration.

disease a form of ill-health or illness with a set of symptoms.

diploid cell one that possesses two complete sets of chromosomes; the abbreviation for diploid is 2n.

DNA Deoxyribonucleic acid, a polynucleotide that contains the pentose sugar deoxyribose.

double circulation a circulatory system in which the blood travels twice through the heart on one complete circuit of the body; the pathway from heart to lungs and back to the heart is known as the pulmonary circulation, and that from heart to the rest of the body and back to the heart as the systemic circulation.

ecosystem all of the living organisms of all species, and all of the non-living components, that are found together in a defined area and that interact with one another.

emphysema a disease in which alveoli are destroyed, giving large air spaces and decreased surface area for gaseous exchange; it is often associated with chronic bronchitis.

endemic a term used to describe an infectious disease that is always present in a population.

endocytosis the movement of bulk liquids or solids into a cell, by the indentation of the plasma membrane to form vesicles containing the substance; endocytosis is an active process requiring ATP.

enzyme a protein produced by a living organism that acts as a catalyst in a specific reaction by reducing activation energy.

enzyme specificity the ability of an enzyme to catalyse reactions involving only a single type of substrate; specificity results from the need for the substrate molecule to bind with the active site of the enzyme, and only substrates with particular shapes are able to bind.

epidemic a term used to describe a disease that many people develop over a short time period.

epidemiology the study of patterns of disease in populations and the factors that influence the spread of diseases.

essential amino acid an amino acid that cannot be made in the body and must therefore be present in the diet.

essential fatty acid a fatty acid that cannot be made in the body and must therefore be present in the diet; there are two, linoleic acid and linolenic acid.

eukaryotic cell a cell containing a nucleus and other membrane-bound organelles.

exocytosis the movement of bulk liquids or solids out of a cell, by the fusion of vesicles containing the substance with the plasma membrane; exocytosis is an active process requiring ATP.

facilitated diffusion the diffusion of a substance through protein channels in a cell membrane; the proteins provide hydrophilic areas that allow the molecules or ions to pass through a membrane that would otherwise be less permeable to them.

fibrous protein a protein whose molecules have a relatively long, thin structure that are generally insoluble and metabolically inactive, and whose function is usually structural, e.g. keratin and collagen.

gaseous exchange the movement of gases between an organism and its environment, e.g. the intake of oxygen and the loss of carbon dioxide; gaseous exchange often takes place across a specialised surface such as the alveoli of the lungs.

gene a length of DNA that codes for a particular protein or polypeptide.

globular protein a protein whose molecules are curled into a relatively spherical shape and that is often water soluble and metabolically active, e.g. insulin and haemoglobin.

glycosidic bond a C–O–C link between two monosaccharide molecules.

habitat the place where an organism, a population or a community lives.

haemoglobin the red pigment found in red blood cells whose molecules contain four iron ions within a globular protein made up of four polypeptides and that combines reversibly with oxygen.

haploid cell one that possesses one complete set of chromosomes; the abbreviation for haploid is n.

homologous chromosomes a pair of chromosomes in a diploid cell that have the same structure as each other, with the same genes (but not necessarily the same alleles of those genes) at the same loci, and that pair together to form a bivalent during the first division of meiosis.

hydrogen bond a relatively weak bond formed by the attraction between a group with a small positive charge on a hydrogen atom and another group carrying a small negative charge, e.g. between two $-O^{\delta-}H^{\delta+}$ groups.

hypertension abnormally high blood pressure.

immune response the action of lymphocytes in response to the entry of an antigen into the body.

immune system the body's defence system.

immunity protection against infectious diseases, gained either actively or passively.

immunological memory the ability of the immune system to respond quickly to antigens that it recognises as having entered the body before.

incidence the number of people who are diagnosed or who develop a disease within a certain time period.

infectious disease a disease caused by an organism such as a bacterium or virus.

inherited disease a disease caused by a genetic fault that is passed on from generation to generation.

inhibitor, competitive a substance that reduces the rate of activity of an enzyme by competing with the substrate molecules for the enzyme's active site. Increasing the concentration of the substrate reduces the degree of inhibition.

inhibitor, non-competitive a substance that reduces the rate of activity of an enzyme, but where increasing the concentration of the substrate does not reduce the degree of inhibition. Many non-competitive inhibitors bind to areas of the enzyme molecule other than the active site itself.

iodine in potassium iodide solution test a test for the presence of starch; the solution is added to the unknown substance, and a change from brown to blue-black indicates the presence of starch.

lactate (*or* **lactic acid**) the end product of anaerobic respiration, often produced by muscles during exercise.

lymph an almost colourless fluid, very similar in composition to blood plasma but with fewer plasma proteins, that is present in lymph vessels.

lymphocyte a type of white blood cell that is involved in the immune response; unlike phagocytes they become active only in the presence of a particular antigen that 'matches' their specific receptors or antibodies.

magnification the number of times greater that an image is than the actual object. Magnification = image size ÷ object size.

memory cells lymphocytes which develop during an immune response and retain the ability to respond quickly when an antigen enters the body on a second, or any subsequent, occasion.

mental disease a disease that affects the mind.

mitosis the division of a nucleus such that the two daughter cells acquire exactly the same number and type of chromosomes as the parent cell.

natural immunity immunity gained by being infected (**active**) or by receiving antibodies from the mother across the placenta or in breast milk (**passive**).

niche the role of an organism in an ecosystem.

non-infectious disease a disease that is not caused by an organism.

nutrient a substance that is required in the diet, e.g. proteins, carbohydrates, fats, vitamins and minerals; water and fibre are not generally regarded as nutrients.

obesity a form of malnutrition in which energy consumption is much higher than energy expenditure, leading to storage of excessive amounts of fat; a person who is 20% or more above the recommended weight for their height is considered to be obese.

organ a structure within a multicellular organism that is made up different types of tissues working together to perform a particular function, e.g. the stomach in a human or a leaf in a plant.

organelle a functionally and structurally distinct part of a cell, for example a ribosome or mitochondrion.

osmosis the net movement of water molecules from a region of high water potential to a low water potential, through a partially permeable membrane, as a result of their random motion.

oxygen debt the volume of oxygen that is required at the end of exercise to metabolise lactate that accumulates as a result of anaerobic respiration in muscles.

pandemic a disease that spreads across continents or the whole world.

passive immunity immunity gained without an immune response; antibodies are injected (artificial) or pass from mother to child across the placenta or in breast milk (natural).

pathogen an organism that causes infectious disease.

peptide bond a C–N link between two amino acid molecules.

phagocyte a type of cell, some of which are white blood cells, that ingests and destroys pathogens or damaged body cells.

phloem tissue tissue containing phloem sieve tubes and other types of cell, responsible for the translocation of assimilates such as sucrose through a plant.

phospholipid a substance whose molecules are made up of a glycerol molecule, two fatty acids and a phosphate group; a bilayer of phospholipids forms the basic structure of all cell membranes.

physical disease a disease that results in temporary or permanent damage to the body.

plaque fatty material in the lining of an artery.

population all of the organisms of the same species present in the same place and at the same time that can interbreed with one another.

prevalence the number of people with a disease in a population at a certain time.

primary structure the sequence of amino acids in a polypeptide or protein.

producer an autotrophic organism; an organism that obtains its food from inorganic sources by photosynthesis or chemosynthesis.

prokaryotic cell a cell that does not contain a nucleus or any other membrane-bound organelles; bacteria are prokaryotes.

Purkyne tissue an area of tissue in the septum of the heart that conducts the wave of excitation from the atria to the base of the ventricles.

quaternary structure the three-dimensional arrangement of two or more polypeptides, or of a polypeptide and a non-protein component such as haem, in a protein molecule.

resolution the ability to distinguish between two objects very close together; the higher the resolution of an image, the greater the detail that can be seen.

rickets weakening of bones in children, resulting from a deficiency of vitamin D.

RNA ribonucleic acid, a polynucleotide that contains the pentose sugar ribose.

secondary structure the structure of a protein molecule resulting from the regular coiling or folding of the chain of amino acids, for example an alpha helix or beta pleated sheet.

self-inflicted disease a disease resulting from a person's own actions, e.g. those related to smoking or drinking excessive alcohol.

semi-conservative replication the method by which a DNA molecule is copied to form two identical molecules, each containing one strand from the original molecule and one newly synthesised strand.

sieve tube element a cell found in phloem tissue, with non-thickened cellulose walls, very little cytoplasm, no nucleus and end walls perforated to form sieve plates, through which sap containing sucrose is transported.

sinoatrial node a patch of muscle in the wall of the right atrium of the heart, whose intrinsic rate of rhythmic contraction is faster than that of the rest of the cardiac muscle, and from which waves of excitation spread to the rest of the heart to initiate its contraction during the cardiac cycle.

social disease a disease which is influenced by people's social environment.

stroke damage to the brain caused by bursting or blockage of an artery.

systolic blood pressure the maximum blood pressure in an artery when the ventricles of the heart contract; at rest this is usually about 120 mmHg.

T lymphocyte a lymphocyte that does not secrete antibodies; T helper cells stimulate the immune system to respond during an infection, and killer T cells destroy human cells that are infected with pathogens, such as bacteria and viruses.

tertiary structure the structure of a protein molecule resulting from the three-dimensional coiling of the already-folded chain of amino acids.

tidal volume the volume of air breathed in or out during a single breath.

tissue a layer or group of cells of similar type, which together perform a particular function.

tissue fluid the almost colourless fluid that fills the spaces between body cells; tissue fluid forms from the fluid that leaks from blood capillaries, and most of it eventually collects into lymph vessels where it forms lymph.

translocation the transport of assimilates such as sucrose through a plant, in phloem tissue; translocation requires the input of metabolic energy.

transmission the transfer of a pathogen from one person to another.

transpiration the loss of water vapour, by diffusion down a water potential gradient, from a plant to its environment; most transpiration takes place through the stomata on the leaves.

triglyceride a lipid whose molecules are made up of a glycerol molecule and three fatty acids.

trophic level the level in a food chain at which an organism feeds.

vaccination giving a vaccine containing antigens for a disease either by injection or by mouth; vaccination confers artificial active immunity.

vein a blood vessel with relatively thin walls, and containing valves, that carries blood back towards the heart.

vital capacity the maximum volume of air that can be breathed out after breathing in as deeply as possible.

water potential the tendency of a solution to lose water; water moves from a solution with high water potential to one with low water potential. Water potential is decreased by the addition of solute, and increased by the application of pressure. Symbol is ψ.

xerophthalmia scarring of the cornea caused by a deficiency of vitamin A.

xerophyte a plant adapted to survive in conditions where water is in short supply.

xylem tissue tissue containing xylem vessels and other types of cells, responsible for support and the transport of water through a plant.

xylem vessel a dead, empty vessel with lignified walls and no end walls, through which water is transported.

Index

Terms shown in **bold** also appear in the glossary (see page 253). Pages in *italics* refer to figures.

activation energy, 43–4, *43*
active immunity, 227–8
active site, 42–3, *42*
active transport, 59–60, *59*, 142–4, *143*
adrenaline, 180
aerobic exercise, 179–82
aerobic fitness, 182–3
aerobic respiration, 179
AIDS/HIV, 209–12
allele, 82–3, *82*, 150
allergen, 188, 232
allergy, 232–4, *233*
altitude sickness, 117–18
alveoli, 61–2, *61*, 174–5, *174–5*
Alzheimer's disease, 152
amino acids
  essential in diet, 162
  R groups of, 31, *31*, 34, 236
  structure, 31, *31*
ammonification, 99
amylopectin, 25, *26*
amylose, 25, *26*
anaerobic respiration, 179
angina pectoris, 195
animal tissues, 17, 19
anorexia nervosa, 167–8, *168*
antibiotic, 155, 215–16, *216*
antibody, 220, 224–5, *224*, 226
anticodon, 75
antigen, 220
antigenic concealment, 230
antigenic variation, 229
antitoxins, 224
aorta, 104, *104*, 106, 121, *121*
apoplast pathway, 131, *131*
artery, *105*, 106
arterioles, 106
asexual reproduction, *87*
assimilates, 138
asthma, 233–4, *233*
atherosclerosis, 193–4

ATP, 93, 179
atria, 122
atrial systole, 122, *122*
atrio-ventricular node, 125
atrio-ventricular valves, 122, *123*
autosomes, 80

B lymphocyte, 221–4, *222–3*
basement membrane, 17, 19
bicuspid valve, 122
bilayers, 51–2, *52*
biological catalysts, 42
biological molecules, 22, *22*
blood, 111–12
blood pressure, 106, 177–9, *178*
blood vessels, 104–8, *104*
body mass index (BMI), 169–70
Bohr shift, 114–15
breathing rate/depth, 175, *176*
bronchi, *61*, 173, *174*
bronchial carcinoma, 190–1
bronchioles, *174*
bronchitis, chronic, 188–9
budding, 87
bulk transport, 60

callose, 141
cancer, 88–90, *88*, *90*, *see also* lung cancer
capillary, 106–7, *107*
carbohydrates, *159*, 163, 23
carbon dioxide transport, 115, *116*
carbon monoxide, 117, 187–8
carbonic anhydrase, 114
carboxyhaemoglobin, 117
carcinogen, 88–9
cardiac cycle, 122–3, *122*, 124–5
cardiac muscle, 120–1, *121*, 124
cardiovascular disease, 193–5, *see also* coronary heart disease
cardiovascular system, 103–8
carrier, 83, 149
Casparian strip, 131, *132*
catalase, 44, *44*
cell
  animal, *3*, 4, 11–14, *11*

  plant, *4*, *5*, 14–15
  size of structures, 5, *6*, 7
cell biology, 3
cell cycle, 83–4, *84*
cell division 84, *85-6*
cell theory, 2–3
cell wall, 5, *15*, 28, *28*
cellulose, 27–8, *27–8*
centriole, *3*, 4, 12
centromere, 81–2
cerebral infarction, 195, *195*
chlorenchyma, *18*
chloroplast, 5, *15*
chloroquine, 207
cholera, 203–5
cholesterol, 53–4, 193–4
chromatid, 81
chromatin, 4, 12
chromosome, 79–83, *80-1*
chronic **bronchitis**, 188–9
chronic obstructive pulmonary disease, 190–1, *201*
cilia, 14, *14*
ciliated epithelium, 19, *19*, 173, *174*
circulatory system, 103–4, *104*
codon, 75
collagen, 35, *36*, 37
collenchyma, *18*
colostrum, 228
community, 92
companion cell, 140, *140*, 144
compartmentalisation, 4
competitive inhibition, 48–9, *48*
complementary DNA (cDNA), 77
concentration gradient, 54–5
condensation reaction, 24, *24*
consumer, 94
coronary arteries, *120*, 121
coronary heart disease
  causes of, 194–5
  global distribution of, 196, *196*
  risk factors for, 196–9
  treatment and prevention of, 199–200
co-transporter molecule, 143
cystic fibrosis, 83, 150–1, *150*

cytokinesis, 84, *85–6*
cytology, 3
cytoplasm, 4

deamination, 99
decomposers, 94
deficiency diseases, 149–50, 168–9
degenerative diseases, 152
dementia, 152
denitrifying bacteria, 100
detritivores, 94
detritus, 94
diastolic pressure, 177
diet
  balanced, 158–9
  calculating requirements in,
    159–65
  and coronary heart disease,
    198–9
dietary reference values (DRVs),
  160–5, *160*
diffusion, 54–5, 103
dipeptide, 31
diploid cell, 81
dipole, 27
disaccharides, 24, *24*
disease
  categories of, 148–53, *149*
  global patterns of, *154*, 155–6
disulphide bonds, 34
DNA
  replication of, 67, *69*
  structure of, 65–7, *68*
  triplet codes, 70–1, 237
DNA ligase, 77

ecology, 92
ecosystem
  definition of, 92–3
  energy flow in, 93–6, *94*
  matter recycling in, 96–100
electrocardiogram (ECG), 125–6,
  125
electromagnetic spectrum, 8–9, *8*
electron microscope, 3
electron microscopy, 7–11
electrons, 9
emphysema, 189–90, *190*
end-product inhibition, 49, *49*
endemic, 155
endocytosis, 60
endoplasmic reticulum, 12–13, *12*
energy flow, 93–4, *94*

energy losses, 95–6
enzyme
  active site of 42–3, *43*
  catalytic action of, 42–3, *42*
  factors affecting reaction rate,
    45–7
  inhibition of, 48–9, *48–9*
  course and rate of reactions, 45,
    45
enzyme–substrate complex, 43, *43*
epidemic, 155
epidemiology, 153
epithelial tissues, 17, 19, *19*
eukaryote, 16–17, *16*
exercise
  aerobic, 179–82, *180*
  aerobic fitness, 182–4
  benefits of, 184
  oxygen demand in, 180–2, *181*
exocytosis, 60, *60*

facilitated diffusion, 55
fatty acids, 29–30, *29*, 162–3
fetal haemoglobin, 115–16, *116*
fibre, in diet, 163
fibrillation, 125–6, *125*
fibrous protein, 35–7, *36*
flagella, 14
fluid mosaic model, 52–3, *53*
food chain, 94–6, *95*
food labels, 165
food web, 94, *95*

gaseous exchange, 61–2
gene, 74, 80, 82–3, *82*
gene technology, 75–8
gene therapy, 77–8, 151
genome, 74
globular protein, 34–5, *35*
glucose, 23–4, *23*
glycerol, 28
glycogen, 26, *26*
glycolipids, 54
glycoproteins, 54
glycosidic bond, 24, *24*
goblet cells, 173
Golgi apparatus, 4, 13
grana, 5, *15*
gross primary productivity, 96

Haber process, 98
habitat, 92
haem group, 35, *35*

haemoglobin, 34–5, *35*, 112–17, 179
haemoglobin dissociation curve,
  113–15, *113*
haemoglobinic acid, 114
haemophilia, 77–8
haploid cell, 81
hay fever, 233
health, 148
health statistics, 153–4
heart, 120–2, *120-1, see also* cardiac
  cycle, cardiac muscle
heart attack, 195
heart failure, 195
α-helix, 32–3, *32*
herd immunity, 229
hexoses, 23
histamine, 221, 232–3
histology, 17
homeostasis, 109
homologous pairs, 80, 82–3
human factor VIII, 77–8
Human Genome Project, 74, 151
Human Immunodeficiency Virus
  (HIV), 209–12, *209*
hydrogen bond, 27, 34
hydrolysis, 24, *24*
hydrophilic molecules, 27
hydrophobic molecules, 27
hydrostatic pressure, 136
hypertension, 178–9

immune cells, 220–7
immunity, 219–20, 227–8
immunoglobulins, 224
immunological memory, 223–4
infectious diseases, 149, 203
inflammation, 233
inherited diseases, 150–1
inhibitor
  competitive, 48–9, *48*
  non-competitive, 48, *49*
inorganic ions
  functions of, 39
  uptake by plant root, 62, *63*
insulin production, 75, *76*, 77
ionic bonds, *33*, 34
isomers, 24

Kaposi's sarcoma, 210
karyotype, 80, *80*
keratin, 34
killer T cells, 226
kwashiorkor, 166

lactate, 180
leaf, *18*, *134*
leucocytes, 112, *112*
life cycles, *83*
light microscopy, 3–4
lightning, 98
lipids, 28–30, 159, 162–3
lipoproteins, 193–4, *193*
locus, 82, *82*
lung **cancer**, *89*, 190–1, 192–3
lung disease
  causes of , 188
    links with smoking, 191–3
    types of, 188–91
lung volumes, *176*
lungs, 61–2, *61*, 172–3, *176*
lymph, 109–10
lymph nodes, 110
lymphatic system, 109–10, *109–10*
lymphocyte, 112, 221–7, *227*
lysosomes, 13

macromolecules, 22
macronutrients, 158
macrophages, 173, *220*, 221
magnification, 7, *7*
malaria, 205–8
malnutrition, 158, 165–9
marasmus, 166
mass flow, 136, 141–3, *142*
mast cells, 225, 232
measles, 231, *232*
mefloquine, 207
meiosis, 83
membranes
  freely permeable, 3
  partially permeable, 3, 55–6, *56*
  structure of, 52–3, *53*
memory cells, 223, 226
mental disorders, 152
mesophyll cells, 135, *135*
messenger RNA (mRNA), 74, *74*
metabolism, 93, 22
metastasis, 190
methicillin resistant *Staphylococcus
  aureus* (MRSA), 216
micelles, 51, *52*
micronutrients, 158, 165
mitochondria, 4, 13–14, *14*
mitosis, 83–4, *85–7*
mitral valve, 122
molecular biology, 21–2

molecular formula, 23
monocytes, *220*, 221
monosaccharides, 23–4, *23*
mutation, 88–9
mutualism, 98
mycorrhiza, 130
myocardial infarction (MI), 195
myoglobin, *33*, 116–17, *116*, 179

net primary productivity, 96
neutrophils, 220–1
niche, 93
nicotine, 188
nitrifying bacteria, 99–100
nitrogen cycle, 97–100, *97*
nitrogen metabolism, 99
nitrogenase, 98
non-competitive inhibition, 48, 49
non-infectious diseases, 149
non-polar molecules, 27
nuclear division, 79, 83–4, *85–7*
nuclear envelope, 11–12
nucleolus, 4
nucleotides, 66–7, *66*
nucleus, 4, 11–12, *12*

obesity, 169–70, *170*
oedema, 110
oncogene, 88
opportunistic infections, 209
oral rehydration therapy, 204, *204*
organ, 17
organelle, 4, 11–14
osmosis
  in animal cells, 57, *57*
  mechanism of, 55–6, *56*
  in plant cells, 57–9, *58*
osteomalacia, 169
oxygen debt, 181, *181*
oxygen deficit, 181, *181*
oxyhaemoglobin, 35

pandemic, 155
parenchyma, *18*
passage cells, 131
passive immunity, 228
pentoses, 23
peptide bond, 31–2, *31*
phagocyte, 112, 220–1
phagocytosis, 60, *60*, 221, *221*
phloem tissue, 138, *138*, 140–1, 144
phospholipid, 30, 51–2, *52*, 53
photosynthesis, 93

physical diseases, 149
pinocytosis, 60
plan diagram, 17
plant cell
  requirements of, 128–9
  structure of *4*, *5*
  ultrastructure of, 14–16
plant tissues, *18*
plaque, 194, *194*
plasma, 108
plasma cells, 223, *223*
plasma membrane
  structure of, 3–4, *14*, 52–3, *53*
  transport across, 54–60, 142–4
plasmid, 77
plasmodesmata, 5, *15*
Plasmodium, 205–6, *205*, 208
plasmolysis, 58–9, *58*
β-pleated sheet, *32*, 33
pneumocystis pneumonia, 210
polar molecules, 27
polio, 231, *231*
polymerisation, 22
polymers, 22
polynucleotides, 67, *68*
polypeptides, 31–2
polysaccharides, 24–8
population, 92
potometer, 137, *138*
pregnancy, 164
primary immune response, 223
primary productivity, 96
producers, 94
prokaryote, 16–17, *16*
prosthetic group, 35
protein energy malnutrition, 166
protein synthesis, 70–5
proteins
  in the diet, 162
  fibrous, 35, *36*, 37
  functions of, 30-1
  globular, 34–5, *34*
  in membranes, 53–4, *53*
  primary structure of, 32, *32*
  quaternary structure of, 34
  secondary structure of, 32–3,
    32–3
  tertiary structure of, 33–4, *33*
  test for, 37
protoctist, 17
pulmonary arteries, 104, *104*, 121,
  121
pulmonary veins, 104, *104*, 121, *121*

pulse rate, 177, 183, *183*
Purkyne tissue, 125

quinine, 207

R groups, 31, *31*, 34, 236
radiation, 89
receptor molecules, 54
recombinant DNA, 77
red blood cells, 35, 111–12, *111*
residual volume, 175
resolution, 7–9
respiration, 179
respiratory system, 61–2, *61*, 172–5
restriction enzyme, 77
retroviruses, 77
reverse transcriptase, 77
Rhizobium, 97–8
ribonuclease, *32*
ribosomes, 6, 7, 9, 12–13, *13*
rickets, 169, *169*
ring structures, 23–4, *23*
ring vaccination, 230
RNA, 13, 65–7, *74*
root
    uptake of ions, *62*, 63
    uptake of water, 130–5, *130–1*
root hairs, 62, 63, 130
root nodules, 98, *98*
root pressure, 137

sap, 140–1, *141*, 144
saturated fatty acids, 29–30, 163
scanning electron microscope,
    9–10, *10*
secondary immune response, 223
self-inflicted diseases, 153
**semi-conservative DNA
    replication**, 67, 70–1
semilunar valves, 107–8, *107*, 123
sex chromosomes, 80, *80*
sexual reproduction, 83, *83*
SI units, 5
sickle cell anaemia, *35*
sieve tubes, 140, *140*, 144
sinoatrial node, 124–5, *125*
smallpox, 230–1, *230*
smoking
    and cardiovascular disease,
        196–8

and lung disease, 188–93
    tobacco smoke, 117, 187–8
social diseases, 152–3
solute potential, 56
sphygmomanometer, 177, *178*
spindle fibres, 85, *85*, 86, *86*
spirometer, *176*
squamous epithelium, *3*, 19, *19*
starch, 25–6, *26*
starvation, 165–9
stem structure, *134*
step test, 182–3, *183*
stomata, 135, *135*
stroke, 195, *195*, 200, *201*
structural formula, 23
structural proteins, 35, *36*, 37
subclavian veins, 110, *110*
suberin, *132*
substrate, 43, *43*, 46, *46*
sugars, 23–4, *23*
surface tension, 38, *38*
symplast pathway, 131, *131*
system, 17
systolic pressure, 177

T helper cell, 209, 226, *227*
T lymphocyte, 221–2, 225–6, *227*
tar, 187
tetanus, 227–8
thrombus, 194
thylakoids, *15*
thymus, 221
tidal volume, 176, *176*
tissue, 17–19
tissue fluid, 108–9
tobacco smoke, 117, 187–8
tonoplast, 5
trachea, *61*, 173, *174*
tracheids, 134–5
transcription, *72*
transfer RNA (tRNA), *74*, 75
translation, *73*
translocation, 138–44
transmission electron microscope,
    9, *10*
transpiration, 135–6, *135–6*, 137–8,
    138
transport proteins, *53*, 54, 59, *59*
transport systems, 102–3, *103*
triglyceride, 28–30, *28–9*
trioses, 23

triplet codes, 70–1, 237
trophic level, 94
tuberculosis (TB), 212–15
tumours, 88, 90, *90*
tunica externa, *105*, 106, *194*
tunica intima, *105*, 106, *194*
tunica media, *105*, 106, *194*
turgor, 58, 136

unsaturated fatty acid, 29–30

vaccination, 155, *155*, 227–30
vacuole, 5
variable region (antibody), 224, *224*
variola virus, 230–1
vector, 77
vein, 105, *105*, 107–8, *107*
vena cava, 104, *104*, 121, *121*
ventilation rate, 175
ventricles, 122
ventricular diastole, 122, 123
ventricular systole, 122–3, *122*
venules, 107
Vibrio cholerae, 203–4, *204*, 205, 230
vital capacity, 176, *176*
vitamin A deficiency, 168–9, *168*
vitamin D deficiency, 169
vitamins, 159, 163

water
    structure and properties, 37–8,
        37–8
    body requirements, 163
water potential, 56
water transport, in plants
    leaf to atmosphere, 135–6, *135–6*
    pathway of, *129*
    root hair to xylem, 130–5, *130–1*
    soil to root hair, 130
    xylem to leaf, 136–7
white blood cells, 112, *112*
World Health Organisation, 148,
    154, 178

xerophthalmia, 168, *168*
xerophytes, 138, *139*
xylem tissue, *18*, *132*, 133–5
xylem vessel, 133, *133*, 144

zidovudine, 210–11